Theory of Machines and Computations

Theory of Machines and Computations

Edited by

Zvi Kohavi
Faculty of Electrical Engineering
Technion–Israel Institute of Technology
Haifa, Israel

and

Azaria Paz
Department of Computer Science
Technion–Israel Institute of Technology
Haifa, Israel

Proceedings of an
International Symposium on the
Theory of Machines and Computations
Held at Technion in Haifa, Israel
on August 16-19, 1971

Academic Press New York and London 1971

ACADEMIC PRESS, INC.
111 Fifth Avenue, New York, New York 10003

United Kingdom Edition published by
ACADEMIC PRESS, INC. (LONDON) LTD.
24/28 Oval Road, London NW1 7DD

LIBRARY OF CONGRESS CATALOG CARD NUMBER: 72-176298

PRINTED IN THE UNITED STATES OF AMERICA

CONTENTS

SECTION II. FORMAL AND STOCHASTIC LANGUAGES

1. Formal Languages

2. Stochastic Automata and Languages

SECTION III. FINITE AUTOMATA

1. Algorithms and Bounds

CONTRIBUTORS

Numbers in parentheses indicate the pages on which the authors' contributions begin.

I. Aleksander, Electronics Laboratory, University of Kent at Canterbury, Canterbury, Kent, England (409)

H. Arango, Departamento de Electrotecnia, Universidad Nacional del Sur, Bahía Blanca, Bs. As., Argentina (353)

Edward Ashcroft, Department of Computer Science, University of Waterloo, Waterloo, Canada (3)

François Bancilhon, Centre d'Automatique, Ecole Nationale Superieure des Mines, Paris, France (153)

Zamir Bavel, Department of Computer Science, University of Kansas, Lawrence, Kansas (255)

Taylor L. Booth, Computer Science Group, Electrical Engineering Department, University of Connecticut, Storrs, Connecticut (169)

Allan Borodin, Department of Computer Science, University of Toronto, Toronto, Canada (45)

Melvin A. Breuer, Electrical Engineering Department, University of Southern California, Los Angeles, California (313)

Robert Cori, Institut de Programmation, Université de Paris, Paris, France (115)

Michel Depeyrot, Centre d'Automatique, Ecole Nationale Superieure des Mines, Paris, France (153)

S. Even, Applied Mathematics Department, The Weizmann Institute of Science, Rehovot, Israel (71)

Michel Fliess, Institut de Programmation, Université de Paris, Paris, France (123)

A. D. Friedman, Bell Telephone Laboratories, Incorporated, Murray Hill, New Jersey (327)

G. Frosini, Instituto di Elaborazione dell'Informazione del C.N.R., Pisa, Italy (395)

G. B. Gerace, Instituto di Elaborazione dell'Informazione del C.N.R., Pisa, Italy (395)

Y. Give'on, Department of Mathematics, University of the Negev, Beer-Sheva, Israel (275)

Sheila A. Greibach, Department of System Science, University of California, Los Angeles, California (125)

G. T. Herman, Department of Computer Science, State University of New York at Buffalo, Amherst, New York (209)

John Hopcroft, Computer Science Department, Stanford University, Stanford, California (189)

A. Itai, Applied Mathematics Department, The Weizmann Institute of Science, Rehovot, Israel (71)

Zvi Kohavi, Faculty of Electrical Engineering, Technion–Israel Institute of Technology, Haifa, Israel (197)

Tomas Lang, Department of Electrical Engineering, University of Chile, Santiago, Chile (377)

L. S. Levy, University of Delaware, Newark, Delaware (127)

Saul Levy, IRIA, Rocquencourt, France (43)

C. L. Liu, Department of Electrical Engineering and Project MAC, Massachusetts Institute of Technology, Cambridge, Massachusetts (87)

E. M. McCreight, Boeing Seientific Research Laboratories, Boeing Company, Seattle, Washington (19)

E. H. Mamdani, Department of Electrical and Electronic Engineering, Queen Mary College, University of London, London, England (409)

Zohar Manna, Computer Science Department, Stanford University, Stanford, California (3)

P. R. Menon, Bell Telephone Laboratories, Incorporated, Murray Hill, New Jersey (327)

CONTRIBUTORS

A. R. Meyer, Project MAC, Massachusetts Institute of Technology, Cambridge, Massachusetts (19)

John F. Meyer, Department of Electrical and Computer Engineering and Department of Computer and Communication Sciences, The University of Michigan, Ann Arbor, Michigan (229)

Claudio R. Moraga, Universidad Tecnica Federico Santa Maria, Valparaiso, Chile (363)

Jacques Morgenstern, Department de Mathematiques, Universite de Nice, France (59)

Amar Mukhopadhyay, Department of Computer Science, The University of Iowa, Iowa City, Iowa (387)

M. Pascual, Departamento de Electrotecnia, Universidad Nacional del Sur, Bahia Blanca, Bs. As., Argentina (353)

Azaria Paz, Department of Computer Science, Technion—Israel Institute of Technology, Haifa, Israel (167)

J-F. Perrot, Institut de Programmation, Université de Paris, Paris, France (287)

Amir Pnueli, Applied Mathematics Department, The Weizmann Institute of Science, Rehovot, Israel (3)

Sudhakar M. Reddy, Department of Electrical Engineering, The University of Iowa, Iowa City, Iowa (387)

Larry H. Reeker, Computer and Information Science and Linguistics Departments, The Ohio State University, Columbus, Ohio (143)

Corina Reischer, Department of Mathematics, University of Iassy, Iassy, Rumania (207)

Bernd Reusch, Gesellschaft für Mathematik und Datenverarbeitung, Bonn, Germany (243)

Jean Richard, Institut de Programmation, Université de Paris, Paris, France (115)

J. Santos, Departamento de Electrotecnia, Universidad Nacional del Sur, Bahia Blanca, Bs. As., Argentina (353)

G. Saucier, Institut de Mathématique Appliquees, Université de Grenoble, Grenoble, France (411)

Mario Schkolnick, Department of Electrical Engineering, University of Chile, Santiago, Chile (377)

Charles L. Seitz, Computer Science Department, University of Utah, Salt Lake City, Utah (341)

Dan A. Simovici, Department of Mathematics, University of Iassy, Iassy, Rumania (207)

Richard A. Thompson, Computer Science Group, Electrical Engineering Department, University of Connecticut, Storrs, Connecticut (169)

D. Tsichritzis, Department of Computer Science, University of Toronto, Toronto, Canada (99)

J. Winograd, Faculty of Electrical Engineering, Technion–Israel Institute of Technology, Haifa, Israel (197)

S. Winograd, IBM, Thomas J. Watson Research Center, Yorktown Heights, New York (67)

P. Wolfe, IBM, Thomas J. Watson Research Center, Yorktown Heights, New York (67)

Bernard P. Zeigler, Department of Computer and Communication Sciences, The University of Michigan, Ann Arbor, Michigan (229, 295)

PREFACE

This volume consists of the papers presented at the International Symposium on the Theory of Machines and Computations, held at Technion—Israel Institute of Technology, Haifa, Israel in August 1971. They are representative of a wide variety of subjects in the areas of computability theory, formal languages, automata theory, and switching theory.

The papers were chosen by an international program committee from a large number of submitted contributions. Each author was responsible for the typing and preparation of his manuscript for the photocopying process by which this volume is printed.

The editors would like to thank the committees' members for their help in the organization of the symposium and the screening of the manuscripts.

The program committee consisted of:

J.W. Carlyle, UCLA, Los Angeles, California
P.C. Fischer, University of Waterloo, Waterloo, Ontario, Canada
S. Ginsburg, University of Southern California, Los Angeles, California
M.A. Harrison, University of California, Berkeley, California
J. Hartmanis, Cornell University, Ithaca, New York
Z. Kohavi, Technion, Haifa, Israel
R.E. Miller, IBM Research Center, Yorktown Heights, New York
A. Paz, Technion, Haifa, Israel
M.P. Schutzenberger, Université de Paris, Paris, France
J.D. Ullman, Princeton University, Princeton, New Jersey
M. Yoeli, Technion, Haifa, Israel

The members of the organizing committee were:

Z. Kohavi, Technion, Haifa, Israel
A. Paz, Technion, Haifa, Israel
M.O. Rabin, Hebrew University, Jerusalem, Israel
M. Yoeli, Technion, Haifa, Israel

Thanks are due to Technion for supporting the symposium and to Academic Press for undertaking the publishing of this volume.

SECTION I

COMPUTABILITY THEORY

DECIDABLE PROPERTIES OF MONADIC FUNCTIONAL SCHEMAS

Edward Ashcroft
Computer Science Dept.
University of Waterloo
Waterloo, Canada

Zohar Manna
Computer Science Dept.
Stanford University
Stanford, Calif., U.S.A.

Amir Pnueli
Applied Mathematics Dept.
Weizmann Institute
Rehovot, Israel

Abstract

We define a class of (monadic) functional schemas which properly includes 'Ianov' flowchart schemas. We show that the termination, divergence and freedom problems for functional schemas are decidable. Although it is possible to translate a large class of non-free functional schemas into equivalent free functional schemas, we show that this cannot be done in general. We show also that the equivalence problem for free functional schemas is decidable. Most of the results are obtained from well-known results in Formal Languages and Automata Theory.

I. Monadic Functional Schemas

An _alphabet_ Σ_S of a (monadic) functional schema S consists of one individual variable x, a finite set of monadic function variables $\{F_i\}$ (with a designated _initial_ function variable F_o)[1], a finite set of monadic function constants $\{f_i\}$, and a finite set of monadic predicate constants[1] $\{p_i\}$. Note that individual constants are not allowed.[1]

The research reported here was supported in part by the Advanced Research Projects Agency of the Office of the Secretary of Defense (SD-183).

A *term over* Σ_S is any term in the normal sense constructed from the monadic function variables $\{F_i\}$, monadic function constants $\{f_i\}$ and the variable x, e.g., $f_1(F_o(f_2(x)))$. A *conditional term over* Σ_S is any finite expression of the form

$$\underline{\text{if}}\ p_i(x)\ \underline{\text{then}}\ \tau_1\ \underline{\text{else}}\ \tau_2 ,$$

where p_i is any predicate constant of Σ_S, and τ_1 and τ_2 are any terms or conditional terms over Σ_S. A *definition of* F_i *over* Σ_S is of the form

$$F_i(x) \Leftarrow \tau ,$$

where τ is any term or conditional term over Σ_S. A (*monadic*) *functional schema* S (over an alphabet Σ_S) consists of a finite set of definitions over Σ_S, one for each function variable F_i in Σ_S. Whenever the special function variable F_∞ is used, its definition is considered to be $F_\infty(x) \Leftarrow F_\infty(x)$. This definition is usually omitted.

Example 1: Let us consider the functional schema S_1:

$$F_o(x) \Leftarrow \underline{\text{if}}\ p_1(x)\ \underline{\text{then}}\ \underline{\text{if}}\ p_2(x)\ \underline{\text{then}}\ F_\infty(x)\ \underline{\text{else}}\ F_1(f_1(x))$$
$$\underline{\text{else}}\ x$$

$$F_1(x) \Leftarrow \underline{\text{if}}\ p_3(x)\ \underline{\text{then}}\ F_o(f_2(x))\ \underline{\text{else}}\ f_1(x) .$$

Since we are using a very restricted alphabet, parentheses and the individual variable x may be omitted without causing any confusion. Therefore the functional schema S_1 can be rewritten as:

$$F_o \Leftarrow \underline{\text{if}}\ p_1\ \underline{\text{then}}\ \underline{\text{if}}\ p_2\ \underline{\text{then}}\ F_\infty\ \underline{\text{else}}\ F_1 f_1$$
$$\underline{\text{else}}\ I$$

$$F_1 \Leftarrow \underline{\text{if}}\ p\ \underline{\text{then}}\ F_o f_2\ \underline{\text{else}}\ f_1 ,$$

where I stands for the 'identity function'.*/

*/ It is worth noting that most of the results in this paper would be trivial if we did not allow the 'identity function'.

An interpretation $\mathcal{I}$ of a functional schema S consists of:

1. a non-empty set of elements D (called the domain),
2. an element ξ_0 of D used as the initial value of x, and
3. assignments to the constants of Σ_S :
   (i) a total monadic function (from D into D) for each function constant f_i , and
   (ii) a total monadic predicate (from D into $\{T,F\}$) for each predicate constant p_i .

For a given interpretation $\mathcal{I}$, the pair $(S,\mathcal{I})$, called a functional program, can be computed by evaluating F_0 with input ξ_0 in the usual way (see McCarthy [1963]). The computation either (i) terminates yielding an element of D denoted by $\underline{val}(S,\mathcal{I})$, or (ii) diverges (i.e., does not terminate) in which case $\underline{val}(S,\mathcal{I})$ is said to be undefined. The method of computation is described more fully later for special types of interpretations called 'Herbrand interpretations'.

A functional schema S is said to terminate/diverge if for every interpretation $\mathcal{I}$, $\underline{val}(S,\mathcal{I})$ is defined/undefined. Two functional schemas S_1 and S_2 are said to be equivalent if for every interpretation $\mathcal{I}$ either both $\underline{val}(S_1,\mathcal{I})$ and $\underline{val}(S_2,\mathcal{I})$ are undefined or both are defined and $\underline{val}(S_1,\mathcal{I}) = \underline{val}(S_2,\mathcal{I})$.

The same class of functional schemas has been discussed by DeBakker and Scott [1969].

It is straightforward to show that every functional schema in which any term contains at most one function variable, occurring on the left-hand side of the term (as in Example 1 above), can be translated to an equivalent 'Ianov' flowchart schema (Ianov [1960], see also Rutledge [1964]). However, such simple functional schemas as

$$F_0 \Leftarrow \underline{\text{if}}\ p\ \underline{\text{then}}\ I\ \underline{\text{else}}\ f_1 F_0 f_2$$

have no equivalent Ianov flowchart schema. Hence, the results in this paper generalize known results about Ianov flowchart schemas.

II. Herbrand Interpretations*/

A Herbrand interpretation $\mathcal{I}^*$ of a functional schema S consists of:

1. The domain D^* which is the set of all expressions "τ_c", where τ_c is a constant term constructed from the individual variable x and the function constants f_i of Σ_S, e.g., "x", "$f_1(x)$", "$f_2(f_1(x))$";
2. The expression "x"$\in D^*$ used as the initial value of x;
3. Assignments to the constants of Σ_S:
   - (i) For every function constant f_i in Σ_S, we assign the total function mapping every expression "τ_c"$\in D^*$ into the expression "$f_i(\tau_c)$"$\in D^*$,
   - (ii) For every predicate constant p_i in Σ_S, we assign some total predicate over D^*, i.e., for every "τ_c"$\in D^*$ the value of p_i("τ_c") is either T or F.

Note that all Herbrand interpretations of a given functional schema differ only in the assignments to the predicate constants. Henceforth we omit the quotation marks whenever this causes no confusion.

The computation of $(S, \mathcal{I}^*)$ is best described by a (finite or infinite) sequence of terms α_i. The first term α_o of the sequence is $F_o(x)$. In general, suppose α_n $(n \geq 0)$ contains the subterm $F_i(\xi)$ where $\xi \in D^*$, i.e., F_i is the right-most function variable in α_n. Then α_{n+1} is obtained by substituting a term τ for $F_i(\xi)$ where τ is obtained as follows. First x is replaced by ξ in the definition of F_i, and then the term τ is chosen from this definition using the values of $p_j(\xi)$ supplied by the interpretation of the predicate constants p_j. The computation terminates as soon as we reach a constant term τ_c. Then $\underline{val}(S, \mathcal{I}^*) = \tau_c$.

---

*/ Herbrand interpretations are identical to the 'free interpretations' of Luckham, Park and Paterson [1970].

Herbrand interpretations are important because many properties of functional schemas can be described and proved just by considering Herbrand interpretations rather than all interpretations. For example,

(i) a functional schema terminates/diverges (under every interpretation) if and only if it terminates/diverges under every Herbrand interpretation;

(ii) two functional schemas are equivalent (under every interpretation) if and only if they are equivalent under every Herbrand interpretation.

III. Termination and Divergence of Functional Schemas

We show that.

THEOREM 1. It is decidable whether or not a functional schema terminates or diverges (for every interpretation).

Proof. The proof depends on the well-known results in Formal Language Theory that it is decidable for any context free grammar whether or not all (rightmost) derivations are finite and whether or not all (rightmost) derivations are infinite.

For this purpose we associate with every functional schema S a context-free grammar G_S such that:

there is a one-to-one correspondence between the set of all computations of S for all Herbrand interpretations, and the set of all (rightmost) derivations of G_S. Furthermore, a computation of S diverges if and only if the corresponding derivation of G_S is infinite.

Given a functional schema S with n predicates $p_1, p_2, \dots, p_n$, function variables $\{F_i\}$ and function constants $\{f_i\}$, we define G_S as follows:

1. The non-terminals are of the form

$$[w_b, F_k, w_a] \qquad F_k \in \{F_i\} \text{ and } w_a, w_b \in W ,$$

where W is the set of all strings of length n over $\{T,F\}$. The intuitive meaning of $[w_b, F_k, w_a]$ is that it will generate all possible constant terms τ_c such that τ_c is computed by S starting from

$F_k(x)$, under some Herbrand interpretation for which the values of $p_1,\ldots,p_n$ for x are w_a and for τ_c are w_b .

In addition, we have a special initial non-terminal A .

2. The <u>terminals</u> are the function constants $\{f_i\}$.

3. The <u>productions</u> are obtained from S as follows:

(i) $A \to [w_b,F_o,w_a]$ for all $w_a,w_b \in W$.

(ii) For every non-terminal $[w_b,F_k,w_a]$ we add productions as follows:

Locate in definition of F_k that term which is selected by w_a . Let the term be

$$\alpha_m \ldots \alpha_2\ \alpha_1$$

where each α_i is either a function variable or a function constant. We construct all productions of the form

$$[w_b,F_k,w_a] \to [w_b,\alpha_m,w_{m-1}][w_{m-1},\alpha_{m-1},w_{m-2}]\ldots[w_2,\alpha_2,w_1][w_1,\alpha_1,w_a]$$

where $w_1,w_2,\ldots,w_{m-1} \in W$,

after replacing each $[w,\alpha_i,w']$, where α_i is a function constant, by α_i .

In the special case where the term is I and $w_a = w_b$ we generate the single production

$$[w_a,F_k,w_a] \to \Lambda \quad (\Lambda \text{ is the empty word}).$$

Finally, we go through G_S and repeatedly remove all productions containing some non-terminal which is not the left-hand side of any production and all productions in which the non-terminal on the left-hand side cannot be reached from A .

G_S now clearly has the required properties. Q.E.D.

IV. Functional Schemas in Standard Form

We introduce now an interesting subclass of functional schemas which has a special syntactic form. This form is relevant to our later discussion.

A functional schema S is said to be in <u>standard form</u> if

1. Every conditional term in S is of the form

   $\underline{\text{if}}$ p $\underline{\text{then}}$ τ_1 $\underline{\text{else}}$ τ_2

   where τ_1 and τ_2 are distinct (i.e., there are no 'redundant' tests) and each of τ_1 and τ_2 is of one of the following forms:

   (a) a conditional term not containing p_j (i.e., there are no 'redundant' terms), (b) F^j_∞, (c) I, or (d) a term in which F_∞ does not occur and the rightmost symbol is a function constant.

2. Every definition in S (except for F_∞) contains a conditional term.

3. No function variable in S always diverges (except for F_∞).*/

Note that our definition of standard form has the flavor of Greibach Normal Form in Formal Languages Theory.

The interest in this form arises from the fact that every functional schema can be effectively transformed to an equivalent functional schema in standard form. This is done easily by first recognizing all 'divergent' function variables (using the technique described in the previous section) and replacing all terms in which they occur by F_∞. Then we repeatedly replace every function variable occuring as the rightmost symbol of a term by its definition, applying straightforward simplifications, as illustrated in Example 3 below.

<u>Example 2</u>: The functional schema S_2 where

$F_0 \Leftarrow$ $\underline{\text{if}}$ p $\underline{\text{then}}$ $F_0F_1f_1$ $\underline{\text{else}}$ f_2

$F_1 \Leftarrow$ $\underline{\text{if}}$ p $\underline{\text{then}}$ F_1f_3 $\underline{\text{else}}$ I ,

is clearly in standard form.

---

*/ i.e., no matter which function variable in Σ_S is taken as the initial function (except for F_∞), the schemas do not diverge.

Example 3: The functional schema S_3 where

$$F_0 \Leftarrow \underline{\text{if}}\ p\ \underline{\text{then}}\ f_1F_1\ \underline{\text{else}}\ f_2$$

$$F_1 \Leftarrow \underline{\text{if}}\ p\ \underline{\text{then}}\ F_1f_3\ \underline{\text{else}}\ f_4$$

is not in standard form because of the term f_1F_1. This term can be removed by first replacing F_1 in f_1F_1 by its definition to obtain:

$$F_0 \Leftarrow \underline{\text{if}}\ p\ \underline{\text{then}}\ \underline{\text{if}}\ p\ \underline{\text{then}}\ f_1F_1f_3\ \underline{\text{else}}\ f_1f_4\ \underline{\text{else}}\ f_2\ ,$$

and then simplifying it to

$$F_0 \Leftarrow \underline{\text{if}}\ p\ \underline{\text{then}}\ f_1F_1f_3\ \underline{\text{else}}\ f_2\ .$$

Thus, we obtain the functional schema S_3', which is clearly in standard form and equivalent to S_3:

$$F_0' \Leftarrow \underline{\text{if}}\ p\ \underline{\text{then}}\ f_1F_1'f_3\ \underline{\text{else}}\ f_2$$

$$F_1' \Leftarrow \underline{\text{if}}\ p\ \underline{\text{then}}\ F_1'f_3\ \underline{\text{else}}\ f_4\ .$$

V. Freedom of Functional Schemas

A functional schema S is said to be free if for every Herbrand interpretation $\mathcal{I}^*$ of S the computation of $(S,\mathcal{I}^*)$ does not test a predicate with the same term (from D^*) more than once.

Examples:

1. The functional schema S_1 (Example 1 above) is clearly free.
2. The functional schema S_2 (Example 2 above) is not free, since there is a Herbrand interpretation $\mathcal{I}^*$ for which the computation of $(S_2,\mathcal{I}^*)$ is of the form

$$F_0(x) \rightarrow F_0(F_1(f_1(x))) \overset{(a)}{\rightarrow} F_0(f_1(x)) \overset{(b)}{\rightarrow} f_2(f_1(x))\ldots .$$

Predicate p tests term $f_1(x)$ at both steps (a) and (b).

3. The functional schema S_3 (Example 3 above) is not free, since there is a Herbrand interpretation $\mathcal{I}^*$ for which the computation of $(S_3, \mathcal{I}^*)$ is of the form

$$F_0(x) \overset{(a)}{\rightarrow} f_1(F_1(x)) \overset{(b)}{\rightarrow} f_1(F_1(f_3(x))) \rightarrow \cdots .$$

Predicate p tests term x at both steps (a) and (b).

There is a crucial difference between the non-freedom demonstrated in the functional schema S_2 and that of S_3. In Example 3 the non-freedom results from the substitutions at step (b) for the function variable F_1 which resulted from the substitution at step (a). In Example 2 the non-freedom results from the substitution at step (b) for the function variable F_0 which was already present before step (a). Note that in this case the function variable F_1 substituted for at step (a) produces the identity function. This will always be the case when non-freedom of the second type occurs.

Functional schemas in standard form cannot have non-freedom of the first type but may have non-freedom of the second type. Thus, by bringing a functional schema to standard form we always eliminate any non-freedom of the first type (but unfortunately preserving any non-freedom of the second type). Since the second type of non-freedom involves the identity function, it follows that any functional schema not containing I can be made free by putting it into standard form.

Although a large class of functional schemas containing I can still be translated to equivalent free frunctional schemas, this cannot be done in general as follows from

<u>THEOREM 2</u>: <u>The non-free schema</u> S_4 <u>where</u>

$$F_0 \Leftarrow \underline{\text{if}}\ p\ \underline{\text{then}}\ F_1F_0f\ \underline{\text{else}}\ I$$

$$F_1 \Leftarrow \underline{\text{if}}\ p\ \underline{\text{then}}\ f\ \underline{\text{else}}\ \underline{\text{if}}\ q\ \underline{\text{then}}\ f\ \underline{\text{else}}\ I\ ,$$

<u>has no equivalent free functional schema</u>.

<u>Proof</u>: Consider the following two families $\{\mathcal{I}_n^*\}$ and $\{\mathcal{J}_n^*\}$, $n \geq 1$, of Herbrand interpretations, where

$$\mathcal{I}^*_n = \begin{cases} p(f^i(x)) = T & \text{iff } i < n \\ q(f^i(x)) = T & \text{iff } i \neq n \end{cases}$$

$$\mathcal{V}^*_n = \begin{cases} p(f^i(x)) = T & \text{iff } i < n \\ q(f^i(x)) = T & \text{for all } i . \end{cases}$$

Note that two corresponding interpretations $\mathcal{I}^*_n$ and $\mathcal{V}^*_n$ differ by only one value, that of $q(f^n(x))$. It is clear that $\underline{val}(S_4, \mathcal{I}^*_n) = f^n(x)$ and $\underline{val}(S_4, \mathcal{V}^*_n) = f^{2n}(x)$ for all $n \geq 1$.

Suppose there exists a free functional schema G in standard form that is equivalent to S_4. We shall derive a contradiction by showing that there exists a positive integer n_o for which $\underline{val}(G, \mathcal{V}^*_{n_o}) \neq f^{2n_o}(x)$.

Let n be an arbitrary positive integer. If we apply interpretations $\mathcal{I}^*_n$ and $\mathcal{V}^*_n$ to G we must reach in both cases a term of the form $\alpha_n(f^n(x))$, since for $f^i(x)$, $i < n$, G cannot distinguish between $\mathcal{I}^*_n$ and $\mathcal{V}^*_n$.

Since for $\mathcal{I}^*_n$ this term must produce $f^n(x)$, it follows that every symbol in α_n is a function variable that 'collapses' to identity for predicate values determined by $\mathcal{I}^*_n$ for the term $f^n(x)$. Thus, since G is free and no predicate in G can test under interpretation $\mathcal{I}^*_n$ the term $f^n(x)$ twice, the number of symbols in α_n can be no more than the number of distinct predicate constants $\{p_i\}$ in G.

Therefore, there must exist two distinct positive integers n_1 and n_2, $n_1 \neq n_2$, such that α_{n_1} is identical to α_{n_2}. By definition of $\{\mathcal{V}^*_n\}$, the continuation of the computation of $\alpha_{n_1}(f^{n_1}(x))$ under $\mathcal{V}^*_{n_1}$ is identical to that of $\alpha_{n_2}(f^{n_2}(x))$ under $\mathcal{V}^*_{n_2}$. Therefore, since $n_1 \neq n_2$, either $\underline{val}(G, \mathcal{U}^*_{n_1}) \neq f^{2n_1}(x)$ or $\underline{val}(G, \mathcal{U}^*_{n_2}) \neq f^{2n_2}(x)$. Contradiction. Q.E.D.

Despite the above result, we still have

<u>THEOREM 3</u>: <u>It is decidable whether a functional schema is free or not</u>.

<u>Proof</u> (sketch): The proof consists of showing that a functional schema S is non-free if and only if non-freedom occurs in a computation under some Herbrand interpretation within a number K of steps, where K depends only on S. The decision method is then to explore all the different ways in which computation can proceed for K steps under any Herbrand interpretation. Since there are a finite number of such ways it is possible to decide whether or not non-freedom will ever occur.

We can assume that every non-divergent variable in S is defined by a conditional term, since S can be put in this form without affecting freedom in any way.

If non-freedom occurs it will be of the first or the second types. It can easily be shown that if non-freedom of the second type is ever to occur in S, then for some Herbrand interpretation the functional schema must have a subcomputation of the form

$$\cdots \rightarrow \tau F_{j_m} F_{j_{m-1}} \cdots F_{j_1} \tau_c \overset{(a)}{\rightarrow} \tau F_{j_m} \cdots F_{j_2} \tau_c \rightarrow \cdots \rightarrow \tau F_{j_m} \tau_c \overset{(b)}{\rightarrow} \cdots,$$

where τ_c is a constant term and $m \leq n+1$ (n is the number of distinct predicate constants in Σ_S.) Non-freedom occurs between steps (a) and (b), i.e., at (b) some predicate constant is testing τ_c which also tested τ_c at step (a). Note that $F_{j_1}, \ldots, F_{j_m}$ all must collapse to identity for τ_c under this interpretation.

We can prove that such a subcomputation must occur (if at all) within a bounded number of steps, by using the following easily-proved result of Formal Language Theory:

Let G be a context-free grammar, and let $\alpha\beta\gamma$ be any sentential form of G, where β is a substring of terminals and non-terminals of length m and γ is a terminal substring. Then there must exist a sentential form $\alpha'\beta\gamma'$ of G (γ' is a terminal substring), which is (rightmost) derivable in no more than $mLMN$ steps, where

L is the number of non-terminals in G,

M is the maximal number of non-terminals on the right-hand side of any production of G, and

N is the upper bound on the minimum number of steps needed for each non-terminal of G to produce a terminal string, if any; (i.e., every non-terminal of G can generate a terminal string, if at all, within N steps).

The above bound can similarly be stated for functional schemas giving the required bound K. (Note that in our case $m \leq n+1$.) It can be easily shown that any non-freedom of the first type must also be discovered within this number of steps, and hence the method of exploring the initial segments of all possible computations can decide whether non-freedom (of any type) is present. Q.E.D.

VI. Equivalence of Free Functional Schemas

THEOREM 4: It is decidable whether or not two free functional schemas are equivalent (for every interpretation).

Proof: Suppose we are given two free functional schemas S and S'. Since the translation of functional schemas into standard form never introduces new non-freedom, we can assume without loss of generality that S and S' are in standard form.

We construct a Deterministic Push-Down Automata (DPDA) A, whose input tape is a representation of some Herbrand interpretation and which simulates the computation of S and S' under this interpretation. A accepts an input tape if and only if S and S' are inequivalent under the corresponding interpretation. Since it is decidable whether or not the language accepted by a DPDA is empty (see, for example, Hopcroft and Ullman [1969]), it follows that the equivalence problem for free functional schemas is decidable.

The construction of A makes use of some ideas developed by Rosenkrantz and Stearns [1970] (see also Korenjak and Hopcroft [1966]).

Suppose S and S' use n predicate constants $p_1, p_2, \ldots, p_n$. The input alphabet consists of words of length n over $\{T,F\}$ where we intend that when A reads such a word (input symbol), the i-th letter denotes the current truth value of p_i. Hence, every possible input tape corresponds to some Herbrand interpretation, and vice versa.

To simulate the joint action of S and S' for a given Herbrand interpretation, we let A have a two-track push-down stack. Each track will hold a modified version of the current term in the computation sequence of the corresponding schema under the given interpretation.

The modification of the computation terms is such that if S and S' are equivalent, both tracks are of the same length during corresponding computations of S and S'. This enables us to put both tracks in a single push-down stack. To understand this modification we introduce the notion of the 'thickness' $T(\tau)$ of a term τ (that does not contain F_∞), namely the shortest possible constant term computable from τ for some Herbrand interpretation. For free schemas, $T(\tau_1\tau_2) = T(\tau_1) + T(\tau_2)$, since no decision made while computing τ_1 may affect the freedom of choice in computing τ_2. The required modification of a term to give its stack representation is to make $T(F_i)$ copies of each function variable F_i. Thus the length of stack representing term τ is $T(\tau)$. Note that if the corresponding terms in the computation of two equivalent functional schemas are τ_1 and τ_2, then $T(\tau_1) = T(\tau_2)$; so the modified terms have the required property. To erase a function variable F_i from such a stack, the automaton A will in fact erase $T(F_i)$ copies of F_i, which is a feasible action of a multi-state DPDA.

The only problem that may arise is that it is possible that $T(F_i) = 0$, which is the case when the definition of F_i contains I. In this case we would like to add F_i to the preceding stack position and hence not increase the length of the stack. Note that if, for the next function variable F_j , we have again $T(F_j) = 0$, F_j will also be added to the same stack position; and so on. However, for free functional schemas the number of function variables we have to add to the same stack position will never exceed the number n of predicate symbols. This is because there can never be more than n successive function variables collapsing to I (otherwise some predicate would be tested more than once on the same term). We therefore can resolve the above difficulty by making each position in a track wide enough to hold n+1 distinct symbols. Then symbols of thickness zero are written on the preceding position, with the other symbols already residing there. In order to make no exception for the bottom position of the stack, we may agree to test the equivalence of fF_0 and fF'_0 instead of F_0 and F'_0 .

The behavior of the DPDA A is as follows.

For each input symbol, A simulates all the possible actions of S and S . If the topmost letter of the corresponding track is a function constant, no change is made. Otherwise, it must be a function variable F_i and we modify the top of that track according to the term in the definition of F_i selected by the current input symbol. These actions will terminate either with some new stack-track with a function constant at the top or F_∞ will be encountered. The crucial point is that for free functional schmeas in standard form, the variation that occurs during these actions in the stack is bounded and can be temporarily remembered in a finite control until both operations for S and S' are completed.

Before moving to the next input letter, A now proceeds as follows:

(i) If F_∞ is encountered for both tracks, we pass to a rejecting state, (i.e., S and S' are equivalent under the given interpretation).

(ii) If we encounter F_∞ for one track and not in the other, we pass to an accepting state (i.e., S and S' are inequivalent for some Herbrand interpretation under which the other track goes to a constant term).

(iii) If the two tracks are not of the same length, we pass to an accepting state (i.e., S and S' are inequivalent for some Herbrand interpretation under which the shorter track produces its shortest constant term).

(iv) If the two function constants at the top of the two tracks are different, we pass to an accepting state.

(v) Otherwise, (i.e., same length tracks with the same topmost function constant) we remove the topmost letters. If both stacks are still non-empty, we move to the next input symbol, otherwise both tracks are empty and we pass to a rejecting state.

Thus the two given free functional schemas S and S' are equivalent if and only if the DPDA A accepts no input tapes, which is a known decidable problem. Q.E.D.

References

J. W. De-Bakker and D. Scott [1969]. A Theory of Programs. Unpublished memo.

J. E. Hopcroft and J. D. Ullman [1969]. Formal Languages and Their Relation to Automata. Addison-Wesley.

Y. I. Ianov [1960]. "The Logical Schemes of Algorithms". In Problems in Cybernetics, Vol. 1, Pergamon Press, New York, pp. 82-140.

A. J. Korenjak and J. E. Hopcroft [1966]. Simple Deterministic Languages, IEEE 7th Annual Symposium on Switching and Automata Theory. pp. 36-46.

D. C. Luckham, D. M. R. Park and M. S. Paterson [1970]. "On Formalized Computer Programs". Journal of Computer and System Sciences, Vol. 4, pp. 220-249.

J. McCarthy [1963]. "A Basis for a Mathematical Theory of Computation". In Computer Programming and Formal Systems, North-Holland, Amsterdam, pp. 33-70.

D. J. Rosenkrantz and R. E. Stearns [1970]. "Properties of Deterministic Top-Down Grammars". Information and Control 17, pp. 226-256.

J. D. Rutledge [1964]. "On Ianov's Program Schemata". J. ACM 11, 1, pp. 1-9.

COMPUTATIONALLY COMPLEX AND PSEUDO-RANDOM ZERO-ONE VALUED FUNCTIONS†

A.R. Meyer*
Massachusetts Institute of Technology

E.M. McCreight
Boeing Scientific Research Labs

Introduction

The existence of hard-to-compute zero-one valued functions is supported by a good deal of experience. An example is the characteristic function of the predicate " x is a prime." To decide whether x is prime requires by all known methods (namely, variations of Eratosthenes' sieve) time proportional to $\sqrt{x}$ and storage space proportional to log x bits for infinitely many x. It is not known whether this much time or space is actually necessary [2]. All presently

---

†Portions of this work were carried out at Carngie-Mellon University, while the authors were in the Department of Computer Science. Portions of these results were reported in preliminary form in [1].

*Work reported herein was supported in part by Project MAC, an M.I.T. research program sponsored by the Advanced Research Projects Agency, Department of Defense, under Office of Naval Research Contract Number Nonr-4102(01).

known existence proofs about large lower bounds on computation of zero-one valued functions are based on diagonal arguments, and this may necessarily be the case. Experience suggests that any intuitively simple description of a function implies a simple computation procedure for the function.

A specious argument for the existence of arbitrarily complex zero-one valued functions illustrates some of the difficulties involved in finding computationally complex functions without diagonal constructions. Suppose the question "Is x a prime?" really does require time proportional to $\sqrt{x}$ for infinitely many x. It might then seem that any general method for answering the question, "Is 2^x-1 a prime?" would, at least for infinitely many x, reduce to the simple but time consuming task of computing $y = 2^x-1$ and then testing whether y is prime. This argument can't be justified, since there are in fact, fast special methods for detecting Mersenne primes. The flaw in the argument is apparent from the fact that it applies equally well to the trivial question "Is 2^x prime?".

In section 3 we outline the construction of zero-one valued functions which are hard to compute at almost all arguments, and whose complexity can be precisely characterized in terms of the amount of storage space required to compute them.

Having constructed a function which is hard to compute, one would like to know <u>why</u> it is complex, besides the fact that by a diagonal construction it differs from all functions which are not complex. For example, one might conjecture that zero-one valued functions are hard to compute because of a "complex" or "random" pattern of zeroes and ones in their successive values. In section 4 we show that this is not true. There are <u>almost everywhere</u> (in the strong sense of <u>all but finitely many</u> exceptions) hard to compute functions which equal zero except at a vanishing fraction of their arguments. Such functions may be arbitrarily hard to compute, but of course can be approximated in practically no space or time at all with 100% limiting accuracy by a constant function equal to zero.

It is not clear how to give a precise formulation to the question of <u>why</u> predicates are complex. However one can sometimes show that one function is hard because it encodes another function known to be hard. We use this technique in section 5 to obtain a proof of Friedberg's decomposition theorem for recursively enumerable sets, a simple proof of a related theorem due to Young, and a theorem about classifying functions by bounds on complexity.

Any zero-one valued function can be computed quickly without auxiliary storage space at any finite number of arguments by some program. One merely builds a finite table of values of the function into the program itself. In section 6 we construct zero-one valued functions for which any program computing the function requires a large amount of tape and time except at a number of arguments equal to the size of the program. We conclude that there is no way to compute such functions quickly except by already having their values in tables. It then follows that such functions cannot even be approximated by easily computed functions, and that such functions exhibit the properties of random zero-one valued functions.

2. Space-Bounded Turing Machines

The machine model we shall use for measuring the computational complexity of functions is an ordinary one tape Turing machine, with inputs and outputs coded in binary representation. A Turing machine M computes a partial recursive function φ_M if, started with the binary representation of x on its tape surrounded by blanks (with the read-write head of M on the high order digit of x), M halts with the binary representation of $\varphi_M(x)$ on its tape and the rest of the tape blank; if $\varphi_M(x)$ is undefined then either M does not halt, or halts without leaving the representation of an integer on its tape.

The space function S_M of M is defined so that $S_M(x)$ equals the larger of the total number of tape squares ever visited by the read-write head of M during the computation on input x, and the number of squares required for input x; $S_M(x)$ is undefined if $\varphi_M(x)$ is undefined. Note that $S_M(x)$ is undefined by this convention even if M uses only a finite number of tape squares but loops or halts with an ill-formed output.

Two convenient consequences of these conventions will be used in later sections. First, $\varphi_M(x) \leq 2^{S_M(x)}$ simply because the largest output which can be represented in S tape squares is 2^S-1. Second, $S_M(x) \geq \ell(x) = \max\{1, \lceil \log_2 x + 1 \rceil\}$ because $\ell(x)$ squares are required to represent x on the tape.

A Turing machine will be allowed to write additional symbols besides 0,1, and blank. Given any Turing machine M one can now design another machine M' which uses only half as much space by allowing M' enough symbols to represent two symbols of M by one of its own symbols. This method of decreasing space works for all except input and output symbols, giving us the following lemma [3,4].

Linear Speed-Up Lemma. For any Turing machine M and any $\epsilon > 0$ there is a Turing machine M' such that $\varphi_M = \varphi_{M'}$ and $S_{M'}(x) \leq \underline{\max}\{\ell(x), \ell(\varphi_M(x)), \epsilon \cdot S_M(x)\}$ for all x.

We shall appeal to speed-up for justification of informal descriptions of Turing machines which are supposed to operate within various bounds on space. To show that a function can be computed in space S it is sufficient to compute it in space bounded by any constant multiple of S. Moreover, it is not hard to show that a Turing machine of the type we have defined can simulate a multiheaded Turing machine with any finite number of unbounded multidimensional storage arrays, for example, using only a constant multiple more space than the multi-machine, and hence can simulate the multi-machine without any space loss at all. In a sense we are appealing to an extended form of Church's Thesis in which we hypothesize that any procedure which can effectively be carried out by some finite computing agency within space S can be performed by a Turing machine within space S. The reader need not subscribe to this thesis, which is almost certainly false stated in such generality, but we shall make some substantial demands on his intuition about the possibility of designing Turing machines which operate within certain space bounds.

Let M_0, M_1,... be some effective enumeration of Turing machines. We write φ_i for φ_{M_i} and S_i for S_{M_i}. Hartmanis and Stearns observe that one can design a universal two input Turing machine which given inputs i and x simulates M_i on input x step by step [3,4]. In general M_i may have more symbols than the fixed universal machine, so that the universal machine must encode each symbol of M_i with several of its own symbols causing a constant factor space loss.

If M_i has $\sigma(i)$ states and symbols it can run for at most $\sigma(i)^n$ steps on n tape squares before entering an infinite loop. Since $\sigma(i)^n$ can be represented in binary using $n \cdot \log_2\sigma(i)$ tape squares, a universal machine can also detect when M_i enters a finite loop, and the space required by the universal machine is again bounded by a constant factor of the number of tape squares involved in this non-halting computation of M_i. We now can state a second important lemma.

Universal Space-Bounded Lemma. There is a Turing machine M which given inputs i and x computes $\varphi_i(x)$ in space bounded by $k_i \cdot S_i(x)$ for some constant k_i independent of x. Moreover if the ith Turing machine loops on input x having visited N(x) tape squares, M halts having used at most $k_i \cdot N(x)$ tape squares.

We shall use P_n (R_n) to designate the partial (total) recursive functions of n variables. All functions are (possibly partial) functions from the nonnegative integers N to N. A predicate P(x) on N is true almost everywhere (a.e.) iff it is true for all but finitely many x. For $\varphi \in P_1$ and any partial function ψ, Comp $(\varphi) \geq \psi$ (a.e.) means that domain $(\psi) \supset$ domain (φ) and $\varphi_i = \varphi$ implies $S_i \geq \psi$ (a.e.). Similarly Comp $(\varphi) \leq \psi$ means domain $(\psi) \subset$ domain (φ) and there exists $\varphi_i = \varphi$ such that $S_i \leq \psi$. (Because a Turing machine can be programmed to print out any finite set of values without using additional space beyond that required for the input, there is no need to distinguish Comp $(\varphi) \leq \psi$ (a.e.) from Comp $(c) \leq \psi$.) Let $1 \dot{-} x = 0$ if $x > 0$; $1 \dot{-} x = 1$ if $x = 0$. A function φ is constructable iff $\varphi = S_i$ for some i. We remark that φ is constructable iff Comp $(\varphi) \leq \varphi$.

For any total function t, the class $\mathcal{J}(t)$ is the set of total functions computable within space t, i.e., $\{\varphi_i \in R_1 \mid S_i \leq t\}$.

3. A Compression Theorem for Computation Space

The original construction of a zero-one valued function which is hard to compute almost everywhere is due to Rabin [5]. Blum generalized Rabin's proof to obtain zero-one valued functions such that the complexity of c was "compressed" between two bounds [6]. In the following theorem we combine Blum's construction, some techniques of Hartmanis and Stearns, and some new programming tricks to obtain the sharpest possible compression theorem for Turing machine space.

Theorem 1. Let $S \in P_1$ be any constructable function. There exists a zero-one valued function $c \in P_1$ such that

(i) domain (c) = domain (S)

(ii) Comp $(c) \leq S$, and

(iii) if $\varphi_i = c$, then $S_i \geq \epsilon \cdot S$ for some $\epsilon > 0$.

Thus the complexity of c is proportional to S, which characterizes the complexity of c as precisely as is possible given linear speed-up. There is a machine which computes c in space S and this machine is optimal in the sense that any other machine computing c requires more space than some linear speed-up of the optimal machine. (It even turns out that one can effectively calculate the factor by which the optimal machine must be sped-up in order to consume less space than a given machine for c, but we shall not prove this.)

Proof. We describe a procedure for computing c(x) in space bounded by $4 \cdot S(x)$. Linear speed-up then implies part (ii). In the computation of c certain indices $i \in N$ will be cancelled when an integer x has been discovered such that

$\varphi_i(x) \neq c(x)$. The computation is arranged so that i will be cancelled if $S_i \leq \epsilon \cdot S$ for every $\epsilon > 0$ at infinitely many arguments in the domain of S. Hence if $\varphi_i = S$, then $S_i \geq \epsilon \cdot S$ (a.e.) for some $\epsilon > 0$. By decreasing ϵ one obtains $S_i \geq \epsilon \cdot S$ (everywhere) which implies part (iii). Given input x the value of c(x) is computed as follows:

1. Preserving the input x on the tape, mark off an adjacent interval of S(x) tape squares without using additional squares outside the interval. (This is possible because S is constructable). If S(x) is undefined, then c(x) will also be undefined.
2. Perform the following process for n = 0, 1, ... within the interval marked off in part 1 until all the space in the interval is used up: carry out n steps in the computation of each of c(0), c(1), ..., c(n) and keep a record of all indices which are discovered to be cancelled in these computations. Let C_x be the final set of cancelled indices discovered in this way.
3. Mark off a second interval of S(x) tape squares. Write in this interval the least integer $i \notin C_x$, without using any additional tape squares outside the two marked intervals. If this is not possible, erase the tape and print c(x) = 0.
4. Mark off a third interval of S(x) tape squares. Let i be the integer in the second interval. Use the universal machine described in section 2 to simulate M_i on input x in this third interval until it halts, or it is discovered to be looping, or the simulation requires more space than the size of the interval.

   If M_i halts, <u>cancel</u> i, erase the tape, and print $c(x) = 1 \dot{-} \varphi_i(x)$. If M_i is discovered to be looping, <u>cancel</u> i, erase the tape, and print $c(x) = 0$. If the simulation of M_i requires too much space, erase this third interval, and try to replace i in the second interval by the least $j > i$, $j \notin C_x$. If this is possible, replace i by j and repeat step 4. If j is too large to fit in the second interval, erase the tape and print $c(x) = 0$.

END.

The reader will have to convince himself that the preceding instructions can actually be carried out by a Turing machine. By definition such a Turing machine uses three intervals of size $S(x)$ plus the space occupied by the input x. Moreover $c(x)$ is defined iff $S(x)$ is defined.

To complete the proof suppose $S_i(x) \leq \epsilon \cdot S(x)$ for every $\epsilon > 0$ and infinitely many $x \in$ domain (S). We need only show that i gets cancelled.

Note that no integer gets cancelled infinitely often. For if integer j is cancelled in the computation of $c(x_0)$ for some x_0, then $j \in C_x$ for all x such that the computation of $c(x_0)$ can be successfully carried out in part 2 of the computation of $c(x)$. But if x is sufficiently large there will be enough space to carry out the computation of $c(x_0)$ in part 2 of the computation of $c(x)$. (We are using the fact that $S(x)$ is constructable, and so must be at least as large as the space required to write input x.) Hence $j \in C_x$ for all sufficiently large x. By construction no member of C_x is cancelled during the computation of $c(x)$.

Let k_i be the constant such that the universal machine can simulate M_i within space $k_i \cdot S_i$. For $x \in$ domain (S) such that $S_i(x) \leq (1/k_i)S(x)$, choose x sufficiently large that no $j < i$ gets cancelled in the computation of $c(x)$ and also sufficiently large that i can be written in an interval of $S(x)$ tape squares. Then M_i will be successfully simulated in part 4 of the computation of $c(x)$ and hence i will be cancelled.

Q.E.D.

Corollary 1. For any constructable $S \in R_1$, the following statements are equivalent for any total function t:

(a) $\mathcal{F}(S) \not\subset \mathcal{F}(t)$,

(b) $\liminf_{x\to\infty} [t(x)/S(x)] = 0$

(c) there is a zero-one valued function $c \in \mathcal{F}(S) - \mathcal{F}(t)$.

Proof. Immediate.

We remark that Theorem 1 was observed independently by Borodin, Constable and Hopcroft, and by Trachtenbrot [7], [8].

4. Sparse Complex Functions

If almost every value of a zero-one valued function is hard to compute, it might seem plausible the values are not only hard to compute exactly, but also hard to compute approximately. In other words, any easy to compute quesses about values of the function ought to be wrong about half the time. This is false, as we now demonstrate.

Definition. A function c is d-sparse for some function d if and only if $c(x) = 1$ implies that $c(y) = 0$ for $x < y \leq x + d(x)$.

Thus if c is a zero-one valued d-sparse function for some function d such that $\liminf_{x\to\infty} d(x) = \infty$, then the average value of $c = \lim_{x\to\infty} \left(\sum_{y=0}^{x} c(y)/x\right) = 0$. As d grows more rapidly, the limit zero will be approached more rapidly.

Theorem 2. For any functions $d, t \in R_1$, there exists a d-sparse zero-one valued $c \in R_1$ such that Comp $(c) \geq t$ (a.e.).

Proof. Given $d, t \in R_1$, the function c is computed in stages beginning with stage zero. The value of c(x) is determined at some stage $z \leq x$. Not all stages get executed.

Stage x. Find the smallest uncancelled $i \leq x$, and for that i find the smallest y_i, $x \leq y_i \leq x + d(x)$, such that $S_i(y_i) < t(y_i)$.

If there is such an i and $y_i = x$, then define $c(x) = 1 \dot{-} \varphi_i(x)$, define $c(y) = 0$ for $x < y \leq x + d(x)$, cancel i, and go to stage $x + d(x) + 1$. Otherwise, define $c(x) = 0$ and go to stage $x + 1$. END

The search for i and y_i called for at stage x is finite and clearly effective. Moreover, the value of $1 \dot{-} \varphi_i(x)$ is computed at stage x only after it is known that $S_i(x) < t(x)$, and hence this computation of $1 \dot{-} \varphi_i(x)$ will terminate. Thus the computation of every stage is effective and will terminate, so that $c \in R_1$.

If $c(x) = 1$ is defined at stage x, then $c(y) = 0$ for $x < y \leq x + d(x)$ is also defined at stage x. Therefore, c is zero-one valued and d-sparse.

If i gets cancelled at any executed stage x, then $c(x) = 1 \dot{-} \varphi_i(x) \neq \varphi_i(x)$. Hence, if $\varphi_i = c$, then i never gets cancelled.

Note that each i is cancelled at most once. Choose $x_i \geq i$ such that all $j < i$ which ever get cancelled at an executed stage have already been cancelled by stage x_i. Then for any $x \geq x_i$, i will be cancelled at stage x if $S_i(x) < t(x)$. Hence, $\varphi_i = c$ implies $S_i(x) \geq t(x)$ for $x \geq x_i$. Q.E.D.

Given integers $n \geq m > 0$, define $c'(x) = c(x)$ if the remainder of $x \div n$ exceeds m; $c'(x) = 1 \dot{-} c(x)$ otherwise. If c is d-sparse for $d(x) \geq x$, then it is easy to see that $\lim_{x \to \infty} (\sum_{y=0}^{x} c'(y)/x) = m/n$. Moreover, the space required to compute c is the same as that required to compute c' and vice-versa. Thus we have

Corollary 2. For any $t \in R_1$, and any rational number q, $0 \leq q \leq 1$, there exists a zero-one valued $c' \in R_1$ such that Comp $(c') \geq t$(a.e.) and the average value of c' =

$$\lim_{x \to \infty} \left(\sum_{y=0}^{x} c'(y)/x \right) = q.$$

5. Reducibility Among Computations

The existence of almost everywhere complex zero-one valued functions is often sufficient to establish the existence of other inherently complex computations. For example, given any $f \in R_1$, there exist arbitrarily complex functions $f' \in R_1$, such that $f \leq f' \leq f + 1$. Namely, let $f'(x) = f(x) + c(x)$ for some complex $c \in R_1$; since $c(x) = f'(x)-f(x)$, the space required to compute f' must at least be equal to the space required to compute c, less the space required to compute f. Since c can be chosen arbitrarily complex, so can f'.

The preceding argument is a proof by reducibility. Object A is said to be reducible to object B if the ability to answer questions about B enables one to answer questions about A by various effective methods. If questions about A are known to be undecidable, and also A is reducible to B, then corresponding questions about B must be undecidable. In order to get more detailed information about computational complexity, one need only demonstrate that object A is "rapidly" reducible to object B; then if questions about A are known to be computationally complex, so must corresponding questions about B. The proof of Corollary 2 in the previous section is another illustration of this obvious technique.

In this section we shall prove two theorems which are related only in that their proofs fit the informal description of reducibility arguments. We have not attempted to formalize the notion of complexity bounded reducibilities, though it is easy to generate an assortment of definitions (generally inequivalent) patterned after the reducibilities familiar in recursive function theory [9].

Our first result is in the spirit of the "gap" theorems of Borodin, Trachtenbrot, and Constable [10], [11], [12]. These theorems imply for example that there exist rapidly increasing functions $t \in R_1$ such $\mathcal{F}(t) = \mathcal{F}(2^t)$. That is, one can't compute any functions using the much larger amount of space 2^t than one can compute in space t. There is a "gap" in the complexity range between t and 2^t in which no new functions appear. Of course if t were constructable, so would 2^t be constructable, and then Corollary 1 would imply that $\mathcal{F}(2^t) \supsetneq \mathcal{F}(t)$. Thus gaps don't occur above constructable functions.

The following theorem shows that there can be a gap (even when t is constructable) between t and another function t' which is never less that t and is enormously greater than t most of the time (but not a.e.). (Bass obtains further results of this sort in [13].)

A set of nonnegative integers will be called d-sparse if its characteristic function is d-sparse, as defined in section 4.

Theorem 3. For any functions $r, t, d \in R_1$, there exists a function $t' \in R_1$, such that

(i) $t'(x) \geq t(x)$ for all x,
(ii) $t'(x) \geq r(x)$ except for a d-sparse set of x, and
(iii) $\mathcal{F}(t) = \mathcal{F}(t')$.

Proof. Given $t = \varphi_j$, let $c \in R_1$ be any d-sparse zero-one valued function such that $\text{Comp}(c) \geq 2^{S_j}$ (a.e.).

Define $t'(x) = t(x) + (1 \dot{-} c(x))\cdot(r(x) + 1)$. Obviously t' satisfies (i) and (ii).

Part (iii) follows easily from a stronger statement: if S is constructable and $S \leq t'$(a.e.), then $S \leq t$(a.e.).

To prove the stronger statement, suppose that $S(x) \leq t'(x)$ for all $x \geq n$. Consider a Turing machine which operates according to the following description:

"Given input x, compute t(x) using space $S_j(x)$.
Then see if $S(x) \leq t(x)$ using at most t(x) additional tape squares. If $S(x) \leq t(x)$ or $x < n$, compute and print out c(x). Otherwise, print out zero."

Note that $c(x) = 0$ if and only if $t'(x) > t(x)$. Hence, if $S(x) > t(x)$ and $x \geq n$, then $t'(x) \geq S(x) > t(x)$ and $c(x) = 0$. Therefore, the Turing machine described above computes the function c. Moreover, for $x \geq n$, whenever $S(x) > t(x)$ the value zero for c(x) is printed out in space $S_j(x) + t(x) \leq 2 \cdot 2^{S_j(x)}$ (We have used the observation that $t(x) = \varphi_j(x) \leq 2^{S_j(x)}$:) But the values of c(x) cannot be printed out in this little space for infinitely many x, because Comp (c) $\geq 2^{S_j}$ (a.e.). Therefore $S \leq t$ (a.e.).

Q.E.D.

We now consider the space required in enumerating sets. For any set $A \subset N$, we define $S_i^A(x)$ to be the cumulative amount of space required by the ith Turing machine to generate x elements in A.

Definition. For any set $A \subset N$, define

$$S_i^A(x) = \sum_{y < y_x} S_i(y)$$

where y_x is the least integer for which $A \cap \{\varphi_i(z) \mid z < y_x\}$ contains x elements.

By convention $S_i^A(0) = 0$ and $S_i^A(x)$ is undefined if $\varphi_i(y)$ is undefined for some $y < y_x$, and is also undefined if range (φ_i) contains fewer than x members of A. The complexity of enumerating exactly the set A is measured by S_i^N when range $(\varphi_i) = A$. Thus we write Enum (A) $\geq t$ (a.e.) if range $(\varphi_i) = A$ implies $S_i^N \geq t$ (a.e.).

Friedberg has shown that every nonrecursive, recursively enumerable set is a disjoint union of two nonrecursive, recursively enumerable sets [14]. Young proves the analogous theorem that any infinite recursively enumerable set is the disjoint union of sets which are arbitrarily hard to enumerate [15]. A natural way to decompose a set into more complex sets is to enumerate the given set and place successive elements into either of two sets on the basis of some complex decision. We use a reducibility argument to verify this idea, and then observe that the same proof yields both Young's and Friedberg's results.

Definition. For A, $B \subset N$ and any function t, the set A is t-blocked by B providing $B \cap \text{range}(\varphi_i) = \emptyset$ implies $S_i^A \geq t$ (a.e.).

Theorem 4.* Let A be an infinite recursively enumerable set, and suppose A = range (g) for some one-one function $g \in R_1$. For any $t \in R_1$ and any sufficiently complex (a.e.) zero-one valued function $c \in R_1$, define

$$A_0 = \{g(x) \mid c(x) = 0\} \text{ and}$$

$$A_1 = \{g(x) \mid c(x) = 1\}.$$

---

*Parts (i), (ii), and (iii) of Theorem 4 are a reformulation, using the space measure, of Young's theorem for his definition of enumeration techniques [15]. One can show that the complexity of any set in the space measure is related effectively to its complexity in an enumeration technique, so that Theorem 4 directly implies Young's theorem.

In constructing the sets A_0, A_1 by diagonalization, Young also notes that among the first n elements in the enumeration of A, at least n/4 are members of A_0, and similarly for A_1. By Corollary 2, our definition of A_0 and A_1 enables one to choose any complementary limiting densities for A_0 and A_1 in the enumeration of A.

(i) A_0, A_1 are disjoint infinite recursively enumerable sets whose union is A.

(ii) Enum $(A_0) \geq t$ (a.e.) and Enum $(A_1) \geq t$ (a.e.).

(iii) A_0 and A_1 t-block each other.

(iv) If A is not recursive, then neither A_0 nor A_1 is recursive.

Proof. If c is sufficiently complex it must equal both zero and one infinitely often, hence A_0, A_1 are infinite. The rest of (i) is immediate.

Part (ii) follows directly from (iii) and the fact that A_0 and A_1 are disjoint.

To prove (iii), suppose $g = \varphi_j$ and define $t'(x) = \max \{t(y) \mid y \leq x+1\}$. We show that if Comp $(c) \geq S_j + 2t'$ (a.e.), then A_0 is t-blocked by A_1. By symmetry A_1 is t-blocked by A_0, and part (iii) then follows.

Suppose $A_1 \cap$ range $(\varphi_i) = \emptyset$. Consider a Turing machine which computes c according to the following description.

"Given input x, compute g(x) using space $S_j(x)$.

Then carry out the following two computations in parallel, devoting an equal amount of space to each, until one of them terminates:

(1) Compute $\varphi_i(0), \varphi_i(1), \ldots$ in order until $\varphi_i(y) = g(x)$ turns up.

(2) Compute c(x).

If computation (1) terminates first, print out zero.

If computation (2) terminates first, print out c(x)."

Note that if $g(x) \in$ range (φ_i), then $g(x) \notin A_1$, and so $c(x) = 0$. Therefore, the Turing machine described above computes the function c. Moreover, if g(x) turns up in the enumeration of range (φ_i), the value zero is printed out in at most the space $S_j(x)$ required to compute g(x), plus twice the space $S_i^{\{g(x)\}}(1)$ required to enumerate range (φ_i) until g(x) appears.

Since Comp (c) $\geq S_j + 2t'$ (a.e.), we must have $S_j(x) + 2 \cdot S_i^{\{g(x)\}}(1) \geq S_j(x) + 2 \cdot t'(x)$ (a.e.), and hence $S_i^{\{g(x)\}}(1) \geq t'(x)$. That is, the space required for g(x) to appear in the enumeration of range (φ_i), if g(x) appears at all, must exceed t'(x) for almost all x. (These inequalities are vacuously true if $S_i^{\{g(x)\}}(1)$ is undefined.)

Now observe that if $S_i^{A_0}(y+1)$ is defined for some y, then among the first y + 1 elements of A_0 which appear in range (φ_i), there must be an element $g(x) \in A_0$ for some $x \geq y$. Hence $S_i^{A_0}(y+1) \geq S_i^{\{g(x)\}}(1) \geq t'(x) \geq t'(y) \geq t(y+1)$ for almost all y. That is $S_i^{A_0} \geq t$ (a.e.), and we have shown that A_0 is t-blocked by A_1.

To prove part (iv), suppose A_1 is recursive.

As in the proof of part (iii), let $g = \varphi_j$, and choose $t'(x) = S_j^{\{g(x)\}}(1)$. Since A_1 is recursive, $\bar{A}_1$ = range (φ_i) for some $\varphi_i \in R_1$, and since $A_1 \cap$ range $(\varphi_i) = \emptyset$, we conclude as before that $S_i^{\{g(x)\}}(1) \geq t'(x) = S_j^{\{g(x)\}}(1)$ for almost all x. That is, almost all elements of A require more space to appear in range φ_i, if they appear at all, than they require to appear in range (g).

We can now decide membership in A as follows. If $x \in A_1$, then $x \in A$. Otherwise, enumerate range (φ_i) until x appears, and devote the same amount of space to enumerating range (g). If x appears in range (g), then $x \in A$.

If x does not appear in range (g) in the allotted space, then $x \notin A$ unless it is one of the finitely many elements in A which appear in range (φ_i) before appearing in range (g).

Thus if A_1 (or, by symmetry, A_0) is recursive, so is A.

Q.E.D.

6. Pseudo-Random Sequences

If one thinks of the detection of <u>all</u> primes as a single problem, one's attention is directed at the long run efficiency of general detection procedures, rather than at the behavior of the procedures which operate on any particular finite set of integers. Such thinking is very natural in mathematics, but in the mundane context of computing it may not be appropriate. One can argue that the limiting behavior of computations of finite functions will not be the same as the behavior of computations of infinite functions, although there is not as yet a satisfactory theory of computation for finite functions.

Turing machine tape is an inadequate measure of the complexity of finite functions, since the entire function can be encoded into the program of a machine. This difficulty can be partly overcome by counting the space required to represent a program, in addition to the space required to execute it [cf. 16].

Computational complexity of functions in the sense of this paper, which might be called the global complexity of computation, differs significantly from the limiting complexity of finite approximations to functions even when program size is counted. Sparse functions for example may be arbitrarily complex globally, but small programs can compute large initial segments of a sparse function from the small table of arguments at which the function is non-zero. Informally, global complexity reflects the difficulty of finding a table of the first x values of a function, whereas the complexity of the function restricted to $\{0, 1, \ldots, x-1\}$ reflects the difficulty of storing these values in an easily retrievable form once they are known. The two notions generally yield widely divergent results, though in this section we prove a theorem relating them.

M. Blum has pointed out in a personal communication that Rabin's original construction of a complex zero-one valued function c actually yields a sharper result: $\varphi_i = c$ implies that S_i is large except for at most 2i arguments. The first n values of a zero-one valued function c can obviously be represented by a table of n bits, so one would expect the index of such a table in any standard indexing to be roughly equal to 2^n. Blum raises the question whether there is a zero-one valued function c such that $\varphi_i = c$ implies that S_i is large except at roughly $\log_2 i$ arguments. Theorem 5 demonstrates that there are such functions.

Lemma 5. Let $f \in R_1$ be such that $\sum_{i=0}^{\infty} 2^{-f(i)} = a$ for some real number a. Let $g \in R_1$ be nondecreasing and unbounded. For any $t \in R_1$, there exists a zero-one valued function $c \in R_1$ such that for all i, if $\varphi_i = c$, then $S_i(x) > t(x)$ for all but $f(i) + g(i) + \log_2 a$ values of x.

Proof. The function c is computed in stages. The value of c(x) is defined at stage x. At stage zero, each index i is uncancelled and has an associated rational weight $w(i) = 2^{-f(i)}$. At subsequent stages indices may become cancelled and weights may be increased.

Stage x. Let

$I = \{i \mid g(i) \leq x, \text{ i is uncancelled, and } S_i(x) \leq t(x)\}$.

For n = 0,1, let

$I_n = \{i \in I \mid \varphi_i(x) = n\}$,

and let

$$s_n = \sum_{i \in I_n} w(i). \quad (\text{If } I_n = \emptyset, \text{ let } s_n = 0.)$$

If $s_0 > s_1$, define c(x) = 1, cancel all $i \in I_0$, and double w(i) for all $i \in I_1$. Otherwise, define c(x) = 0, cancel all $i \in I_1$, and double w(i) for all $i \in I_0$. Go to stage x+1. END

Clearly $c \in R_1$, and c is zero-one valued. At stage zero the cumulative weights of all uncancelled indices equals a. At stage x, the cumulative weights of all uncancelled indices is decreased by $\underline{\max}\{s_0, s_1\}$ and increased by $\underline{\min}\{s_0, s_1\}$. Therefore the cumulative weights of all uncancelled indices at any stage remains bounded above by a. Hence, the weight of an uncancelled index i cannot be doubled more than $f(i) + \log_2 a$ times; otherwise its weight would exceed a.

Suppose $\varphi_i = c$. Then i never gets cancelled at any stage. Therefore the weight of i gets doubled at each stage x at which $g(i) \leq x$ and $S_i(x) \leq t(x)$. It follows that $S_i(x) \leq t(x)$ for at most $g(i) + f(i) + \log_2 a$ different values of x.

Q.E.D.

<u>Theorem 5</u>. Let $M_0, M_1, \ldots$ be any effective enumeration of Turing machines. Given any recursive function t one can construct a zero-one valued recursive function c such that any machine M_i which computes c requires t(x) tape squares to compute c(x) for all but $\log_2 i + o(\log_2 i)$ values of x.

<u>Proof</u>. Let $g(i) = \lfloor \log_2 \log_2(i+1) \rfloor$ and $f(i) = \lfloor \log_2(i+1) + 2 \log_2 \log_2(i+1) \rfloor$ in Lemma 5.

Q.E.D.

For enumerations of machines in increasing order of "length" the bounds of Theorem 5 can be approximately achieved. If instead of machines we think of programs which may contain constants, then the length of a program should grow precisely as the length of the representation of the constant. This motivates the following

<u>Definition</u>. Let $M_0, M_1, \ldots$ be an effective enumeration of machines. Let $M_{\sigma(i,x)}$ be the index of the machine which on input y copies the binary representation of x next to y and then performs exactly the computation of M_i on the pair of inputs x and y. The enumeration is a

<u>length-order enumeration</u> iff $\sigma(i,x) \leq (x+1)\cdot f(i)$ for some $f \in R_1$, and all i,x.

It is not hard to exhibit length-order enumerations. If we apply Theorem 5 to a length-order enumeration to obtain a sufficiently complex function c, it turns out that the function c exhibits properties associated with "random" zero-one valued infinite sequences. To verify this observation we elaborate a technique of Chaitin [17].

We first show that the average value of c must exist and equal $\frac{1}{2}$. The idea is that otherwise there would be small easily decoded descriptions for relatively large initial segments of c, which would enable small programs for c to use little space for a large number of arguments.

Order the binary sequences of length n in increasing order of weight (number of ones in the sequence), with sequences of the same weight ordered lexicographically. One can easily construct a machine which prints out the mth length n sequence $(1 \leq m \leq 2^n)$ in order of weight given inputs m and n, using space $n + \ell(m) + \ell(n)$. The following basic result of information theory will be essential: given $\epsilon > 0$, there exists $\delta > 0$ such that for all n the number of binary sequences of length n with weight at most $(1-\epsilon)\, n/2$ is less than $2^{(1-\delta)n}$ [17,18].

<u>Lemma 6</u>. Let $c \in R_1$ satisfy Theorem 5 for a length-order enumeration with $t(x) \geq 2^x$. The average value of c exists and equals $\frac{1}{2}$.

<u>Proof</u>. Let h(n,m) be the integer whose binary representation is obtained by inserting zeroes between each digit in the binary representation of n, and placing a one after the last digit followed by the binary representation of m. (For example, $h(5,2) = h((101)_2,(10)_2) = (10001110)_2$.) Note that $h(n,m) \leq p(n)(m+1)$ for some polynomial p.

Let M_k be the Turing machine which operates as follows: "Given inputs y and x, find n,m such that h(n,m) = y using only the tape squares occupied by y. (If there are no such n,m halt immediately.) If $x \geq n$, compute and print $c(x)$ as output. If $x < n$, print as output the xth digit of the length n sequence which is m^{th} in order of weight."

On inputs x, y for $x < n$ and $y = h(n,m)$ for some $m \leq 2^n$, M_k need only use $n + \ell(y) + \ell(x) \leq b \cdot n$ tape squares for some constant b independent of n.

Suppose the average value of c exists and is not equal to $\frac{1}{2}$, or does not exist. There is no loss of generality in either case if we assume that for some $\epsilon > 0$ there are infinitely many n for which the weight of the sequence $\bar{c}_n = c(0), c(1), \ldots, c(n-1)$ is at most $(1-\epsilon)\, n/2$. Then the sequence $\bar{c}_n$ is the m_n^{th} in order of weight among length n sequences for $m_n \leq 2^{(1-\delta)n}$. Therefore for infinitely many n, $M_{\sigma(k,h(n,m_n))}$ computes the function c, and uses space at most $b \cdot n$ on inputs $x < n$. But $b \cdot n < t(x) = 2^x$ for $x > \log_2 n + \log_2 b$, so abbreviating $\sigma(k,h(n,m_n))$ as $\sigma(n)$, we have for infinitely many n

$$\varphi_{\sigma(n)} = c \text{ and } S_{\sigma(n)}(x) < t(x) \text{ for } n\text{-}o(n) \text{ values of } x.$$

But by the bound on h and the definition of length-order enumerations we have

$$\log_2(\sigma(n)) \leq (1-\delta)n + o(n)$$

which contradicts our choice of c in Theorem 5. Q.E.D.

No recursive function can properly be called "random" because there is a way to "predict" its values <u>a priori</u>, namely compute them. We propose a weak notion of randomness with respect to certain prediction methods in the spirit of Von Mises' notion of "collectives" or gambling sequences [19,20].

<u>Definition</u>. A zero-one valued function c is <u>a priori random</u> with respect to a zero-one valued function g iff the average value of $g \oplus c$ (mod 2 sum) exists and equals $\frac{1}{2}$.

Theorem 6. For $t \in R_1$, $t(x) \geq 2^x$, let $c \in R_1$ be the zero-one valued function satisfying Theorem 5 using a length-order enumeration of Turing machines. Then c is *a priori* random with respect to any zero-one valued $g \in R_1$ such that Comp (g) < t.

Proof. The proof is essentially the same as Lemma 5. Replace the sequence $\bar{c}_n$ in the proof of Lemma 5 by $\bar{c}_n \oplus \bar{g}_n$ (coordinatewise mod 2 sum), and let machine M_k print out $g(x) \oplus$ (the xth digit of the mth length n sequence) for $x < n$. Q.E.D.

The proof of Theorem 5 implies that for increasing constructable functions t there are zero-one valued functions $c \in \mathcal{F}(2^{2^t})$ satisfying Theorem 5 for certain simple length-order enumerations. By Theorem 6 such functions c are random with respect to $\mathcal{F}(t)$, and in fact are random even with respect to procedures which need not predict c(x) for every x, and which may use the values of c(0), c(1),..., c(x-1) in computing a prediction for the value of c(x), providing the computation of the prediction requires space less than t [cf. 21, 22].

Our results are closely related to more general definitions of randomness proposed by Kolmogorov, Martin-Lof, and Chaitin [17, 20, 23, 24, 25, 26]. A detailed discussion must be postponed because of space limitations [27].

References

1. A.R. Meyer and E.M. McCreight, Properties of Bounds on Computation, *Proc. Princeton Conf. on Inf. Sci.* (1969), 154-156.
2. J. Hartmanis and H. Shank, Two Memory Bounds for the Recognition of Primes by Automata, *Math. Sys. Th.* 3 (1969), 125-129.
3. J. Hartmanis and R.E. Stearns, On the Computational Complexity of Algorithms, *Trans. Am. Math. Soc.* 117 (1965), 285-306.

4. R.E. Stearns, J. Hartmanis, and P.M. Lewis II, Hierarchies of Memory-Limited Computations, IEEE Conf. Rec. on Switch. Th. and Log. Design (1965), 179-190.
5. M.O. Rabin, Degree of Difficulty of Computing a Function, Hebrew Univ. Tech. Report 2 (1960).
6. M. Blum, A Machine-Independent Theory of the Complexity of Recursive Functions, J. Assoc. Comp. Mach. 14 (1967), 322-336.
7. A.Borodin, R. Constable, and J. Hopcroft, Dense and Non-Dense Families of Complexity Classes, IEEE Conf. Rec. on Switch. and Aut. Th. (1969), 7-19.
8. B.A. Trachtenbrot, On Autoreducibility, Soviet Math. Dokl. 11, 3 (1970), 814-817.
9. H.Rogers, Theory of Recursive Functions and Effective Computability, McGraw-Hill (1967).
10. A. Borodin, Computational Complexity and the Existence of Complexity Gaps, thesis, Dept. of Comp. Sci., Cornell Univ. (1970).
11. B.A. Trachtenbrot, Complexity of Algorithms and Computations (in Russian), Novosibirsk Univ. (1967).
12. R.L. Constable, The Operator Gap, IEEE Conf. Rec. on Switch. and Aut. Th. (1969), 20-26.
13. L.J. Bass, Hierarchies Based on Computational Complexity, thesis, Dept. of Comp. Sci., Purdue Univ.(1970).
14. R.M. Friedberg, Three Theorems on Recursive Enumeration, J. Symb. Log. 23 (1958), 309-316.
15. P.R. Young, Toward a Theory of Enumerations, J. Assoc. Comp. Mach. 16 (1968), 328-348.
16. D. Pager, On the Efficiency of Algorithms, J. Assoc. Comp. Mach. 17 (1970), 708-714.
17. G.J.Chaitin, On the Length of Programs for Computing Finite Binary Sequences, J. Assoc. Comp. Mach. 13 (1966), 547-569.
18. C.E. Shannon and W. Weaver, The Mathematical Theory of Communication, Univ. of Ill., Chicago (c. 1949).
19. R. von Mises, Probability, Statistics and Truth (trans. from German), Macmillan, New York (1957).
20. D. Loveland, A New Interpretation of the von Mises Concept of Random Sequence, Zeit f. math. Logik und Grund. d. Math. 12 (1966), 279-294.
21. M.Levin, M. Minsky, and R. Silver, On the Problem of the Effective Definition of "Random Sequence", Mass. Inst. Tech. Comp. Center, memo 36 (revised)(1962).

22. R.A. DiPaola, Random Sets in Subrecursive Hierarchies, _J. Assoc. Comp. Mach._ _16_ (1969), 621-630.
23. P. Martin-Lof, The Definition of Random Sequences, _Inf. and Control_ _9_ (1965), 602-619.
24. C.P. Schnorr, Uber die Definition von effektiven Zufallstests, _Z. Wahrscheinlishkeitstheorie_ _15_ (1970), 297-312.
25. G. Bruere-Dawson, Pseudo-random Sequences, _Mass. Inst. of Tech._, Project MAC Technical mem. 16 (1970).
26. A.N. Kolmogorov, Three Approaches to the Quantitutive Definition of Information, English trans. in _Int. J. Computer Math._ _2_ (1968), 157-168.
27. E.F. Beschler, (Asst. Vice Pres., Academic Press) Letter to the Contributors International Symposium on the Theory of Machines and Computations (1970).

COMPUTATIONAL EQUIVALENCE

Saul Levy
IRIA, Rocquencourt
FRANCE

ABSTRACT

The notion of effectively calculable function has been approached and studied from several directions. General recursiveness, λ-defineability, Post Cannonical Systems, Combinatory definability, and Turing Computability are the best known notions and they have all been shown formally to be equivalent one to the other (in the sense that they all define the same class of effective computations). These formal proofs taken together with "Church's Thesis" have lead to the general acceptance of all these notions as indeed capturing the idea of "effective computability". Characteristic of all these approaches is a mechanistic procedure which acts with a finite amount of information to compute the desired functions. The modern stored program electronic computer is a mechanization of a "reasonable approximation" to a mechanistic "clerk" who carries out the procedures described in any of the systems mentioned above. In that sense, each of the representations of a function in any of those systems has an analogue in the computer program, and the power and the limitations embodied in each of those systems carries over to the corresponding computer programs. The subject of this research is a study of the properties of a particular notion of algorithm which is much closer in form and appearance to the commonly accepted notions of computer programs than any of the formalisms mentioned above. These algorithms are called "programs" to reflect this bias, and we shall be concerned particularly with relations of computational equivalence between programs. Deciding computational equivalence is the core of any attempts at mechanical simplification or verification of computer programs and in this study we will assess the relative difficulty involved in trying to decide several types of "equivalence relation".

HORNERS RULE IS UNIQUELY OPTIMAL

Allan Borodin

Department of Computer Science
University of Toronto

Abstract

It is shown that with respect to the basic arithmetics $(+,-,\times,\div)$, Horner's rule is a uniquely optimal method for computing a polynomial $\sum_{i=0}^{n} a_i x^i$. The proof of uniqueness follows the known techniques for establishing the optimality of Horner's rule; specifically, "growth" arguments are combined with arguments regarding "active operations".

I Introduction

The problem of determing the least number of arithmetics required to compute a polynomial was first discussed by Ostrowski [7]. Ostrowski's "first problem" was to show that Horner's rule is optimal; that is, show that at least n multiplications and n additions or subtractions are required to compute $\sum_{i=0}^{n} a_i x^i$. He established the multiplication bound for $n \leq 4$ and suggested how to prove the addition-subtration bound for all n. Garsia [2] and Pan [8] successly extended the result to show that for all n, $\sum_{i=0}^{n} a_i x^i$ does require at least n multiplications or divisions.

Ostrowski's "second problem" was the conjecture that Horner's rule is "essentially" uniquely optimal; that is, show that any scheme for computing $\sum_{i=0}^{n} a_i x^i$ that requires only n multiplications "reduces" to Horner's rule. In this paper, we shall show that the techniques used to establish optimality can be extended to prove the unique optimality of Horner's rule. Indeed, we shall show that Horner's rule is the <u>only</u> way to compute $\sum_{i=0}^{n} a_i x^i$ in n multiplications or divisions and n additions or subtractions. In doing so, we shall consider a lower bound for the number of multiplications or divisions required to compute a "general polynomial" $P(\vec{a}, x) = \sum_{i=1}^{k} \ell_i(\vec{a})x^i + r(x)$, where each ℓ_i is a linear combination of the parameters $a_1,\ldots,a_s$ and $r(x)$ is a rational function of x. Thus we are considering the $\{a_i\}$ as well as x to be variables. In particular, we shall not be concerned with schemes for specific polynomials nor with schemes involved "preconditioning" [5,1,8] of the $\{a_i\}$.

II Definitions and a Review of the Proof of Optimality

Let F be any infinite field and let D be an infinite subset of F. D will be the domain of the inputs $a_1,\ldots,a_s,x$. Let $\ell(\vec{a})$ indicate $\sum_{j=1}^{s} c_j a_j$ and let $r(x)$ denote $(\sum_{j=0}^{v} d_j x^j) \div (\sum_{j=0}^{w} e_j x^j$ where all the c_j, d_j, e_j are in F. For example, D can be the positive integers and F the reals.

As in [8], we consider algorithms (programs) consisting of a sequence of instructions of the form $f_i = g_i \circ h_i$ where $\circ$ stands for one of the binary operations $(+, -, \times, \div)$ on F. Each f_i is a new variable, each g_i and h_i is either a fixed constant in F, a previously computed f_j $(j < i)$, or an input variable $(a_1,\ldots,a_s,x)$ from the domain D. A program computes $P(\vec{a},x)$ if there exists an $f_i = P(\vec{a},x)$ for all $a_1,\ldots,a_s,x$.

We let $*$ denote either $\times$ or $\div$ and following Pan [8], we distinguish between <u>inactive</u> and <u>active</u> operations. A $*$ operation $f_i = g_i * h_i$ is inactive if one of the following holds:

i) h_i is equivalent to a constant in F.

ii) g_i is equivalent to a constant in F and the operation is $\times$.

iii) g_i and h_i are both equivalent to rational functions of x (with coefficients in F).

All other $*$ operations are active. Thus $p_1 = x \div (1+x)$ is inactive while both $p_2 = 1 \div a_j$ and $p_3 = p_1 \times p_2$ are active. For purposes of this paper, we shall not "count" multiplication by a constant in F; this is, $*$ operations of either type i or ii.

Pan showed that without "preconditioning of the coefficients", n active $*$ operations were required to compute $\sum_{i=1}^{n} a_i x^i$. Hopcroft and this author observed that the Pan proof could be restated (and more easily proved) as follows:

$\ell_1(\vec{a}),\ldots,\ell_u(\vec{a})$ are said to be <u>linearly independent</u> if there does not exist a non trivial set $c_1,\ldots,c_u$, c_i in F: $\sum_{i=1}^{u} c_i \ell_i$ = constant 0 in F.

<u>Fact 1</u>: Let $P(\vec{a},x) = \sum_{i=1}^{n} \ell_i(\vec{a})x^i + r(x)$ and assume that there are u linearly independent ℓ_i. Then u active $*$ operations are required to compute $P(\vec{a},x)$. Thus n active $*$ operations are required to compute $\sum_{i=1}^{n} a_i x^i$.

<u>Proof</u>: The proof consists of an induction on u and follows the line of reasoning in Knuth [2] and also in Winograd [9]. The following Lemma is essential.

<u>Lemma</u>: Let $\ell_1(a_1,\ldots,a_s),\ldots, \ell_u(a_1,\ldots,a_s)$ be linearly independent. Let $a_1 = \ell(a_2,\ldots,a_s)$. Then there are at least $u - 1$ linearly independent ℓ_i' where $\ell_i'(a_2,\ldots,a_s) = \ell_i|_{a_1=\ell(\vec{a})} = \ell_i(\ell(a_1,\ldots,a_s), a_2,\ldots,a_s)$.

<u>Proof of Lemma</u> [3]: Think of the a_i as generating a u dimensional vector space S over F, and consider $\ell_1,\ldots,\ell_u$ to be u linearly independent vectors in S. Let S_1 be the subspace generated by the $\{\ell_i\}$. Now consider the linear mapping ϕ induced by $\phi(a_1) = \ell(a_2,\ldots a_s)$ and $\phi(a_i) = a_i$ $2 \le i \le s$. The kernel of ϕ has dimension one, and therefore the kernal of ϕ restricted to S_1 has dimension at most one. $\phi(S_1)$ is then the space generated by $\ell_1',\ldots,\ell_u'$ and has dimension = dim S_1 - dim ker $\phi|_{S_1} \ge u - 1$.

QED Lemma

We now sketch the proof of Fact 1.

<u>$u = 1$</u>

Without an active $*$ operation, it is only possible to compute functions having the form $\ell(\vec{a}) + r(x)$.

Induction Step

Let $[\ell_1(\vec{a}) + r_1(x)] * [\ell_2(\vec{a}) + r_2(x)]$ be the first active * operation. Without loss of generality (wlg.), assume $\ell_2(\vec{a}) \neq$ constant. Set (in the program) $\ell_2(\vec{a}) + r_2(x) = e$ where e is a constant chosen so that no proper division will become improper (for example, this could occur if there were an assumption that $a_n \neq 0$ and the first operation was $p_1 = x \div a_n$).

If $\ell_2(\vec{a}) = \sum_{i=1}^{s} d_i a_i$ and $d_j \neq 0$ then we can effectively set $\ell_2(\vec{a}) + r_2(x) = e$ by setting

$$a_j = -\frac{1}{d_j}\left(\sum_{\substack{i=1 \\ i\neq j}}^{s} d_i a_i + r_2(x) - e\right)$$

$$= \tilde{\ell}(a_1,\ldots,a_{j-1}, a_{j+1},\ldots,a_s) + \tilde{r}(x)$$

Now consider $P(a_1,\ldots,a_s,x)\big|_{a_j=\tilde{\ell}+\tilde{r}}$

$$= \sum_{i=1}^{n} \ell_i(\ )\big|_{a_j=\tilde{\ell}+\tilde{r}} + r(x)$$

$$= \sum_{i=1}^{n} \ell_i(\ )\ {}_{a_j=\tilde{\ell}} + r'(x)$$

$$= \sum_{i=1}^{n} \ell'_i(\ ) + r'(x) = P'$$

Thus, by making the substitution we have removed one active * operation and we are now computing P'. By the Lemma, there are at least u-1 linearly independent ℓ'_i in P'. Applying the induction hypotheses, there must be at least u-1 remaining active * operations, and thus there were at least u active * operations in total.

Fact 2: The results mentioned in this paper do not hold in general if the restriction on D is relaxed. That is, suppose D were the finite set $\{0,1\}$. Since $x^n \equiv 1$ for all $n \geq 1$, any general polynomial can be computed in one active multiplication. Note that we do not make the finer distinction between symbolically computing (using only field properties of F) and evaluation (using specific properties of the given F or D).

III Establishing Uniqueness

Although arguments based only on active * operations do enable us to establish lower bounds such arguements alone can not produce "good" lower bounds for many problems. Consider the computation of $x^n + \sum_{i=1}^{k} a_i x^i$ with $k << n$.

Theorem 1: Let $P(\vec{a},x) = \sum_{i=1}^{k} \ell_i(\vec{a})x^i + r(x)$

$$k=0 \text{ or } \ell_k(\vec{a}) \neq \text{constant}$$

Let $r(x) = q(x)/s(x)$ and $\deg r = \deg q - \deg s$
Let $n = \max\ (k, \deg r)$
Let $u \leq$ number of independent ℓ_i
If $u = 0$ and $n > 2^m$ or if $u \geq 1$ and either $k > u \cdot 2^m$ or $n > k + 2^m$, then the evaluation of $P(\vec{a},x)$ requires least $u + m + 1$ * operations.

Proof: For each m we prove the theorem by induction on u.

$u = 0$

Obviously, using $\leq m$ * operations, we can not generate a rational function of degree $> 2^m$.

Induction Step

Assume that there are u (≥ 1) linearly independent ℓ_i. Let $[\ell(\vec{a}) + t(x)]$ * $[\ell'(\vec{a}) + t'(x)]$ be the first active * operation.

Note that Fact 1 insures such an operation. Moreover, using Fact 1, we may assume that at most m inactive operations preceded, and therefore that $\deg t \leq 2^m$ and $\deg t' \leq 2^m$.

Wlg., assume $\ell'(\vec{a}) \neq$ constant. Set (in the program) $\ell'(\vec{a}) + t'(x) = e$ where e is some appropriately chosen constant. (As before, e is chosen to avoid improper divisions; moreover, e is chosen with respect to cases 3 and 4 of the proof below.)

If $\ell'(\vec{a}) = \sum_{i=1}^{s} d_i a_i$ and $d_j \neq 0$ then we can effectively set $\ell'(\vec{a}) + t'(x) = e$ by setting $a_j = -\frac{1}{d_j}\left(\sum_{\substack{i=1 \\ i\neq j}}^{s} d_i a_i + t'(x) - e\right)$ in the definition of P.

Now consider $P(a_1,\ldots,a_s,x)\big|_{\ell'(\vec{a})+t'(x) = e} = P'(a_1,\ldots,a_{j-1},a_{j+1},\ldots,a_s,x)$. By making this substitution, we have <u>effectively removed one * operation</u> and we are now computing P'. Let n', k', u' be the appropriate "descriptors" for P'. Note that $u - 1 \leq u' \leq u$ and $k' \leq k$. We now consider the number of remaining * operations (that is, the number preceding and following the "removed" operation).

<u>Case 1</u>: $n > k + 2^m$

Then $n' = n$ (recall $\deg t' \leq 2^m$) and $\therefore$ $n' > k' + 2^m$. Applying the induction hypotheses, there are at least $(u-1) + m+1$ remaining * operations, and therefore, there were at least $u + m + 1$ * operations, in total.

<u>Case 2</u>: $k' > (u - 1)\cdot 2^m$ $(u - 1) \geq 1$
Apply induction hypotheses.

<u>Case 3</u>: $k > u\cdot 2^m$ and $k' \leq (u - 1)\cdot 2^m$
By a suitable choice of e, we can make $n' \geq k$. It then follows that $n' \geq k > u\cdot 2^m = (u-1)\cdot 2^m + 2^m \geq k' + 2^m$. Apply induction hypotheses.

Case 4: $k > u \cdot 2^m$ and $u - 1 = 0$
Again, we can make $n' \geq k > u \cdot 2^m = 2^m$
Apply induction hypotheses.

Fact 3: The conditions in Theorem 1 cannot be weakened. That is $(\forall u)(\forall m) \exists P(\vec{a}, x) = \sum_{i=1}^{u} a_i x^{2^m \cdot i}$ for which $k = u \cdot 2^m$ and $P(\vec{a}, x)$ can be computed in $u + m$ multiplications. Similarly, for $(\forall u)(\forall m)$ $P(\vec{a}, x) = x^{2^m + u} + \sum_{i=1}^{u} a_i x^i$ has $n = k + 2^m$, and can be computed in $u + m$ multiplications. We do not mean to imply that Theorem 1 provides a precise characterization of what polynomials are computable in $u + m$ * operations, but rather that this is the best we can do relative to the descriptors n, k and u.

Theorem 2: Any way to compute a polynomial $P(x) = \sum_{i=1}^{n} a_i x^i$ in n * operations must have the following form:

$$p_1 = \ell_1(\underline{a_n}) \times \ell_1'(\underline{x})$$

$$p_2 = \ell_2(\underline{p_1}, a_n, \underline{a_{n-1}}) \times \ell_2'(\underline{x})$$

$$\vdots$$

$$p_n = \ell_n(p_1, \ldots, \underline{p_{n-1}}, a_n, \ldots, a_2, a_1) \times \ell'_n(\underline{x})$$

where the ℓ_i, ℓ_i' indicate linear combinations, and an underlined variable indicates that variable must be present.

Proof: By Fact 1, we know that n active * operations are required, and we denote these operations by $p_1, \ldots, p_n$. The other operations (that is, +, -, and "free" multiplications by a constant) are implicitely indicated by the linear combinations. Thus the program has the form:

$$p_1 = \ell_1(a_1,\ldots,a_n,x) * \ell_1'(a_1,\ldots,a_n,x)$$

$$p_2 = \ell_2(p_1,a_1,\ldots,a_n,x) * \ell_2'(p_1,a_1,\ldots,a_n,x)$$

$$\cdot$$

$$\cdot$$

$$p_n = \ell_n(p_1,\ldots,p_{n-1},a_1,\ldots,a_n,x) * \ell_n'(p_1,\ldots,p_{n-1},a_1,\ldots,a_n,x)$$

A) We show the following for $1 \le j \le n$ by an induction on j.

i) a_i $(i < n + 1 - j)$ does not appear in p_j

ii) a_{n+1-j} appears in p_j

iii) the substitution $a_n = c_n$, $a_{n-1} = -c_n x + c_{n-1}, \ldots, a_{n+1-j} = -c_{n+2-j}x + c_{n+1-j}$

effectively eliminates the first j * operations.

<u>$j = 1$</u>

Suppose $a_i (i < n)$ appears in either ℓ_1 or ℓ_1'. Then set a_i (as in Theorem 1), so as to remove the first * operation. We are then computing $P'(\vec{a},x)$ in which $n' = k' = n$ and $u' = n - 1$. Thus $k' > (n-1)\cdot 2^0$ and by Theorem 1, $(n-1) + 1 = n$ more * operations must follow. Since this would give $n + 1$ * operations total, it follows that $a_i (i < n)$ cannot occur in p_1.

Since all operations considered are active, a_n must occur in either ℓ_1 or ℓ_1' (we shall show later that it cannot occur in both, and moreover, that * must be $\times$). We now show that x and a_n cannot occur in the same operand. For if they did, we could then set a_n so as to eliminate the * operation (i.e. set $a_n = -cx$). But then we would be computing $P'(\vec{a},\overset{n}{x})$ for which $n' = n + 1 = k' + 2$ and $u' = n - 1$. Again, applying Theorem 1, there must be $(n-1)+1$ remaining * operations - a contradiction as before.

Induction Step

By the induction hypotheses, we may set $a_n, a_{n-1}, \ldots, a_{n+1-j}$ so that $p_1, \ldots, p_j$ are no longer * operations. After the indicated substitutions, we would be computing $P'(a_1, \ldots, a_{n-j}, x) = c_{n+1-j}x^{n+1-j} + \sum_{i=1}^{n-j} a_i x^i$. Since $p_1, \ldots, p_j$ have been eliminated by these substitutions, p_{j+1} effectively has the form $\ell(a_1, \ldots, a_{n-j}, x) * \ell'(a_1, \ldots, a_{n-j}, x)$. We can then argue exactly as before that $a_i (i < n-j)$ cannot appear in either operand, and also as before that a_{n-j} must appear in at least one of the operands. Thus p_{j+1} effectively has the form $\ell(a_{n-j}, x) * \ell'(a_{n-j}, x)$.

Wlg., assume a_{n-j} appears in ℓ'. To complete the proof of part A, we need to show that the substitution $a_{n-j} = -c_{n+1-j}x + c_{n-j}$ (for any c_{n-j}) will effectively eliminate p_{j+1}. It is obvious that the substitution $a_{n-j} = cx + c'$ for some c (and any c') will effectively eliminate P_{j+1}. Suppose $c \neq -c_{n+1-j}$. Then we would be computing $(c + c_{n+1-j}) \cdot x^{n+1-j} + c'x^{n-j} + \sum_{i=1}^{n-j-1} a_i x^i$. But this would require (by Theorem 1) $n - j$ remaining * operations - a contradiction.

QED part A

Thus the program has the form (assuming for notational convenience only that a_{n+1-j} definitely appears in ℓ_j, rather than say ℓ'_j):

$$p_1 = \ell_1(\underline{a_n}) * \ell'_1(a_n, x)$$

$$p_2 = \ell_2(p_1, a_n, \underline{a_{n-1}}, x) * \ell'_2(p_1, a_n, a_{n-1}, x)$$

$\vdots$

$$p_n = \ell_n(p_1,\ldots,p_{n-1}, a_n,\ldots,\underline{a_1},x) * \ell'_n(p_1,\ldots,p_{n-1}, a_n,\ldots,a_1,x)$$

B We now show by induction on k (where $j=n-k+1$) that

i) all * operations are indeed $\times$
ii) ℓ'_j is $\ell'_j(\underline{x})$; that is, neither the coefficients nor previous p_i appear in ℓ'_j.

<u>k = 1</u>

Since a_1 appears for the first time in p_n, and p_n is the last * operation, it follows immediately that the operation is $\times$, and ℓ'_n is $\ell'_n(p_1,\ldots,p_{n-1},\underline{x})$. Moreover, it follows that if p_i appears in ℓ'_n, then $p_i = \ell(x)$, in which case p_i would represent a wasted * operation - a contradiction.

<u>Induction Step</u>

By hypotheses, assume that i) and ii) hold for $p_{j+1},\ldots,p_n$. Now consider p_j.

Since a_{n+1-j} appears for the first time in ℓ_j, and all succeeding operations have the form $p = \ell(\ ) \times \ell'(\underline{x})$, it follows that the * operation in p_j must be $\times$ and that x must appear in ℓ'_j. For otherwise, it would not be possible to form the term $a_{n+1-j}\cdot x^{n+1-j}$. Similarly, no a_i can appear in ℓ'_j, for we could not remove the $a_i a_{n+1-j}$ term that would be formed (recalling the assumptions on the succeeding operations). Finally, it follows in a similar manner that if p_i appears in ℓ'_j then $p_i = \ell(x)$.

QED part B

Thus the program has the form:

$$p_1 = \ell_1(\underline{a_n}) \times \ell_1'(\underline{x})$$

$$p_2 = \ell_2(p_1, a_n, \underline{a_{n-1}}, x) \times \ell_2'(\underline{x})$$

$$\vdots$$

$$p_n = \ell_n(p_n, \ldots, p_{n-1}, a_n, \ldots, \underline{a_1}, x) \times \ell_n'(\underline{x})$$

It now follows immediately that p_j must be present in p_{j+1} $(1 \le j \le n-1)$, in order to produce the term $a_{n+1-j}x^{n+1-j}$.

QED Theorem 2

Fact 6: A stronger form for Theorem 2 is possible. Informally, the only way to evaluate $\sum_{i=1}^{n} a_i x^i$ in n multiplications is by Horner's rule with some "wasted additions" and "compensating subtractions".

Cor. 1: The only way to evaluate $\sum_{i=1}^{n} a_i x^i$ in n * operations and n - 1 additions (or $\sum_{i=0}^{n} a_i x^i$ in n * operations, n additions) is by Horner's rule.

Proof: It is known [1,7] that n-1 additions or subtractions are required. At least n-1 additions are indicated in theorem 2 since both p_j and a_{n+1-j} are present in ℓ_j. In order to achieve n-1 additions, neither a_i $(i \ne n+1-j)$ nor p_i $(i \ne j-1)$ can be present in p_j. Moreover, the indicated linear combinations cannot have any constant terms. Thus the form must be:

$$p_1 = c_1' a_n \times c_1'' x$$

$$p_2 = (c_2 p_1 + c_2' a_{n-1}) \times c_2'' x$$

$$\vdots$$

$$p_n = (c_n p_{n-1} + c_n' a_1) \times c_n'' x$$

Of course, if multiplication by a constant is not "free", then the only way to achieve n * operations and n-1 additions is precisely Horner's rule.

Cor. 2: An nth degree polynomial ($n > 2$) and its first derivative cannot both compute in n * operations.

Proof: Follows directly from the definition of the derivative and the form dictated by Theorem 2.

IV Conclusion

A somewhat routine extension of known techniques has allowed us to establish the unique optimality of Horner's rule. In particular, we have shown that (to some extent) arguments based on growth and arguments based active operations may be combined. Of course, with respect to proofs of optimality, there are many problems which must go beyond these basic techniques. It may be possible to further extend existing techniques to problems where the "second order term" is at question (ex; the number of real arithmetics required for complex polynomial evaluation, or for simultaneous evaluation of a polynomial and the derivative). However, it seems apparent that other arithmetic problems where the "basic order of difficulty' is at question (ex; matrix multiplication, polynomial interpolation) will require fundamentally different concepts and techniques.

[1] Belaga, E.C. "Some Problems in the Computation of Polynomials", Dokl. Akad. Nauk. SSSR VS 123, (1958).

[2] Garsia, A.M. reffered to in Knuth, The Art of Computer Programming - Vol. 2, see prob. 38 in 4.6.4.

[3] Greub, W.H. Linear Algebra - Second Ed., Academic Press, Inc. (1963).

[4] Hopcroft, J. and L. Kerr, "On Minimizing the Number of Multiplications Necessary for Matrix Multiplications", IEEE Conf. Record of the 10th Annual Symposium of Switching and Automata Theory, (1969).

[5] Motzkin, J.S. "Evaluation of Polynomials and Evaluations of Rational Functions", Bull. Amer. Math. Soc., Vol. 61 (1955).

[6] Munro, I., "Some Results Concerning Efficient and Optimal Algorithms", to appear in Third Annual ACM Symposium on the Theory of Computers, Shaker Heights, 1971.

[7] Ostrowski, A.M., "On Two Problems in Abstraact Algebra Connected with Horner's Rule", Studies Presented to R Von Mises, Acad. Press, New York, (1954).

[8] Pan, V.Ya, "Method of Computing Values of Polynomials", Russian Math Surveys 21 (1966).

[9] Winograd, S., "On the Number of Multiplications Required to Compute Certain Functions" Proc. National Academy of Sciences 58:5 (1967).

ON LINEAR ALGORITHMS

Jacques Morgenstern
Département de Mathématiques
Université de Nice
06-Nice FRANCE

I hope to show in this paper how to bound the number of additions necessary to compute by a linear algorithm a given setof linear functions of several variables.
Besides the help of Pr. ZERNER, I am deeply endebted to Pr WINOGRAD and M. HIRSCHOWITZ for the stimulating talks.

I- ALGORITHMS - DEFINITIONS:

Let us first give a definition of a rational algorithm[(1)]

Definition 1

Let $f_1, f_2, \dots f_n$ be a family of n rational functions over a field K of the r variables $x_1, x_2, \dots x_r$, we shall call algorithm of length m computing the given family, a sequence of rational functions ϕ_i such that:

a) $\phi_i = R'_i * R''_i$ where $*$ is one of the four arithmetical operations; R'_i and R''_i are either one of the ϕ_j with j less than i, or a projection, i e an $\{x_k\}$, or a scalar.

b) For each positive integer k less than or equal to n there exists an integer m_k less than or equal to m such that $f_k = \phi_{m_k}$.

Definition 2

If all the ϕ_i are linear affin functions, the sequence is a linear algorithm.
From now on this will be the case; so that $*$ is either an addition or a multiplication by a scalar of the field K.

PROPOSITION 1

If the $f_1, f_2, \dots, f_n$ are homogeneous linear functions and if A_o is a linear algorithm of minimal length m_o computing the family, then each ϕ_i is homogen.

Proof Let c_1 be the first additive constant appearing at the i_1-th operation in A_o, c_2 the second one appearing at the i_2-th operation etc...If we set $c_i = o$, we can define a new sequence of operations:

(1) $\phi^*_i = R'^*_i \ast R''^*_i$ recursively, the ϕ^*_i being obtained from ϕ_i by nullifying c_r in it, and the others by (1)) we see that all the ϕ^*_i are homogeneous and that if $R'_i - R'^*_i$ and $R''_i - R''^*_i$ belong to K, $\ast$ being either an addition or a multiplication by a scalar, then $\phi_i - \phi^*_i \varepsilon K$. The sequence A^*_o of operations so defined is an algorithm, it computes the f_j, and since $f^*_j = f_j$, it computes the given family in less operations (in fact here additions) than A_o if one of the constants c_s is not zero.

COROLLARY

If $\mathcal{F}$ is a family of homogeneous linear functions of the r variables $x_1, x_2, \ldots x_r$, and if A_o is a linear algorithm computing $\mathcal{F}$ with a minimum number m_1 of additions, then all the ϕ_i are homogeneous.

It will be of some help for what follows to look at a line ear algorithm computing $\mathcal{F}$ as a sequence $\mathcal{F}_0, \mathcal{F}_1 \cdots \mathcal{F}_m$ of families of linear forms such that $\mathcal{F}_0$ contains the projections and the constants and

$$\mathcal{F}_{i+1} = \mathcal{F}_i \cup \{af_k + bf_h\}$$

where a and b are in K and f_k, f_h are in $\mathcal{F}_i$, and $\mathcal{F} \subset \mathcal{F}_m$ this presentation points out the additions.

Definition 3 :

The matrix F associated to a family (f_i) of n linear forms of r variables is the matrix nxr, the coefficient a_{ij} of which is the coefficient of x_j in f_i. The bi-indices (i,j) of the non-zero coefficients of F are the occurrences of the variables in F, their number is H(F).

II- THE ADDITIVE DEGREE OF FREEDOM

We shall now define a positive integer depending on a given family $\mathcal{F}$ of linear forms, and which behaves almost likethe minimum number of additions required to compute the family $\mathcal{F}$. Namely if $D^+(F)$ is this number, it is invariant if we add a form proportional to a form of $\mathcal{F}$, or if we add a projection. Moreover $D^+(F)$ does not decrease if we add any form to the family, and does not increase by more than one if we add a linear combination of two forms of the family .

A family of linear forms is pure if it does not contain either a multiple of a projection or two forms which are proportional. To each family $\mathcal{F}$ of linear forms corresponds at least one pure family $\mathcal{F}^o$ deduced from by deleting projections and redundant forms. Let F be the matrix $\| a_{ij} \|$, $i = 1,2 \ldots n$; $j = 1,2 \ldots r$ associated to a pure family of linear forms; we denote by P(1,r) the power set of (1,2 ...r)

Definition 4 :

A relation of carrier J is an element of $K^n \times P(1,r)$ denoted by $R = (R_o ; J)$ where $R_o = (\lambda_1, \lambda_2, \ldots \lambda_n)$ the λ_i being not all zero and such that $\sum_i \lambda_i \ell_i^J = 0$ where $\ell_i^J = (a_{ij_1}, a_{ij_2}, \ldots a_{ij_s})$; and $J = (j_1, j_2, \ldots j_s)$ The matrix of the relation R is the sub-matrix of F of the coefficients of the ℓ_i^J. We denote by m_R the number of non-zero components of R_o and we say that R is non-trivial if m_R is less than or equal to $\mathrm{card}(J) = |J|$.

Definition 5 :

Let R' be a relation of carrier J' and let $R^1, R^2, \ldots R^\ell$ be ℓ distinctsrelations, $\ell \geqslant 2$, carried by $J \subseteq J'$, all of those ℓ +1 relations being non-trivial . we shall say that R' is a consequence of the family $(R^1, R^2, \ldots R)$ if R'_o belongs to the linear space spanned by R_o, R_o, $\ldots R_o$ over the field K .

Example : Consider a 3x3 matrix whose rows are $\ell_1 = (1,1\ 2)$, $\ell_2 = (2\ 2\ 3)$, $\ell_3 = (3\ 3\ 7)$; consider the sub-lines $\ell'_1 = (1\ 1)$, $\ell'_2 = (2\ 2)$, $\ell'_3 = (3\ \ 3)$, the relation (5,-1,-1 ;(1 2)) from $5\ell_1 - \ell_2 - \ell_3 = 0$ is a consequence of (2,-1,o ; (12)) and (3,0,-1 ;(1 2)) from $2\ell'_1 - \ell'_2 = 0$ and $3\ell'_1 - \ell'_3 = 0$ for instance.

Definition 6 :

Two relations are connected if their matrices have a common coefficient without being such that the carrier of one contains the carrier of the other.

Definition 7 :

A choice σ is an application defined on the set of non-trivial relations $\mathcal{R}$, such that $\sigma(R)$ is a row of the matrix of R or the empty set.

Definition 8 :

A set $\mathcal{R}_u \subset \mathcal{R}$ is coherent iff :

i) For each R and R' in $\mathcal{R}_u$, R and R' are not connected
ii) No relation of $\mathcal{R}_u$ is a consequence of a family in $\mathcal{R}_u$
iii) If $R = (R_o ; J)$ belongs to $\mathcal{R}_u$, there is no $R' = (R'_o ; J')$ in $\mathcal{R}_u$ with $R'_o = R_o$ and $J \subset J'$ stricty.

For a coherent set of relations $\mathcal{R}_u$ and a given choice σ, we call $C_R = (|J^\sigma_R| - m_R + 1)$ the <u>contribution</u> of R in relation with σ where $|J^\sigma_R|$ is the number of non-zero coefficients of $\sigma(R)$ and we denote by $\mathcal{R}_u^\sigma$ the corresponding set of relations with non-negative contribution, and

<u>Definition 9</u> :

If $\mathcal{R}_u$ is a coherent set of relations, a choice is said to be <u>licit</u> with respect to $\mathcal{R}_u$, if it satisfies the following conditions:
i) For each R and R' in $\mathcal{R}_u$, $\sigma(R)$ and $\sigma(R')$ have no common coefficient.
ii) For all R and R' in $\mathcal{R}_u^\sigma$, no row of the matrix of R' is a proper sub-line of $\sigma(R)$.
iii) If $R_1, R_2, \ldots R_m$ are relations of common carrier in $\mathcal{R}_u^\sigma$, then there exists j from (1,m) such that $\sigma(R_j)$ is not a row of the matrix of R_i $i \neq j$.
(Those two last conditions will be used in the reciprocal of the theorem)

Consider now the number $G_u = \max \sum_{R \in \mathcal{R}_u^\sigma} (C_R)$, the sum being over all the relations of $\mathcal{R}_u^\sigma$; the maximum is taken over all the licit choices with respect to $\mathcal{R}_u$.

<u>Definition 10</u> :

<u>The number of links</u> of a matrix F is equal to the number

$$L(F) = L(F^o) = \max_u G_u$$

where $\{\mathcal{R}_u\}_{u \in V}$ is the family of all the coherent sets of relations of F^o, a purified of F (page 3)

<u>PROPERTIES</u> :The number of links of a family remains unchanged if one multiplies a form by a non-zero scalar, if one adds either a projection or a form already in the family.

<u>Proof</u> :Left to the reader

<u>PROPOSITION 3</u> : Let $\mathcal{F}$ be a pure family of linear forms, the number of links of $\mathcal{F}' = \mathcal{F} \cup \{af + bg\}$ where f and g are in $\mathcal{F}$, a and b in K verifies $L(F') - L(F) \geq H(F'^o) - H(F) - 2$ where F'^o is a pure matrix associated to F'.

Proof : a) If $af + bg$ belongs to $\mathcal{F}$ then $L(F') = L(F)$
b) If $af + bg$ is a projection then $L(F') = L(F)$
c) In the other cases, F' being pure, let σ and u be such that $L(F) = G_u = \sum_{R \in \mathcal{R}_u} C_R^{\sigma}$. Consider the relation R^* defined by $h = af + bg$, namely after reordering $R = (o, o, \ldots a, b, -1 ; J)$ where $J = (1, 2, \ldots r)$.
We are going to build a set $\mathcal{R}_{u'}^{\sigma'}$ of coherent relations of F' containing $\mathcal{R}_u^{\sigma}$.
-If R is trivial, that is $H' - H \leq 2$, then $L' \geq L$ by taking $\mathcal{R}_{u'}^{\sigma'} = \mathcal{R}_u^{\sigma}$, and the proposition is proved.
-Suppose R^* non-trivial, $\mathcal{R}_{u'} = \mathcal{R}_u \cup \{R^*\}$ is a coherent set of relations of F' since (see def. 8) :
i) no relation of $\mathcal{R}_u$ can be connected with R^* because the carrier of R is the whole set $(1, 2, \ldots r)$
ii) R^* is not a consequence of other relations of $\mathcal{R}_u$ because h is a new line
iii) R has the greatest carrier.
Moreover if we let $\sigma' = \sigma$ on $\mathcal{R}_u$ and $\sigma'(R^*) = h$, σ' is licit with respect to $\mathcal{R}_{u'}$, since (see def. 9):
i) h is a new line
ii) h is a new line and R has the greatest carrier.
iii) Same reason.
Therefore the set $\mathcal{R}_{u'}^{\sigma'}$ is a coherent set of relations with non-negative contributions and we have

$$G_{u'} \geq G_u + C_{R^*} = L(F) + |J_{R^*}^{\sigma'}| - 3 + 1$$

where $J_R^{\sigma'}$ is equal to $H' - H$ which is greater than 2, so that $L(F') \geq G_{u'}$ leads to

$$L(F') - L(F) \geq H(F') - H(F) - 2$$

Definition 11 :

Let F_1 and F_2 be two r-columns matrices with the same finite number of rows, consider the matrix $F = F_1 + F_2$, if it contains the same rows as F (up to reordering) plus possibly zero rows, we shall say that the pure r-columns matrix $G(F_1, F_2)$ associated to $\left\{ \begin{matrix} F_1 \\ F_2 \end{matrix} \right\}$ obtained by superposition of F_1 and F_2 is a decomposition of F. Let $N(F)$ be the number of rows of F and s the number of rows of F proportional to a non-zero row of $G(F_1, F_2)$, then the additive degree of freedom of F is defined by

$$D^+(F) = \min_{F^+ = F_1 + F_2} \left\{ H(G) - L(G) - N(G) + N(F) - s \right\}$$

Where the minimum is taken over all the decompositions of F ; this number is positive since L(G) is a sum of contributions of the form $|\mathcal{J}^{\sigma}_R| - m_R + 1$ which is less than H(G) - N(G) for the total number non-zero coefficients of $\sigma(R)$ $R \in \mathcal{R}_u$ cannot reach H(G) (see def. 9)

Example :

$$F = \begin{pmatrix} 1 & 1 & 7 \\ 2 & 3 & 2 \\ 9 & 2 & 4 \end{pmatrix}$$ has no relation, but the

decomposition $F_1 = \begin{pmatrix} 1 & 1 & 0 \\ 2 & 2 & 0 \\ 9 & 0 & 0 \end{pmatrix} F_2 = \begin{pmatrix} 0 & 0 & 7 \\ 0 & 1 & 2 \\ 0 & 2 & 4 \end{pmatrix}$

admits two relations therefore $D^+(F) \leqslant 5$.

PROPOSITION 4 :

If one adds any linear form to a given family $\mathcal{F}$ of linear forms, then the additive degree of freedom does not decrease.

Proof: Let $\mathcal{F}$ and $\mathcal{F}' = \mathcal{F} \cup \{f\}$ be the two families.

Consider a minimal decomposition of $\mathcal{F}' : \{\Phi, \varphi, \psi\}$ it is also a decomposition of $\mathcal{F}$: think of $0 = \varphi + (-\varphi)$ so that $\{\Phi, \varphi, \psi\} = C$ is the purified of $\{\Phi, \varphi, \psi, -\varphi, -\psi\}$

We have $D^+(F') = H(C) - L(C) - N(C) + N(F') - s'$
and $D^+(F) \leq H(C) - L(C) - N(C) + N(F) - s$
Suppose that $D^+(F') < D^+(F)$ then it would follow that s'
$s' > s + 1$ which is impossible .

PROPOSITION 5 :

The additive degree of freedom of the pure families $\mathcal{F}$ and $\mathcal{F}' = \mathcal{F} \cup \{af + bg\}$ where f and g are in $\mathcal{F}$ and a,b are in K verify :

$$D^+(F') \leqslant D^+(F) + 1$$

Proof : Let us consider a minimal decomposition of $\mathcal{F} = (G , f , g)$; let it be $A = \{\Phi, \varphi_1, \varphi_2, \psi_1, \psi_2\}^o$

Then the family $B = \{\Phi, \varphi_1, \varphi_2, a\varphi, bg, \psi_1, \psi_2\}^o$ is a decomposition of $\mathcal{F}'$. Therefore we have

$D^+(F) = H(A) - L(A) - N(A) + N(F) - s$ and

$D^+F') \leqslant H(B) - L(B) - N(B) + N(F') - s'$

a) Suppose af + bg does not belong to Φ

i) If neither f nor g belong to Φ then, applying the proposition 3 twice we get $L(B) - L(A) \geq H(B) - H(A) - 4$ and therefore $D^+(F') - D^+(F) \leq 4 - 2 + 1 - 2 = 1$

ii) If f belongs to Φ then applying proposition 3 once we get $L(B) - L(A) \geq H(B) - H(A) - 2$ and therefore

$$D^+(F') - D^+(F) \leq 2 - 1 + 1 - 1 = 1$$

iii) If both f and g belong to Φ then $L(A) = L(B)$ and still

$$D^+(F') - D^+(F) \leq 1$$

b) If af + bg belongs to Φ then $D^+(F') \leq D^+(F)$, and in view of prop. 4 $D^+(F') = D^+(F)$

PROPOSITION 5 bis

If one adds a projection $\{x_i\}$ to a given family $\mathcal{F}$ of linear forms, the additive degree of freedom is not changed.

Proof : By definition .

PROPERTIES : The additive degree of freedom of any family of linear forms $\mathcal{F}$

- remains the same if : i) We multiply one form by a scalar
  - ii) We add a form equal to a form which belongs to $\mathcal{F}$
  - iii) We add a projection
- does not decrease if we add any form to the family: prop4
- does not increase by more than one if we add a linear combination of two forms of $\mathcal{F}$
- is 0 for the empty family, the constants and the projections ; therefore:

THEOREM 1 : Let $\mathcal{F}$ be a family of linear forms whose additive degree of freedom is $D^+(F)$, a linear algorithm computing $\mathcal{F}$ has at least $D^+(F)$ additions .

Proof: Each additive operation of such an algorithm increases the additive degree of freedom of the family by at most one unit. As we need at least as many additions to compute a larger family, the theorem is proved .

(1) S. WINOGRAD For a more general and formal definition Communications on Pure and Applied Mathematics. Vol XXIII

(2) Ting K. Pan Methods of Computing values of polynomials Russian Mathematical Surveys. Vol 21 (1966) p 105

ON THE RATE OF CONVERGENCE OF LOCAL ITERATIVE SCHEMES

S. Winograd and P. Wolfe

IBM Thomas J. Watson Research Center
Yorktown Heights, New York

Extended Abstract

Let $y = f(x)$ be a function of one real variable with a simple root at $x = r$. Many iterative methods for determining r exist in the literature; Traub's book [1] describes most of these, and analyzes their rates of convergence. The iterative process generates a sequence $\{x_k\}$ of approximations of r, where x_{k+1} depends on $x_k, x_{k-1}, \ldots$ and the values of f and possibly some of its derivatives at these points. If the initial approximations are close enough to r then the sequence $\{x_k\}$ converges to r. (This makes the iterative method "local"). The secant method and Newton's method are examples of iterative schemes which are much used in practice. The various methods differ in the amount of information used, the particular way the information is used, and the rate at which $\{x_k\}$ converges to r.

An <u>iterative scheme using d derivatives</u> is a sequence of (partial) functions $\varphi_k: X^{(d+2)k} \to X$, which specify $x_{k+1} = \varphi_k(x_k, x_{k-1}, \ldots, x_1, f(x_k), \ldots, f(x_1), \ldots, f^{(d)}(x_k), \ldots, f^{(d)}(x_1))$.

A <u>local iterative scheme using d derivatives</u> is a

system consisting of an iterative scheme using d derivatives and a family $I_t, J_t^o, J_t^1, \ldots J_t^p$ of sets of nonempty open intervals of the real line (where p is fixed and t ranges over any index set), nested in the sense that if a set of intervals of the above form belongs to the family, then so does the set obtained from it by replacing I_t by any of its open subintervals. A real function f <u>fits the scheme</u> if, for some t,

$$f \text{ vanishes at some point of } I_t, \tag{1}$$

and

$$f^{[i]}(x) \in J_t^i \text{ for all } x \in I_t \text{ and } i = 0, 1, \ldots, p. \tag{2}$$

The most natural form of the family of intervals above is the following: the index t is the collection of positive numbers δ, r, $a_0, a_1, \ldots, a_p$, with $a_0 < a_1$, and

$$\left.\begin{aligned} I_t &= (r-\delta,\ r+\delta)\ , \\ J_t^1 &= \text{either } (a_0, a_1) \text{ or } (-a_1, -a_0)\ , \\ J_t^i &= (-a_i, a_i) \text{ for } i = 2, \ldots, p\ . \end{aligned}\right\} \tag{3}$$

Then if f fits the scheme, r is a root of f; the requirement $f'(x) \in J_t^1$ makes r a simple root, and all the derivatives are bounded by the numbers a_i.

Let the function f fit a given local iterative scheme, having the root $r \in I_t$. The scheme is said to <u>converge</u> for f if, for some k_o, for any sequence of "starting values" $x_1, \ldots, x_{k_o}$ having the property that all points x satisfying $|x-r| \leq \text{Max}\ \{|x_k - r| : k = 1, \ldots, k_o\}$ belong to I_t, the continuation of the sequence determined by the iteration scheme satisfies $x_k \in I_t$ for $k \geq k_o$ and converges to r.

The hypotheses (1,2) restricting the functions to which the scheme is applied are an extension of the standard hypotheses used to obtain the convergence of specific algorithms. They do, in fact, embrace almost all existing algorithms. Let us call an iteration scheme a polynomial interpolatory scheme (of maximal degree p) if, for each k, there is a polynomial g_k of degree at least one and at most p which is an Hermite interpolatory polynomial for the function f at some previous set of points, the most recent of which is, say, x_{j_k}; if $j_k \to \infty$ as $k \to \infty$; and if x_{k+1} is that root of g_k closest to x_k (or to x_{j_k}). We assert that any polynomial interpolatory scheme is a local iterative scheme, and converges in the neighborhood of a simple root of a reasonable function. More precisely:

THEOREM: Let a polynomial interpolatory scheme of maximal degree p be given. For any $\delta > 0$ and $a_0 \neq 0$ there exist $a_1, \ldots, a_p$ so that the local iterative scheme consisting of the given scheme and the family of intervals given by (3) is a local iterative scheme which converges for any function in C^{p+1} which fits the scheme.

Our basic result establishing an upper bound on the speed of convergence of any iterative scheme is:

THEOREM: Given any local iterative scheme using d derivatives, and any starting values $\{x_k : k \leq k_0\}$ there exists an analytic function f fitting the scheme with root r such that

$$\liminf_{k \to \infty} \frac{|x_{k+1} - r|}{\prod_{j=1}^{k} |x_j - r|^{d+1}} > 0,$$

where x_k for $k > k_0$ is determined by the scheme. Further,

$$\limsup_{k \to \infty} \frac{|x_{k+1} - r|}{|x_k - r|^{d+2}} \geq 1 \quad (4)$$

and there exists B such that

$$|x_k - r| \geq B^{(d+2)^k} \quad (5)$$

for all k. The constant B has the form

$$C|x_1 - r|^{(d+1)/(d+2)^2} .$$

The formulas (4) and (5) express the fact that order of convergence of the scheme as applied to f is no higher than d+2. A lower bound on the speed of convergence has, of course, been established [1]: the scheme which takes x_{k+1} as the appropriate root of the polynomial of degree m(d+1)-1 agreeing with f through the dth derivative at each of the previous m points has an order of convergence the largest root of the equation

$$\lambda^m = (d+1) \Sigma_{i=0}^{m-1} \lambda^i ;$$

that order tends toward d+2 (from below) as $m \to \infty$.

Reference

[1] J. F. Traub, Iterative Methods for the Solution of Equations, Prentice-Hall (1964).

The research on this report was partially supported by the Office of Naval Research, Contract No. N0014-69-C-0023 and Contract No. N00014-71-C-0112.

QUEUES, STACKS AND GRAPHS

S. Even and A. Itai

The Weizmann Institute of Science
Rehovot, Israel

Abstract

The problem of realizing a given permutation through a network of queues in parallel and through a network of stacks in parallel is considered. Each one of these problems is translated into a coloration problem of a suitable graph. In the case of parallel queues, the resulting graph is a permutation graph, and therefore very easy to color. The number of queues necessary to realize the permutation is equal to the chromatic number of the graph. The case of parallel stacks defines two different problems, depending on whether or not we insist on completion of the stacks loading before unloading them. If we accept this condition, the resulting graph is again a permutation graph. However, if we allow unloading of stacks before loading is complete the resulting graph, called the union graph, may not be a permutation graph. An alternative way of defining a union graph as the graph describing the intersection of chords in a circle is shown. In spite of the fact that the set of all union graphs is a proper subset of all graphs, no efficient algorithm to color them has yet been found.

1. Queues in Parallel

A queue is a linear storage device. It has one entrance and one exit. The elements exit in the same order in which they have entered (FIFO). The elements may be stored any length of time and the number of elements that can be stored in any one queue is assumed to be unbounded.

Assume we have, in a queue A, the elements $1,2,\ldots,n$ in their natural order and we want to transfer them into a queue B in such a way that their order is $P(1),P(2),\ldots,P(n)$, where P is some permutation. Clearly, $P^{-1}(i)$ is the place (the number of the place when the places are enumerated from left to right) in which i appears in B after the transfer.

Assume we have m intermediate queues $Q_1,Q_2,\ldots,Q_m$. We may take the first element in A and transfer it to some Q_i (it exits A and enters Q_i). This may be followed by transferring the second element to some Q_j, where i may or may not be identical with j, etc. We shall refer to a transfer from A to some Q_i as <u>loading</u>. No transfers from one Q_i to another (or the same) Q_j is allowed. The only place elements may enter upon exiting a Q_i is to enter B. This type of transfer is called <u>unloading</u>. No unloading of B is allowed. Naturally, this configuration is referred to as a <u>system of m queues in parallel</u>.

Two different modes of operations are defined by either insisting that all n elements be loaded before unloading begins, or not.

It is clear that every permutation P on n elements is realizable through a system of n queues, by first loading each element on a separate intermediate queue and then unloading $P(1)$, then $P(2)$, etc. Our aim is to find the smallest m such that a system of m queues in parallel will suffice to realize the given P. Following Even, Lempel and Pnueli [1], a <u>permutation graph</u> $\vec{G}(N,\vec{R})$ is defined for P where the set of vertices N is $\{1,2,\ldots,n\}$ and the set of directed edges $\vec{R}$ is given by $\vec{R} = \{i \to j \mid i < j \text{ and } P^{-1}(i) > P^{-1}(j)\}$.

<u>Lemma 1</u>: In every realization of P by a system of queues in parallel, if $i \to j$ in $\vec{G}$ then i and j do not pass through the same intermediate queue.

<u>Proof</u>: If $i \to j$ then $i < j$. Thus i exits A before j. If they enter the same Q_k then i is before j in the queue. Thus, $P^{-1}(i) < P^{-1}(j)$. A contradiction.

Q.E.D.

Clearly if $i \not\rightarrow j$ and $i < j$, then $P^{-1}(i) < P^{-1}(j)$ and there exists a realization in which i and j do pass through the same queue.

Lemma 2: If P is realizable through a system of m queues in parallel, then there exists a partition of N to m blocks such that no two elements in one block are connected in $\vec{G}$.

Proof: Define the block B_i to consist of all the elements which pass through Q_i, and use Lemma 1. Q.E.D.

Lemma 3: If N has a partition into m blocks such that no two elements in one block are connected in $\vec{G}$ then P is realizable through a system of m queues in parallel.

Proof: We can load all the elements of a block B_k into Q_k. Clearly, in each queue the elements are in their natural order. (Loading is completed before unloading begins.)

There can be no element b which precedes $P(1)$ in its queue. (This would have implied that $b < P(1)$, and since $P^{-1}(b) > 1$, it would have implied that $b \rightarrow P(1)$, and they cannot belong to the same block.) Thus, $P(1)$ can be unloaded. Assume $P(1), P(2), \ldots P(\ell)$ have been unloaded. $P(\ell+1)$ is the first element in its queue, by a similar argument.

Q.E.D.

Note that in the realization of the proof we first complete the loading before unloading begins. Thus, if a realization without this restriction exists with m queues, by Lemma 2 we have a partition into m blocks such that no two elements in one block are connected in $\vec{G}$, and by the proof of Lemma 3 we get a realization satisfying the restriction. Thus, we have proved the following:

Lemma 4: Every permutation which is realizable by a system of m queues in parallel is also realizable by the same system with completion of loading before unloading begins.

Thus, the problem of finding the smallest m such that P is realizable by a system of m queues in parallel is equivalent to minimal coloration of $\vec{G}$. Very efficient algorithms for coloring permutation graphs were given by Even, Lempel and Pnueli [1].

2. Stacks in Parallel-Loading Before Unloading

A stack is also a linear storage device. It has only one orifice. The elements exit in the reverse order of their entrance (LIFO). Here too, the elements may be stored any length of time and the number of elements that can be stored in one stack at any time is unbounded.

Again we shall assume that the elements of N are stored on an input queue A in their natural order, and that they have to be transferred to an output queue B in the order specified by P. Assume we have m intermediate stacks $S_1, S_2, \ldots, S_m$. We may transfer from A to any one of the stacks, and from any stack to B. No transfer between stacks or reloading A or unloading B is allowed. This is called a system of m stacks in parallel.

The graph $\vec{G}'(N,\vec{R}')$ is defined by

$$\vec{R}' = \{i \to j \mid i < j \text{ and } P^{-1}(i) < P^{-1}(j)\}.$$

$\vec{G}'(N,\vec{R}')$, as the notation suggests, is also a directed graph and is the complement of $\vec{G}$. (That is, if $i < j$ then $i \to j$ in G' if and only if $i \not\to j$ in $\vec{G}$).

Lemma 5: In every realization of P by a system of stacks in parallel, with completion of loading before unloading begins, if $i \to j$ in $\vec{G}'$ then i and j do not pass through the same stack.

Proof: If $i \to j$ then $i < j$. Thus i exits A before j. If they enter the same S_k then j is stored on top of i. Thus, $P^{-1}(j) < P^{-1}(i)$. A contradiction.

Q.E.D.

Clearly, if $i \not\to j$ in $\vec{G}'$ and $i < j$, then $P^{-1}(i) > P^{-1}(j)$ and there exists a realization by stacks in parallel, with completion of loading before unloading, in which i and j pass through the same stack. Indeed, j

is stored on top of i , but it is also unloaded before i.

Lemma 6: If P is realizable by a system of m stacks in parallel, with loading completed before unloading begins, then N can be partitioned into m blocks such that no two elements in one block are connected by an edge in $\vec{G}'$.

The proof follows immediately by Lemma 5.

Lemma 7: If N can be partitioned into m blocks such that no two elements which are connected by an edge in $\vec{G}'$ are in the same block, then P is realizable by a system of m stacks in parallel, where loading is completed before unloading begins.

The proof is similar to the proof of Lemma 3. Thus, the problem of finding the smallest number of stacks in a system of parallel stacks, for realizing a given permutation P , when we insist on completion of loading before unloading begins, is equivalent to the coloration problem of $\vec{G}'$. Even, Lempel and Pnueli [1] showed that $\vec{G}'$ is a permutation graph, and thus the problem of its coloration is very easy to solve.

3. Stacks in Parallel - Without Restrictions on Unloading

Unlike the situation in queues in parallel, the removal of the restriction on completion of loading before unloading begins creates a completely new problem. Consider, for example, the identity permutation I ($I(i) = i$ for $i=1,2,\ldots,n$) . $\vec{G}'$ is a completely connected graph (an edge between every two vertices) and therefore its chromatic number is n . However, one stack is sufficient to realize it: Load 1, unload 1, load 2, unload 2, etc.

Our aim is to define a graph whose coloration problem is equivalent to that of finding the smallest number of stacks necessary in a parallel system for realizing a given permutation P .

Define for every $k=1,2,\ldots,n$ a graph $\vec{G}^k(V^k,\vec{R}^k)$ as follows:

$$V^k = \{i \mid i < k \text{ and } P^{-1}(k) < P^{-1}(j)\}$$

$$\vec{R}^k = \{i \to j \mid i,j \in V^k \text{ and } i < j \text{ and } P^{-1}(i) < P^{-1}(j)\}.$$

The <u>union graph</u>, $\vec{G}_U(V,\vec{R})$ is defined by

$$V = \bigcup_{k=1}^{n} V^k \quad \text{and} \quad \vec{R} = \bigcup_{k=1}^{n} \vec{R}^k .$$

Each $\vec{G}^k$ is a subgraph of $\vec{G}'$ of the previous section. Therefore, $\vec{G}_U$ is also a subgraph of $\vec{G}'$, but is not necessarily identical to it.

<u>Example 1</u>: $P = [3,5,1,2,4]$. $\vec{G}'(N,\vec{R}')$ is shown below.

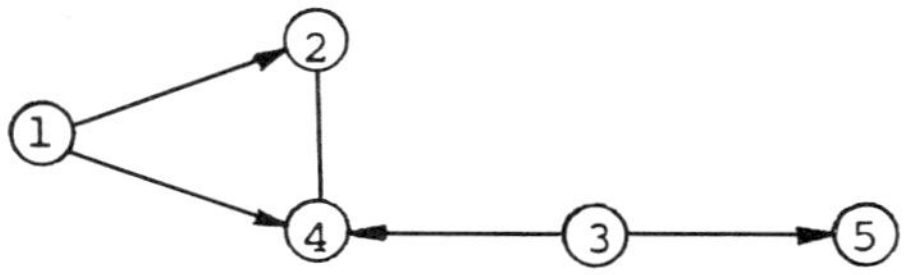

Now, $\vec{G}^1$, $\vec{G}^2$ and $\vec{G}^4$ are empty.

$\vec{G}^3$ consists of the vertices 1 and 2:

$\vec{G}^5$ is shown below.

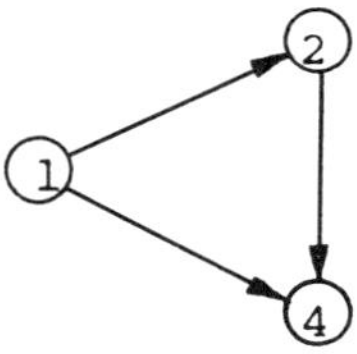

Thus, the union graph, $\vec{G}_U$ is identical with $\vec{G}^5$ and is not equal to $\vec{G}'$.

<u>Lemma 8</u>: If $i \to j$ in $\vec{G}_U$ then there is no realization of P by a system of stacks in parallel in which i and j pass through the same stack.

<u>Proof</u>: If $i \to j$ in $\vec{G}_{U}$, then there exists an element k such that $i \to j$ in $\vec{G}^{\to k}$. Thus, $i < j < k$ and $P^{-1}(k) < P^{-1}(i) < P^{-1}(j)$. Therefore, i and j are loaded on the stacks before k leaves A and k is unloaded from the stack it passes through before i and j leave the stacks in which they are stored. Thus, if both i and j are stored on the same stack, j is stored on top of i and must be unloaded first. This contradicts $P^{-1}(i) < P^{-1}(j)$.

Q.E.D.

Let S be a set of elements which pass through a given stack in some realization. Lemma 8 implies that $S \cap V$ is an independent set in $\vec{G}_U$ (a set of vertices such that no two of them are connected by an edge). Thus, a realization of P by a system of stacks in parallel implies a coloration of the vertices of $\vec{G}_U$.

Conversely, let $\{C_1', C_2, \ldots, C_m\}$ be a coloration of the vertices of $\vec{G}_U$. (Each C_i is the set of vertices which are colored by the i-th color. Clearly, no two vertices in one C_i are connected by an edge in $\vec{G}_U$.) Let $C_1 = C_1' \cup (N-V)$. Thus, $\{C_1, C_2, \ldots, C_m\}$ is a partition of N.

<u>Lemma 9</u>: If $\{C_1, C_2, \ldots C_m\}$ is a partition of N such that $\{C_1 \cap V, C_2 \cap V, \ldots, C_m \cap V\}$ is a legal coloration of $\vec{G}_U$ then there exists a realization of P by a system of m stacks $S_1, S_2, \ldots, S_m$ in parallel in which the elements of C_ℓ pass through S_ℓ.

<u>Proof</u>: Let us use the following rule: Assume $P(1), P(2), \ldots, P(k-1)$ are already on B. If $P(k)$ is available (on top of one of the S_i's) for unloading, unload it and repeat the rule. If not, load the next element in line on A to its corresponding stack and repeat the rule.

Let us prove now, by induction on k, that it will never happen that $P(1), P(2), \ldots, P(k-1)$ are already on B, $P(k)$ is out of A and yet it is not available for unloading.

First consider $P(1)$. If it is already out of A,

then its exit out of its stack cannot be blocked, because when it first enters the stack, the rule guarantees that it is immediately unloaded. Now, assume the statement is true for $i = 1,2,\ldots,k-1$, and that $P(1),P(2),\ldots,P(k-1)$ are already on B and $P(k)$ is already out of A. If $P(k)$ is not on top in its stack, then some element a is on top of it. Let the elements on B be $P(1),P(2),\ldots,P(i-1)$ when a is loaded. By the inductive hypothesis $P(i)$ is not loaded yet. Thus, $P(i) > a$. We also know that $i < k$, $a > P(k)$ and $P^{-1}(a) > k$. Summarizing, we have

$$P(k) < a < P(i) \quad \text{and} \quad P^{-1}(P(i)) < P^{-1}(P(k)) < P^{-1}(a).$$

Thus in $\vec{G}^{P(i)}$, $P(k) \rightarrow a$ and $P(k)$ and a cannot have the same color in $\vec{G}_U$.

Q.E.D.

Lemmas 8 and 9 imply that the problem of finding the smallest m such that P is realizable by a system of m stacks in parallel, when unloading is permitted before loading is completed, is equivalent to the problem of finding minimum coloration of its union graph. Let us now show an example of a union graph which is not a permutation graph. In fact it is not even transitive.

<u>Example 2:</u> $P = [5,2,7,4,1,6,3]$.

$\vec{G}^1$ and $\vec{G}^3$ are empty.

$\vec{G}^2$ is (1)

$\vec{G}^4$ is (1) ⟶ (3)

$\vec{G}^5$ is (1) ⟶ (3) ⟵ (2) ⟶ (4)

$\vec{G}^6$ is (3)

$\vec{G}^7$ is (4) ⟶ (6) ⟵ (1) ⟶ (3)

Thus, $\vec{G}_U$ is as follows:

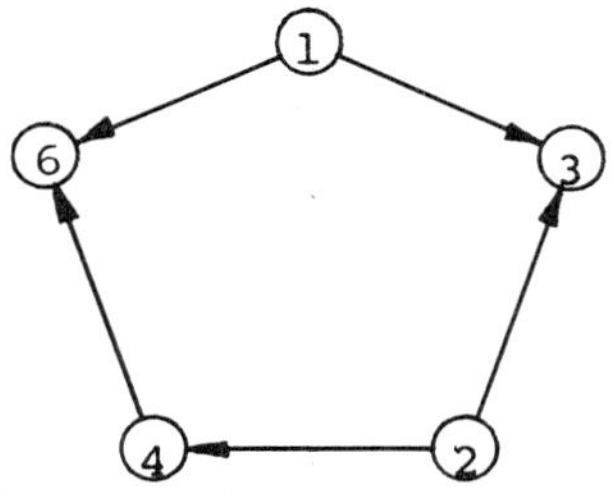

Clearly, there is no way of redirecting its edges to make it transitive.

One may suspect that every undirected graph is the layout of some union graph, and that the coloration problem for union graphs is as hard as for graphs in general. Unfortunately, we have not found an efficient algorithm for coloring union graphs as yet. However, pessimism is not justified. First, the fact that the edges of the union graph are directed may be of help, as in the case of transitive graphs [1]. Second, there exist undirected graphs which are not the layout of any union graph. One such graph is the following:

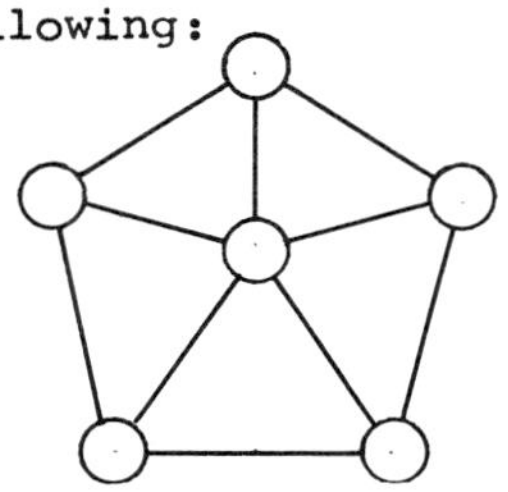

We postpone the proof of this fact to the next section.

<u>Lemma 10</u>: If $i \to j$ in $\vec{G}_U$ and both i and j are vertices of $\vec{G}^k$, then $i \to j$ in $\vec{G}^k$.

<u>Proof</u>: Since $i \to j$ in $\vec{G}_U$ then there exists an ℓ such that $i < j < \ell$ and $P^{-1}(\ell) < P^{-1}(i) < P^{-1}(j)$. However, since i and j are in $\vec{G}^k$, then $i < k$, $j < k$ and $P^{-1}(k) < P^{-1}(i)$ and $P^{-1}(k) < P^{-1}(j)$. It follows that

$$i < j < k \quad \text{and} \quad P^{-1}(k) < P^{-1}(i) < P^{-1}(j) .$$

Thus, $i \to j$ in $\vec{G}^k$. Q.E.D.

A graph H is called a vertex-subgraph of a graph G if the set of vertices of H is a subset of the set of vertices of G and all the edges of G connecting vertices which appear in H are also edges of H. H has no other edges. (This is sometimes called a section graph.)

Lemma 10 implies that each $\vec{G}^k$ is a vertex-subgraph of $\vec{G}_U$.

Lemma 11: If $\ell \in V$ then there exists a $k \neq \ell$ such that $\vec{G}^\ell$ is a vertex-subgraph of $\vec{G}^k$.

Proof: Since $\ell \in V$, there exists a k such that $\ell \in V^k$. Thus, $\ell < k$ and $P^{-1}(k) < P^{-1}(\ell)$. If $i \in V^\ell$ then $i < \ell$ and $P^{-1}(\ell) < P^{-1}(i)$. Thus, $i < k$ and $P^{-1}(k) < P^{-1}(i)$ and $i \in V^k$. Furthermore, if $i \rightarrow j$ in $\vec{G}^\ell$ then $i < j < \ell$ and $P^{-1}(\ell) < P^{-1}(i) < P^{-1}(j)$. Thus, $i < j < k$ and $P^{-1}(k) < P^{-1}(i) < P^{-1}(j)$. Therefore $i \rightarrow j$ in $\vec{G}^k$.

Q.E.D.

Corollary: $\vec{G}_U$ is the union of graphs $\vec{G}^k$ such that $k \notin V$.

The following lemma is not difficult to prove.

Lemma 12: Every vertex-subgraph of the union graph of some permutation is the union graph of some permutation.

4. Circle Graphs and their Relation to Union Graphs

Let C be a set of chords drawn in a circle. Define the corresponding undirected circle graph G(C,R) by representing each chord by a vertex; two vertices are connected by an edge if and only if the corresponding chords intersect.

Example 3:

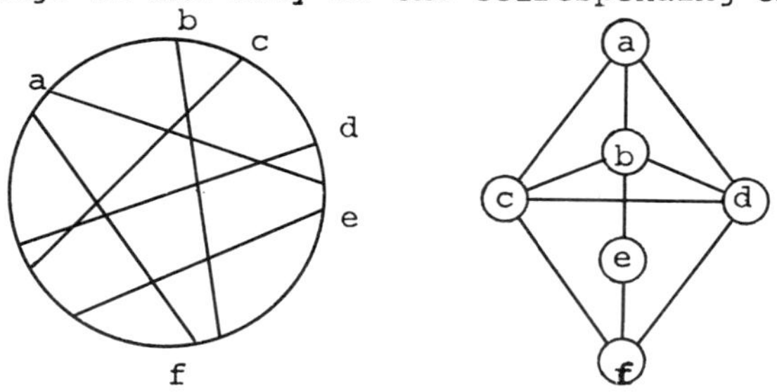

Let us show now an undirected graph which is not the circle graph of any circle with chords:

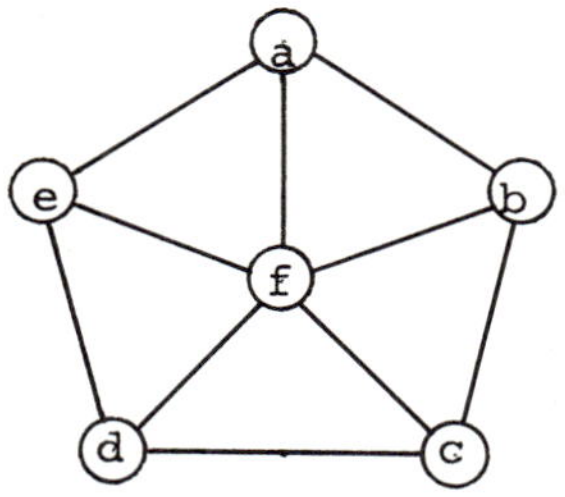

The only way of getting a circuit a—b—c—d—e—a in a circle graph is by drawing five chords as follows:

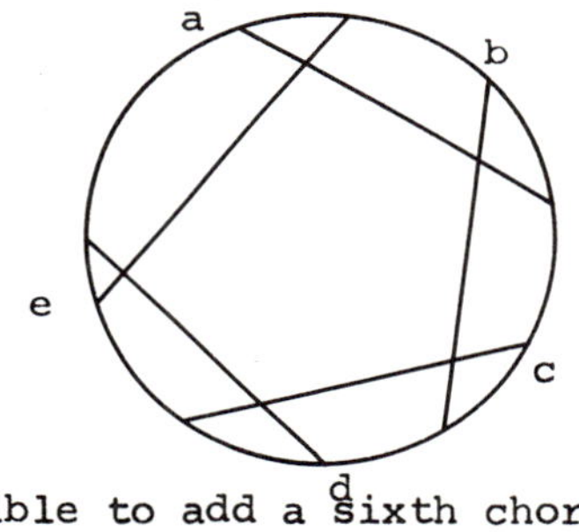

It is now impossible to add a sixth chord which will intersect all the existing five chords.

Next, let us describe an algorithm for generating a permutation whose union graph has a layout isomorphic to the given circle graph of a given circle with chords. (We assume the number of chords is not zero.)

<u>Algorithm 1</u>:

(1) Choose a point on the circle which is not an end point of a chord. Call it q (the first artificial vertex). Also set $i \leftarrow 1$.

(2) Move (clockwise, starting at q) along the circle until you reach an end point of a chord, p .

(3) Let p have the label i and the other end point of the same chord have the label i' . Increment i ($i \leftarrow i + 1$) .

(4) Move (clockwise, starting at p) along the circle. If you reach an unlabeled end point of a chord, call it p and go to Step (3). If you reach a labeled end point of a chord (it must have a primed label), let q have the label i' and increment i (i ← i + 1) .

(5) Move (clockwise, starting at the last labeled end point found in Step (4)), ignore additional labeled end points of chords as you go along. If you reach an artificial vertex, stop. If you reach an unlabeled end point of a chord p (a new chord) put a new artificial vertex, q , on the arc between the last end point encountered and q and go to Step (3).

The resulting permutation is achieved by reading the primed vertices off the circle, starting from the first artificial vertex and tracing clockwise.

<u>Example 4</u>: Consider a circle with five chords which has a pentagon as its circle graph:

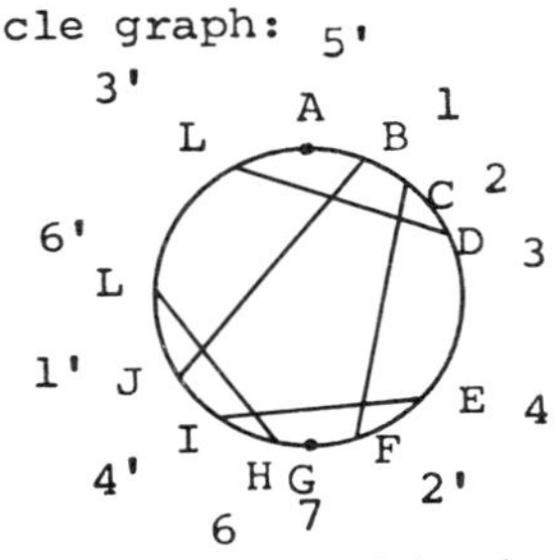

Assume we start at point A ; this is the first artificial vertex. (If we start between B and C we get a different permutation.) Going clockwise, we label B as 1 and J' as 1' ,C as 2 and F as 2' , D as 3 and L as 3' , E as 4 and I as 4' . Next we encounter F which is already labeled 2' . The present value of i is 5 , thus A is labeled 5' . We continue to trace from F and encounter an end point of a new chord, H . Thus, we put a new artificial vertex, G , between F and H . We label H as 6 and K as 6' . Next, we encounter I which is already labeled 4' . We label G as 7' and continue tracing from I . No unlabeled vertices are encountered until we reach the artificial vertex A and stop. The resulting permutation is:

$$P = [5,2,7,4,1,6,3]$$

See Example 2.

Theorem 1: Assume P is a permutation which is derived from a circle with chords through Algorithm 1. The underlying undirected graph of the union graph of P is identical with the circle graph.

Proof: Assume the algorithm assigns the end points of a given chord the labels i and i'. There exists an artificial vertex before i' (the one nearest to it) with a label k', where $k > i$. Thus, i is a vertex in the union graph.

An artificial vertex is assigned a number after all the vertices which precede it are labeled. Thus, its label is higher than these and it is not a vertex in the union graph.

Thus, we have already shown that the circle graph and the union graph have the same set of vertices.

Next, assme that $i — j$ in the circle graph; that is, the chord i intersects the chord j in the circle. (Here the chord names are as assigned in the algorithm.) Thus, the labels i, j, i', j' appear in this order on the circle. Consider the last artificial vertex before j, say k'. The algorithm implies that $k > j$ and therefore, $i \to j$ in the union graph.

Finally, assume $i \to j$ in the union graph. Thus, there exists a k, not in the union graph (by the Corollary following Lemma 11) such that $i < j < k$ and $P^{-1}(k) < P^{-1}(i) < P^{-1}(j)$. Thus, i' appears before j' on the circle, and k' appears before i'. If i' appears before j, then there must be an artificial vertex between i' and j, and $k < j$. Therefore i,j,i',j' must appear in this order and $i — j$ in the circle graph.

Q.E.D.

Now assume we are given a permutation P. The following algorithm will construct a circle with chords such that the underlying undirected graph of the union graph of

P is identical with the circle graph. Let V be the set of vertices in the union graph. Let us call the numbers in N-V <u>artificial vertices</u> (they will turn out to be similar to the artificial vertices defined in Algorithm 1).

<u>Algorithm 2:</u>

(1) Draw a circle. Choose n points around it and label them P(1), P(2),...,P(n), in this order, with primes.

(2) Set $k \leftarrow P(1)$ and $i \leftarrow 1$. (k is an artificial vertex.)

(3) If i is an artificial vertex, reset k to be the next artificial vertex following i in P , and go to Step (5).

(4) Draw vertex i in the arc between k' and the next primed vertex, after other unprimed vertices which have already been drawn in this arc.

(5) Increment i $(i \leftarrow i + 1)$. If $i < n$, go to Step (3). Otherwise, stop.

<u>Example 5:</u> Let P = [5,3,4,7,2,1,6] . Its union graph is

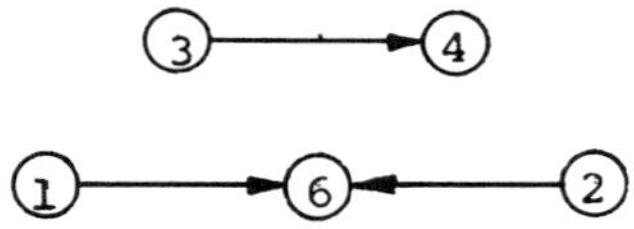

and the artificial vertices are 5 and 7 .

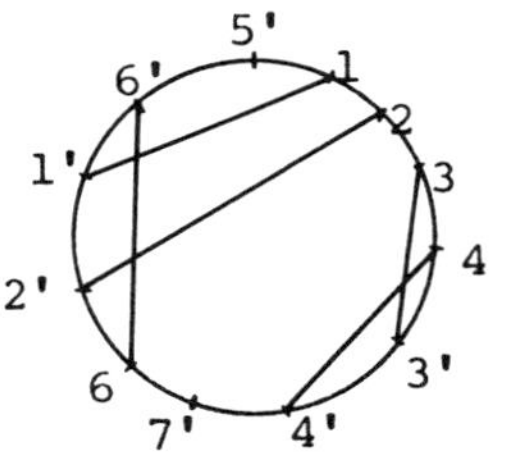

First we draw the points 5',3',4',7',2',1',6' on the circle in this order. We start with k = 5 and i = 1 . Next, vertices 1,2,3 and 4 are drawn by Steps (3), (4), (5) applied four times. Now i = 5 and 5 is an artificial vertex. We set $k = 7$, $i = 6$ and vertex 6 is drawn between 7' and 2'. Now $i = 7$, and we stop. The resulting chords and labels are shown above.

<u>Theorem 2</u>: Let P be any permutation. Algorithm 2 will construct a circle with chords whose circle graph is identical with the underlying undirected graph of P's union graph $\vec{G}_U(V,\vec{R})$.

<u>Proof</u>: For every i, i' is drawn on the circle in Step (1). Note that n (the highest integer in P) is always artificial and that the subsequence of artificial vertices of P is always an increasing sequence. Assuming that $n > 1$, it will never happen that Step (3) is applied to $i = n$, and if $i < n$, then there is a next artificial vertex to become the value of k.

The algorithm will also draw every non artificial vertex i. Now, assume $i \to j$ in $\vec{G}_U$. Thus there exists a least artificial vertex k such that $i < j < k$ and $P^{-1}(k) < P^{-1}(i) < P^{-1}(j)$. Thus, i' is drawn before j' on the circle. Clearly, i is drawn before j, and when the running artificial vertex is k, j is drawn before i'. Thus the four vertices i, j, i', j' appear in this order and i—j in the circle graph.

If i—j in the circle graph, and $i < j$, then i, j, i', j' appear in this order on the circle. Also, j comes after some artificial vertex $k > j$. Thus, $i < j < k$ and $P^{-1}(k) < P^{-1}(i) < P^{-1}(j)$, and $i \to j$ in $\vec{G}_U$.

Q.E.D.

<u>Corollary</u>: Every circle graph is the layout of some union graph, and the layout of every union graph is a circle graph.

Thus, the coloration of circle graphs is the same problem as the coloration of union graph. Also, since we have shown a graph which is not a circle graph (Example 3), the same graph is not the layout of any union graph.

The interested reader may find related results in references 2,3 and 4. Some of our results, and additional results on related subjects are reported in 5. The circle graph has been suggested to us by Yagil [6].

References

1. S. Even, A. Lempel, and A. Pnueli, "Permutation Graphs and Transitive Graphs", to appear in the JACM.

2. D. E. Knuth, The Art of Computer Programming. Vol. 1, Addison-Wesley (1969), pp. 234-239 and 531-534.

3. D. E. Knuth, The Art of Computer Programming, Vol. 3. To appear.

4. A. Pnueli, A. Lempel, and S. Even, "Transitive Orientation of Graphs and Identification of Permutation Graphs", Canadian J. of Math. Vol. 23, No. 1, pp.160-175 (1971).

5. R. Tarjan, "Sorting Using Networks of Queues and Stacks". Unpublished.

6. S. Yagil, "Linear Programming for Traffic Light Optimization". I.B.M. Technical Information Exchange, April (1966).

CONSTRUCTION OF SORTING PLANS*

C. L. Liu

Department of Electrical Engineering and Project MAC
Massachusetts Institute of Technology
Cambridge, Massachusetts 02139
U.S.A.

1. Introduction

By sorting a set of objects†, we mean to arrange them in such a way that a certain ordering relationship between them is satisfied. An algorithm leading to a correct arrangement of these objects is called a sorting algorithm. In this paper, we study the problem of designing sorting algorithms. That is, given an ordering relationship according to which a set of objects is to be arranged, we want to determine a procedure (more specifically, a sequence of steps) that will yield the desired result.

We introduce first some notations: Let A be a finite set which is a set of <u>locations</u>. Let Z denote the set of integers. Let ϕ be a function mapping A into Z. For $a \in A$, $\phi(a)$ is the <u>content</u> of location a. We call the ordered pair (A,ϕ) a <u>configuration</u>. Let ϕ be a one-to-one function mapping A onto A which defines a <u>permutation of the contents</u> of the locations. For $a \in A$, $\pi(a)$ is the location to which the content of a, $\phi(a)$, will be moved. Let ϕ_π be a function from A into Z

---

*Part of this work was done at the Aiken Computation Laboratory, Division of Engineering and Applied Physics, Harvard University. Part of this work was done at Project MAC, an M.I.T. research project sponsored by the Advanced Research Projects Agency, Department of Defense, under Office of Naval Research Contract N00014-70-A-0362-0001.

†We limit our discussion to the sorting of integers (or any set of objects over which there is a natural linear ordering).

such that

$$\phi_\pi(a) = \phi(\pi^{-1}(a))$$

We say that (A,ϕ_π) is a configuration induced from (A,ϕ) by π.

Let P be a partial ordering relation over A. A configuration (A,ϕ) is said to be consistent with P if a_1Pa_2 implies that $\phi(a_1) \leq \phi(a_2)$ for all a_1, a_2 in A. By sorting a configuration (A,ϕ) with respect to P, we mean to determine a permutation π on A such that (A,ϕ_π) is consistent with P. It is not difficult to see that for a given configuration (A,ϕ) and a partial ordering relation P the permutation π and thus the configuration (A,ϕ_π) are not necessarily unique. We shall use (A,ϕ_P) to denote the configuration induced from (A,ϕ) by some π such that (A,ϕ_P) is consistent with P. We say that (A,ϕ_P) is a configuration induced from (A,ϕ) by P.

A partial ordering relation C over A is called a shift if (i) a_1Ca_2 and a_1Ca_3 implies that either a_2Ca_3 or a_3Ca_2† and (ii) a_2Ca_1 and a_3Ca_1 implies that either a_2Ca_3 or a_3Ca_2† for any a_1,a_2,a_3 in A. A maximal sequence of locations $a_{11},a_{12},\ldots,a_{1m}$ such that $a_{1k}Ca_{1k}$, $a_{1k}Ca_{1(k+1)}, a_{1k}Ca_{1(k+2)},\ldots,a_{1k}Ca_{1m}$, for $k = 1,2,\ldots,m$ is called a chain of the shift C. Thus corresponding to a shift the locations in A are partitioned into chains. For a given configuration (A,ϕ) and a shift C over A, a configuration consistent with C can readily be obtained by rearranging the integers in the locations in each chain into ascending order according to C. As a matter of fact, we shall adopt the convention that for a given configuration (A,ϕ) and a shift C over A, the configuration (A,ϕ_C) is the one induced from (A,ϕ) by the permutation that permutes the contents of the locations in each chain so that the partial ordering relation C is satisfied. A sequence of shifts

---

†Since C is a partial ordering relation, it is clear that this is an "exclusive or" relationship for $a_2 \neq a_3$.

over A, $C_k, C_{k-1}, \ldots, C_2, C_1$, is said to be a <u>sorting plan</u> for P if for any arbitrary ϕ, the configuration $(A, \phi_{C_k C_{k-1} \ldots C_2 C_1})$ is consistent with P†.

The physical significance of these abstract notations should now become obvious: Given a set of integers stored in a set of locations as described by the configuration (A, ϕ), we can rearrange the integers so that the partial ordering relation P will be satisfied by following a sorting plan $C_k, C_{k-1}, \ldots, C_2, C_1$. That is, we rearrange the integers stored in A according to C_k, we then rearrange these (rearranged) integers according to C_{k-1}, and so on. Eventually, after we rearrange the integers according to C_1, we will have the integers sorted according to P.

2. Analysis of Sorting Plans

The construction of sorting plans is based on some results on the analysis of sorting plans developed in Liu [3]. We shall state these results without proof. Let (A, ϕ) be a given configuration. Let P be a partial ordering relation and C be a shift over A. Suppose that we have sorted the integers in A so that the partial ordering relation P is satisfied. We want to know the partial ordering relation that these integers will satisfy if the contents of the locations in each chain of C are rearranged according to C.

For a partial ordering relation P over A, a location a_1 is said to <u>precede</u> a location a_2 in P if $a_1 P a_2$. We also say that the location a_2 <u>is preceded</u> by the location a_1. Given a shift C over A, we define the <u>rank</u> of a location to be the number of locations preceding it in C. Clearly, the rank of each location is a positive integer. Moreover, in a chain of m

---

†We write $\phi_{C_k C_{k-1}}$ to mean $(\phi_{C_k})_{C_{k-1}}$, and $\phi_{C_k C_{k-1} \ldots C_2 C_1}$ to mean $((((\phi_{C_k})_{C_{k-1}}) \ldots)_{C_2})_{C_1}$.

locations, there is a location of rank 1, a location of rank 2,..., and a location of rank m.

Let P be a partial ordering relation and C be a shift over A. We define a binary relation Q over A as follows: Let a_1 be a location in a chain A_1 and a_2 be a location in a chain A_2 of the shift C. Let the rank of a_1 be i and the rank of a_2 be j. Then a_1Qa_2 if and only if every j locations in A_2 are preceded, in the partial ordering relation P, by i or more locations in A_1. The binary relation Q is said to be a composition of the shift C and the partial ordering relation P which will be denoted $C \otimes P$. It can be shown that:

Theorem 1: Let a_1 and a_2 be two locations in the same chain of C. Then a_1Qa_2 if and only if a_1Ca_2.

Theorem 2: Q is a partial ordering relation over A.

Theorem 3: For any configuration (A,ϕ_P), the configuration (A,ϕ_{PC}) is consistent with Q.

Theorem 4: Q is the largest partial ordering relation that (A,ϕ_{PC}) is consistent with.

Thus, these theorems answer the question raised earlier on the partial ordering relation the integers in A will satisfy if they were arranged according to P and then are rearranged according to C.

We introduce the notion of a shift preserving a partial ordering relation. Let $Q = C \otimes P$. We say that C <u>preserves</u> P if $P \subseteq Q$. We have the next two theorems which are due to Gale and Karp [2]:

Theorem 5: A shift C preserves a partial ordering relation P if and only if

(i) For $a_1 \neq a_2$, a_1Ca_2 implies that $\neg(a_2Pa_1)$.

(ii) For a location a_1 of rank i in a chain A_1 and a location a_2 of rank j in a chain A_2 with $A_1 \neq A_2$, a_1Pa_2 implies that, in the partial ordering relation P, every j locations in A_2 are preceded by i or more locations in A_1.

Theorem 6: Let $Q = C \otimes P$. If C preserves P, then $Q = P \circ C = C \circ P$.

3. Construction of Sorting Plans

The results presented in Section 2 lead to a recursive procedure for designing sorting plans. Let R be a partial ordering relation over A according to which the integers in A are to be sorted. If we choose a shift C over A such that $a_1 C a_2$ implies that $\neg(a_2 R a_1)$, for $a_1 \neq a_2$, then we can determine a partial ordering relation P such that $R \subseteq C \otimes P$. The decomposition step can then be repeated to decompose P until a sorting plan consisting of a sequence of shifts over A is determined. Let us illustrate the idea with a simple example: Let $A = \{a_1, a_2, \ldots, a_9\}$ and R be the partial ordering relation shown in Fig. 1(a)[†]. Let C_1 be the shift shown in Fig. 1(b) where the three chains are labelled A_1, A_2, A_3. We construct P in Fig. 1(c) so that the conditions (i) every two locations in A_2 are preceded by two or more locations in A_1 (ii) every three locations in A_3 are preceded by one or more locations in A_2 are satisfied. (Note that condition (i) implies that every two locations in A_2 are preceded by one or more locations in A_1 and every three locations in A_2 are preceded by two or more locations in A_1.) We then decompose P by first choosing the shift C_2 in Fig. 1(d) and then determining the partial ordering relation C_3 in Fig. 1(e) such that $P \subseteq C_2 \otimes C_3$. Since C_3 is a shift, C_3, C_2, C_1 is a sorting plan for R. That is, $R \subseteq C_1 \otimes (C_2 \otimes C_3)$.

The procedure suggested above does not include a systematic construction of the partial ordering relation P. Thus, in constructing P care must be exercised so that P is indeed a partial ordering relation. (Specifically, the antisymmetric law must be satisfied.) Theorem 7 in the following provides a systematic decomposition procedure.

[†]Partial ordering relations will be described by their Hasse diagrams.

Let R be a partial ordering relation over A. Let C be a shift such that $C \subseteq R$. Clearly, $(R - C)^*$ is a partial ordering relation. ($(R - C)^*$ denotes the transitive reflexive closure of $R - C$.) We have:

Theorem 7: The shift C preserves the partial ordering relation $(R - C)^*$.

Proof: To simplify the notations, let $P = (R - C)^*$. First, for $a_1 \neq a_2$, $a_1 C a_2$ implies that $\neg(a_2 P a_1)$. Next, let $a_{11}, a_{12}, a_{13}, \ldots, a_{1i}$ be locations in a chain A_1, where a_{1r} is of rank r for $r = 1,2,\ldots,i$. Let $a_{2j}, a_{2(j+1)}, a_{2(j+2)}, \ldots, a_{2n}$ be locations in another chain A_2, where a_{2r} is of rank r for $r = j, j+1, \ldots, n$. Suppose that $a_{1i} P a_{2j}$. Note that $a_{1u} P a_{2v}$ for $u = 1,2,\ldots,i$ and $v = j, j+1, \ldots, n$. That is, every one of the locations $a_{2j}, a_{2(j+1)}, \ldots, a_{2n}$ is preceded by the locations $a_{11}, a_{12}, \ldots, a_{1i}$ in P. Since every subset of j locations in A_2 must contain one or more of the locations $a_{2j}, a_{2(j+1)}, \ldots, a_{2n}$, every subset of j locations in A_2 are preceded by i or more locations in A_1. Therefore, according to Theorem 5, C preserves P. □

Corollary 7.1: $C \otimes (R - C)^* = R$

Proof: To simplify the notations, let $Q = C \otimes (R - C)^*$. Since $C \subseteq Q$ and $(R - C)^* \subseteq Q$, $R \subseteq Q$. Since $C \subseteq R$, $(R - C)^* \subseteq R$, $Q = C \circ (R - C)^* \subseteq R$. Therefore, $Q = R$. □

Repeated applications of Theorem 7 lead to a decomposition of the partial ordering relation R into a collection of shifts $C_k, C_{k-1}, \ldots, C_2, C_1$ such that $C_k, C_{k-1}, \ldots, C_2, C_1$ is a sorting plan for R. To be explicit, we choose first C_1 such that $C_1 \subseteq R$, we then choose C_2 such that $C_2 \subseteq (R - C_1)^*$, and then choose C_3 such that $C_3 \subseteq ((R - C_1)^* - C_2)^*$, and so on. To assure that R will be decomposed into a <u>finite</u> collection of shifts, we want to select the shifts such that $C_1 \cap (R - C_1)^* = A^0$, $C_2 \cap ((R - C_1)^* - C_2)^* = A^0$, $C_3 \cap (((R - C_1)^* - C_2)^* - C_3)^* = A^0$, and so on†. In other words, in selecting the shift C_i we should follow the rule that if $(a_1,a_2) \in C_i$ then for any location a_3 such that $(a_1,a_3) \in (((R - C_1)^* - C_2)^* \ldots - C_{i-1})^*$ and $(a_3,a_2) \in (((R - C_1)^* - C_2)^* \ldots - C_{i-1})^*$, we should have $(a_1,a_3) \in C_i$ or $(a_3,a_2) \in C_i$.

Note that for any sorting plan $C_k, C_{k-1}, \ldots, C_1$ constructed according to this procedure, C_{k-1} preserves C_k, C_{k-2} preserves $C_{k-1} \otimes C_k$, and so on. In other words, in such a sorting plan every shift preserves the partial ordering relation resulted from previous steps in the sorting plan. Theorem 8 in the following suggests a variation to the construction procedure so that sorting plans containing shifts that do not preserve the result of previous sorting steps might also be discovered.

Let P be a partial ordering relation and C be a shift over A. Let τ be a one-to-one mapping from A onto A such that a and $\tau(a)$ are locations in the same chain of C for every a in A. In other words, τ is a permutation of the locations in each chain. We define a relation P' over A such that $a_1P'a_2$ if and only if $\tau(a_1)P\tau(a_2)$. Clearly, P' is also a partial ordering relation.

Theorem 8: $C \otimes P = C \otimes P'$.

Proof: Every j locations in a chain A_1 are preceded by i or more locations in another chain A_2 in the partial ordering relation P' if and only if every j locations in A_1 are preceded by i or more locations in A_2 in the partial ordering relation P. □

Theorem 8 enables us to modify the construction procedure that is based on Theorem 7. Specifically, after selecting C_1 and determining $P = (R - C_1)^*$, we can construct P' as in Theorem 8 so that $C_1 \otimes P = C_1 \otimes P'$

---

† A^0 denotes the binary relation $\{(a_i,a_i) \mid a_i \in A\}$.

by choosing a permutation of the locations in the chains of C_1. In general, C_1 no longer preserves the partial ordering relation P'. We can now go on to decompose P' into shifts as we did before. Again, at any point of the recursive decomposition of P' we may permute the locations in the chains of a shift arbitrarily. If we let $C'_k, C'_{k-1}, \ldots, C'_1$ denote a sorting plan obtained this way, then we have

$$C'_1 \otimes (C'_2 \otimes \ldots \otimes (C'_{k-1} \otimes C'_k))) \supseteq R$$

although a shift C'_i might not preserve the partial ordering relation $C'_{i+1} \otimes (C'_{i+2} \otimes \ldots \otimes (C'_{k-1} \otimes C'_k))$.

The result in Theorem 8 is only an instance of many possible ways of modifying a partial ordering relation P that is preserved by a shift C. It suffices to say that any modification of P such that the condition on the number of locations in one chain preceding a subset of locations in another chain is not violated will lead to a correct sorting plan. This point is illustrated in Example 2 in Section 4.

4. Illustrative Examples

We show in this section two examples illustrating the application of the results derived above.

Example 1: Suppose we want to design a sorting plan for sorting six integers linearly. Let R be the partial ordering relation shown in Fig. 2(a), and C_1 be the shift shown in Fig. 2(b). We obtain $(R - C_1)^*$ as shown in Fig. 2(c). Let C_2 be the shift shown in Fig. 2(d). We obtain $((R - C_1)^* - C_2)^*$ as shown in Fig. 2(e). Let C_3 be the shift shown in Fig. 2(f) and C_4 be the shift shown in Fig. 2(g). Since C_3 preserves the shift C_4, and $C_4 \otimes C_3 = ((R - C_1)^* - C_2)^*$, we conclude that C_4, C_3, C_2, C_1 is a sorting plan for sorting six integers linearly.

This example can be extended to the construction of a sorting plan for any number of integers. Interesting enough, the result turns out to be equivalent to the odd-even merge algorithm due to Batcher [1]. For further details, see Liu [3].

Example 2: We can also derive Batcher's result [1] on merging two sorted lists which are not of the same length. For the sake of simplicity, let us, instead of deriving the general result, show how to merge a sorted list of seven integers and a sorted list of three integers. Let R be the partial ordering relation shown in Fig. 3(a)†, and let C_1 be the shift shown in Fig. 3(b). We obtain $(R - C_1)^*$ as shown in Fig. 3(c). Let C_2 be the shift shown in Fig. 3(d), and C_3 be the shift shown in Fig. 3(e). Since C_2 preserves C_3, and $C_2 \otimes C_3 = (R - C_1)^*$, C_3, C_2, C_1 is a sorting plan for R. However, it can easily be seen that for the shift C_3' shown in Fig. 3(f) $C_2 \otimes C_3' = C_2 \otimes C_3 = (R - C_1)^*$. Therefore, C_3', C_2, C_1 is also a sorting plan for R. Note that C_3' has two chains, one contains seven locations and the other contains three locations.

References

1. K.E. Batcher, "Sorting Networks and Their Applications," Proceedings of the Spring Joint Computer Conference, April 1968, pp. 307-314.

2. D. Gale and R.M. Karp, "A Phenomenon in the Theory of Sorting," IEEE Conference Record of the 1970 Eleventh Annual Symposium on Switching and Automata Theory, October 1970, pp. 51-59.

3. C.L. Liu, "Analysis and Synthesis of Sorting Algorithms," (to appear).

† Note that we label the locations in such a way that the final result will become clearer.

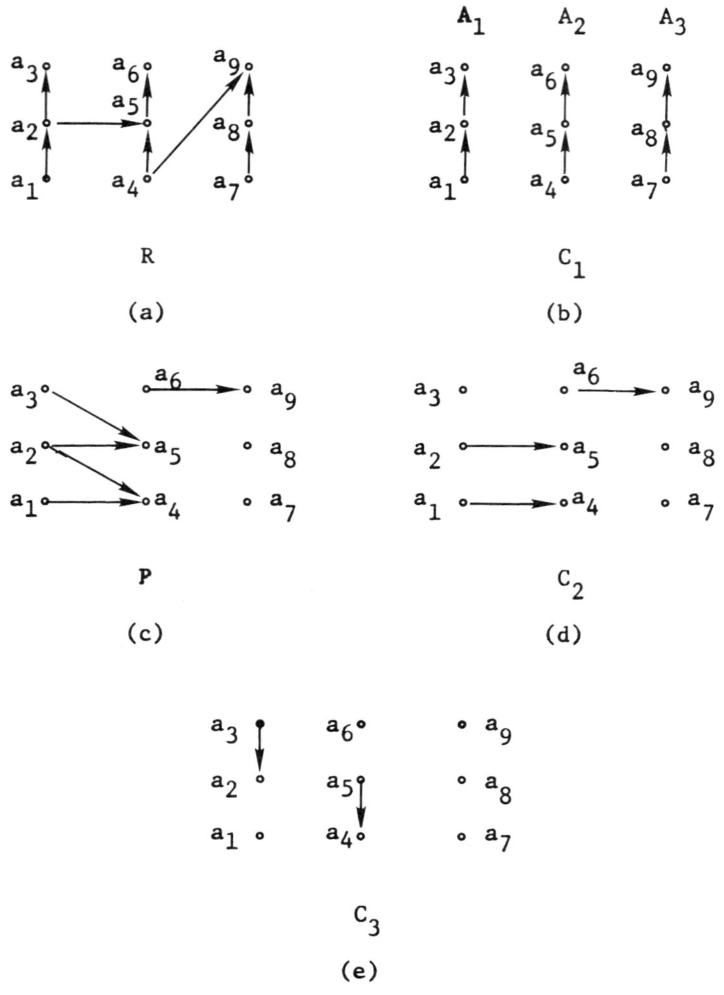

Figure 1

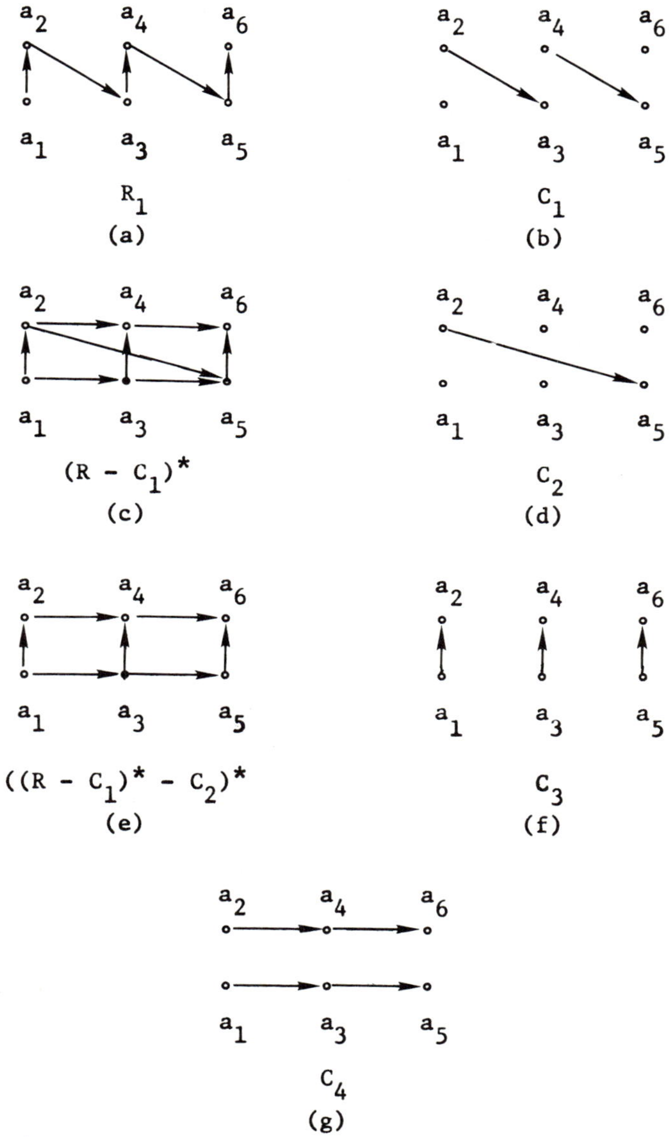
a2 a4 a6
a1 a3 a5
R1
(a)
a2 a4 a6
a1 a3 a5
C1
(b)
a2 a4 a6
a1 a3 a5
(R - C1)*
(c)
a2 a4 a6
a1 a3 a5
C2
(d)
a2 a4 a6
a1 a3 a5
((R - C1)* - C2)*
(e)
a2 a4 a6
a1 a3 a5
C3
(f)
a2 a4 a6
a1 a3 a5
C4
(g)

Figure 2

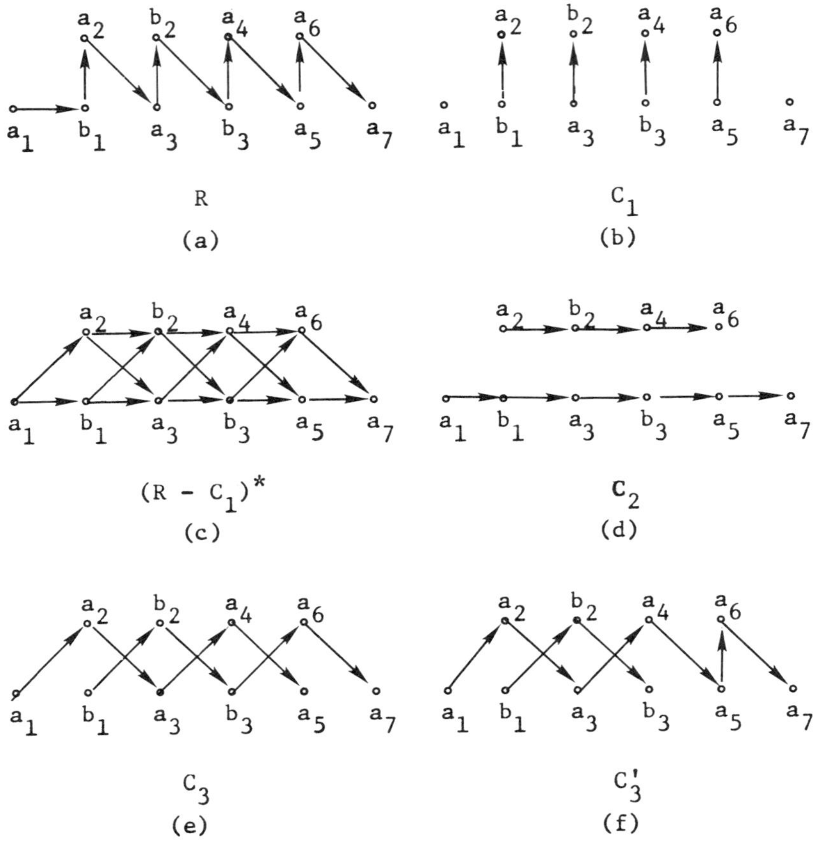

Figure 3

IFF PROGRAMS

D. Tsichritzis

Computer Science Department*
University of Toronto
Toronto, Canada

Abstract

The properties of programs with very simple control structure are investigated. Specifically programs with only <u>if</u>...<u>then</u>...<u>else</u>... control statements and polynomial assignment statements are introduced as IFF programs. Although most of the general decision problems are unsolvable partial solutions can be given for their optimization.

1. Introduction and Definitions

We will investigate the properties of programs generated from assignment statements and the control statement <u>if</u>...<u>then</u>...<u>else</u>... (forward IF). We will call such programs <u>IFF programs</u>. IFF programs are essentially piecewise definitions of functions using simpler functions. They can offer efficient ways of storing tables and approximating functions.

There are some advantages in the simple control of IFF programs.

a) They always terminate.
b) There is a bound on their running time.
c) Their control sequence is very simple.

We choose to consider IFF programs as interpreted models, where the arguments take integer values and the

* This work was supported by the National Research Council of Canada, Grant No. A7146.

assignment functions are chosen among a simple class of functions A. In order to obtain the conditions tested in the <u>if</u> part of the control we incorporate in our model the relation $>$ (or $\geq$, or $\leq$, or $<$).

<u>Definition 1.1</u>

Consider a set of functions A. Let C_A be the set of conditions $f(\bar{x}) > g(\bar{x})$ where $f,g \in A$. The set of IFF programs P can be defined recursively:

```
<P> ::= y = <A>
<P> ::= begin if <C_A> then <P> else <P> end
```

As long as the function $x_1 - x_2$ is in A testing the value of a function in A against a cutpoint is enough to generate all the conditions. We will usually choose as a cutpoint the number zero. If we do not use any delimiters (<u>begin</u>,<u>end</u>) in the programs we assume association to the left.

<u>Example E1</u>. Consider the following IFF program defining the function $y = f(x)$.

```
        if   g1(x) > 0  then
        if   g2(x) > 0  then
        if   g3(x) > 0  then  y = h1(x)  else  y = h2(x)
  else  if   g4(x) > 0  then  y = h3(x)  else  y = h4(x)
  else  if   g5(x) > 0  then  y = h5(x)  else  y = h6(x)
```

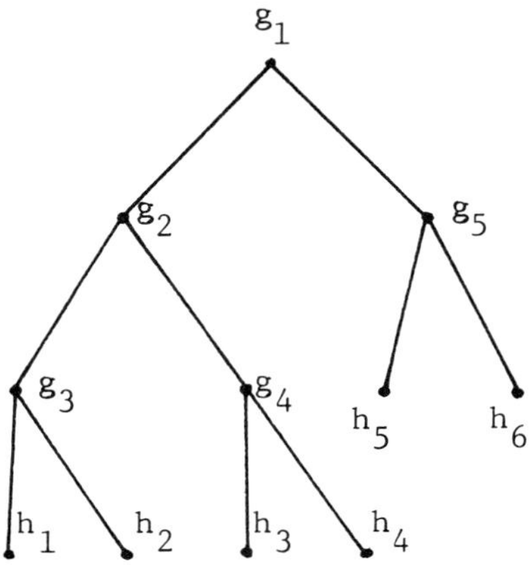

g_1	g_2	g_3	g_4	g_5	*
1	1	1	d	d	h_1
1	1	0	d	d	h_2
1	0	d	1	d	h_3
1	0	d	0	d	h_4
0	d	d	d	1	h_5
0	d	d	d	0	h_6

* The symbol d (don't care) is used as a shorthand notation. The table can be expanded by substituting {0,1} for d.

The program E1 can be represented in a natural way by a computation tree. Each leaf gives a definition of the function for the corresponding path. Every other node corresponds to a condition $g(x) > 0$. We move to the left if the condition is satisfied to the right otherwise. By convention we use the letter g for conditions and h for final assignments.

Consider now an alternative way of defining the function using a table. The columns of the table correspond to conditions $g_i(x) > 0$, $i = 1,\ldots,5$. The rows are all binary sequences of length five. A function h is associated with each row. The value of the function f(x) represented by the table is computed by the following algorithm.

<u>Step 1</u> Test $g_i(x)$ for every i and define $a_i = 1$ if $g_i(x) > 0$, 0 otherwise.

<u>Step 2</u> Pick the function h_j corresponding to row $a_1 \ldots a_5$.

<u>Step 3</u> $f(x) = h_j(x)$.

The computation of f(x) defined by the table can be described using pseudo-Algol and the delimiters <u>parbegin</u>, <u>parend</u> [2,4].

Note the difference between the <u>if</u> <u>then</u> <u>else</u> (computation tree) definition and the <u>parbegin</u> <u>parend</u> (table) definition. The first is purely sequential the second highly parallel. We will call them respectively <u>sequential form</u> and <u>parallel form</u>.

It is very easy to show that from a given set of functions A both forms compute the same functions.

2. General Properties

We will denote by B = F(A) the class of functions defined by IFF programs with control and assignment functions g and f in a class of functions A. The class A will usually be the closure under composition of an initial class of simple functions. Note that if A includes a switching function like $w(x_1,x_2,x_3) = x_1$, if $x_3 = 0$, x_2 if $x_3 > 0$ and it is closed under composition, B is identical to A. In such a case the structure of B corresponds to the way we compose the switch function in A. We will choose A in such a way that it does not contain w either explicitly as an initial function, or implicitly formed by composition.

It is obvious that if we start from a simple class of statements in our program and use only IF control statements we will not be able to compute all recursive functions. To begin with, functions in B grow at the same rate as functions in A. Hence any majorizing function of A will also majorize B. It is easy to prove that if A is r.e. then there are even recursive predicates not in B. It follows that, if A is obtained from a finite number of initial functions and composition, then there are recursive predicates not in B.

Note that if B = F(A), then F(B) = F(F(A)) = B. Namely a second extension of a class using IFF programs does not give any more functions.

The equivalence of IFF programs is usually undecidable. It is easy to prove the following statement. The equivalence problem of B is decidable if and only if both the equivalence problem of A and the emptiness problem of a set of relations $g(x) > 0$, $g(x)$ in A are decidable.

We would like to choose A in such a way that the statements are FORTRAN-like. It is also customary in theoretical work to use only the nonnegative integers N as domain and range of the functions. These goals are incompatible with our desire to exclude switching functions from A.

Consider A = Closure $\{SF, x_1+x_2, x_1-x_2, [x_1/x_2], x_1 \cdot x_2, x_1^{x_2}\}$, where SF (starting functions) are the functions $\phi(x) = 0$, $s(x) = x+1$, $u_i^n(x_1,\ldots,x_n) = x_i$ useful in order to generate all constants and pass the arguments. The function $[x_1/x_2]$ is defined to be some constant c if $x_2 = 0$. It is easy to show that not only A but even subsets of A contain a switch function implicitly [4].

We will have to allow negative integers since the discontinuity at zero introduces the switch function. We choose as statements polynomials of the variables for two reasons. First they are very commonly used in programming. Second there is a lot known about the behavior and the structure of polynomials. From now on the class A is going to be:

A = Closure $\{SF, x_1+x_2, x_1-x_2, x_1 \cdot x_2\}$, domain all integers I.

3. Polynomial Statements

We will investigate the properties of the class of functions B generated by IFF programs with polynomial statements in A. It is obvious that there are much more functions in B than in A. For instance the function $f(x) = 0$ if $x > 0$, 1 if $x \leq 0$ cannot be expressed as a polynomial.

We can choose different structural static measures of complexity for IFF programs computing functions in B.

a) The nodes of the computation tree.
b) the conditional statements of the computation tree.
c) The maximum path in the computation tree.
d) The number of columns of the table.
e) The number of rows of the table.

All the above measures are related. The number of columns (conditions) in a table is chosen, since all conditions need be resolved for each computation of the function defined by the table.

Definition 3.1

A_n is the class of functions in B defined by at most n columns (condition statements) in a definition table.
$A_0 = A$, $\bigcup_n A_n = B$.

Theorem 3.1

Two conditions are enough to obtain all functions in B with one variable. $f(x) \in B \rightarrow f(x) \in A_2$.

Proof

Suppose $f(x) \in B$ then there is a table representation of f with $g_1, \ldots, g_K$ associated with the columns and $h_1, \ldots, h_{2^k}$ associated with the rows.

Consider the real roots of $g_1(x), \ldots, g_k(x)$ and define:

$m = [\max \{r | g_j(r) = 0 \text{ for some } j\}]^+$, where $[y]^+$ stands for the "first integer $\geq y$".

It follows that for every $x > m$ all $g_j(x)$ will remain >, or $\leq$ of zero.

In a similar way define

$t = [\min \{r | g_j(r) = 0 \text{ for some } j\}]^+ - 1.$

It follows that for every $x \le t$ all $g_j(x)$ will remain $>$, or $\le$ of zero.

According to the definition of f(x) it follows that for $x > m$, $f(x) = h_i(x)$ and for $x \le t$, $f(x) = h_j(x)$ for some fixed i and j. Hence f(x) is defined by the table:

	x-m	x-t	
x>m	1	1	$h_i(x)$
x>m,x<t	1	0	empty row
m≥x>t	0	1	h(x)
x≤t	0	0	$h_j(x)$

where h(x) is the Langrange polynomial which agrees with f(x) at the finite number of integers $m \ge x > t$.

Note that if $g_1,\ldots,g_k$ do not have any real roots the function f is trivially in A.

Theorem 3.1 can be generalized to functions $f(\bar{x})$ defined by single variable conditions $g_1(x),\ldots,g_k(x)$. It follows that one variable functions do not form a structural hierarchy according to the number of <u>if</u> <u>then</u> <u>else</u> statements. Two control statements are enough. Some functions require two control statements.

<u>Proposition 3.2</u>

There are functions f(x) s.t. $f(x) \in A_2$, $f(x) \notin A_1$.

<u>Argument</u>

Consider the function f(x) s.t. $f(x) = x^n$ for $x > 2n$, $f(x) = x^{n-1}$ for $x < 0$ and $f(x) = 0$ for $0 \le x \le 2n$. It is easy to express f(x) in A_2.

The function f(x) cannot be expressed as a polynomial since it has different degree for $x > 2n$ and $x < n$. Suppose $f(x) \in A_1$ defined by the following table:

g(x)	
0	$h_1(x)$
1	$h_2(x)$

It is clear that $h_1(x)$ and $h_2(x)$ has each degree at most n in order to agree with f(x) as $x \to \infty$ and $x \to -\infty$. But they have to agree with f(x) in the region $0 \le x \le 2n$, hence one of them has at least n+1 roots, which is a contradiction.

Lemma 3.3 [3,4]

Consider two polynomials $h(x,y)$ and $h'(x,y)$ of maximum degree n in (x,y) which agree on n+1 lines $y = r_0x+t_0$, $y = r_1x+t$, ..., $y = r_nx+t_n$, where $r_i \neq r_j$ for every $i \neq j$. It follows that $h(x,y)$ and $h'(x,y)$ are identical.

Theorem 3.4

Consider the set of 2^k lines $y = r_ix$, $r_i = \tan \frac{2\pi i}{2^k}$ $i = 0,\dots,2^k-1$, dividing the (x,y) plane in 2^k regions, and let the function $f(x,y)$ defined as x^j for the R_j region, $j = 1,\dots,2^k$. The function $f(x,y)$ is in B but it cannot be expressed using k-1 or less conditions; that is $f(x,y) \in B$ but $f(x,y) \notin A_{k-1}$.

Proof

To prove that $f(x,y) \in B$ is trivial, since it can be expressed easily using the 2^k lines as conditions.

Suppose $f(x,y) \in A_{k-1}$. Let $g_1,\dots,g_{k-1}$ be the conditions in the table defining f and G_i, $i = 1,\dots,2^{k-1}$ the corresponding regions. Let n be defined as

$n = \max_i \{\text{degree of } g_i, 2^k\} + 1$.

Choose t different lines $y = s_ix$ in each region R_j where $t = 2^kn$. For all these lines by definition $f(x,y) = x^j$. Each of the lines will eventually lie in a unique region G_i.

In each region G_i we will have on the average $\frac{2^kt}{2^{k-1}} = 2t$ lines. Hence one region G_j will have at least 2t lines. Then there must be at least two regions R_p and R_q with at least n lines each in G_j. Suppose only one region R_i had more than n, the maximum it could have is t, and the rest of the regions R have $(2^k-1)(n-1)$ at most, but then $t + (2^k-1)(n-1) < 2t$, which is a contradiction.

Let $f(x,y) = h(x,y)$ in the region G_j. Hence $h(x,y) = x^p$ for the n lines of the region R_p and

$h(x,y) = x^q$ for the n lines of the region R_q. But the degree of $h(x,y) < n$ and $h(x,y) = x^p$, $h(x,y) = x^q$, $p \neq q$ for n lines. This cannot be true according to Lemma 3.3.

Theorem 3.4 can also be proved for an arbitrary number n of regions. Namely for n regions we need at least $[\log_2 n]^+$ conditions.

Theorem 3.5

For every $k = 1,2,\ldots$ there is a sequence of conditions $\{g_1(x,y),\ldots,g_k(x,y)\}$ which cut the plane in 2^k regions $R_1,\ldots,R_{2^k}$. Each region R_{i+1} lies between the lines $y = x \tan \frac{2\pi i}{2^k}$ and $y = x \tan \frac{2\pi(i+1)}{2^k}$.

Proof

Note that k conditions can cut the plane in at most 2^k regions. We will show that the limit can be attained, moreover the regions are infinite.

Consider the functions

$$g_1(x,y) = x$$
$$g_2(x,y) = y$$
$$g_3(x,y) = x^2(y/x - \tan \tfrac{\pi}{4})\cdot(y/x - \tan \tfrac{3\pi}{4})$$
$$\vdots$$
$$g_n(x,y) = x^{2^{n-2}}(y/x - r_1)(y/x - r_2)\ldots(y/x - r_{2^{n-2}})$$

where $r_i = \tan [\frac{2\pi}{2^{n-1}}(i-1+\frac{1}{2})]$ $i=1,\ldots,2^{n-2}$.

The sequence $\{g_1(x,y),\ldots,g_n(x,y),\ldots\}$ has the following properties

a) $g_n(x,y) = 0$ consists of 2^{n-2} straight lines $y = r_1x, \ldots, y = r_{2^{n-2}}x$.

b) The regions $g_n(x,y) > 0$, $g_n(x,y) \leq 0$ alternate between the lines $y = r_{i+1}x$, $y = r_ix$ for $i=1,\ldots,2^{n-2}$.

We will prove inductively that for every k the conditions $\{g_1,\ldots,g_k\}$ divide the plane in 2^k regions $R_1,\ldots,R_{2^k}$, where R_{i+1} is between $y/x = \tan \frac{2\pi i}{2^k}$, $y/x = \tan \frac{2\pi(i+1)}{2^k}$.

It is easy to verify for $\{g_1,g_2,g_3\}$. Suppose it is

true for $\{g_1,\ldots,g_n\}$ and let $g_{n+1}(x,y) = x^{2^{n-1}}(y/x - r_1)\ldots(y/x - r_{2^{n-1}})$. The asymptotes of of $g_{n+1}(x,y)$ are $y = r_i x$, $i = 1,\ldots,2^{n-1}$ where

$$r_1 = \tan\left(\frac{2\pi}{2^n}\frac{1}{2}\right)$$

$$r_i = \tan\left[\frac{2\pi}{2^n}\left(i-1+\frac{1}{2}\right)\right]$$

$$r_{2^{n-1}} = \tan\left[\frac{2\pi}{2^n}\left(2^{n-1}-1+\frac{1}{2}\right)\right].$$

Hence the asymptotes of $g_{n+1}(x,y)$ will split the regions $R_1,\ldots,R_{2^n}$ right in half. Moreover in the two parts of a region R_i the function $g_{n+1}(x,y)$ will be respectively $>$ and ≤ 0. It follows that the conditions $\{g_1,\ldots,g_{n+1}\}$ will divide the plane in $2 \cdot 2^n = 2^{n+1}$ regions $R_1,\ldots,R_{2^{n+1}}$. Each region R_{i+1} lies between the lines $y/x = \tan\frac{2\pi i}{2^{n+1}}$, $y/x = \tan\frac{2\pi(i+1)}{2^{n+1}}$.

Consider now the function $f(x,y)$ defined by conditions $\{g_1,\ldots,g_k\}$ and $f(x,y)$ being $f(x,y) = x^i$ for the R_i region $i = 1,\ldots,2^k$.

The function $f(x,y)$ cannot be defined using only k-1 conditions according to Theorem 3.4.
Hence $f(x,y) \in A_k$, $f(x,y) \notin A_{k-1}$ and $A_k \supsetneq A_{k-1}$.

Corollary 3.6

The number of conditions establishes a hierarchy $A_k \supsetneq A_{k-1}$, $k = 1,2,\ldots$

We will investigate some other properties of the class B.

Proposition 3.7

The equivalence problem of $B = F(A)$ is unsolvable.

Argument

Given any polynomial $h(\bar{x})$ consider the functions $f_1(\bar{x})$, $f_2(\bar{x})$ in B represented by the computation trees. $f_1(\bar{x}) \neq f_2(\bar{x})$ iff $h(\bar{x}) = 0$ has at least one integer solution. Hence we reduce the equivalence problem of B to

Hilbert's tenth problem which has been recently proved to be unsolvable (Mateyacevich) [1].

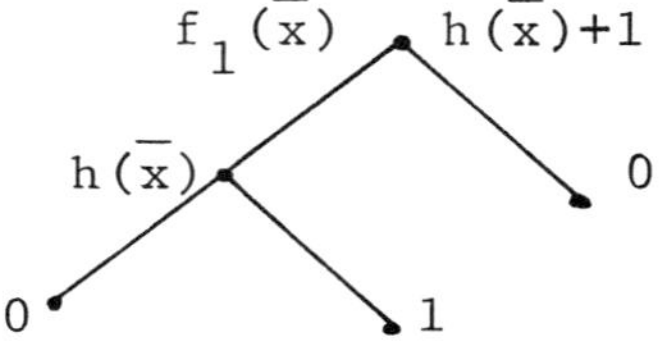

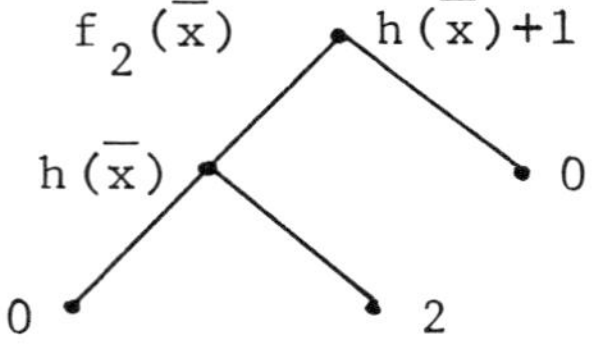

The membership problem of the class B can also be proved to be unsolvable [4].

4. Program Transformations

We will try to obtain "optimization procedures" for IFF programs although the general optimization problem is unsolvable. In some special cases we will give methods to remove redundancies and improve the programs.

Proposition 4.1 [4]

Given a function $f(\bar{x}) \in B$ it is recursively unsolvable to determine the minimum n s.t. $f(\bar{x}) \in A_n$.

Suppose we have a one variable function $f(x) \in B$ then according to theorem 3.1 $f(x) \in A_2$. There is a procedure to check whether $f(x) \in A_0$ or A_1 [4].

Lemma 4.2 [4]

Consider a polynomial $g(x,y) = p_n(x,y) + p_{n-1}(x,y) + \dots + p_1(x,y) + c$. The curve $g(x,y) = 0$ is closed (can be contained in a circle $x^2 + y^2 = r^2$) if and only if for every real w, $p_n(1,w) \neq 0$ and $p_n(0,1) \neq 0$ (the curve has no points at infinity). The directions at infinity (d.a.i.) are given by $y = ax$ if $p_n(1,a) = 0$ and $x = 0$ if $p_n(0,1) = 0$.

If a curve is not closed (has points at infinity) it does not necessarily mean that the direction at infinity is an asymptote in the geometric sense. Namely it does not necessarily have the property that the points on the curve get very close to the line as we go far from the origin. An easy example is the parabola $y = x^2$.

Theorem 4.3

Consider a function $f(x,y) \in B$ defined by a table with conditions $g_1(x,y),\dots,g_k(x,y)$. We can substitute all conditions $g_i(x,y)$ s.t. $g_i(x,y) = 0$ is a closed curve on the plane, with one condition $g(x,y) = x^2 + y^2 - r^2$.

Outline of Proof

We substitute the closed curves with the circle which contains them and use in the definition of $f(x,y)$.

1) For the points outside the circle the same function $h(x,y)$ as before.
2) For the points inside the circle the generalization of Lagrange's polynomial for two variables [3].

It is of interest to investigate some cases where the conditions $g(x,y)$ can be replaced by their asymptotes, since it is far easier to test a linear condition.

Lemma 4.4 [4]

Consider a straight line $y = ax + b$ where a,b both rational. Then there may be integer points (x,y) on the line but there are no integer points within a fixed distance $\delta > 0$ from the line.

Theorem 4.5

If $g(x,y) = 0$ has only asymptotes $y = a_i x + b_i$ where a_i, b_i rational for every i, then the condition $g(x,y)$ can be substituted by straight line conditions.

Outline of Proof

With every asymptote we associate a distance δ according to Lemma 4.4. Far enough form the origin the curve $g(x,y) = 0$ is closer than δ to all its asymptotes. It can be shown on the other hand that after a certain point the curve cannot cut the asymptote. Hence we can substitute the curve by its asymptote. Moreover from Lemma 4.4 we are assured that no integer points are between the asymptote and the curve.

In order to ensure that we are far from the origin we incorporate four lines as conditions: $y + k = 0$, $y - k = 0$, $x + k = 0$, $x - k = 0$ for large enough k.

Hence we can substitute $g(x,y)$ as a condition with four lines (a large square) and its asymptotes. Three lines (large triangle) can be used instead of four.

Unfortunately some conditions cannot be substituted by a set of lines. A good example is the parabola $y = x^2$. Straight lines can only approximate the condition.

Consider a set S of integer coordinate points in the (x,y) plane. Consider the set of concentring circles $x^2 + y^2 = r^2$ for $r = 1,2,\ldots$ and let N_r be the set of integer coordinate points inside the circle $x^2 + y^2 = r^2$. We will associate a <u>frequency</u> of occurrence of points in S q(S).

$$q(S) = \lim_{r\to\infty} \frac{|N_r \cap S|}{|N_r|} \text{, when the limit exists.}$$

$|N|$ denotes the number of points in N.

We will say that a set contains <u>sparse points</u> if q(S) = 0. The measure q(S) has some interesting properties [4].

<u>Theorem 4.6</u>

Consider a function $f(x,y) \in B$ and let $g_1(x,y),\ldots,g_n(x,y)$ be the conditions used to define it. We can give a definition using only straight lines corresponding to the directions at infinity (d.a.i.'s) of $\{g_i(x,y)\}$ which expresses f(x,y) up to sparse points.

<u>Outline of the proof</u>

First we can dispose of $g_i(x,y)$ corresponding to closed curves since they can only affect sparse points.

Consider the conditions g(x,y) and their d.a.i.'s. We can use the d.a.i.'s instead of g(x,y) to delimit the regions and this only affects sparse points according to the properties of the frequency q(S) [4].

Note that if m is the maximum degree of $g_i(x,y)$ for $i = 1,\ldots,n$, then the number of d.a.i.'s is less than n.m. Hence we need at most n.m straight lines.

According to properties of the frequency q sometimes we can interpret q as the probability of an integer point falling within a region.

If we obtain all the d.a.i.'s of the conditions used to define f(x,y), the probabilities q are obtained from the angles between the d.a.i.'s.

<u>Theorem 4.7</u>

Consider a function $f(x,y) \in B$. If f(x,y) is defined through a table we can compute the probability of f(x,y) being defined from a certain row. If f(x,y) is defined by a computation tree we can compute the branching probability of the tree.

5. Concluding Remarks

We continue investigating IFF programs, representing finite domains of functions. Consider a list of length n defining the values of an arbitrary function on a finite domain. It would be very nice if we can express the same function over the finite domain using a definition table with conditions $\{g_1,\ldots,g_k\}$ and functions $h_1,\ldots,h_t$, where $k,t \ll n$. This is a method of data compression ("squeezing"). We are investigating:

a) Properties which a list of data should have in order to be "squeezable" in the above sense.

b) Algorithms to test (a) and transform a list of data into a definition table efficiently.

References

1) Davis M. "An explicit Diophantine defintion of the exponential function" Unpublished manuscript.

2) Dijkstra E.W. "Co-operating Sequential Processes" Report EWD 123, Mathematical Dept. T.H.E. (Sept. 1965).

3) Isaacson I. and Keller H.B. "Analysis of Numerical Methods" John Wiley, 1966.

4) Tsichritzis D. "IFF programs" Technical Report No. 27 Department of Computer Science, University of Toronto, Canada.

SECTION II

FORMAL AND STOCHASTIC LANGUAGES

SOME LANGUAGES RELATED TO PLANAR MAPS

Robert Cori and Jean Richard

Institut de Programmation
PARIS , FRANCE

Abstract

A bijection is defined between rooted planar maps, with a fixed number of vertices, and the words of a context-free language . Formal power series built from the previous language are shown to verify equations of a certain type, which are then solved, the results implying the algebraicity of the power series solution and giving enumerational formulas .

Introduction

The enumeration of rooted planar maps has been developped by W.T.Tutte and his school, since the Census papers of 1962, using recurrence formulas from which generating power series are computed . These are always algebraic. A new method was introduced by M. Gross [5] for the enumeration of the different ways one can dissect a polygon into triangles .This method consists in building a bijection between the maps to enumerate and the words of a certain context-free language, the generating function is then obtained by taking a commutative image of the language. This method was also used by W.Kuich [6] for the enumeration of trees ; we apply it here for general maps .

I Definition of the code of a planar map

A planar map, as defined by W.T.Tutte [10] , is a partition of the sphere into a finite number of subsets of three kinds : vertices, edges, and faces . A <u>half-edge</u> of a map is defined by an edge and one of its vertices, a loop giving raise to two half-edges. The map is said to be <u>rooted</u> if a half-edge is distinguished and called the root. A map will be said to be <u>simple</u> if one of its faces is incident with all the edges. In the sequel we enumerate simple maps with conditions for the choice of its root (as described below), as the enumerational formula for them is much more elegant.

Rooted simple maps : the root of a simple map must verify :

- If the root belongs to a loop, then the other half-edge of it is met immediately after the root when turning counter clockwise around the vertex origin .

- If the root belongs to an edge joining two distinct vertices, such that there exists another edge joining them, this edge is met immediately after the root when turning counter clockwise around the vertex origin (the map being considered drawn in the plane such that the infinite face is incident with all the edges).

A rooted plane tree is a rooted planar map having only one face . It is also characterized by the fact that the number of vertices is one over the number of its edges.

To define the code of planar maps (see [1]), we introduce the following infinite sequence of letters : $x_0, \bar{x}_0, x_1, \bar{x}_1, \ldots$ and the alphabets : $X_k = \{x_0, \bar{x}_0, \ldots, x_k, \bar{x}_k\}$ $(k \geqslant 0)$. The free monoid generated by X_k will be denoted by X_k^* and the submonoid generated by any subset A of X_k^* by A^* .

- The map with a single vertex and no edges is considered as a degenerated planar map coded by the empty word of X_0^* .

- In the general case, let (M, b_0) be a rooted planar map with root b_0 , having n edges and k + 1 vertices .We define first two bijections (numberings), one between the half-edges of M and the set $[2n] = \{1,2,\ldots,2n\}$, the other one between the vertices of M and the set $\{0\} \cup [k]$ .The root is numbered 1 and the vertex origin of it 0. Then, if i of the half-edges are numbered : $1,2,\ldots,i$ and j of the vertices $0,k,k-1,\ldots, k-j+2$, we follow the numbering by applying the first one of these three procedures which is possible to apply :

Procedure A : If the half-edge opposite to the half-edge i is incident with a vertex which is not yet numbered, this half-edge is numbered i+1 and the vertex incident with it k-j+1 .

Procedure B : If the half-edge met immediately after the half-edge i turning counter clockwise around the vertex origin of i is not yet numbered, we then number it i+1 .

Procedure C : We consider the half-edges i-1,i-2,...,until a half-edge i'is met such that turning counter clockwise around the vertex origin of i' a half-edge not yet numbered is met; that half-edge is then numbered i+1 .

As the graph associated to the map M is connected, all the vertices and half-edges are numbered by these procedures. We then associate to the map (M,b_o) the word f of length 2n belonging to X_k^* defined by : the ith letter of f is x_j iff the half-edge numbered i is incident with the vertex numbered j and if the opposite half-edge is numbered i' with $i'>i$; it is $\bar{x}_j$ if $i'<i$.

Remark that the mapping of the set of rooted planar maps of k+1 vertices onto the set of codes, which form a language L_k, is one to one . We will denote by S_k the set of words in bijection with simple maps and by A_k the set of words in bijection with rooted plane trees.

II Relations verified by L_k, S_k, A_k.

In the sequel the union of two subsets A and B of X_k^* will be denoted by A + B and the symbol $\dot{+}$ will mean disjoint union. In order to set up these relations we need the following:

Definitions : 1 Let ∇_k be the operator of $\mathcal{P}(X_k^*)$ (the set of all subsets of X_k^*) in itself defined on words by :

$$\nabla_k 1 = 1$$

$$\nabla_k(x_i g) = x_i \nabla_k g \qquad \nabla_k(\bar{x}_i g) = \bar{x}_i \nabla_k g \quad \text{for all } i \neq o \text{ and } g \in X_k^*$$

$$\nabla_k(x_o g) = x_o g + x_k \nabla_k g$$

$$\nabla_k(\bar{x}_o g) = \bar{x}_o g + \bar{x}_k \nabla_k g$$

and for any subset A of X_k^* by : $\nabla_k A = \bigcup_{f\in A} \nabla_k f$.

2 Let τ_j be the mapping of X_1^* in X_{j+1}^* consisting in replacing in every word f of X_1^* the letters x_a $(a>o)$ and $\bar{x}_a$ respectively by x_{j+a} and $\bar{x}_{j+a}$.

Remark that ∇_k is a transduction in the terminology of C.C. Elgott and J. E. Mezei [3] , a sequential transducer mapping in the one of S.Ginsburg [4] .

Theorem 1 [1] : The languages L_k verify the following relations :

$$L_o = 1 \dot{+} x_o L_o \bar{x}_o L_o \qquad (1)$$

$$L_k = \dot{\sum_{p=o,k}} x_o \tau_{k-p}(L_p) \bar{x}_o L_{k-p} \dot{+} x_o \bar{x}_k \nabla_k L_{k-1} \qquad (2)$$

where products are unambiguous ones . Moreover L_k is a context-free language for every $k \geqslant 0$.

The proof of these relations is to be found in [1] .
We only prove that L_k is context-free by induction : L_0 is trivialy context-free ; it is the Dyck language on two letters, an important tool in the theory of context-free languages . If then the L_p are supposed context-free for $p < k$, $\nabla_k L_{k-1}$ is also context-free as ∇_k is a transduction , and L_k verify the following relation (where L'_k is context-free):

$$L_k = x_0 L_0 \bar{x}_0 L_k \dotplus x_0 L_k \bar{x}_0 L_0 \dotplus L'_k$$

hence it is context-free .

Theorem 2 The languages S_k verify the following relations :

$$S_0 = 1 \dotplus x_0 \bar{x}_0 S_0 \qquad (3)$$

$$S_k = x_0 \bar{x}_0 S_k \dotplus x_0 \bar{x}_k \nabla_k S_{k-1} \quad (k > 1) \qquad (4)$$

Moreover S_k is regular .

To prove this theorem we need the following lemma :

Lemma : $S_k = L_k \cap (Y_k \bar{Y}_k)^*$ where $Y_k = \{x_0, \ldots, x_k\}$ and $\bar{Y}_k = \{\bar{x}_0, \ldots, \bar{x}_k\}$

This is a consequence of the fact the numbering of a rooted simple map is obtained by discribing counter clockwise the face incident with all the edges, then a half-edge and its opposite are numbered i and i+1 (or i-1) .

Proof of theorem 2 : As $L_0 = 1 \dotplus x_0 L_0 \bar{x}_0 L_0$, $S_0 = L_0 \cap (x_0 \bar{x}_0)^*$ verifies :

$$S_0 = 1 \dotplus (x_0 L_0 \bar{x}_0 L_0) \cap (x_0 \bar{x}_0)^* = 1 \dotplus x_0 \bar{x}_0 S_0$$

And for $k > 1$ $\quad S_k = L_k \cap (Y_k \bar{Y}_k)^* =$

$$\sum_{p=0,k} (x_0 \, \mathcal{T}_{k-p}(L_p) \, \bar{x}_0 \, L_{k-p}) \cap (Y_k \bar{Y}_k)^* \dotplus x_0 \bar{x}_k (\nabla_k L_{k-1} \cap (Y_k \bar{Y}_k)^*)$$

as x_0 is a left factor of any word of L_p ($p > 0$), it is also a left factor of $\mathcal{T}_{k-p}(L_p)$ hence the intersection $x_0 \, \mathcal{T}_{k-p}(L_p) \, \bar{x}_0 \, L_{k-p} \cap (Y_k \bar{Y}_k)^*$ is empty, only remains the first term : $x_0 \bar{x}_0 S_k$. As ∇_k does not change the places of the "upper-lined" letters the least term is $x_0 \bar{x}_k \nabla_k S_{k-1}$.

S_o is evidently regular; suppose that S_{k-1} is regular, then $S_k^o = S_o x_o \bar{x}_k \nabla_k S_{k-1}$ also is, as ∇_k is a transduction.

<u>Theorem</u> 3 [2] : The A_k verify the following relations:

$$A_o = 1 \tag{5}$$

$$A_k = x_o \bar{x}_k \nabla_k A_{k-1} \tag{6}$$

and they are thus finite.

<u>Proof</u> : Clearly $A_k = S_k \cap (X_k)^{2k}$ as the number of letters of the code f of a rooted plane tree is twice the number of its edges and as a tree with k+1 vertices has 2k half-edges.

Hence $A_o = S_o \cap 1 = 1$

For $k > 1^o$

$$A_k = S_k \cap (X_k)^{2k} = x_o \bar{x}_o (S_k \cap (X_k)^{2k-2}) \dotplus x_o \bar{x}_k (\nabla_k S_{k-1} \cap (X_k)^{2k-2})$$

the first term is empty as S_k has only words of length at least 2k, as ∇_k does not change the length of the words, the second term gives : $A_k = x_o \bar{x}_k \nabla_k A_{k-1}$.

III Generating power series

Let X be the alphabet $X = \{x,y\}$; $\mathbb{Z}\langle\langle x,y\rangle\rangle$ the set of formal power series is the non commuting variables x,y and with coefficients in the ring $\mathbb{Z}$ of rational integers . We use the definition of algebraic and rational power series given by M.P.Schützenberger [9] .

Let π be the morphism of X_k^* into $\mathbb{Z}\langle\langle X\rangle\rangle$ defined by :

$\pi(x_o) = \pi(\bar{x}_o) = x$; $\pi(x_j) = \pi(\bar{x}_j) = y$ for $j \neq o$

And for $A \in X_k^*$, $\pi(A)$ is defined by $\pi(A) = \sum_{f \in A} \pi(f)$.

π verifies : $\pi(A \dotplus B) = \pi(A) + \pi(B)$

$\pi(AB) = \pi(A)\pi(B)$ if the product A.B is unambiguous .

Remark that for any A, $\pi \nabla_k A = \nabla \pi A$, where ∇ is defined in $\mathbb{Z}\langle\langle X\rangle\rangle$ by :

$$\nabla 1 = 1$$

$$\nabla(xf) = xf + y\nabla f \qquad \nabla(yf) = y\nabla f$$

and the definition is extended by linearity . ∇ may also be defined by $\nabla = (1 - \Lambda)^{-1} = \sum \Lambda^n$, where Λ is given by $\Lambda y^p = 0 \quad \Lambda(y^p xg) = y^{p+1} g$ for all $p \geqslant o$ and $g \in X^*$.

Let us now define the following power series :

$$L = \sum_{k \geq 0} \Pi(L_k) \qquad S = \sum_{k \geq 0} \Pi(S_k) \qquad A = \sum_{k \geq 0} \Pi(A_k)$$

<u>Property 1</u> : The commutative images of L,S,A : λ, σ, α are the generating power series in the usual sense; for instance $\lambda(x,y) = \sum \lambda_{n,m} x^n y^m$, where $\lambda_{n,m}$ is the number of rooted planar maps with $(n+m)/2$ edges such that the degree of the vertex origine of the root is n. Hence $\lambda(y,y)$, $\sigma(y,y)$, $\alpha(y,y)$ are the generating power series of the rooted planar maps, rooted simple planar maps, rooted plane trees having n edges.

The theorems 1,2,3 give the following

<u>Property 2</u> :

$$L = 1 + xLxL + xy \nabla L \tag{7}$$

$$S = 1 + xxS + xy \nabla S \tag{8}$$

$$A = 1 + xy \nabla A \tag{9}$$

To solve these equations, we use the following theorems [7],[8]

<u>Theorem 4</u> The equation $\zeta = A + B \nabla \zeta$ (where A and B belong to $\mathbb{Z}\langle\langle X \rangle\rangle$ and $B(0,0) \neq 1$) has a unique solution given by :

$\zeta = A + B(1 - \nabla_M B)^{-1} \nabla_M A$, $M = 1 + M\, B(yM,y)$

where $\nabla_M = (1 - M\Lambda)^{-1} = \sum_{n \geq 0} M^n \Lambda^n$, if M is a formal power series in y. Moreover if A and B are algebraic, then also is.

<u>Theorem 5</u> : The equation $\zeta = 1 + T(\zeta) + B \nabla \zeta$ (where $T(\zeta)$ belongs to $\mathbb{Z}\langle\langle x, y, \zeta \rangle\rangle$, such that T does not contain any term of the form $a\zeta^n$, $n \geq 1$, $a \in \mathbb{Z}$ and $B(0,0) \neq 1$) has a unique solution. If moreover $T(\zeta)$ and B are algebraic, then the commutative image of ζ also is.

<u>Applications</u> :

1 - By theorem 5, λ is algebraic. One may prove also that :

$$\lambda(y,y) = \sum_{n \geq 0} \frac{2.3^n (2n)!}{n!(n+2)!} y^{2n} \qquad [10]$$

2 - By therem 4, S and A are algebraic and are given by :

$$S = (1 - xMx - xyM^2)^{-1} \text{ where } M = 1 + y^2 M^3$$

$$A = (1 - xyN)^{-1} \qquad \text{where } N = 1 + y^2 N^2$$

and one obtains :

$$\sigma(y,y) = \sum_{n \geqslant 0} \frac{2.(3n+1)!}{n!(2n+2)!} y^{2n}$$

$$\alpha(x,y) = \sum_{n,m \geqslant 0} \frac{n(m-1)!}{(\frac{n-m}{2})! \ (\frac{n+m}{2})!} x^n y^m \qquad [2] .$$

References

1. R. Cori, Graphes planaires et systèmes de parenthèses Thèse 3e cycle Paris, (1969).
2. R. Cori, C.R. Acad. Sci. Paris 271, 771 (1970).
3. C.C. Elgott and J.E. Mezei, I.B.M. J.Res. Devel. 9,47 (1965)
4. S.Ginsburg, The mathematical theory of Context-free languages Mc Graw-Hill , New-York (1966) .
5. M. Gross, I.C.C. Bull. 5, 141 (1966).
6. W. Kuich, Indag. Math. 32, 268 (1970) .
7. J. Richard, Séminaire Schützenberger, Lentin, Nivat Secrétariat Mathématiques Paris (1970-1971).
8. J. Richard, C.R.Acad.Sci. Paris 272, 203 (1971).
9. M.P. Schützenberger, Proc.Amer. Math. Soc. 13, 885, (1962).
10. W.T. Tutte, Can. J. Math. 15,249 (1963).

FORMAL LANGUAGES AND FORMAL POWER SERIES

Michel FLIESS
Institut de Programmation, Paris V[e]

Abstract

The theory of rational and algebraic formal power series in noncommuting variables is a very useful tool to study new families of languages and to get new results on more classical ones. For example, we show among others that the family of stochastic languages is closed neither under union nor under intersection, but that the complement of a one-letter stochastic language is again stochastic.

SIMPLE SYNTACTIC OPERATORS ON FULL SEMIAFLS*

Sheila A. Greibach

Department of System Science
University of California, Los Angeles

Abstract

The class of simple syntactic operators is defined. If a full AFL $\mathscr{L}$ is not closed under a simple syntactic operator $\otimes$, then repeated applications of $\otimes$ to $\mathscr{L}$ produces an infinite hierarchy of full AFLs and the closure of $\mathscr{L}$ under $\otimes$ is not full principal. If $\mathscr{L}_1$ and $\mathscr{L}_2$ are incomparable full AFLs, then the least full AFL containing $\mathscr{L}_1$ and $\mathscr{L}_2$ is not closed under any simple syntactic operator. If L is any generator of a full AFL $\mathscr{L}$ closed under any simple syntactic operator, then all of $\mathscr{L}$ may be expressed as finite state translations of L (without applying concatenation or star). It is shown that substitution, insertion, intercalation and homomorphic replication are all simple syntactic operators.

*The research represented in this paper was supported in part by the National Science Foundation under Grant Number GJ-803.

Tree Adjunct, Parenthesis, and Distributed Adjunct Grammars

L.S. Levy*

1. Summary - This paper reviews the definition of a new form of tree grammar, the tree adjunct grammar [1]. Using tree adjunct grammars, we obtain two results:

i) The parenthesis language decision problem [2] was solved in [3]. Our solution, involving a new and simpler algorithm, is developed from the tree adjunct grammar.

ii) Distributed adjunct languages were defined in [4] where it was conjectured that they were incomparable with context free languages. We refute this conjecture, establishing the distributed adjunct languages as properly containing the context free languages, and [4] properly contained in the context sensitive languages.

2. Review of Tree Adjunct Grammars - Tree adjunct grammars (TAG's) are closely related to the tree grammars of Brainerd [5] and Rounds [6], although the grammatical derivations using the trees are much closer in spirit to the work of Parikh [7].

We define a minimal derivation tree as a tree of depth 1, whose root is labeled with a nonterminal V and whose yield is the right hand side of a V-production.

A derivation tree is defined recursively as either a minimal derivation tree, or a tree obtained from two derivation trees T_1 and T_2 by replacing an occurrence of root(T_2) in the frontier of T_1 by T_2 itself.

---

* University of Delaware

Starting with the set of minimal derivation trees, corresponding to the rules of the grammar, we can recursively enumerate the set of derivation trees. We define the set of *basic derivation trees* as the finite subset of derivation trees such that on no path from the root to the frontier is any nonterminal duplicated (other than the root label which may occur at most twice along a path), and which includes precisely:

i) The set of V-trees each of whose yield is in $\Sigma^* V \Sigma^*$, called the set of *adjunct trees*, τ_A;

ii) The set of S-trees each of whose yield is in Σ^* and which has no internal nodes labeled by S, called the set of *center trees*, τ_C. (It is easy to see that the enumeration of the basic derivation trees terminates).

Example 2.1. We illustrate the set of basic derivation trees for the grammar G:{S→aTb;T→TT;T→ab; T→ba;T→Sa.}

τ_C:

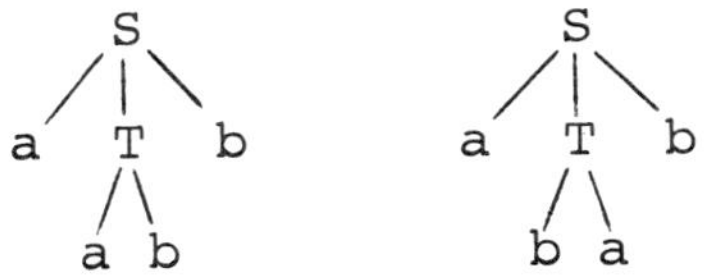

τ_A:

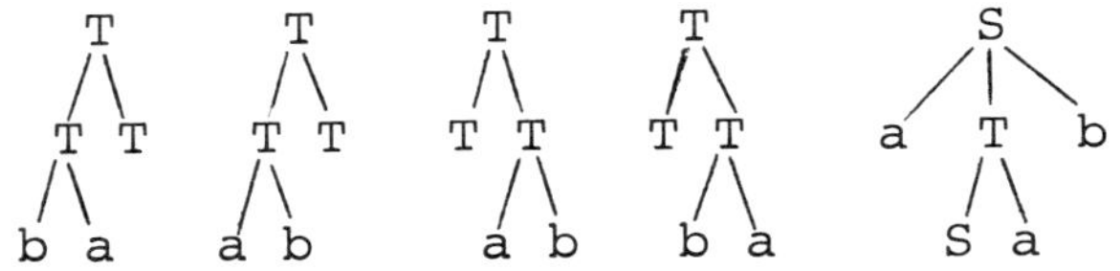

Figure 2.1. Set of trees in the tree adjunct grammar for G of Example 2.1.

Using the set of basic trees we can describe the set of context free derivations in G as follows:

i) Every center tree is a derivation tree.

ii) If T is a derivation tree and T' is obtained from T by detaching the subtree T" at some internal node ν, labeled V, attaching a V-tree in τ_A to ν, and attaching T" to the V-node on the frontier of T", then T' is a derivation tree.

iii) Nothing else.

Example 2.2. We show the adjoining of an adjunct tree to a derivation tree to obtain a new derivation tree:

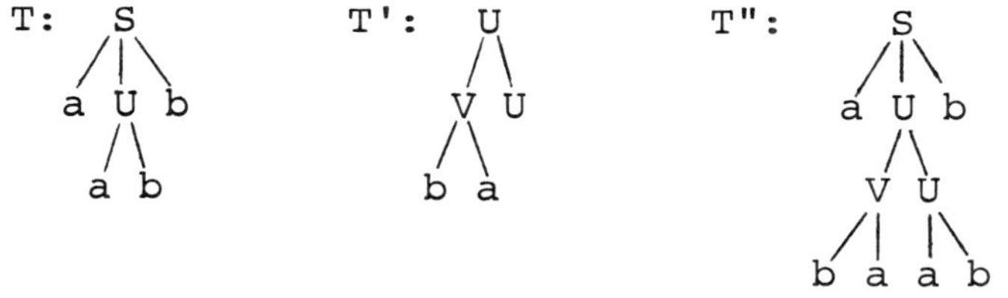

Figure 2.2. A derivation step: T" obtained by adjoining T' to T.

It can be seen from the preceding development that the set of derivation trees in the TAG is the same as the set of derivation trees in the original context free grammar; and that for every context free grammar, a tree adjunct grammar can be effectively derived which generates exactly the set of derivation trees in G.

3. The Parenthesis Language Decision Problem-In this section, the solution to the problem of deciding whether a given context free language is a parenthesis language is developed. This problem was posed by McNaughton [2] and a solution presented by Knuth [3]. The alternate solution presented here is based on the TAG, which, as noted above, is effectively derivable.

Let V_N be the set of nonterminals,

V_T' be the set of terminals except {(,)}

$V_T = V_T' \cup \{(,)\}$

δ a finite subset of $\{V_N \cup V_T'\}^*$

A <u>parenthesis grammar</u>, G, is the set δ and rules of the form $V \to (A)$ where A is in $(V_N \cup V_T')^*$. The language L(G) is the set of strings over V_T derivable from δ.

A <u>parenthesis language</u> is a language for which there is a parenthesis grammar.

Define, for any string σ in V_T^*, the head deficiency, $h(\sigma)$, and tail deficiency, $t(\sigma)$. $h(\sigma)$ is the number of left parentheses to be added to the left of to match the unbalanced right parentheses in σ; $t(\sigma)$ is the number of right parentheses to be added on the right.

Define for any x in V_N, $\bar{h}(x)$ and $\underline{h}(x)$ as the upper and lower bounds, respectively, on $h(\sigma')$ for any σ' such that $x \overset{*}{\Rightarrow} \sigma'$, if L(G) is to contain only balanced strings. Similarly for $\bar{t}(x)$ and $\underline{t}(x)$.

For each x in V_N, $\bar{h}$, $\bar{t}$, $\underline{t}$ can be directly calculated from the set of center trees, and serve as finite bounds for the iterative calculation.

Next, an iterative computation of $H_n(x)$, $T_n(x)$ occurs, where $H_n(x)$ is the set of head deficiencies obtained on the nth iteration, and $T_n(x)$ is the set of tail deficiencies. Either H, T^n converge and stay within the bounds established, in which case L(G) is a balanced language, or they do not in which case L(G) is not balanced and hence not a parentheses language. (H_0, T_0 are calculated directly from the TAG).

If L(G) is balanced then the necessary and sufficient condition that it be a parenthesis language is that in every x-tree in τ_A whose yield is $\sigma_1 x \sigma_2$, we have $t(\sigma_1) \geq 1$ and $h(\sigma_2) \geq 1$.

Details of the algorithm are given in Appendix I, with an illustrative example.

4. String Adjunct Languages - Local and Distributed

Adjunct grammars have been defined in [4]. We review the basic ideas without formal definition, here.

The only operation allowed on strings in an adjunct grammar is the adjoining of a string of class σ_1 to the left or right of a distinguished symbol in another string σ_2, 0 or more times; the resulting string being of class σ_2. The language is the set of strings in a union of string classes. For example, the rule ([ ],[ ],r_1)means adjoin any string of class [ ] to the right of the first symbol in the string [ ], the resulting string being of class [ ]. It can be shown that the language is the Dyck language over {[,]}.

Distributed adjunction is a generalization of this operation, in which segments of a string of class σ_1 are adjoined (without being permuted) to the left or right of a sequence of designated symbols in a string σ_2, the resulting string being of class σ_2. In the segmentation of a string of class σ_1, all adjuncts of any symbol must appear in the same segment as the symbol to which they are adjoined. (When no segmentation is allowed, we call the adjunction local). Thus the rule p=(aabbcc, (d)(e)(f), $\ell_1\ell_3\ell_5$) generates $\{d^n a^2 e^n b^2 f^n c^2 | n \geq 0\}$.

(The rule p is interpreted as follows: Let σ be any string in the syntactic class def, α = udvwexyfz, where u,v are the strings (possibly null) which have been built up adjoining d; w,x adjoining e; and y,z adjoining f. If σ' is any built up string in the syntactic class aabbcc, σ'=TaUaVbWbXcYcZ, then after applying the rule p, we have σ''=TudvaUaVwexbWbXyfzcYcZ).

In order to facilitate derivations, null symbols were introduced [4]. Null symbols cannot be adjoined to, but serve to distinguish classes of strings. Thus ν ab is different from ab, where ν is a null symbol. In the language itself the null symbols are deleted (by a homomorphic mapping). Only one special case is known [8], where the null symbols can actually be shown to be needed to obtain the weak generative power.

It was shown [4] that regular languages, local adjunct languages, and context free languages constitute a proper hierarchy RL $\subsetneq$ LALN[1] $\subsetneq$ CFL and that DALN[2] $\subsetneq$ CSL but was conjectured that the CFL's and the DALN's are incomparable. In the next section, we show that this is not so. In fact the CFL's are properly contained in the class of DALN's.

5. Every CFL is a Distributed Adjunct Language.

We prove, in this section, that every context-free language is generable by a distributed adjunct grammar with null symbols. This refutes a conjecture by Joshi, Kosaraju, and Yamada [4], and establishes the hierarchical relationship:

$$\text{RL} \subsetneq \text{LALN} \subsetneq \text{CFL} \subsetneq \text{DALN} \subsetneq \text{CSL} .$$

The proof is based on the tree adjunct grammars, and the result [1] that for every context-free grammar an equivalent TAG can be effectively derived. The desired result follows from the fact (to be shown) that for every TAG, an equivalent DAGN can effectively be derived.

The equivalent DAGN is obtained directly from the set of trees of the TAG. We also give an algorithm for obtaining a DAGN derivation

---

1. Local Adjunct Languages derived using Null symbols
2. Distributed Adjunct Languages derived using Null symbols

corresponding to a TAG derivation. The algorithm uses a <u>derivation indexed tree</u> in the TAG, which is just a tree derived by the grammar with labels indicating the sequence of steps in the derivation. The corresponding sequence of steps in the DAGN are then obtained.

As a preliminary technical measure, it is necessary to transform the context free grammar into the Rosenkrantz normal form [9], in which the right hand side of each production starts and ends with a terminal symbol. The transformation to Rosenkrantz normal form is effective, and we have the following lemma:

<u>Lemma 5.1</u> Let G be a context free grammar in Rosenkrantz normal form, and let τ be the corresponding TAG, then in every tree in τ the left-most and right-most descendants of any interior node are labeled with terminal symbols.

We shall call a TAG, τ, in which the left-most and rightmost descendants of any interior node are terminal symbols, a <u>normal form TAG</u>.

5.1 Construction of a DAGN from a TAG

Let τ be a normal form TAG. We describe next an algorithm for constructing a DAGN, G, such that $L(G) = L(\tau)$.

To each tree in τ attach a unique null symbol ν_i, and for each tree T_i in τ_c, the string associated with T_i is $\sigma(T_i)=\nu_i$ yield (T_i); for each tree T_j in τ_A, the <u>bracketed string</u> associated with T_j is $\sigma_b(T_j) = \overline{(\nu_j \ell_j)(r_j)}$ and the <u>de-bracketed string</u> associated with T_j is $\nu_j \ell_j r_j$ where yield $(T_j) = \ell_j x r_j$ ℓ_j, r_j in V_T^+, x in V_N.

$\sum_c$, the set of center strings of G is given by:

$$\sum_c = \{\sigma(T_i) \mid T_i \text{ in } \tau_c\}$$

The set of adjunct strings, Σ_A, is:

$$\Sigma_A = \{\sigma_b(T_j) \mid T_j \text{ in } \tau_A\}$$

The adjunction rules, in general, are:
Let T be any tree in τ; for each occurrence of an interior node of T labeled x (i.e. excluding the frontier but including the root), and for each T' in τ_x (i.e. the set of adjunct trees whose root is labeled x) include the rules

$$(\ \sigma(T)\ ,\ \sigma_b(T')\ ,\ \ell_{x1} r_{x2}\ )$$

where ℓ_{x1}, r_{x2} are adjunction points to the left and right respectively, of the frontier of the subtree headed by the occurrence of x; i.e. if yield (T) = t and the yield of the subtree headed by this occurrence of x is x', where $t=\ell' x' r'$, then $x_1 = |\ell'|+1$, $x_2 = |\ell'|+|x'|$.

5.2 Equivalence of DAGN and TAG

The construction is effective. Equivalence of the DAGN, G', with the TAG, G, from which it is obtained will follow if every derivation in G has a corresponding derivation in G' and vice versa. It is easy to show that every derivation in G' has a corresponding derivation in G. Since this follows directly from the tree description of derivations in G', we omit the proof here.[1]

On the other hand, we must also show that any derivation in the TAG, G, has a corresponding derivation in the DAGN, G'. To do this we construct a derivation indexed tree which described derivations in the TAG. (Note that a tree generated by a TAG corresponds to a derivation in a CFG, but does not indicate its own derivation from the

1. The proof is based on the derivation tree of the DAGN; see [4] and [10]. The crucial fact is that all the DAGN rules of G' are context free because of the way they are defined whereas, in general, DAGN rules are context sensitive.

basic trees in the TAG).

A derivation indexed tree in a TAG, T_d, is just like a tree in a TAG, T, except that an internal node labeled V in T, is labeled (V, n) in T_d, where n is a non-negative integer. The assignment of labels in T_d is as follows:

a) A node in the center tree labeled V is labeled (V, 0) in the derivation tree.

b) At the $i^{\underline{th}}$ step of the derivation, an adjunction of a tree is performed by detaching a subtree and interposing another (adjunct) tree. In adjoining the tree, we label each variable node V of the adjoined tree (V, i)(including its root but excluding the variable leaf node).

In the completed derivation indexed tree for any word in $L(\tau)$ each variable node is labeled with the number of a derivation step, and each derivation step number occurs at least once. Given a derivation indexed tree it is clear that the derivation can be reconstructed, and for each derivation in the TAG there is a (unique) derivation indexed tree.

From the derivation indexed tree we can construct a <u>DAGN derivation sequence tree</u>. Let σ_j be the distributed adjunct string corresponding to the adjunct tree adjoined in the $j^{\underline{th}}$ step of the TAG derivation. σ_o is the center string. Whenever $i<j$ and a node indexed by i is a direct descendant of a node indexed by j in the derivation indexed tree, then σ_j is adjoined to σ_i.

The adjunctions in the distributed adjunct grammar proceed from the bottom up. The actual adjunction rule can, indeed, be recovered from the derivation indexed tree. Define the i-yield of the tree as the concatenation of those leaves labeled by terminals which are direct descendants of nodes labeled (V, i). Then the o-yield is the center string in the DAGN, and the i-yield, $i \geq 1$, is the ith adjunct string, σ_i, except that the null symbol has been deleted.

Define a deletion mapping, as a tree homomorphism which erases a set of nodes and their direct descendants which are labeled by terminals. For our purposes, the deletion mappings are defined in terms of sets of indices, and we shall delete all nodes and their direct descendants except those specified. The built-up tree for index i is the deletion mapping for the set of all of i's descendants in the DAGN derivation sequence tree of the TAG, and the corresponding DAGN string (without phrasing indicated) is the yield of the tree. Determination of the adjunction rules used is straightforward from the trees obtained via the deletion mappings.

Thus we see that we can indeed reconstruct in the DAGN, the derivation in the TAG, giving us:

Theorem 5.2-For every context free grammar, G, a (weakly equivalent) DAGN, G', can be effectively derived such that L(G)=L(G').

Corollary 5.3-The set of context free languages is properly contained in the set of distributed adjunct languages with null symbols.

Define a k-DALN as a language generated by a distributed grammar with at most k adjunction points in a rule. Then we have the following:

Corollary 5.4-Every regular set is a 1-DALN; and every CFL is a 2-DALN.

Also, it is easy to show that:
Proposition 5.5-For every k, there is a (k+1)-DALN which is not a k-DALN.

Thus the k-DALN's constitutes an infinite proper hierarchy.

References

[1] Joshi, A.K., and Takahashi, M. "A Characterization of the Derivation Trees of a Context Free Grammar and an Intercalation Theorem" to be issued as a Moore School Report.

[2] McNaughton, R. "Parentheses Grammars", JACM (1967) p. 490-500.

[3] Knuth, D.E. "A Characterization of Parenthesis Languages" Information & Control (1967) p. 269-289.

[4] Joshi, A.K., Kosaraju, S.R., and Yamada, H. "String Adjunct Grammars" (1969) IEEE Symposium on Switching & Automata.

[5] Brainard, W.S. "Tree Generating Systems and Tree Automata" Ph.D. Dissertation, Purdue, 1967.

[6] Rounds, W.C. "Context-Free Grammars on Trees", 1969 ACM Symposium on Theory of Computing, p. 143-148.

[7] Parikh, R.J. "On Context-Free Languages" 1966, JACM p. 570-581.

[8] Levy, L.S. "Tree Automata and Adjunct Grammars" to be issued as a Moore School Report.

[9] Rosenkrantz, D.J. "Matrix Equations and Normal Forms for Context Free Grammars" (1967) JACM, p. 501-507.

[10] Levy, L.S. "Generalized Local Adjunction and Replacement in Adjunct Languages" Moore School Report No. 70-29.

Appendix I.

Algorithm for Parenthesis Language Decision Problem

Define $a \dot{-} b = \max \{a - b , 0\}$. For any tree T, in τ_c

T = 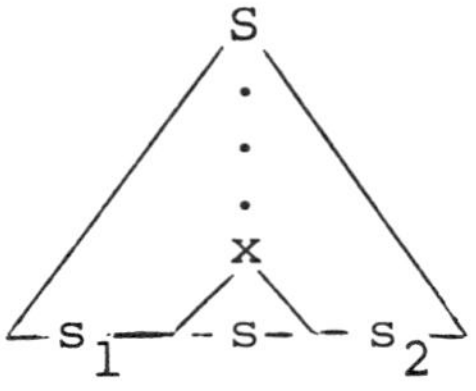

$s_1 s s_2$ is the yield of the tree, where s is the yield of the subtree headed by x.

Figure A.1 Definition of s_1 , s_2

we require $t(s_1) \dot{-} h(s_2) \leq h(x) \leq t(s_1)$, (since the yields of the center trees are in the language, they must be balanced).

Thus

$$\underline{h}(x) \geq \max_{\tau_c} \{t(s_1) \dot{-} h(s_2)\}$$

$$\overline{h}(x) \leq \min_{\tau_c} \{t(s_1)\}.$$

Similarly,

$$\underline{t}(x) \geq \max \{h(s_2) \dot{-} t(s_1)\}$$

$$\overline{t}(x) \leq \min \{h(s_2)\}$$

Define

$$H_0(x) = \{h(s) \mid x \overset{*}{\Rightarrow} s \text{ in } \tau, \ s \text{ in } V_t^*\}$$

$$T_0(x) = \{t(s) \mid x \overset{*}{\Rightarrow} s \text{ in } \tau, \ s \text{ in } V_t^*\}$$

where $\tau = \tau_c \cup \tau_A$.

Define $H_n(y|x)$ as the set of head deficiencies computer for occurrences of y in adjunct trees where $y \overset{*}{\Rightarrow} s_1 x s_2$ using the values of $H_n(x)$. If we never have $y \overset{*}{\Rightarrow} s_1 x s_2$, then $H_n(y|x)$ is taken to be the empty set. Then we define $H_{n+1}(x) = H_n(x) \cup \{H_n(x|y) \mid y \text{ is in } V_n\}$. $T_n(x)$ is defined similarly.

A necessary and sufficient condition that L(G) contain only balanced strings is that for all x for which $\underline{h}$, $\overline{h}$, $\underline{t}$, $\overline{t}$, are defined and for all n

$$\max H_n(x) \leq \overline{h}(x) \qquad \max T_n(x) \leq \overline{t}(x)$$

$$\min H_n(x) \geq \underline{h}(x) \qquad \min T_n(x) \geq \underline{t}(x)$$

The computation of H_n and T_n is iterative and ends either when $H_{n+1} = H_n$ and $T_{n+1} = T_n$ for all x or else some H_n or T_n is "out of bounds".

An additional condition that the balanced language be a parenthesis language is that in any self embedding sequence $x \overset{*}{\Rightarrow} s_1 x s_2$, $t(s_1) \geq 1$ and $h(s_2) \geq 1$. This condition may be checked directly by inspection of the set of adjunct trees.

<u>Example A.1</u> As an example of the application of the algorithm presented here, we apply it to the grammar used as an illustration in [3], p. 279-281.
The grammar is:

A → Ba A → (bB) A → (c(

B → (dA))(() B → (B)))(Ae) ;δ = B))

The TAG is:

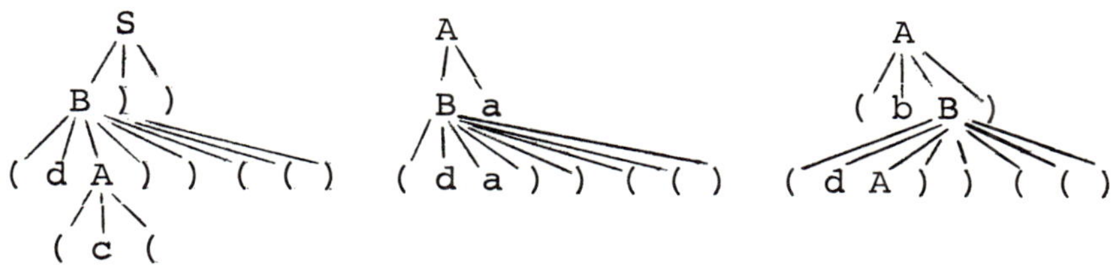

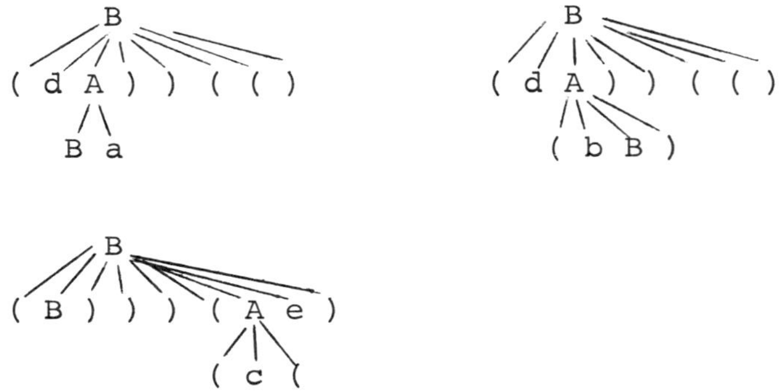

Figure A.2. TAG for Example A.1.

Direct computation shows

$\underline{h}(A) = 0,\ \overline{h}(A) = 1,\ \underline{t}(A) = 2,\ \overline{t}(A) = 3$

$\underline{h}(B) = \overline{h}(B) = 0,\ \underline{t}(B) = \overline{t}(B) = 2$

Based on the center tree

$$H_0(A) = H_0(B) = 0$$

$$T_0(A) = T_0(B) = 2$$

Then based on the adjunct trees

$$H_1(A) = H_1(B) = 0$$

$$T_1(A) = T_1(B) = 2$$

The additional condition on the adjunct trees is also easily checked. Thus L(G) is a parenthesis language.

Appendix II.
Examples of steps in TAG to DAGN transformation

Here, we illustrate some of the steps in the algorithm of Section 5. (Detailed definitions of distributed adjunct grammars and languages are given in [4] and [10]).

1. Start with the context free grammar: S→abc;

S→aSbSc

2. The TAG is:

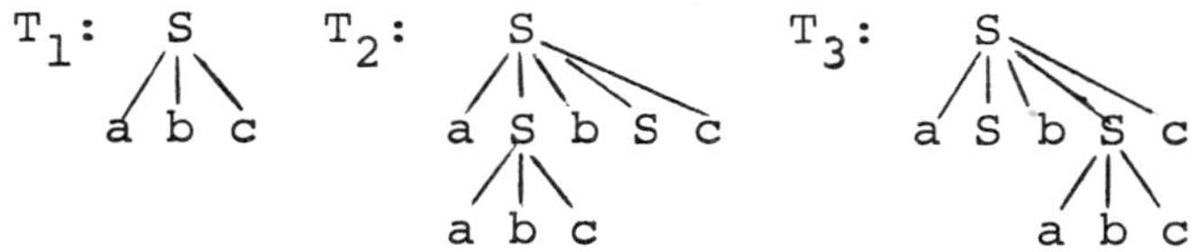

3. The DAGN is: $\sum_C$ = set of center strings = $\{\sigma(T_1)\}=\{\nu_1 abc\}$

$\sum_A$=set of adjunct strings=$\{\sigma_b(T_2),\sigma_b(T_3)\}$ = $\{(\nu_2 aabcb)(c),(\nu_3 a)(babcc)\}$

Letting $A=\sigma(T_1)$;$B=\sigma(T_2)$;$C=\sigma(T_3)$;$D=\sigma_b(T_2)$;$E=\sigma_b(T_3)$, the rules of the DAGN are: $(A,D,\ell_1 r_3)$, $(A,E,\ell_1 r_3)$, $(B,D,\ell_1 r_6)$, $(B,D,\ell_2 r_4)$, $(B,E,\ell_2 r_4)$, $(C,D,\ell_1 r_6)$, $(C,D,\ell_3 r_5)$, $(C,E,\ell_1 r_6)$, $(C,E,\ell_3 r_5)$.

4. A typical derivation indexed tree is:

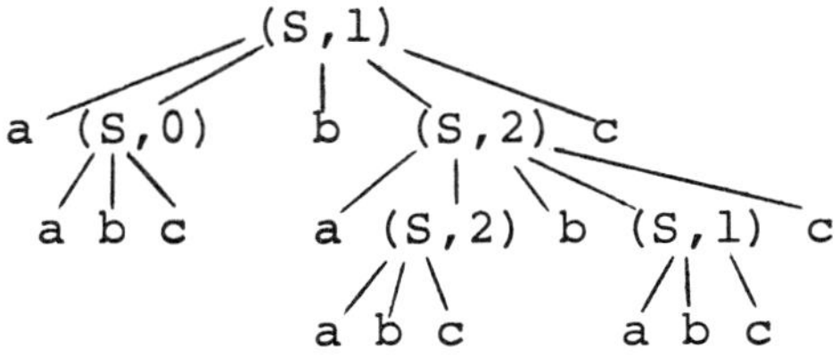

and the corresponding DAGN derivation sequence is:

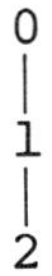

5. The appropriate deletion mappings are:

$D_{(\{2\})}T=$

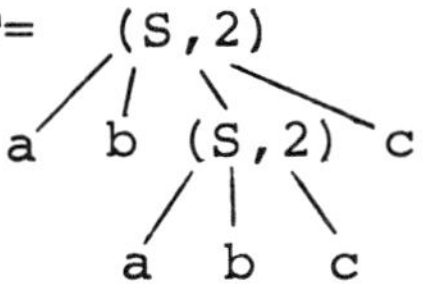

$D_{(\{2,1\})}T=$

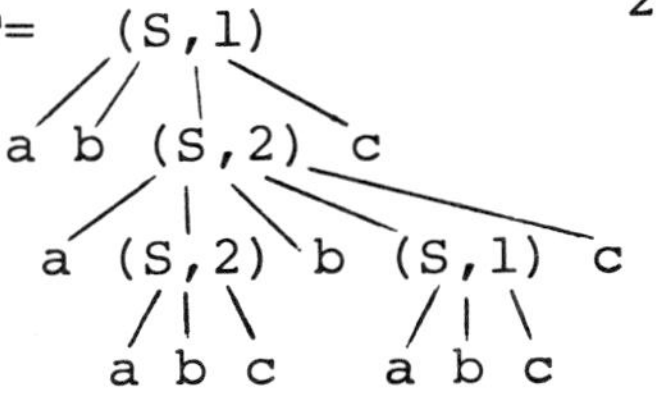

6. The DAGN derivation sequence is:
D is adjoined to C, using the rule $(C,D,\ell_3 r_5)$ and C segmented as E is adjoined to A using the rule $(A,E,\ell_1 r_3)$.

STATE GRAPHS AND CONTEXT FREE LANGUAGES

Larry H. Reeker
The Ohio State University*
Columbus, Ohio

Abstract

This paper sketches a theory of infinite state graphs for non-regular languages, analogous to the finite state graphs for regular languages. For the context free case, a characterization is provided, and relations to other characterizations are noted.

1. Introduction

The author has found it worthwhile as a pedagogical technique to consider infinite graphs which 'accept' context free and context sensitive languages. These graphs often facilitate proofs of theorems and allow ready extension of finite state concepts and techniques to the infinite case. Results tying infinite graphs to generative grammars may also be of use in the theory of infinite graphs, and vice-versa.

Some of the areas mentioned here have been explored by the author in a series of working papers (Reeker, 1969, 1970a, 1970b, 1970c, 1970d). The present paper presents some of the results that are related to context free languages. A knowledge of standard definitions is assumed.

2. Series of Finite State Machines

Infinite automata can be treated as series of finite automata, and doing so sometimes facilitates proofs by mathematical induction. Here we will deal only with acceptors. The input alphabet will be $A = \{a_1, a_2, \ldots, a_k\}$.

---

*Computer and Information Science and Linguistics Departments. This work supported under NSF grant GN-534.

We will assume a single initial state.

Definition 2.1. An acceptor series (AS) M consists of a series of finite state acceptors $[M_1, M_2, \ldots,]$ over a common alphabet A, with the following properties: [Let the states of M_i be $S_i = \{\sigma_1{}^i, \ldots, \sigma_{n_i}{}^i\}$, and the acceptance states F_i. Let the transition function of M_i be τ_i].

1) $S_i \subseteq S_{i+1}$, for each M_i and M_{i+1}.

2) If σ^i is in M_i, then it is in M_{i+1} also, renamed σ^{i+1}.

3) For all i, $F_i \subseteq F_{i+1}$.

4) τ^{i+1} is a consistent extension of τ^i to S^{i+1}.

It is possible to study any such series in which M_{i+1} is related in some manner (preferably computable) to M_i. In our examples, we will confine ourselves to rather simple relations. It is often worthwhile to make the further convention that the members of the AS be associated with a language in such a manner that M_i accepts all strings of length i or less. Clearly, it is not possible in general to produce effectively such a series of machines accepting a language that is not context sensitive.

The acceptor series approach is related to the formal power series approach (Ginsburg and Rice, 1961; Schützenberger, 1962; Chomsky and Schützenberger, 1963), the elements of the AS forming a refinement of the classes obtained when the power series is defined on the basis of length of generation, as in the last reference above.

The intuitive quality of graphs of context free grammars has been remarked by many over the years (for example, Kalmár, 1969). But if repeated substitutions are made in such graphs, one generates graphs (either finite or infinite) in a manner exactly analogous to the method of power series, mentioned above. And these graphs have characteristic properties which we shall examine below.

3. Letichevskii's Characterization; Derivatives

Letichevskii (1965) has characterized context free languages by means of recognition by deterministic 'abstract pushdown automata'. This has the virtue of giving a deterministic characterization for context free languages, but the abstract characterization is rather difficult to use in practice. Clearly, the abstract pushdown automata do not correspond directly to pushdown automata, since they are always deterministic.

Salomaa (1970) has pointed out that in determining states of Letichevskii's automata, all letters of a string except the first are left untouched. Reeker, 1969, presented an analogous method of obtaining a deterministic machine directly from the grammar by identifying sets of strings with identical left quotients (Ginsburg and Spanier, 1963). This may be accomplished by an extension of the method of derivatives for regular expressions (Brzozowski, 1964). In addition to Brzozowski's definition tions, we need the following:

Definition 3.1. Let X_i be a nonterminal symbol in a context free grammar G. Then we define $R(X_i)$ to be the set of all strings Y_k of terminals and nonterminals such that productions $X_i \to Y_k$ are in G.

Definition 3.2. Let X_i be a nonterminal symbol of a grammar G, and a_j be a terminal symbol of the same grammar. Then the derivative of X_i with respect to a_j [symbolized $D(a_j,X_i)$] is the union of all derivatives of members of $R(X_i)$.

Definition 3.3. Let G be a grammar with root symbol S. Then the set of left quotients of L(G) with respect to a terminal symbol a_j is given by $D(a_j,S)$.

If all equivalent left quotient expressions could be identified, the technique for finding a series of machines to accept L(G) (to any arbitrary length) would be analogous to that for regular expressions, and would always lead to a series of minimal state deterministic machines, as follows:

Procedure 3.4. Take derivatives of S with respect to all terminal symbols $\{a_1,\ldots,a_n\}$ of G. If $D(a_j,S) = D(a_k,S)$, then $\tau_1(\tau_1,a_j) \underline{=} \tau_1(\tau_1,a_k)$. The set of equivalence classes under $\underline{=}$ is the set of states of M_1; the equivalence classes containing the empty string λ comprise the final states of M_1. For M_i, replace single terminals by i-symbol terminal sequences.

Clearly, the problem of equivalence of the set of all quotient expressions is algorithmically unsolvable, since there is no decision procedure for equality of context free languages. However, we can always determine when two such expressions <u>differ</u>, so we obtain (perhaps non-minimal) members of an AS for L(G).

4. Graphs for Context Free Languages

Let us now modify our representation of the AS from a series of finite machines to a single infinite machine. We shall be concerned with the (infinite) state graph of this machine.

If an AS has a largest member, say M_n, then the graph of M_n will be finite state, or regular. It is interesting to note that there are infinite AS's which correspond to finite state languages (though not to finite languages).

Definition 4.1. Let a graph G be defined as follows:

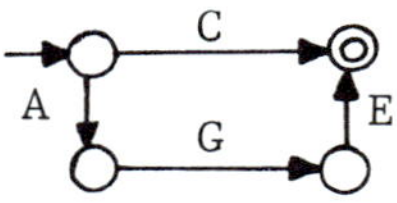

Then we will call G a ladder graph. Notice that the definition is by recurrence on the graph G.

Definition 4.2. The following will be called context free (CF) graphs:

1) regular graphs
2) ladder graphs
3) any context free graph with an edge replaced by another context free graph, correspondingly lettered edges in definition 4.1 being replaced by identical graphs.

Theorem 4.3. Given a context free language L, a (possibly nondeterministic) context free graph G can be found which includes all members of some AS, M, for L. [We will say that M and G are associated.]

Proof. Consider the case $S \overset{*}{\Rightarrow} ASE|C$, which is general enough, since we can let A, E and C again generate arbitrary languages. By taking derivatives (generalized with respect to arbitrary strings of nonterminals and terminals in the obvious manner), we obtain successive machines of an AS which can be represented by a graph of the form shown in 4.1, above. This shows that the graph associated with a grammar with a single embedded symbol is a CF graph. The grammar can be separated into a finite number of embedded productions, and a finite number of others. All cases where an embedded symbol is not present are amenable to the standard finite state technique. A case such as $S \overset{*}{\Rightarrow} ASBSD|C$ can be considered as above, with E replaced by BSD, as long as reference back to the original graph is allowed. We then obtain

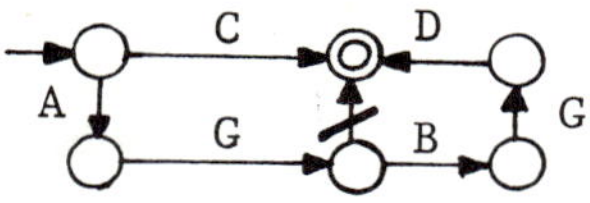

Example 4.5. The linear languages have very simple CF graphs, since embeddings can take place only in the central portion of each graph. Taking derivatives of the linear grammar $S \to aSa|bSb|c$, we obtain

$D(a,S) = Sa$
$D(b,S) = Sb$
$D(c,S) = \lambda$
$D(aa,S) = D(a,S)a = Saa$
...
$D(a^i,S) = Sa^i$ (by induction, sim. for b^i)
$D(ab,S) = Sba$
$D(x,S) = Sx^R$ (where x^R is the reverse of x,
$D(xc,S) = x^R$ $x \varepsilon \{a,b\}^*$)

The machine G obtained is as shown in Fig. 1. If, however, c is replaced with the empty string λ, the graph becomes nondeterministic. If we take derivatives and form a new AS, we can obtain a series of deterministic machines, but it is no longer represented by a context free graph. The problem is that the deterministic AS grows too fast to be represented by a CF graph.

5. Growth Rate

Alternatively, as a proof of the representation theorem (4.4), one can start with a graph for a Dyck language and show that intersection with a finite state language and homomorphism preserve the 'shape' of the graph. Using this technique, it is possible to show that there exists a graph for the language with constant-bounded growth rate. The growth rate of a graph representing an AS is defined as follows:

Definition 5.1. Let M be an AS in the notation used earlier. Then let

(i) $G(i)$ be the number of states in M_i

(ii) $N(i)$ be the number of paths from initial to final states in M_i not counting loops

(iii) $R(i) = G(i)/N(i)$

The functions G, N, and R are called the growth, yield, and growth rate, respectively, of M.

The concept of growth rate can be used to show that

certain languages are not context free. For example, the growth rate of the graph in Fig. 2 is not constant-bounded, though it is minimal. Thus $\{a^ib^ic^i\}$ is not context free.

6. Equivalences and Operations

Several equivalences between CF graphs are shown in Fig. 3. To prove such equivalences, one returns to the AS, performing induction on the index of the machines in the series.

In addition to their intrinsic interest, as statements about particular infinite graphs, these equivalences may be used to rearrange graphs, or decompose them, as shown in the example of Fig. 4.

One also returns to the AS to define operations on the graphs:

Definition 6.1. The intersection [union, concatenation, etc.] of a CF graph is obtained by taking the intersection [union, concatenation, etc.] of their associated AS's. If two AS's are $M = \{M_1, M_2, \ldots\}$ and $N = \{N_1, N_2, \ldots\}$, then $M \wedge N = \{M_1 \wedge N_1,\ M_2 \wedge N_2, \ldots\}$ [and similarly for other operations].

It is instructive to apply these operations to some standard examples. The intersection of the CF graphs for $\{a^*b^ic^i\}$ and $\{a^ib^ic^*\}$ gives, as one would expect, the graph of Fig. 2. The union of the same languages gives a nondeterministic CF graph.

7. Graphs and Pushdown Automata

It can be shown that all CF graphs accept context free languages, thus completing the characterization begun in (4) above.

Theorem 7.0. Given a CF graph G, a pushdown store automaton to accept the language defined by G can be obtained effectively.

Proof: A regular graph requires no pushdown symbols, but a ladder graph requires a 1-symbol pushdown, which counts the number of occurrences of A (in Def. 4.1) and eventually matches each with an E. Now if A or E are themselves composed of ladder graphs or regular graphs, the situation is repeated, perhaps requiring another pushdown store, etc.

Notice, however, that a single pushdown can be used to

handle all of the pushdowns mentioned in the paragraph above. Each time a new ladder is entered, a new counter is used. That is, if one has been pushing 0's in one ladder, then 1's are pushed in the embedded ladder, and vice-versa.

There is one case where more than one stack symbol will be needed at a single node to count different types of symbols, and that is the situation illustrated in Fig. 1. An examination of that case will show that it is merely another case of embedding a ladder within another, this time at C, instead of A or E, but that a single cou counter can not be made to suffice in any embedding at C, unless the embedding really has no effect later. Pursuing this line of reasoning, we get

Corollary 7.1. A language is acceptable by an automaton equipped with a single counter if the minimum state CF graph for that language has at most a single infinite continuation at each point.

An example of the procedure used in the proof of 7.0 is illustrated in Fig. 5.

8. Extensions

The technique of using a locally-finite, denumerable flow graph to represent a series of acceptors - and thus a language - is readily extensible to non-CF languages. For context sensitive languages, the growth (as defined in 5.1, above) must be bounded by an exponential function of the input length (though the converse is not necessarily true).

9. Acknowledgement

I would like to thank Abraham Ginzburg for early encouragement in work on this approach.

10. References

Brzozowski, J. A., Derivatives of regular expressions, _J. Assoc. Computing Mach._, 11, 481-494, 1964.

Chomsky, N. and Schützenberger, M. P., The algebraic theory of context free languages, in _Computer Programming and Formal Systems_, Braffort and Hirschberg, eds., 1963.

Ginsburg, S. and Rice, H. G., Two families of languages related to ALGOL, _J. Assoc. Computing Mach._, 9, 350-371, 1962.

Ginsburg, S. and Spanier, E. H., Quotients of context free languages, *J. Assoc. Computing Mach.*, 10, 487, 1963.

Kalmár, L., An intuitive representation of context free languages, International Conference on Computational Linguistics, Sweden, 1969, Preprint No. 66.

Letichevskii, A. A., The representation of context free languages in automata with a push-down type store, *Kibernetika* 1, 80-84 (transl. in *Cybernetics*), 1965.

Reeker, L. H., Extended finite state representation of infinite machines, CISRC Tech. Rept. 69-20, Ohio State University, 1969.

------, Extended state parsing techniques for context free languages, CISRC Quarterly Rept., March, 1970. (a)

------, Extended state representation of infinite machines, CISRC Annual Rept., June 1970. (b)

------, Extended state parsing, II, CISRC Annual Rept., June 1970. (c)

------, The extended state characterization of context free languages, CISRC Quarterly Rept., September, 1970. (d)

Schützenberger, M. P., Certain families of elementary automata and their decision problems, *Proceedings of the MRI Symposium*, Brooklyn Polytechnic, 1962.

Salomaa, A., *Theory of Automata*, Pergamon, 1969.

11. Figures

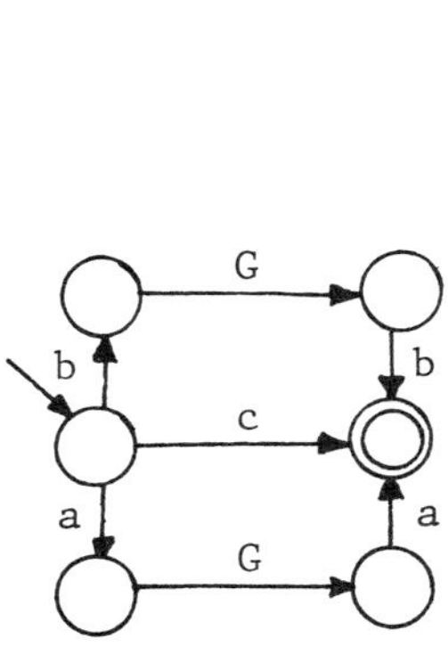

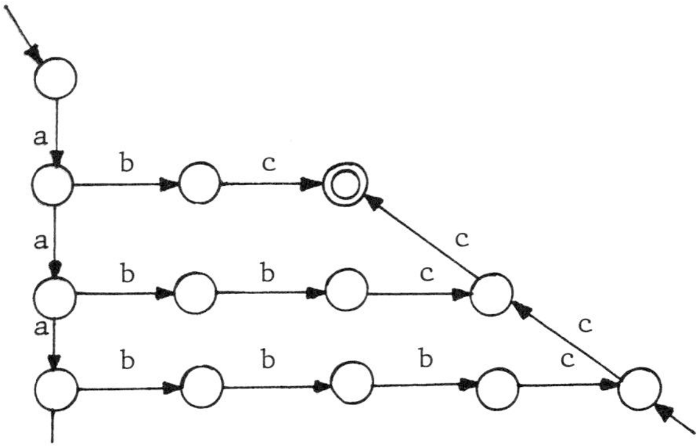

Fig. 1. (left) Graph of $\{\omega c \omega^R \mid \omega \varepsilon \{a,b\}^*\}$.

Fig. 2. (right) Graph of $\{a^i b^i c^i\}$.

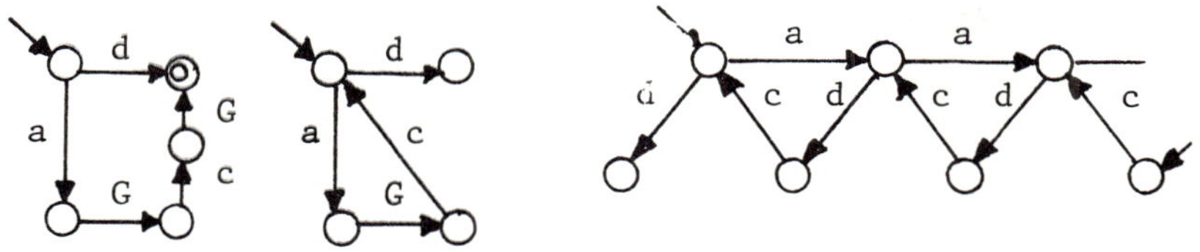

(a) All three are equivalent

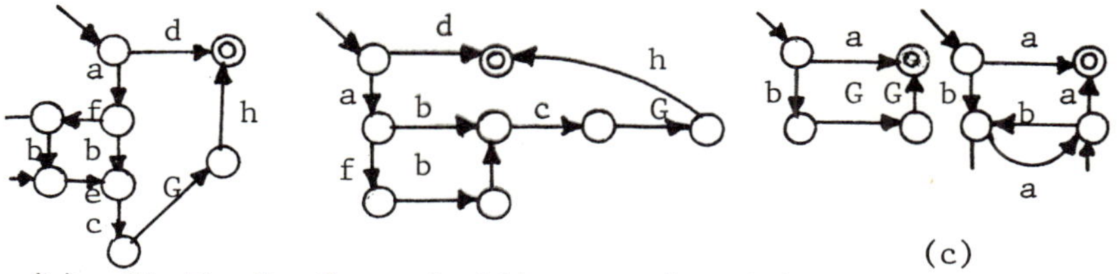

(c)

(b) Similarly for embedding on the right

Fig. 3. Some CF Graph Equivalences.

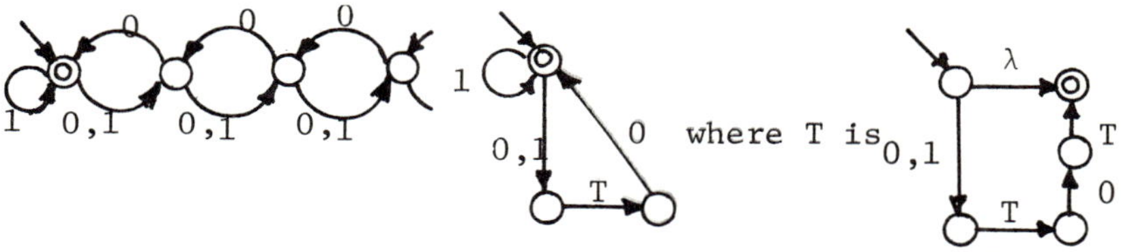

Fig. 4. The graph on the left is decomposed into the parts on the right.

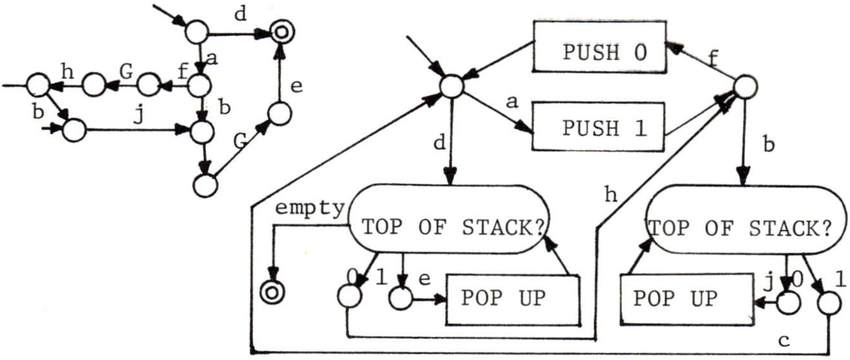

Fig. 5. A graph and the pushdown automaton obtained from it (as in 7.0)

DISPERSION MATRICES AND STOCHASTIC AUTOMATA MORPHISMS

François Bancilhon and Michel Depeyrot

Abstract

Dispersion morphisms acting upon the internal representation of stochastic automata preserves their external description (behavior functions). They are used here to solve some problems of minimality and ambiguity of stochastic machines.

1. Introduction to stochastic automata morphisms.

Since Gilbert's presentation of an identification algorithm [1] for a function of a finite Markov chain a thorough investigation of the state-minimization of stochastic automata has been initiated. Two outstanding contributions have been published since, with the definition of a new automaton model [2] best-fitted for these questions, and with the exhibition of the dominance problem [6] whereby a stochastic machine in reduced form can be covered by a machine having a smaller number of states.

A categorical approach was applied to this problem in [8] where the relationship between singularity of behavior functions (external description) and ambiguity of internal representations was found out. The technique then introduced is applied here to the state minimization problem with the aid of a natural representation of stochastic morphisms by a pseudo-stochastic matrix pair (B^L, B) such that $B^L B = I$.

2. Dispersion matrices.

This paragraph provides a few definitions and propositions concerning the main tool of this paper, namely dispersion morphisms.

Definition 2.1. An aggregation matrix is a row-monomial rectangular matrix over $\{0,1\}$.
This concept has been thoroughly investigated [11] for automata decomposition. In the stochastic case we need the continuous extension of this definition:
Definition 2.2. A pseudostochastic matrix B is a dispersion matrix if it is $c \times r$ with full rank r, where a matrix B is said to be pseudostochastic whenever $Be = e$, and e is the $r \times 1$ column vector whose elements are all ones. B is stochastic if it is pseudostochastic and all its elements are positive.
Definition 2.3. The affine inverse M^L of a pseudostochastic matrix M is a pseudostochastic matrix which is a generalised inverse of M, i.e. such that:

$$MM^LM = M \quad \text{and} \quad M^LMM^L = M^L$$

Propositions:

a) The affine inverse of a dispersion matrix B is a left-inverse B^L admitting e as a right invariant. Since B is of full rank r, there exists B^L such that

$$B^LB = I_r, \qquad B^LBe = I_re,$$

$$B^Le = e,$$

$$B^L \text{ pseudostochastic;}$$

b) B^L is an $r \times c$ pseudostochastic matrix of full rank r, $B^LB = I_r$, rank $(B^L) = r$.
Notice that the idempotent $J_c = BB^L$ is neither symetrical nor of full rank ingeneral.
Counter example 1:

$$B = \begin{bmatrix} 1/2 & 1/2 \\ 1 & 0 \\ 0 & 1 \end{bmatrix} \quad B^L = \begin{bmatrix} 0 & 1 & 0 \\ 0 & 0 & 1 \end{bmatrix} \quad J_c = \begin{bmatrix} 0 & 1/2 & 1/2 \\ 0 & 1 & 0 \\ 0 & 0 & 1 \end{bmatrix}$$

The affine inverse is not unique. In fact given B^L, B is unique but to given B there correspond several B^L's. If B is stochastic and row polynomial, then B^L is properly pseudostochastic (there is a negative element in B^L). The only square stochastic matrices whose inverses are stochastic are permutation matrices.

Assertions:

a) Dispersion morphisms form a homotopy [7] i.e. a continuous chain of morphisms.

b) Dispersion matrices form a semigroupoid under the usual product i.e.:

$$B_{k_1\times b_2} = B^1_{k_1\times b_1} \times B^2_{k_2\times b_2} \quad \text{iff} \quad b_1 = k_2$$

c) Pseudostochastic regular matrices (n×n) form a group.

d) Stochastic matrices of dimension n×n form a semigroup.

3. Transition output Automata.

Definition 3.1. The transition output automaton is a quintuple: $\Sigma_T = (Z,R,[0,1],\tau,\gamma)$ where R is the finite state space ($|R| = c$); $Z = X\times Y$ where X is the finite input alphabet ($|X| = a$) and Y the finite output alphabet ($|Y| = b$). Let the convex hull of R be $^cR = \{\pi : \langle\pi,e\rangle = 1;\ \pi_i \geq 0\}$ where e is a (c×1) vector whose elements are all equal to 1.

$\tau : R \times Z \to {}^cR$ is the transition function which associate to (r,x,y) a distribution-state whose i-th element is $pr(y,r_i|x,r)$.

$\gamma : R \times Z \to [0,1]$ is the answer functional which associates to (r,x,y), $pr(y|x,r)$.

3.2. Algebraic representation. The i-th element of R, r_i is represented by a row vector (1×c), whose j-th element is δ_{ij}. A distribution state is a row vector π belonging to ^cR whose i-th element is the probability for the machine to be in state r_i. Let Z^* be the free monoid generated by Z, let $\bar{z}$ denote the elements of Z^* and let E be the set of (c×c) sub-markovian matrices:

$E = \{A_{c\times c} : a_{ij}$ belonging to $[0,1]$, $\sum_j a_{ij} \leq 1,\ \forall i, \forall j\}$.

Let m be the map:

$$m : Z^* \to E$$
$$\bar{z} \to m(\bar{z})$$

defined by $m_{ij}(\bar{y}|\bar{x}) = pr(\bar{y},r_j|r_i,\bar{x})$ (probability of receiving the output sequence $\bar{y}$ and to be in the state r_j, knowing the initial state r_i and the applied input sequence $\bar{x}$) it is easy to prove that m is a semigroup homomorphism i.e.: $m(\overline{zz'}) = m(\bar{z})m(\bar{z}')$. The transition function and the answer functional can be derived from $m(z)$ by $\tau(r,(y|x)) = rm(y|x)$ and $\gamma(r,(y|x)) = rm(y|x)e$.

3.3. Tensor representation. The automaton tensor is a $c \times c \times (ab)$ parallelepipedic display $R[Z] \triangleq [r_{igh}]$ where $r_{igh} = m_{ij}(z_h)$. A stratum is an $(ab) \times c$ matrix associated to a pure state r_i: $(r_i) = [r_{i..}]$.

3.4. External representation. Let π belong to ${}^cR$, $\mu_\pi : Z^* \to [0,1]$ defined by $\mu_\pi(\bar{z}) = \pi m(\bar{z})e$ is the behavior function induced by the distribution state π of the automaton. It can be readily proven that:

$$\mu_\pi(\bar{y}, \bar{x}) = pr(\bar{y}|\bar{x}, \pi)$$

(probability of receiving the output sequence $\bar{y}$ given the initial distribution state π and the applied input sequence $\bar{x}$).

4. Relations between states and between automata.

4.1. Definitions.

a) Two distribution states π and π' of an automaton Σ_T are indistinguishable ($\pi \equiv \pi'$) iff $\mu_\pi \equiv \mu_{\pi'}$, i.e. iff they induce the same behavior function. (We reserve the adjective equivalent for automata in state-output form).

b) An automaton is in reduced form [3, 5] iff no different pure states are indistinguishable : $r_i \equiv r_j \Rightarrow r_i = r_j$.

c) An automaton is minimal [3, 5] iff no pure state is indistinguishable from a distribution state having zero probability on this state : $\pi \equiv r_i \Rightarrow \pi_i \neq 0$. Out of this hierarchy of definitions a novel concept can be derived.

d) An automaton is non-ambiguous iff no distinct distribution state π and π' are indistinguishable : ($\pi \equiv \pi' \Rightarrow \pi = \pi'$) otherwise it is ambiguous. From those definitions we see that :

Non ambiguity $\Rightarrow$ minimal form $\Rightarrow$ reduced-form.

e) An automaton is <u>redundant</u> iff it is minimal and ambiguous.

f) An automaton is <u>straight</u> iff it its strata are linearly dependant, otherwise it is oblique.

Rank of an automaton [6]: Let H be the semi-infinite matrix whose columns are $\{e, m(z_1)e, \ldots, m(\overline{z})e, \ldots\}$.

The <u>rank of the automaton</u> is the rank of H; it is easy to see that rank $(\Sigma_T) \leq c$.

<u>Theorem</u>: An automaton is ambiguous iff its rank is less than its number of states.

Proof: i) The automaton is ambiguous iff we can find π and π' belonging to ${}^cR$ such that:

$$\pi m(\overline{z})e = \pi' m(\overline{z})e \quad \text{for any } \overline{z} \Rightarrow (\pi - \pi')m(\overline{z})e = 0,$$

so rank (H) $<$ c.

ii) rank (H) $\underline{<}$ c, there exists σ such that $\sigma m(\overline{z})e = 0$ for any $\overline{z}$ so $\langle\sigma, e\rangle = 0$ take any π belonging to ${}^cR$ $\pi m(\overline{z})e = (\pi+\sigma)m(\overline{z})e$, so the automaton is ambiguous.

4.2. <u>Relations between automata.</u>

a) Two automata are <u>partially interchangeable</u> if they at least admit one common behavior function.

b) The c-automaton Σ_T <u>dominates</u> the c'-automaton Σ'_T iff for any π' belonging to ${}^{c'}R'$ there exists π belonging to ${}^cR$ such that $\mu_\pi \equiv \mu'_{\pi'}$.

c) The c-automaton Σ_T dominates the c'-automaton Σ'_T <u>with degree</u> n iff

i) Σ_T dominates Σ'_T

ii) there exist $i_1, i_2, \ldots, i_n$ belonging to $\{1, 2, \ldots, c\}$ and $i'_1, i'_2, \ldots, i'_n$ belonging to $\{1, 2, \ldots, c\}$ such that $i_j \neq i_k$, $i'_j \neq i'_k$, if $i \neq k$, and $\mu_{r_{i_k}} = \mu'_{r'_{i'_k}}$ for any $k = 1, 2, \ldots, n$.

d) Two automata Σ_T and Σ'_T are <u>totally interchangeable</u> if Σ_T dominates Σ'_T and Σ'_T dominates Σ_T.

5. The detection of ambiguity and the interchangeability morphism.

<u>Theorem 5.1.</u> Any straight automaton is ambiguous.
Proof: If the strata are linearly dependent there exists v $(1\times c)$ such that $v\,R[Z] = 0$ which gives: $v\,m(z) = 0$ for any z so:

$$v \sum_{i=1}^{b} m(y_i|x) = 0,$$

and

$$v \sum_{i=1}^{b} m(y_i|x)e = \langle v, e\rangle = 0,$$

hence $v\,m(\bar{z}) = 0$ for any $\bar{z}$, $v\,m(\bar{z})e = 0$ for any $\bar{z}$.

Let $\pi' = \pi + \alpha v$, there exists α real such that π' belong to ${}^{c}R$ and $(\pi + v)m(\bar{z})c = \pi m(\bar{z})e$

Q.E.D.

The converse is not always true, one can find in the litterature examples of oblique non minimal automata [6, 10], but no example of an oblique redundant automaton. The following example is taken from [13]:

<u>Example 2.</u> $X = \{x\}$, $Y = \{y_1, y_2\}$, $|X| = 1$; $|Y| = 2$; $|Z| = 2$; $c = 4$.

$$m(y_1|x) = \begin{bmatrix} .1 & .1 & .1 & .1 \\ 0 & 0 & 0 & 0 \\ .1 & .2 & .1 & .1 \\ .175 & .225 & .2 & .1 \end{bmatrix} \qquad m(y_2|x) = \begin{bmatrix} .1 & .1 & .2 & .2 \\ 0 & 0 & 1 & 0 \\ 0 & .1 & .1 & .3 \\ .2 & 0 & 0 & .1 \end{bmatrix}$$

We have: $[1/3, 0, 2/3, 0]m(\bar{z})e = [0, 1/3, 0, 1/2]m(\bar{z})e$ so the automaton is <u>ambiguous</u>. It is <u>oblique</u> because $\det(m(y_2|x)) \neq 0$.

$$H = \begin{bmatrix} 1 & .4 & .16 \\ 1 & .0 & .0 \\ 1 & .5 & .16 \\ 1 & .7 & .24 \end{bmatrix}$$

is such that no row vector is a positive linear combination of the other rows, which proves that the automaton is minimal. Q.E.D.

Theorem 5.2. Any ambiguous c-automaton is partially interchangeable with a $(c-1)$ pseudo-automaton (the elements of $m(z)$ being not necessarily positive).

Proof: One can find two vectors σ and σ' in ${}^{c}R$ such that $\sigma m(\bar{z})e = \sigma' m(\bar{z})e$, for any $\bar{z}$ of Z^*, which we can write $(\sigma - \sigma')m(\bar{z})e = 0$. As $\sigma \neq \sigma'$, we can assume up to a permutation that the c-th element of $(\sigma - \sigma')$ is not zero. We thus write:

$$\mu_{r_c}(\bar{z}) = \sum_{i=1}^{c-1} v_i \, \mu_{r_i}(\bar{z}),$$

so

$$\mu_\pi(\bar{z}) = \sum_{i=1}^{c-1} (\pi_i + \pi_c v_i) r_i m(\bar{z})e = \pi A m(\bar{z})e,$$

where $A = \begin{bmatrix} & I_{c-1} & & \begin{matrix}0\\ \vdots\end{matrix} \\ v_1 & \cdots & v_{c-1} & 0 \end{bmatrix}$ then, as $\sum_{i=1}^{c-1} v_i = 1$,

we have :

$$\mu_\pi(\overline{zz'}) = \pi A m(z) m(z')e = \pi A m(\bar{z}) A m(\bar{z}') A e.$$

Let

$$B = \begin{bmatrix} 1 & & \\ & \ddots & \\ & & 1 \\ v_1 & \cdots & v_{c-1} \end{bmatrix} \text{and} \quad B^L = \begin{bmatrix} I_{c-1} & \begin{matrix}0\\ \vdots \\ 0\end{matrix} \end{bmatrix}; \quad B^L B = I_{c-1};$$

$BB^L = A$, so:

$$\mu_\pi(\overline{zz'}) = \pi B B^L m(\bar{z}) B B^L m(\bar{z}') B e.$$

It appears that the pseudo automaton defined by $m'(z) = B^L m(z) B$ induces the same behavior function from $\pi' = \pi B$. Q.E.D.

Corollary. Any non minimal c-automaton is totally interchangeable with a (c-1)-automaton.
Proof: If the automaton is non minimal, up to a permutation we can assume that the v_i are positive or nul. So $m'(z)$ has all his elements positive or nul. Q.E.D.

Theorem 5.3. Ambiguous automata of rank (c-1) satisfy the quadratic equation up to a permutation:

$$[v_1, \ldots, v_{c-1}, -1]R[Z]\begin{bmatrix} 1 & & \\ & \ddots & \\ & & 1 \\ v_1 & \ldots & v_{c-1} \end{bmatrix} = 0.$$

Proof: We can assume up to a permutation

$$\mu_{r_c}(\bar{z}) = \sum_{i=1}^{c-1} v_i \mu_{r_i}(\bar{z}),$$

which can be written as $[v_1, \ldots, v_{c-1}, -1]m(\bar{z})e = 0$ for any $\bar{z} \in Z^*$. Let $K = \mathrm{Ker}\{(m(\bar{z})e)_{\bar{z} \in Z^*}\}$, we have $v = [v_1, \ldots, v_{c-1}, -1] \in K$; hence $[vm(z)]m(\bar{z})e = 0$ $\forall\ z \in Z$, $\forall\ \bar{z} \in Z^*$, $vm(z) \in K$ as the automaton is of rank (c-1) $\dim(K) = 1$ and $vm(z) = \lambda v$ where λ is real, and as

$$v\begin{bmatrix} 1 & & \\ & \ddots & \\ & & 1 \\ v_1 & \ldots & v_{c-1} \end{bmatrix} = 0$$

the quadratic equation is satisfied. Q.E.D.

Notice that the straight case is obtained when the quadratic equation is degenerated ($vR[Z] = 0$). So the theorem can be extended to any straight ambiguous automaton. In case the rank is less than (c-1) a generalized quadratic equation must be used [13].

Theorem 5.4. Any ambiguous automaton of rank (c-1) is partially interchangeable with a straight pseudo-automaton whose c-th state is unreachable.
Proof: From theorem 4.2 we know that $m(z)$ is partially interchangeable with $m'(z) = m(z)A$; as it satisfies the quadratic equation $[v_1, \ldots, v_{c-1}, -1]R'[Z] = 0$, the

strata are linearly dependent. Q.E.D.

6. The search algorithm for a dominant automaton with degree (c-2).

Given an automaton whose rank is (c-1) we now want to find a degree (c-2) dominant automaton. There is a simple search algorithm whenever this problem admits a particular solution.

Procedure.

1) Test the quadratic equation up to a permutation

$$\tilde{v}\, R[Z]K = \tilde{v}K = 0$$

where $\tilde{v} = [\mathbf{v}, -1]$ and where $K = \begin{bmatrix} I_{c-1} \\ v \end{bmatrix}$

2) If $\exists\, \tilde{v}_{i_1} \neq 0$ such that $\tilde{v}_{i_1} \tilde{v}_j \leq 0, \forall j \neq i_1$ the automaton is not minimal and a (c-1) dominant automaton (totally interchangeable in this case) is given by:

$$m'(z) = [I_{c-1}, 0]m(z)K.$$

3) If not the automaton is minimal redundant, let

$$\tilde{v}_{i_1} = \max\{\tilde{v}_i : \tilde{v}_i > 0\}$$

$$\tilde{v}_{i_2} = \min\{\tilde{v}_i : \tilde{v}_i < 0\}$$

Let $\tilde{\pi}$ be defined by:

$$\tilde{\pi}_i = \tilde{v}_i \quad \text{if} \quad \tilde{v}_i \leq 0 \quad \text{and} \quad i \neq i_2$$

$$\tilde{\pi}_i = 0 \quad \text{if} \quad \tilde{v}_i > 0 \quad \text{and} \quad i \neq i_1$$

$$\tilde{\pi}_{i_1} = v_{i_1}$$

$$\tilde{\pi}_{i_2} = 0$$

test whether $\langle\tilde{\pi}, e\rangle > 0$.

If not, there is no (c-2) dominant automaton. If $\langle\tilde{\pi}, e\rangle > 0$, define:

$\pi = \tilde{\pi}/<\tilde{\pi}, e>$ and $\pi' = (\tilde{\pi} - \tilde{v})/<\tilde{\pi}, e>$, we now have two distribution states π and π' such that $\mu_\pi \equiv \mu_{\pi'}$, and that r_{i_1} and r_{i_2} can be expressed respectively as convex distributions of $\{(r_i)_{i\neq i_1,i_2}, \pi\}$ and $\{(r_i)_{i\neq i_1,i_2}, \pi'\}$ which mean that the cone generated by $(r_i)_{i=1,\ldots,c}$ is contained in the cones generated by $\{(r_i)_{i\neq i_1,i_2}; \alpha\pi+(1-\alpha)\pi'\}$

Then a (c-2) dominant pseudo-automaton is

$$m'(z) = B^L m(z) B$$

where B^L is obtained from the identity matrix by suppressing the i_1-th and i_2-th rows after adding a (c+1)st row equal to π, and B is obtained from the identity matrix by suppressing the i_1-th and i_2-th columns and replacing the i_1-th and i_2-th rows by the convex distributions of r_{i_1} and r_{i_2} over (r_i, π) and (r_i, π'). (Notice that $B^L B = I_{c-1}$). So, if $m'(z)$ is submarkovian it is a solution to our question. Q.E.D.

<u>Exemple 3</u>. We apply our technique to the solution of a case presented by Nieh and Carlyle [9].
The first machine satisfies to the quadratic equation

$$[\alpha, -1, \beta] R^{\Sigma_1}[Z] \begin{bmatrix} 1 & 0 \\ \alpha & \beta \\ 0 & 1 \end{bmatrix} = [0, 0] \quad \text{with}$$

$\alpha = 1/3$ and $\beta = 2/3$; it induces the morphism matrix pair:

$$B_1^L = \begin{bmatrix} 1 & 0 & 0 \\ 0 & 0 & 1 \end{bmatrix} \quad ; \quad B_1 = \begin{bmatrix} 1 & 0 \\ 1/3 & 2/3 \\ 0 & 1 \end{bmatrix}$$

which gives the equivalent machine:

$$\Sigma'_1 = \left\{ \begin{bmatrix} 0 & 0 \\ 1/4 & 1/2 \end{bmatrix} \; ; \; \begin{bmatrix} 1/9 & 8/9 \\ 1/36 & 8/36 \end{bmatrix} \right\}$$

The second machine satisfies to the generalized quadratic equation:

$$[1/3,\ -1,\ 1/3,\ 1/3]R^{\Sigma_2^2}[Z]\begin{bmatrix}1 & 0\\ 1/3 & 2/3\\ 0 & 1\\ 0 & 1\end{bmatrix} = 0.$$

The morphism matrix pair is:

$$B_2^L = \begin{bmatrix}1 & 0 & 0 & 0\\ 0 & 0 & 1/2 & 1/2\end{bmatrix} \quad ; \quad B_2 = \begin{bmatrix}1 & 0\\ 1/3 & 2/3\\ 0 & 1\\ 0 & 1\end{bmatrix}$$

such that $\Sigma'_2 = \Sigma'_1$; the complexity measure of the reduced machine is $C(M) = 100$.

Example 4.

We now give an example for the redundant case which is due to Paz:

$$R[Z] \triangleq \left\{\begin{matrix}\begin{bmatrix}1/4 & 1/8 & 1/8 & 0\\ 3/8 & 3/16 & 3/16 & 0\\ 1/4 & 1/8 & 1/8 & 0\\ 0 & 0 & 0 & 0\end{bmatrix} & \begin{bmatrix}0 & 1/4 & 1/4 & 0\\ 0 & 1/8 & 1/8 & 0\\ 0 & 1/4 & 1/4 & 0\\ 0 & 1/2 & 1/2 & 0\end{bmatrix}\\ \\ \begin{bmatrix}0 & 0 & 0 & 0\\ 0 & 1/8 & 1/8 & 1/4\\ 0 & 3/16 & 3/16 & 3/8\\ 0 & 1/8 & 1/8 & 1/4\end{bmatrix} & \begin{bmatrix}1/2 & 0 & 0 & 1/2\\ 1/4 & 0 & 0 & 1/4\\ 1/8 & 0 & 0 & 1/8\\ 1/4 & 0 & 0 & 1/4\end{bmatrix}\end{matrix}\right\}$$

The automaton is straight, the quadratic equation is degerate: $[-1/2,\ 1,\ -1,\ 1/2]R[Z] = 0$.
So the redundancy relation generates the combination $r'_5 = r_2 - r_1/2 = r_3 - r_4/2$, which can be normalised as $r_5 = 2r_2 - r_1 = 2r_3 - r_4$ so the convex distributions are $r_2 = 1/2(r_1 + r_5)$ and $r_3 = 1/2(r_4 + r_5)$. The dispersion morphism is defined by:

$$B = \begin{bmatrix} 1 & 0 & 0 \\ 1/2 & 0 & 1/2 \\ 0 & 1/2 & 1/2 \\ 0 & 0 & 1 \end{bmatrix} \qquad B^L = \begin{bmatrix} 1 & 0 & 0 & 0 \\ 0 & 0 & 0 & 1 \\ -1 & 2 & 0 & 0 \end{bmatrix}$$

and the dominant machine is:

$$R'[Z] = \left\{ \begin{matrix} \begin{bmatrix} 5/16 & 1/8 & 1/16 \\ 0 & 0 & 0 \\ 5/8 & 1/4 & 1/8 \end{bmatrix} & \begin{bmatrix} 1/8 & 1/4 & 1/8 \\ 1/4 & 1/2 & 1/4 \\ 0 & 0 & 0 \end{bmatrix} \\ \\ \begin{bmatrix} 0 & 0 & 0 \\ 1/8 & 3/16 & 3/16 \\ 1/4 & 3/8 & 3/8 \end{bmatrix} & \begin{bmatrix} 1/2 & 0 & 1/2 \\ 1/4 & 0 & 1/4 \\ 0 & 0 & 0 \end{bmatrix} \end{matrix} \right\}$$

7. Conclusion.

The identification-realisation problem solved in the full rank case has no yet received a complete answer if $r < c$. It appears that dispersion morphism provide an adequate approach to solve it as follows. Consider a c-automaton of rank r and suppose there is a distribution state π such that rank $(\pi \overline{m(z)})$ is at least equal to r; it is shown in [1] and generalised in [2] that given μ_π, one can built an interchangeable pseudo-automaton $m'(z)$ having same behavior function.

i) If $r = c$, this interchangeable automaton is $m'(z) = m_P(z) = P^{-1}m(z)P$ and the homotopical search presented in [8, 12] can be applied to find a matrix P so that $m_P(z)$ would be positive.

ii) If $r = c-1$ we can assume that there exist P $(r\times r)$ and v $(1\times(c-1))$ so that:

$$m'(z) = m_P(z) = P^{-1} \begin{bmatrix} 1 & & \\ & \ddots & \\ & & 1 \quad 0 \end{bmatrix} m(z) \begin{bmatrix} 1 & & \\ & \ddots & \\ & & 1 \\ & v & \end{bmatrix} P$$

and the problem amounts to finding either an inverse dispersion morphism $(B_{c\times r}, B^L_{r\times c})$ so that $m(z) = Bm_P(z)B^L$ would be a $(c-1)$ dominant automaton, or a matrix P such that $m_P(z)$ is positive, hence that $m_P(\overline{z})$ is a dominant automaton of $m(\overline{z})$.

iii) If $r < c-1$ it suffices to proceed recursively or use a generalized quadratic equation [13].

It is enlightening to compare this morphism technique to the linear programming approach of [6] using the more recents [8] concepts of ambiguity and redundancy. The power of the quadratic equation has been demonstrated through the last couple of examples where it provides facilities not previously available for automaton analysis.

References

1. E. J. Gilbert, On the identifiability problem for functions of finite Markov chains. Ann. Math. Stat., pp. 688-697, (1959).
2. J. W. Carlyle, On the external Probability Structure of Finite State Channels, Info. & Cont., pp. 385-397, (1964).
3. G. C. Bacon, Minimal-state stochastic finite-state systems, IEEE - C. T. 11, pp. 307-308, (1964).
4. S. Even, Comments on the minimization of stochastic machines, IEEE - E. C. 14, pp. 634-637, (1965).
5. M. A. Arbib, Realization of stochastic systems, IEEE Seventh Symposium on Switching and Automata theory, (1966).
6. G. H. Ott, Reconsider the state minimization problem for stochastic finite-state systems, IEEE Seventh Symposium on switching and Automata theory, (1966).
7. P. J. Hilton and S. Wylie, Homology theory - An introduction to algebraic topology, Cambridge U. P., (1967).
8. M. Depeyrot, Operand investigation of stochastic systems, Stanford Doctoral Dissertation, (May 1968).
9. T. T. Nieh and J. W. Carlyle, On a measure of complexity for stochastic sequential machines, IEEE ninth Symposium on switching and Automata theory, (1968).
10. A. Paz, Homomorphisms between stochastic sequential machines and related problems, Math. Syst. Th. Vol. 2, N° 3, pp. 223-245, (1968).
11. M. Depeyrot, Un algorithme rapide de décomposition, Colloque International "Systèmes Logiques", Bruxelles, (1969).

12. F. Bancilhon and M. Depeyrot, Réalisation d'un modèle stochastique pour un canal de communication à partir d'expériences d'entrées sorties. (October 1970)
13. F. Bancilhon, These de docteur ingénieur, (to be published).

WHIRL DECOMPOSITION OF STOCHASTIC SYSTEMS

A. Paz

Technion - Israel Institute of Technology

Abstract

Markov systems are dynamical devices with a finite number of internal states, transiting probabilistically from state to state when external inputs (whose variety is assumed to be finite) are fed into it. Many physical or abstract systems can be represented as Markov Systems and this is true in particular for Probabilistic Automata.

This work deals with a specific aspect of decomposition of Markov systems, called whirl decomposition, and based on a "state splitting" technique. It is important to be able to decompose given systems into an interconnection of "simpler" systems [with less states than the given one] for this may facilitate the actual construction of such a system when necessary (the simpler systems can be constructed separately and in parallel and then interconnected). Also simpler systems are easier to investigate and this may facilitate the investigation of a given system.

Using a technique based on"state splitting" it is shown that every n-state Markov system is decomposable into a "whirl-interconnection" of n-1 2-state Markov systems.

ENCODING OF PROBABILISTIC CONTEXT-FREE LANGUAGES

Richard A. Thompson and Taylor L. Booth

Computer Science Group
Electrical Engineering Department
University of Connecticut
Storrs, Connecticut

Abstract

The compact encoding of information generated by probabilistic context-free grammars is discussed and a Coding Automaton M is introduced. Four classes of M are investigated: Character encoders, word encoders, grammar encoders, and parse encoders. The four classes are compared.

Introduction

The encoding/decoding of the data produced by a general information source is a two step process(4): first, redundant information is removed from the source message (source encoding) and second, appropriate redundancy is added so that channel errors may be detected or even corrected (channel encoding). The first step in this process is investigated, where the information source is a context-free grammar. Programming languages, if they are not context-free, may, perhaps, be approximated as context-free languages. With the increase in computer communication, the study of encoding such languages is highly motivated. Besides the transmission problem, the data compression techniques to be developed are appropriate to implement the storage of computer programs in a reduced amount of memory.

1 Preliminary Definitions

<u>Definition 1-1: Probabilistic Language (p-language)</u> Let T

be a finite set. A language $L \subset T^*$ is a p-language if there exists a probability measure p(x) for each $x \varepsilon L$ such that

$$\text{a)} \quad 0 \leq p(x) \leq 1$$

$$\text{b)} \quad \sum_{x \varepsilon L} p(x) = 1.$$

Let a grammar G' be denoted by

$$G' = (T, N, R', \sigma) \quad \text{where}$$

T is the set of terminal symbols, N is the set of non-terminal symbols, R' is the set of rewrite rules, and σ is the start symbol. The usual notation (1,5,6) with upper case, lower case, and Greek letters is used: T={a,b,c,---}, N= {σ,A,B,---}, strings from $(N \vee T)^*$ are indicated by Greek letters, and strings from T^* are indicated by z,y,x,---. Since only context-free grammars are being considered, the rewrite rules have the general format

$$A \rightarrow \alpha .$$

<u>Definition 1-2: A_i-rules</u> Let A_i-rules be that subset of R' containing all rewrite rules with non-terminal symbol A_i on the left-hand side.

<u>Definition 1-3: Probabilistic Grammar (p-grammar)</u> Let a p-grammar G be denoted

$$G = (T, N, R, \sigma)$$

where T,N, and σ are as above. In addition each rewrite rule in R has a probability p associated with it. This is indicated as

$$p: A \rightarrow \alpha$$

where $0 \leq p \leq 1$ is the probability of using the rule to which it is associated. It is also required that

$$\sum_{A_i\text{-rules}} p\,(\text{rule}) = 1 \quad \text{for all } A_i \varepsilon N$$

The probability of a word in a p-language generated by a p-grammar is found by the product of the rule probabilities over the rules used in deriving the word. The conditions under which a p-grammar derives a p-language are known (2,3) and are quite generous.

Any context-free p-grammar may be put in Greibach Normal Form (GNF)(3) where all rules have the general format

$$p: \ A \rightarrow a\alpha \quad \text{where } \alpha \subset N^*.$$

2 Codes and The Coding Automaton

Since this paper is concerned only with source encoding, codes will not be considered in terms of error detection or scrambling. Let B be a code alphabet, usually understood to be

$$B = \{0,1\}$$

Definition 2-1: Code A code over a p-language $L \subset T^*$ is another p-language $C \subset B^*$ where there exists a mapping of L onto C. In general, one of the $y \varepsilon C$ is $y=\lambda$, the null symbol, where $x \varepsilon L$ is mapped onto λ if $p(x)=1$ or 0; that is, x is fully expected or impossible. If $L_\lambda \subset L$ is defined as

$$L_\lambda = \{x/x \text{ maps onto } y=\lambda\}$$

then, to avoid ambiguity, the mapping of $L-L_\lambda$ onto $C-\lambda$ is a one-to-one mapping.

Definition 2-2: Coding If $x \varepsilon L$ maps onto $y \varepsilon C$, where C is a code as defined, then y is called the coding of x. Clearly, $p(y)=p(x)$ and thus C is a p-language.

Definition 2-3: Q-Optimal A code is optimal under some specific condition Q if the average length of an encoded message (acl) is less than that for any other code under the same condition. Thus, a code assigned on a character-by-character basis shall not be compared to one assigned on a word basis.

A general model for a source encoder is presented. It is called a Coding Automaton because many of the techniques used are those of classical push-down automata.

Definition 2-4: Coding Automaton A Coding Automaton M is a generalized deterministic machine (hence, not a transducer) with a one-way read-only input tape, a one-way write only output tape, and a potentially infinite supply of internal scratch tape. With $x \varepsilon L$ on the input tape and with the output tape initially blank, M maps x onto its coding $y \varepsilon C$ and places y on the output tape.

The Coding Automaton, as defined, can be described in the terminology of Information Theory as an encoder for a controllable-rate source (4). In such a source, instead of providing outputs in a free-running mode, the source only gives an output when requested by the encoder. This request is analogous to moving the head on the one-way input tape.

The uniquely-decipherable codes proposed by Huffman are known to be optimal in controllable-rate source encoding(4).

The underlying property of the Coding Automaton, fundamental in both Automata Theory and Information Theory, is Information Losslessness. This concept, well defined for finite-state machines (1,7), must be generalized to the infinite automata models.

Definition 2-5: Status The status of a generalized deterministic machine is that internal information which, together with the input, determines the machines output and new status.

In a finite-state machine, the status is the state. In a push-down machine, the status is the state and the contents of the push-down list. Formally, a generalized machine (such as a Coding Automaton) can be represented:

$$M = (S, I, B, \delta, \omega, s_1) \text{ where}$$

S is the status set (which can be infinite), I is the input alphabet, B is the output alphabet, δ (the next-status function) is a mapping of SxI into S, ω (the output function) is a mapping of SxI into B^*, and s_1 is the initial status of M.

Definition 2-6 Type I Information Lossless (IL1)
A generalized deterministic machine is Type I Information Lossless (IL1) if

$$\omega(a_i, s) \neq \omega(a_j, s)$$

for all $a_i \varepsilon I$ and $a_j \varepsilon I$ and for every status $s \varepsilon S$.

Note that this is an extension of Type I Information Losslessness as defined by Huffman(7). Other types of

Information Losslessness are defined (1,7) but are not required here. Note also that it is undecideable if an arbitrary machine is IL1 because the status set S can be infinite. The following lemma is presented without proof. The proof follows from a corresponding proof for the finite-state case(7).

Lemma 2-1 The input sequence to a generalized deterministic machine can be determined by a knowledge of the initial status and the output sequence if the machine is IL1.

The canonical form for an IL1 machine and its inverse is given in Figure 1. If the IL1 machine of Figure 1(a) is an encoder then the inverse of Figure 1(b) is the corresponding decoder. By Lemma 2-1, the decoder must be initialized before operation. Thus, in the classes of Coding Automata which follow, it suffices to show that, if the encoder is IL1, then the decoder is a trivial extension of the encoder.

3. Classes of Coding Automata

Four classes of Coding Automata are investigated. In the first, character encoding, the code language C is a simple homomorphism of the source language L. The drawback here is that the sequential properties of L are not utilized. In the second, word encoding, an entire word $x \varepsilon L$ is mapped onto its coding $y \varepsilon C$ instead of considering each individual character of x. The drawback here is that L must be approximated by a finite set. In the third class, grammar encoding, the grammatical structure of the source is utilized in selecting sequences of optimal codes. In the fourth class, parse encoding, a word $x \varepsilon L$ is parsed and then the sequence of rule labels is encoded.

Character Encoding

Definition 3-1: Character Encoding Character Encoding is implemented on a Coding Automaton M_C as follows. A single code $H \subset B^*$ is constructed over the set T such that each $a_m \varepsilon T$ maps onto $u_m \varepsilon H$ and M_C has one single state from which it outputs u_m upon reading a_m.

Clearly, the IL1 property is satisfied by M_C. The optimal code H in this situation is known to be a uniquely-decipherable code as described by Huffman(4). A multinomial distribution over the set T is required to construct H; but his can be found from the p-grammar which generates L (9) or it can be measured.

The code language C is such that, if

$$x=a_{m_1} a_{m_2} \cdots a_{m_n}$$

is in L, then

$$y = M_C(x) = u_{m_1} u_{m_2} \cdots u_{m_n}$$

is in C.

Theorem 3-1 Let L be a p-language generated by p-grammar G. Then $C=M_C(L)$ is a p-language which is : a) context-free if G is context-free, b) deterministic if G is deterministic, or c) regular if G is regular.

Proof A grammar which generates C is constructed by substituting u_m for a_m in G. The theorem also follows from Corollary 9-1 of Hopcraft and Ullman(6) which states that the language type is preserved under homomorphism.

Word Encoding

Definition 3-2: Word Encoding Word Encoding is implemented on a Coding Automaton M_W as follows. A single code $C \subset B^*$ is constructed over a set of words and M_W does not output the $y_i \varepsilon C$ corresponding to $x_i \varepsilon L$ until all of x_i has been read.

Clearly, the IL1 property is satisfied by M_W. Again a Huffman code is used for C if C is optimal. A distribution over L is needed but this is defined by the p-language. Word encoding should be superior to character encoding because: 1) the block length is increased, (4) and 2) the sequential behavior of L is utilized. This is not the case, necessarily, because the Huffman code C can only be constructed over a finite set.

If the P-language L is not finite, it may be approximated by one that is.

Definition 3-3: $(1-\varepsilon)$-approximation A p-language L is $(1-\varepsilon)$-approximated by a finite p-language $\tilde{L}$ of size N+1 by first ordering the words in L in decreasing order of their probabilities $p(x_i)$ and then selecting the words in L, in order, to be in $\tilde{L}$ until

$$\sum_{i=1}^{n} p(x_i) = (1-\varepsilon).$$

The (N+1)-st word in $\tilde{L}$ is a dummy word d which occurs with probability ε.

Two Word Encoding procedures are proposed depending on whether encoder error is allowed. In either case C is constructed over $\tilde{L}$ and $x\varepsilon\tilde{L}$ are encoded (optimally) by outputting the corresponding $y\varepsilon C$. It is in encoding $x\varepsilon L-\tilde{L}$ that the two procedures differ.

If encoder error is permitted, then $x\varepsilon L-\tilde{L}$ is mapped onto y_d, the coding for d; the dummy coding is an error message. As $\tilde{L}$ includes more words of L, fewer errors are made. However, due to the nature of Huffman codes, as ε decreases the length of the dummy code l_d increases.

Theorem 3-2 Let $C = M_W(L)$ as described, allowing encoder error. Then,

$$\lim_{\tilde{L}\to L} l_d\varepsilon = 0$$

Proof

From the proof of the Basic Noiseless Coding Theorem as applied to Huffman codes(4), it is noted that for any x being encoded

$$p(x) \leq D^{-(l_x-1)}$$

where l_x is the length of the coding for x and D is the size of B. The theorem follows.

If encoder error is not permitted, then let y_d be used as a prefix to a homomorphism on $x\varepsilon L-\tilde{L}$. It is necessary to append a unique stop code y_s to such code words in order to preserve IL1-ness. Then $x\varepsilon L-\tilde{L}$ are mapped onto a concatenated code word $y_d y_x y_s$ where y_x is constructed as in Character Encoding.

Theorem 3-3 Let $C = M_W(L)$ as described, not allowing encoder error. Then

$$\lim_{\tilde{L}\to L} \sum_{x\in L-\tilde{L}} |y_d y_x y_s| \; p(x) = 0$$

if L has a finite average word length.

Proof

$$l_e = \sum_{x\varepsilon L-\tilde{L}} |y_d y_x y_s| \; p(x)$$

$$= l_d \varepsilon + \sum_{x\varepsilon L-\tilde{L}} |y_x| \; p(x) + |y_s| \; \varepsilon$$

The first term approaches zero by Theorem 3-2 and the last because $|y_s|$ is a constant. Let h be such that $D^h \geq |T|$, then $|y_x| \leq h \; |x|$ and the middle term

$$\sum_{x\varepsilon L-\tilde{L}} |y_x| \; p(x) \leq h \sum_{x\varepsilon L-\tilde{L}} |x| p(x)$$

The right-hand summation is that part of the average word length of L which corresponds to $L-\tilde{L}$ and it approaches 0 if the average word length is finite. The conditions on the p-grammar generating L are known guaranteeing that L has finite average word length (9).

These two theorems show that, in either type of Word Encoding, C can be made arbitrarily optimal by increasing the size of $\tilde{L}$. The grammatical structure of L is totally lost in the encoding and thus nothing can be said about the type of language for C.

Grammar Encoding

In this type of encoding, the sequential behavior of L is utilized. The Coding Automaton is constructed from the p-grammar which generates L. In general, some coding is outputted after each input character is read; that output may correspond to the currently read character (first order) or the k-th previously read character (k-th order). First order Grammar Encoding is defined and then the process is later generalized.

Definition 3-4: First-order Grammar Encoding Grammar Encoding of the first order is implemented on a Coding

Automaton M_G^1 as follows. Let

$$x = a_{m_1} a_{m_2} \text{---} a_{m_r} \text{---} a_{m_n}$$

and let the r-character prefix of x be written

$$x_r = a_{m_1} a_{m_2} \text{---} a_{m_r} .$$

Then, a code $H_{x_r} \subset B^*$ is constructed over the set T based on x_r, the previously read (and encoded) characters. Each $a_j \in T$ maps onto $u_j^{x_r} \in H_{x_r}$ and so the (r+1)-st character $a_{m_{(r+1)}}$ of x is encoded as $u_{m_{(r+1)}}^{x_r}$. In this manner the enrire word is encoded.

In comparison to the expression for y in character encoding, if

$$x = a_{m_1} a_{m_2} \text{---} a_{m_n} ,$$

then

$$y = M_G^1 (x) = u_{m_1}^{\lambda} \; u_{m_2}^{x_1} \text{---} u_{m_n}^{x_{(n-1)}} .$$

<u>Lemma 3-1</u> The code $C = M_G^1(L)$ is optimal under the conditions of such character-by-character encoding if the H_{x_r} are Huffman codes at each step of the encoding process.
<u>Proof</u> The proof is identical to Ott's proof (8) of the same result for Markov processes and is omitted.

Let L, a p-language to be Grammar Encoded, be generated by p-grammar G. There is no loss in generality by considering that G is in GNF and that only left-most derivations by G are used. It should also be noted that G need not be unambiguous. The operation of M_G^1 during the encoding process is described.

Let the rules of G be represented as:

$$P_{(i,j,k)}: A_i \to a_j \; \alpha_{(i,j,k)} .$$

If there are K(i,j) rules which rewrite A_i onto $a_j\alpha$, for arbitrary α, then

$$\sum_{j=1}^{|T|} \sum_{k=1}^{K(i,j)} P_{(i,j,k)} = 1 \quad \text{for all } 1 \leq i \leq |N|$$

A partial derivation of x, after r rules are used, has the format

$$a_{m_1} a_{m_2} \text{---} a_{m_r} \gamma$$

where x_r is generated as shown because G is in GNF and the derivations are left-most and γ is the resulting string of non-terminal symbols. Let there be N_{x_r} such derivations each with a probability w_n, where

$$\sum_{n=1}^{N_{x_r}} w_n = 1.$$

The Coding Automaton M_G^1 records all possible (γ_n, w_n) for $1 \leq n \leq N_{x_r}$. Initially $N_\lambda = 1$, $\gamma_1 = \sigma$, and $w_1 = 1$.

Now each γ_n can be written as

$$\gamma_n = A_{i_n} \beta_n$$

where $A_{i_n} \varepsilon N$ is the left-most non-terminal symbol in γ_n. A probability distribution over $a_{m_{(r+1)}}$ is computed by:

$$\text{Prob}\{a_{m_{(r+1)}} = a_j / x_r\} = \sum_{n=1}^{N_{x_r}} w_n \sum_{k=1}^{K(i_n,j)} P_{(i_n,j,k)}$$

It can be seen that

$$\sum_{j=1}^{|T|} \text{Prob}\{a_{m_{(r+1)}} = a_j / x_r\} = 1$$

From this distribution, H_{x_r} is constructed and, when $a_{m_{(r+1)}}$ is read, $u^{x_r}_{m_{(r+1)}}$ is outputted. The γ_n must be altered before reading $a_{m_{(r+2)}}$.

There are $K(i_n, m_{(r+1)})$ ways that $a_{m_{(r+1)}}$ could be generated from γ_n. Then each γ_n is the "father" to a set of strings with the form

$$\gamma_{(n,k)} = \alpha_{(i_n, m_{(r+1)}, k)} \beta_n$$

due to using the rule

$$A_{i_n} \to a_{m_{(r+1)}} \alpha_{(i_n, m_{(r+1)}, k)}.$$

Each "son" string has a probability computed by

$$w_{(n,k)} = w_n \frac{P(i_n, m_{(r+1)}, k)}{\text{Prob}\ \{a_{m_{(r+1)}} = a_j / x_r\}}$$

It can be seen that

$$\sum_{n=1}^{N_{x_r}} \sum_{k=1}^{K(i_n, m_{(r+1)})} w_{(n,k)} = 1$$

Now if there is no rule

$$A_{i_n} \to a_{m_{(r+1)}} \alpha$$

then the entire γ_n "family" is stricken. If $\gamma_{(n_1,k_1)} = \gamma_{(n_2,k_2)}$ then they are merged and the single string has probability $w_{(n_1,k_1)} + w_{(n_2,k_2)}$.

The remaining strings are reclassified as:

$$(\gamma_n, w_n) \text{ for } 1 \le n \le N_{x_{(r+1)}}$$

and the process continues. By induction, the operation of M_G^1 is completed. It can be seen that M_G^1 is IL1.

The code H_{x_r} is actually a code over a set of subsets

of grammar rules which are applicable at the generation of the (r+1)-st character of x. In the first order case, the subsets are formed on the basis of the single terminal symbol in the rule and, thus, H_{x_r} is also a code over T.

This is due to the unique structure of Greibach Normal Form. This is not the case, in general, in the k-th order. Grammar Encoding of the k-th order is implemented on a Coding Automaton M_G^k which is not formally defined but which is seen to also be ILl.

By looking ahead M_G^k is able to form a code over a finer and finer set of subsets of grammar rules as k increases. Two counter-acting effects are seen. The early codings, $u_{m_{(r+1)}}^{x_r}$ for small r, get larger as k increases because the codes H_{x_r} are over larger sets. The later codings, $u_{m_{(r+1)}}^{x_r}$ for larger r, get smaller as k increases because the process need not keep track of so many different lists γ_n. Thus it is not clear that k-order look-ahead is beneficial or detrimental.

A related technique, which is beneficial, is to encode k-characters at a time. Increasing the block-length always decreases the average code length (4).

<u>Definition 3-5: k-th order GNF</u> A p-grammar G is in <u>Greibach Normal Form of the k-th</u> order, GNF(k), if all the rules in G have one of the forms:

$$p: \ A \rightarrow v \ \alpha$$

$$p: \ A \rightarrow w$$

where

$$v \varepsilon T^k, \ w \ \varepsilon \ \bigvee_{i=1}^{k} T^i$$

Any p-grammar can be put in this form. By applying the techniques of M_G^1, the blocks of characters, v, w, etc. are encoded as single codings. A more optimal code will result.

In M_G^k it may be the case that, at some k=K, the set of subsets of grammar rules is exactly the set of rules with one rule in each subset. If this occurs for all r in all $x \in L(G)$ then G is said to be LL(K).

Definition 3-6: LL(k) A context-free grammar G, hence a p-grammar, is LL(k) if, by scanning $x \in L(G)$ from left to right k characters beyond the point of last replacement, a unique left-most parse is determined.

The LL(k) grammars have interesting properties similar to those of the LR(k) grammars (9). The concept is introduced here because it is an important special case in Grammar Encoding.

Lemma 3-2 A LL(1) p-grammar G in GNF has, at most, one rule which rewrites A_i onto a_i for all A_i and a_i.

Proof: If G is LL(1), then knowledge of a_{m_1} determines the rule which generated a_{m_1}. That rule is

$$\sigma \rightarrow a_{m_1} \alpha$$

But, in general, α can be any string with any A_i as the next non-terminal symbol to be rewritten. The lemma follows.

Lemma 3-3 If M_G^k encodes a p-language generated by a LL(k) p-grammar G, then only one list γ is ever required.

Proof: First consider the case for M_G^1 and LL(1) grammars. By Lemma 3-2 the rules of G can be written

$$P_{(i,j)}: \quad A_i \rightarrow a_j \; \alpha_{(i,j)}$$

Initially, $\gamma = \sigma = A_1$ and

$$\text{Prob}\,\{a_{m_1} = a_j / \lambda\} = P_{(1,j)}$$

After a_{m_1} is read and $u_{m_1}^{\lambda}$ is outputted, the unique rule is known which generated a_{m_1}. It is

$$P_{(1,m_1)}: \quad A_1 \rightarrow a_{m_1} \; \alpha_{(1,m_1)}$$

Then $\gamma=\alpha_{(1,m_1)}=A_i\ \beta_{(1,m_1)}$ where A_i is the left-most non-terminal symbol in $\alpha_{(1,m_1)}$. Then

$$\text{Prob}\ \{a_{m_2} = a_j/a_{m_1}\} = p_{(i,j)}$$

and the process continues with $N_{x_r} = 1$ for all r and all x.

The lemma is extended to M_G^k and LL(k) grammars. The first k characters x_k determine the unique rule used in the derivation, and hence γ. One more character $a_{m_{(k+1)}}$, when appended to x_k and with a_{m_1} dropped, determines the second rule used, etc. Since only k characters must be remembered (the last k) then a finite-state machine suffices and the only list required is for γ.

<u>Theorem 3-4</u> If M_G^k encodes a p-language L generated by a LL(k) p-grammar G, then $C=M_G^k(L)$ is a context-free p-language.

<u>Proof</u>: By Lemma 3-3, M_G^k is seen to be a push-down transducer (pdt) as defined by Ginsburg(5). By Theorem 3.5-1 of that reference, the output language of a pdt is context-free if the input language L is context-free and L is the language accepted by some automaton "associated" with the transducer. In this case, L is "associated" with M_G^k because M_G^k is constructed from G.

<u>Corollary</u> If L_k is regular, then C is also regular.

<u>Proof</u>: Here, M_G^k is a "gsm" and a gsm-mapping of a regular language is a regular language. (5,6)

At any point in the M_G^k-encoding of L (G), where G is LL(k),

$$\text{Prob}\{a_{m_{(r+1)}}/x_r\} = p_{(i,j)}$$

where A_i is the left-most symbol in γ. Thus H_{x_r} is not only constructed over T, it is constructed over the A_i-rules, again due to the structure of Greibach Normal Form.

Then A_i and $a_{m_{(r+1)}}$ uniquely determine the rule used at this point in the derivation and $u^{x_r}_{m_{(r+1)}}$ is simply the coding for that rule. A grammar which generates C is easily constructed by substituting in the rules of G the rules' coding for the terminal symbol. Thus an alternative proof to Theorem 3-4 is apparent. It is not necessary, however, that G be LL(k) in order to uniquely parse each $x \varepsilon L$.

Parse Encoding

Definition 3-7: Parse Encoding Parse Encoding is implemented on a Coding Automaton M_p as follows. A code $H_i \subset B^*$ is constructed over the set of A_i-rules for $1 \leq i \leq |N|$ in the p-grammar which generates the p-language being encoded. Then each rule r_k is assigned a coding u_k where $u_k \varepsilon H_i$ if r_k is an A_i-rule. Then, in a two-step process, the input word $x \varepsilon L$ is parsed into a sequence of rule labels which is then encoded.

Again for optimality the H_i should be Huffman codes over the set of A_i-rules. Note that the set $\{u_k\}$ over all rules is not a code as defined in Definition 2-1 because the coding for an A_1-rule could be the same as that for an A_2-rule. Note also that the output of the parser is a sequence

$$r_{m_1} r_{m_2} \text{---} r_{m_n}$$

with one rule label for each character in x if G is in GNF. This sequence is encoded as a homomorphism onto

$$u_{m_1} u_{m_2} \text{---} u_{m_n}$$

where, in this final step, there is no knowledge of the partial derivation or status of M_p. Thus IL1-ness must be investigated.

The decoder, initialized to $\gamma=\sigma$, interprets u_{m_1} as the coding for a σ-rule. Let that σ-rule be

$$\sigma \to a_{m_1} \alpha$$

Then if $\alpha = A_i \beta$, then u_{m_2} must be the coding for an A_i-rule. The decoder proceeds in this manner and, since the process is fully reconstructed, M_P is seen to be IL1.

Definition 3-8: Parse Language Let a Parse Language $Q_L \subset \hat{R}^*$ be the set of all rule sequences which are parsings of the words in the parent language L. Here $\hat{R}$ is the set of rule labels in the grammar which generates L.

If L is ambiguous, then a parser would only output one of many possible parsings. If such L is a p-language then Q_L will not be a p-language because normality breaks down. But if L is unambiguous, the Q_L is a p-language.

Theorem 3-5 If M_P encodes an unambiguous p-language L generated by p-grammar G, in GNF, then Q_L and $C=M_P(L)$ are: a) context-free if G is context-free, b) deterministic if G is deterministic, and c) regular if G is regular.

Proof: A grammar generating Q_L is found by substituting the rule label for the terminal symbol in all rules of G. A grammar generating C is found by substituting the rule coding for the terminal symbol in all rules of G.

4 Comparison

In the preceding section, four classes of Coding Automata were investigated. In all four clases, Huffman codes were seen to be optimal and IL1-ness was seen to prevail. In Word Encoding the language structure is destroyed and in Grammar Encoding of order k for general grammars, all that can be said is that C is a type-0 language. Techniques are known for determining the average word length of context-free p-languages (9) and thus, if C is context-free, the codes can be compared.

The four classes of Coding Automata are compared by their acl in Figure 2. The highest acl occurs in Character Encoding and the lowest acl occurs in Word Encoding (in the limit as $L \to \tilde{L}$). The acl for Parse Encloding lies in between these two extremes. The acl for Grammar Encoding also lies between these two bounds for every value of k; this is indicated by the shaded area in Figure 2. If the grammar is LL(K) then, for $k \geq K$, Grammar Encoding and

Parse Encoding are identical.

The four classes of Coding Automata have widely varying complexity. Character encoding is extremely simple and Word Encoding, while also simple, requires a vast memory. Grammar Encoding is quite complex and also requires much memory for storing the multiple lists. Parse Encoding would also appear complex but an enormous simplification is possible. Modern compiler techniques include parsing algorithms to verify "grammaticalness". Then, Parse Encoding of a programming language is easily implemented by modifying the compiler to provide outputs. The encoded program statements are then ready for transmission or for memory storage. It is felt that the most practical application of this theory is in this area.

References

1. Booth, Taylor L., Sequential Machines and Automata Theory, John Wiley and Sons, Inc., 1967.
2. Booth, Taylor L., Probabilistic Representation of Formal Languages, IEEE Conference Record of the Tenth Annual Symposium of Switching and Automata Theory, 1969.
3. Ellis, Clarence A., Probabilistic Languages and Automata, Doctoral Thesis, Department of Computer Science, University of Illinois, 1969.
4. Fano, Robert M., Transmission of Information, MIT Press and John Wiley and Sons, Inc. 1961.
5. Ginsburg, Seymor, The Mathematical Theory of Context-Free Languages, McGraw-Hill, Inc. 1966.
6. Hopcraft, John E. and Ullman, Jeffrey D., Formal Languages and their Relation to Automata, Addison-Wesley Publishing Co., Inc. 1969.
7. Huffman, David A., Canonical Forms for Information-Lossless Finite-State Logical Machines, Sequential Machines: Selected Papers Edited by Edward F. Moore, Addison-Wesley Publishing Co., Inc. 1964.
8. Ott, Gene, Compact Encoding of Stationary Markov Sources, IEEE Transactions on Information Theory, Vol. IT-13, No.1 January 1967.
9. Thompson, Richard A, Compact Encoding of Languages Generated by Probabilistic Grammars, Doctoral Thesis, Computer Science Group, Elect. Eng. Dept. U. Conn.1971.

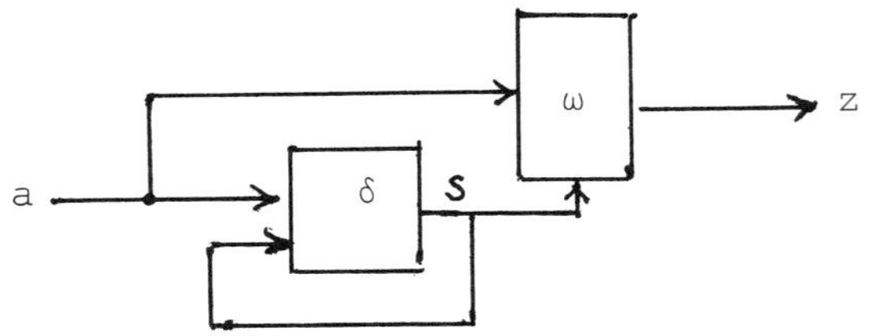

Figure 1 (a) An IL1 Machine

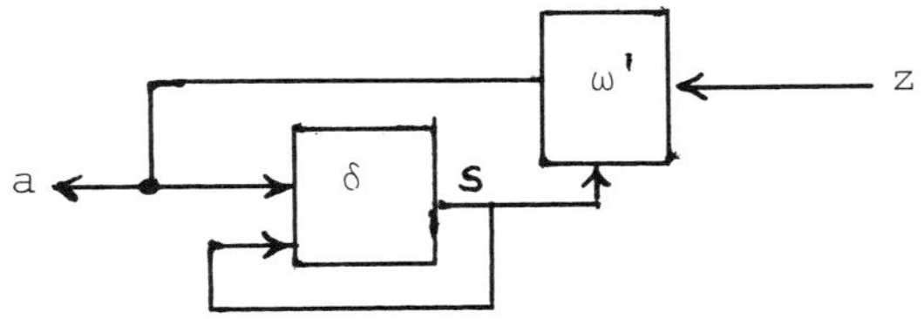

Figure 1 (b) The Inverse of an IL1 Machine

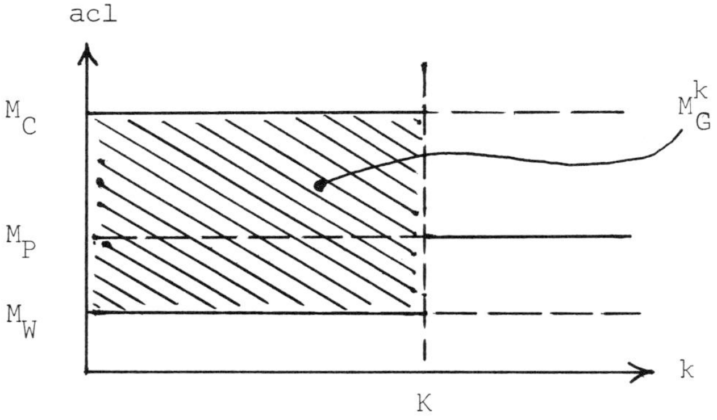

Figure 2 Comparision of Average Code Length (acl) for the Four Classes of M.

SECTION III

FINITE AUTOMATA

AN n log n ALGORITHM FOR MINIMIZING STATES IN A FINITE AUTOMATON

John Hopcroft

Introduction

Most basic texts on finite automata give algorithms for minimizing the number of states in a finite automaton [1, 3]. However, a worst case analysis of these algorithms indicate that they are n^2 processes where n is the number of states. For finite automata with large numbers of states, these algorithms are grossly inefficient. Thus in this paper we describe an algorithm for minimizing the states in which the asymptotic running time in a worst case analysis grows as $n \log n$. The constant of proportionality depends linearly on the number of input symbols. Clearly the same algorithm can be used to determine if two finite automata are equivalent.

The essence of previously published algorithms was to first partition the states according to their outputs. The blocks of the partitions are then repeatedly refined by examining the successor state on a given input for each state in the block. States whose successor states on a given input are in different blocks are placed in separate blocks. When no further refinement is possible, all states in the same block of the partition can be shown to be equivalent. Consider the example in Figure 1. The initial partition is (1,2,3,4,5)(6). Since on input 0, the successor states of states 1, 2, 3 and 4 are in the first block of the partition and the successor of state 5 is in the second block, the first iteration refines the partition into the blocks (1,2,3,4)(5) and (6). Successive refinements yield (1,2,3)(4)(5)(6);

State	Input 0	Input 1	Output
1	2	1	0
2	3	2	0
3	4	3	0
4	5	4	0
5	6	5	0
6	6	6	1

Figure 1

(1,2)(3)(4)(5)(6) and (1)(2)(3)(4)(5)(6). Thus, in this example it is seen that as many as n iterations may be required. Since an iteration requires scanning each state the total number of steps needed to execute the algorithm if implemented in a straightforward fashion on a digital computer is n^2.

The algorithm proposed in this paper may also require n iterations but the work per iteration summed over all iterations yields only n log n. We illustrate the algorithm by an example before specifying it in detail. Extensive use of list processing is employed to reduce the computation time. First the state table is inverted to obtain the table shown in Figure 2. The states are partitioned according to their outputs (1,2,3,4,5)(6). Next a block and an input symbol on which the partition is refined are selected. Assume that block (6) and input 0 are selected. The states in each block are further partitioned depending on whether on input 0 their next state is in block (6) or not. Thus the next partition is (1,2,3,4)(5)(6). Note that had we partitioned on the block (1,2,3,4,5) and input 0 we would have obtained the same result. More generally, once we have partitioned on a block and an input symbol, we need never partition on that block and input symbol again until the block is split and then we need only partition on one of the two subblocks. Since the time needed to partition on a block is proportional to the transitions into the block and since we can always select the half with fewer transitions, the total number of steps in the algorithm is bounded by n log n.

State	Input 0	Input 1	Output
1	-	1	0
2	1	2	0
3	2	3	0
4	3	4	0
5	4	5	0
6	5,6	6	1

previous state

Figure 2

Formal description of the algorithm

Let $A = (S,I,\delta,F)$ be a finite automaton where S is a finite set of states, I is a finite set of inputs, δ is a mapping from $S \times I$ into S and $F \subseteq S$ is the set of final states. No initial state is specified since it is of no importance in what follows. The mapping δ is extended to $S \times I^*$ in the usual manner where I^* denotes the set of all finite length strings of symbols from I. States s and t are said to be equivalent if for each x in I^*, $\delta(s,x)$ is in F if and only if $\delta(t,x)$ is in F.

The algorithm for finding the equivalence classes of S is described below.

Step 1. For each s in S and each a in I construct

$$\delta^{-1}(s,a) = \{t \mid \delta(t,a) = s\} .$$

Step 2. Construct $B(1) = F$, $B(2) = S-F$ and for each a in I and $1 \leq i \leq 2$ construct

$$\hat{B}(B(i),a) = \{s \mid s \in B(i) \text{ and } \delta^{-1}(s,a) \neq \emptyset\} .$$

Step 3. Set $k = 3$

Step 4. For each a in I construct

$$L(a) = \begin{cases} \{1\} & \text{if } |\hat{B}(B(1),a)| \leq |\hat{B}(B(2),a)| \\ \{2\} & \text{otherwise} \end{cases} .$$

Step 5. Select a in I and i in $L(a)$. The algorithm terminates when $L(a) = \emptyset$ for each a in I.

Step 6. Delete i from $L(a)$.

Step 7. For each $j < k$ such that there exists t in $B(j)$ with $\delta(t,a)$ in $\hat{B}(B(i),a)$, perform steps 7a, 7b, 7c, and 7d.

Step 7a. Partition $B(j)$ into

$B'(j) = \{t \mid \delta(t,a) \in \hat{B}(B(i),a)$ and
$B''(j) = B(j) - B'(j)$.

Step 7b. Replace $B(j)$ by $B'(j)$ and construct $B(k) = B''(j)$. Construct the corresponding $\hat{B}(B(j),a)$ and $\hat{B}(B(k),a)$ for each a in I.

Step 7c. For each a in I modify $L(a)$ as follows.

$$L(a) = \begin{cases} L(a) \cup \{j\} & \text{if } j \notin L(a) \text{ and } 0 < |\hat{B}(B(j),a)| \leq |\hat{B}(B(k),a)| \\ L(a) \cup \{k\} & \text{otherwise} \end{cases} .$$

Step 7d. Set $k = k+1$.

Step 8. Return to Step 5.

Correctness of algorithm

The claim is made that on termination of the algorithm two states are equivalent if and only if they are in the same block. Let a be in I . The algorithm must terminate since the only times that an index is added to $L(a)$ are in Step 4 and in Step 7c. Step 4 is executed only once. An index is added at Step 7c only after a refinement of a block of the partition. The number of such refinements is at most n . Each time Step 6 is executed, an index is removed from $L(a)$ for some a . Thus the algorithm must terminate.

It is easily shown by induction on the number of times Step 7a is executed that if s is in $B(i)$ and t is in $B(j)$, $i \neq j$, then s is not equivalent to t . Clearly it is true the first time Step 7a is executed since only two blocks exist, $B(1)$ containing only final states and $B(2)$ containing only nonfinal states. Blocks are refined at Step 7a only when successor states on a given input have previously been shown to be inequivalent.

To see that two inequivalent states cannot be in the same block when the algorithm terminates, assume that states s and t are in $B(i)$ and that s and t are not equivalent. Without loss of generality, assume $\delta(s,a)$ is in $B(j)$ and $\delta(t,a)$ is in $B(k)$ where $j \neq k$. (If $\delta(s,a)$ and $\delta(t,a)$ are in the same block then there exists a shortest x such that $\delta(s,x)$ and $\delta(t,x)$ are in distinct blocks. Clearly an x exists and hence a shortest x since for some x one or the other of $\delta(s,x)$ and $\delta(t,x)$ but not both is in a final state and each block consists solely of final or solely of nonfinal states. Let a be the last symbol of x and write $x = ya$. Then $\delta(s,y)$ and $\delta(t,y)$ are in the same block, $\delta(s,y)$ and $\delta(t,y)$ are not equivalent and $\delta(\delta(s,y),a)$ and $\delta(\delta(t,y),a)$ are in different blocks. Replace s by $\delta(s,y)$ and replace t by $\delta(t,y)$.) Consider the point at which the block containing $\delta(s,a)$ and $\delta(t,a)$ is partitioned so that $\delta(s,a)$ and $\delta(t,a)$ first appear in separate subblocks. At that point one of the two subblocks is placed in $L(a)$. When this subblock is removed from

$L(a)$, the block containing s and t is partitioned with s and t going into separate subblocks. Thus s and t cannot both be in $B(i)$, a contradiction.

Analysis of the running time

The running time of the algorithm is clearly dependent on the implementation. The algorithm has been programmed in ALGOL. Since the implementation consists of approximately 300 ALGOL statements we shall simply indicate how the various steps are implemented and discuss informally their running time. A listing of the program can be found in Reference 2.

The sets such as $\delta^{-1}(s,a)$, $L(a)$, etc. are represented by linked lists in such a way that an item could be added or deleted at the beginning of the list in a fixed number of steps. Vectors are also maintained to indicate if a state is or is not on a given list. This eliminates searching a list simply to determine if the item is on the list and is essential in Step 7c. The sets $B(i)$ and $\hat{B}(B(i),a)$ were represented as doubly linked lists so that an item could be added or deleted anywhere in the list in a fixed number of steps once the position is given. The structure was such that given a state s, its position in $B(i)$ and $\hat{B}(B(i),a)$ can be determined in a fixed number of steps.

Steps 1, 2, 3 and 4 are executed only once and require time proportional to the product of the number of states times the number of input symbols. Steps 5 through 8 form a simple loop. The time necessary to traverse the loop for given a in I and i in $L(a)$ is proportional to the number of state transitions on input a terminating on states in $B(i)$. (To see this, note that Steps 5, 6 and 8 are finite. In Step 7 we do not need to examine $B(j)$ for each $j < k$ to see if there exists a t in $B(j)$ with $\delta(t,a)$ in $\hat{B}(B(i),a)$. Rather we look at each state in $\hat{B}(B(i),a)$ and then consult the inverse state table to find each t such that $\delta(t,a)$ is in $\hat{B}(B(i),a)$. Each time a new t is found, the block containing t is located and t placed on a list of states to be split off from the block. The block is then placed on a list of blocks which have been refined if it is not already on the list. Finally we go down the list of blocks which have been refined and actually partition them. The number of blocks we must look at must be less than the number of state transitions on input a terminating on states in $B(i)$. The time necessary to actually partition a block is proportional to the number of states to be split off. When the number is summed over all blocks which are partitioned it adds up to the number of state transitions on input a terminating on states in $B(i)$.) Let k be the constant of proportionality.

Consider the time spent in the loop of Step 5 through 8 for a given input symbol a. Assume that at Step 5 the blocks of the partition are $B(1), B(2), \ldots, B(m)$ and that $L(a) = \{i_1, i_2, \ldots, i_r\}$. Let $\{i_{r+1}, i_{r+2}, \ldots, i_m\} = \{1, 2, \ldots, m\} - L(a)$ and let $a_i = |\delta^{-1}(B(i), a)|$. The claim is made that the total time spent on traversals of the loop for which input symbol a is selected in Step 5 until the program terminates is bounded by

$$T = k\left(\sum_{j=1}^{r} a_{i_j} \log a_{i_j} + \sum_{j=r+1}^{m} a_{i_j} \log(a_{i_j}/2)\right) .$$

Clearly the bound is valid if the algorithm has terminated. If the loop is traversed for an input symbol other than a, then the time spent is not included in T. However, since the blocks get split and the set $L(a)$ modified we must show that the new value of T, call it $\hat{T}$, is less than or equal to the old value of T. If a block whose index is in $L(a)$ is partitioned, then a term of the form $b \log b$ is replaced by the expression $c \log c + (b-c) \log(b-c)$ which decreases the value of T. If a block whose index is not in $L(a)$ is partitioned, then a term of the form $b \log b/2$ is replaced by the expression

$$c \log c + (b-c) \log((b-c)/2)$$

where $c \leq b-c$. Since $c \leq b/2$ and $(b-c)/2 \leq b/2$,

$$\begin{aligned} c \log c + (b-c) \log(b-c)/2 &\leq c \log b/2 + (b-c) \log b/2 \\ &\leq b \log b/2 . \end{aligned}$$

Thus, in either case $\hat{T}$ is less than T. Finally, assume

$r \neq 0$ and a in I and some ℓ in $L(a)$ has been selected at Step 5. As we showed earlier, the time around the loop is bounded by ka_ℓ . Thus by induction, the total time is bounded by

$$k[a_\ell + a_\ell \log(a_\ell/2) + \sum_{\substack{j=1 \\ j\neq\ell}}^{r} a_{i_j} \log a_{i_j} + \sum_{j=r+1}^{m} a_{i_j} \log(a_{i_j}/2)].$$

We must show that this expression is less than or equal to T . That is, we need to show

$$a_\ell + a_\ell \log(a_\ell/2) \leq a_\ell \log a_\ell$$

Clearly $a_\ell + a_\ell \log(a_\ell/2) = a_\ell(\log(a_\ell/2) + \log 2) = a_\ell \log a_\ell$. This completes the proof of the claim.

The first time Step 5 is executed the formula for T is bounded by $k n \log n$. Multiply by the number of input symbols and adding in the time for Steps 1 through 4 yields a total bound proportional to $n \log n$.

Experimental results and conclusions

In order to obtain timing information, the algorithm was applied to two classes of finite automata. Automata in the first class are given by $A(n) = (\{1,2,\ldots,n\},\{0,1\},\delta,\{1\})$ where $\delta(1,0) = \delta(1,1) = 1$ and $\delta(i,0) = i-1$ and $\delta(i,1) = i$ for $2 \leq i \leq n$. Automata in the second class are given (for even n) by $B(n) = (\{1,2,\ldots,n\},\{0,1\},\delta,\{i|1 \leq i \leq n/2\})$ where $\delta(i,0) = \delta(i,1) = n/2 + 2i-1$ and $\delta(n/4 + i,0) = \delta(n/4 + i,1) = 2i-1$ for $1 \leq i \leq n/4$ and $\delta(n/2 + i,0) = \delta(n/2 + i,1) = 2i-1$ for $n/2 < i \leq n$. The running times on an IBM 360/67 for the two classes are listed in Table 1.

n	A(n)	B(n)
100	$\frac{37}{60}$	$\frac{2}{3}$
1000	$5\frac{50}{60}$	$6\frac{3}{4}$
2000	$11\frac{38}{60}$	$13\frac{2}{3}$

Table 1. time in seconds

Note that A(n) is the example that requires n^2 steps for previous algorithms.

Our algorithm is particularly suited for A(n) and a detailed analysis shows that the running time should grow linearly with the number of states as the experimental evidence indicates. The worst case for our algorithm is typified by B(n) in which blocks are always partitioned equally. The running time for B(n) should grow as n log n for both the current algorithm and for previously published algorithms. The results seem to indicate that the algorithm is practical for minimizing states in finite automata (or testing equivalence of finite automata) of up to several thousand states.

References

1. Harrison, M. A., Introduction to Switching and Automata Theory, McGraw-Hill, New York, 1965.

2. Hopcroft, J. E., "An n log n Algorithm for Minimizing States in a Finite Automaton," Technical Report CS-190, Stanford University, Stanford, California, 1970.

3. McCluskey, E. J., Introduction to the Theory of Switching Circuits, McGraw-Hill, New York, 1965.

BOUNDS ON THE LENGTH OF SYNCHRONIZING SEQUENCES AND THE ORDER OF INFORMATION LOSSLESSNESS

Z. Kohavi and J. Winograd

Faculty of Electrical Engineering
Technion - Israel Institute of Technology
Haifa, Israel.

Abstract

In this paper we establish a number of bounds concerning reduced finite-state machines. In particular, we prove that the least upper bound, L, on the length of synchronizing sequences is bounded by

$$\frac{n^2 + n - 4}{2} \leq L \leq \frac{n(n + 1)(n - 1)}{6}$$

where n is the number of states.

We also prove that there exists a machine with a fixed number of inputs and outputs which is information lossless of maximal order.

The Length of Synchronizing Sequences

A synchronizing sequence of a finite-state machine M is a sequence which takes M to a specified final state, regardless of the output or the initial state. Some machines possess such sequences; others do not.

An upper bound on the length of synchronizing sequences is given in Kohavi [1], where it is shown that if a synchronizing sequence for an n-state machine exists, then its length is at most $(n - 1)^2 n/2$. It was pointed out in [1] that this bound is not the least upper bound, which is probably considerably lower.

In this paper we shall first show that the upper bound

on the length of synchronizing sequences can indeed be lowered by a constant factor. We shall next determine a lower bound for the least upper bound. In other words, we shall establish a range of values and show that the value of the least upper bound must be in that range.

Let the <u>initial uncertainty</u> [1] regarding the state of a machine be its entire set of states, $(S_1 S_2 \ldots S_n)$. The <u>uncertainty</u> regarding the state of the machine after the application of an input sequence X consists of a specific subset of the X-successors of the states contained in the initial uncertainty. If the X-successors of all the states in the initial uncertainty are identical, X is a synchronizing sequence. In this case the X-successor uncertainty is a singleton uncertainty, that is, an uncertainty consisting of only one state.

<u>Theorem 1</u>: If an n-state machine has a synchronizing sequence, or sequences, then it has one such sequence whose length is at most

$$\frac{n(n + 1)(n - 1)}{6}$$

<u>Proof</u>: A necessary condition for a machine to have a synchronizing sequence is that, under at least one input I_k, the I_k-successors of some two states S_i, S_j will be identical. The synchronization of a machine whose initial state is unknown into some state S_c can be accomplished by applying I_k to the machine so that, if it is in either S_i or S_j, it will go to the common successor; and then applying a sequence which transfers another pair of states S_p, S_q into S_i, S_j and again applying I_k to the machine to take it into the common successor, and so on. This process actually reduces the initial uncertainty $(S_1 S_2 S_3 \ldots S_n)$ to the singleton uncertainty (S_c).

Suppose now that $k - 1$ states have already been taken out of the uncertainty which presently thus consists of $n - k + 1$ states. We wish to determine an upper bound on the length of the sequence needed to reduce the uncertainty by another state, that is, to reduce it to $n - k$ states. Suppose also that S_u and S_v are the states that will now be taken by this sequence into a common successor. The present uncertainty, U, thus consists of S_u, S_v and the remaining $n - k - 1$ states. The length of the required sequence depends on the number of pairs of states through which S_uS_v pass before reaching the common successor. This number will be maximized if S_uS_v do not pass through any other pair of states contained in the remaining $n - k - 1$ states of the uncertainty. (Because in such a case we could use that pair of states to reduce the uncertainty.) For the same reason S_uS_v should not pass through any pair of states contained in the successors of these $n - k - 1$ states.

The length of the sequence to be determined will thus be maximized if the uncertainty-successors of U will all contain the same $n - k - 1$ states and only S_uS_v will pass through various pairs of states. The successors of S_uS_v can be any pair of states not contained in these $n - k - 1$ states. Since there are $n - (n - k - 1) = k + 1$ such states, there are $k(k + 1)/2$ pairs of possible successors to S_uS_v. Consequently, at most $k(k + 1)/2$ inputs (which is equal to $1 + 2 + 3 + \ldots + k$) are needed to take out the k-th state from the uncertainty.

To reduce the initial uncertainty $(S_1S_2 \ldots S_n)$ to a singleton uncertainty, a sequence of length

$$1 + (1+2) + (1+2+3) + \ldots + (1+2+3+\ldots+n-1) = \sum_{k=2}^{n} \frac{k(k-1)}{2}$$

is needed. Since $k(k - 1)/2 = 0$ for $k = 1$, we can take the sum from 1 to n, i.e.

$$\sum_{k=1}^{n} \frac{k(k-1)}{2} = \frac{1}{2} \sum_{k=1}^{n} k^2 - \frac{1}{2} \sum_{k=1}^{n} k$$

$$= \frac{1}{2}\left[\frac{n(n + 1)(2n + 1)}{6} - \frac{3n(n + 1)}{6}\right]$$

$$= \frac{n(n + 1)(n - 1)}{6} \quad \Delta$$

<u>Theorem 2</u>: For every n, there exists an n-state machine which has a synchronizing sequence of length

$$\frac{n^2 + n - 4}{2}$$

Proof: A machine that satisfies the theorem is given in Table I. If the initial uncertainty is $(1\ 2\ 3\ \ldots\ n)$, only one input, I_o, is needed to take the first state out of that uncertainty. Thereafter, it is easy to show by means of the testing graph [1], that after k states have been taken out of the initial uncertainty, $k + 2$ inputs are required in order to take out the $k + 1$st state. Consequently, to reduce the initial uncertainty to a singleton uncertainty, we need

$$1 + 3 + 4 + 5 + \ldots + n$$

input. This sum is equal to

$$\frac{n(n+1)}{2} - 2 = \frac{n^2 + n - 4}{2} \qquad \Delta$$

The synchronizing sequence for the machine of Table I is given by

$$(I_o)(I_1I_1I_o)(I_2I_1I_1I_o)(I_3I_2I_1I_1I_o)\ldots(I_kI_{k-1}\ldots I_2I_1I_1I_o)\ldots$$
$$\ldots(I_{n-2}I_{n-3}\ldots I_2I_1I_1I_o)$$

Combining the results in Theorems 1 and 2 we obtain:

Corollary: The least upper bound, L, on the length of synchronizing sequences is bounded by

$$\frac{n^2 + n - 4}{2} \leq L \leq \frac{n(n+1)(n-1)}{6} \qquad \Delta$$

The problem of determining the exact value of L is still open.

Information Losslessness of Finite Order

A machine is said to be information lossless of finite order if the knowledge of the initial state and the first μ output symbols is sufficient to determine uniquely the first input symbol. The integer μ is said to be the order of losslessness if μ is the least integer satisfying the above definition.

The upper bound on the order of information losslessness was established by Huffman [2] and Even [3], who proved that if an n-state machine is information lossless of finite order μ, then

$$\mu \leq \frac{(n - 1)n}{2} + 1$$

Kohavi [1] (see Problem 14-14) proved that this bound cannot be lowered and thus is the least upper bound for μ. The proof was accomplished by constructing a machine which for any given n is information lossless of order μ, where $\mu = 1 + (n - 1)n/2$. The number of inputs and outputs of the machine in [1], however, are functions of n. In fact, it has $n - 1$ inputs and approximately $2n$ outputs. Our aim in this section is to show that for every n there exists a four-input seven-output machine which is information lossless of maximal order, that is, for which $\mu = 1 + (n - 1)n/2$. Such a machine is shown in Table II, where $[g]$ is the largest integer not exceeding g.

The proof that the machine of Table II is indeed information lossless of maximal order, can be accomplished with the aid of the testing graph and table [1,3]. The <u>testing table</u> has seven columns corresponding to the output symbols of the machine and n rows corresponding to its states. The entries in row S_i, column O_j, are the states that can be reached from S_i by single transitions associated with the output symbol O_j. Two states, S_i and S_j, are said to be <u>(output) compatible</u> if they can be reached from some state S_p by transitions associated with identical output sequences. The <u>testing graph</u> G is a directed graph such that:

1. Corresponding to every compatible pair of states there is a vertex in G.

2. An arc is drawn from vertex S_iS_j to vertex S_pS_q, where $p \neq q$, if and only if (S_pS_q) is a compatible implied by (S_iS_j).

It has been shown [1,3] that a machine is information lossless of order $\mu = k + 2$ if and only if: (1) Its testing graph is loop-free and the length of the longest path in the graph is k; (2) There exists no compatible pair of states consisting of repeated entries, e.g., S_mS_m. Consequently, to prove that the machine of Table II is information lossless of maximal order, it is sufficient to show that its testing graph is loop-free and contains no vertex with repeated entries, and that it contains a path of length $k = (n - 1)n/2 - 1$.

The details of the proof will not be given here and instead we shall illustrate the testing graph for the case $n = 7$. The seven-state machine is shown in Table III and its testing table is shown in Table IV. The testing graph (Fig. 1) which contains 21 vertices $(7(7 - 1)/2)$ has no loops and has a path (shown by bolder lines) connecting all these vertices. Consequently, this machine is information lossless of order $\mu = 22$.

A similar graph can be constructed for the machine of Table II for all values of n. In each case the graph will have $n(n-1)/2$ vertices and there will be a path of length $n(n - 1)/2 - 1$ connecting these vertices. Therefore, for any given n, the machine in Table II is information lossless of maximal order.

It seems that it may be possible to find an information lossless machine of maximal order with fewer inputs or outputs. It is not clear, however, whether there exists such a machine with only two inputs and two outputs.

References

[1] Kohavi, Z.: Switching and Finite Automata Theory, McGraw-Hill Book Co., pp. 1-588, 1970.

[2] Huffman, D.A.: Canonical Forms for Information Lossless Finite-State Machines, IRE Trans. Circ. Theory, Vol. CT-6, pp. 41-59, May 1959.

[3] Even, S.: On Information Lossless Automata of Finite Order, IEEE Trans. Elect. Comp., Vol. EC-14, pp. 561-569, Aug. 1965.

Table I

A Machine Having a Synchronizing Sequence of length $\frac{(n^2 + n - 4)}{2}$

P.S.	I_o	I_1	I_2	I_3	I_4		I_{k-3}	I_{k-2}	I_{k-1}	I_k		I_{n-4}	I_{n-3}	I_{n-2}
1	1	3	1	1	1		1	1	1	1		1	1	1
2	1	1	2	2	2		2	2	2	2		2	2	2
3	3	2	4	3	3		3	3	3	3		3	3	3
4	4	4	3	5	4	..	4	4	4	4	..	4	4	4
5	5	5	5	4	6		5	5	5	5		5	5	5
6	6	6	6	6	5		6	6	6	6		6	6	6
7	7	7	7	7	7		7	7	7	7		7	7	7
			⋮					⋮					⋮	
k-2	k-2	k-2	k-2	k-2	k-2		k-1	k-2	k-2	k-2		k-2	k-2	k-2
k-1	k-1	k-1	k-1	k-1	k-1		k-2	k	k-1	k-1		k-1	k-1	k-1
k	k	k	k	k	k	..	k	k-1	k+1	k	..	k	k	k
k+1	k+1	k+1	k+1	k+1	k+1		k+1	k+1	k	k+2		k+1	k+1	k+1
k+2	k+2	k+2	k+2	k+2	k+2		k+2	k+2	k+2	k+1		k+2	k+2	k+2
			⋮					⋮					⋮	
n-2	n-2	n-2	n-2	n-2	n-2		n-2	n-2	n-2	n-2		n-3	n-1	n-2
n-1	n-1	n-1	n-1	n-1	n-1	..	n-1	n-1	n-1	n-1	..	n-1	n-2	n
n	n	n	n	n	n		n	n	n	n		n	n	n-1

Table II

State Table of an Information Lossless Machine of Maximal Order

P.S.	I_1	I_2	I_3	I_4
1	2,0	3,2	2,3	2,5
2	3,0	4,2	3,3	3,5
3	4,0	5,2	4,3	4,5
⋮	⋮	⋮	⋮	⋮
i	i+1,0	i+2,2	i+1,3	i+1,5
⋮	⋮	⋮	⋮	⋮
$\left[\frac{n}{2}\right]-1$	$\left[\frac{n}{2}\right]$,0	$\left[\frac{n}{2}\right]+1$,2	$\left[\frac{n}{2}\right]$,3	$\left[\frac{n}{2}\right]$,5
$\left[\frac{n}{2}\right]$	$\left[\frac{n}{2}\right]+1$,0	$\left[\frac{n}{2}\right]+2$,1	$\left[\frac{n}{2}\right]+1$,3	$\left[\frac{n}{2}\right]+1$,5
⋮	⋮	⋮	⋮	⋮
j	j+1,0	j+2,1	j+1,3	j+1,5
⋮	⋮	⋮	⋮	⋮
n-2	n-1,0	n,1	n-1,3	n-1,5
n-1	n,0	1,1	1,6	n,5
n	1,4	1,2	n,3	2,4

Table III

A 7-State Information Lossless Machine of Maximal Order

P.S.	I_1	I_2	I_3	I_4
1	2,0	3,2	2,3	2,5
2	3,0	4,2	3,3	3,5
3	4,0	5,1	4,3	4,5
4	5,0	6,1	5,3	5,5
5	6,0	7,1	6,3	6,5
6	7,0	1,1	1,6	7,5
7	1,4	1,2	7,3	2,4

Table IV

Testing Table for the Machine in Table III

P.S. \ Output	0	1	2	3	4	5	6
1	2	-	3	2	-	2	-
2	3	-	4	3	-	3	-
3	4	5	-	4	-	4	-
4	5	6	-	5	-	5	-
5	6	7	-	6	-	6	-
6	7	1	-	-	-	7	1
7	-	-	1	7	(1,2)	-	-

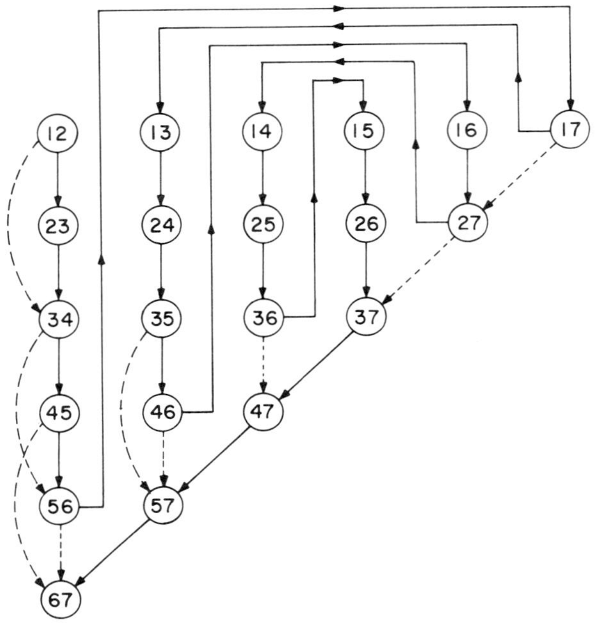

Fig. 1. Testing graph for the machine of Table III.

ON THE EXISTENCE OF A PERIODIC ANALOGUE OF A FINITE AUTOMATON

Corina Reischer and Dan A. Simovici
University of Iassy, Rumania
Department of Mathematics

Abstract

This paper contains the solution of the problem of the existence of an analogue with periodic-variable structure of a given, fixed-structure, connected automaton. The main interest of the existence of such an analogue is the possibility of saving the memory capacity needed for the construction of a given automaton.

First, we establish

Theorem 1. Let $G=(S,\Gamma)$ be a finite, strongly connected graph for which there exists a natural number p such that the length of each circuit is a multiple of p. Then the set of vertices S, can be partitioned into classes S_i, $i=\overline{1,P}$ so that

$$\Gamma S_i = S_{i+1},\ i=\overline{1,p-1} \quad \text{and} \quad \Gamma S_p = S_1.$$

Using a Boolean approach we give an algorithm which performs the search of the sets of the partition. Namely, if G is the incidence matrix of the graph G, m is the least common multiple of the lengths of the circuits connecting any vertex s to s, e is the order of the matrix G, the characteristic vector of the set S_k will be $\chi_{S_k} = G^{me+k}\chi_S$, where χ_S is the characteristic vector of a certain, initial vertex.

By considering the graph G(A) related to a Moore automaton A it is possible to obtain, using theorem 1 and the algorithm which was given earlier, an algorithm which solves the problem.

EVERY FINITE SEQUENTIAL MACHINE IS LINEARLY REALIZABLE

G. T. Herman

Department of Computer Science
State University of New York at Buffalo
Amherst, New York 14226

Abstract

We prove that, using the definitions of realization of one sequential machine by another which appear to be most widely accepted today, every finite sequential machine is linearly realizable over any field of infinite characteristic and even over some fields of finite characteristic. This will give us, as corollaries, answers to two open questions posed in an earlier publication. We shall show that our result is the strongest we can hope for, putting various additional restrictions on the definition of linear realizability would result in the existence of not linearly realizable finite sequential machines.

Introduction

In recent years, a great deal of research has been concerned with the problem of linear realizability of finite sequential machines. Davis [2] gave a survey of a large portion of this research and some aspects of it are also discussed in [4], [6], [7], [9], [12] and [13]. In spite of the large literature on the topic, it is not even clear whether the problem has been solved. The reason for this is that there is a lot of confusion as to the precise statement of the problem.

A statement of the problem which would probably be acceptable to everybody is: "Give an algorithm which for any finite sequential machine M decides whether or not there exists a linear sequential machine M' such that M' is a realization of M." Some would wish to attach that "and if the answer is yes, then the algorithm must produce such an M'."

How can such a simple statement lead to so great a confusion? There are a number of reasons.

(i) The definition of "realization" of a sequential machine by another is not generally agreed on. In Herman [9] three definitions (those from [3] and [8], from [4] and [7] and from [2]) were examined, and they were found to be pairwise different. In extreme cases it was possible to give a finite minimal sequential machine M which is realizable by a finite minimal linear sequential machine according to one definition, but such that there is no linear sequential machine (finite or infinite) which realizes M according to another definition.

(ii) It is also not generally agreed what sort of linear sequential machines are acceptable for realization. Must they be over the field GF(2) of two elements or do we allow any field of characteristic 2? For some, any field with prime number of elements is a reasonable restriction, while others argue that any finite field should be allowed. In [4], [5], [7], [9], [10] and [13] linear sequential machines over infinite fields are discussed. Should we call the sequential machine M linearly realizable if the M' is an infinite linear sequential machine?

(iii) If we allow linear sequential machines over arbitrary fields, in what sense can an algorithm be given which produces M'?

The present paper is an addition to some earlier work of the author (of which [9] and [10] are examples) designed to clear up this confusion. In [9], we have discussed the exact conditions under which realization according to one definition implies realization according to another. In [4], we have discussed how the notion of computable fields (see [11]) can be used to discuss decision problems involving linear sequential machines over some infinite fields, and, in [10], we have extended the concept of computability to deal with elements of an arbitrary field. In the present paper we wish to clarify the effect of the choice of allowable underlying fields under various definitions of realization.

Our most interesting result is (Theorems 1 and 2) that using either of two generally accepted definitions of realization (used e.g. in [3] and [8], and in [4] and [7], respectively) every finite sequential machine is linearly realizable over any field of infinite characteristic and even over some fields of finite characteristic. We shall also show (Theorem 3) that it is not the infinite size of the field which guarantees linear realizability, using the same definitions of realization there exist a finite sequential machine M and an infinite field F, such that M is not linearly realizable over F. In fact, we shall give a complete characterization of fields according to whether or not it is true that all finite sequential machines are linearly realizable over the field in question.

The rest of the paper is devoted to showing that using more restrictive definitions of realization (those given in [4], [6], [7], [12] and [13]) there are finite sequential machines which are not linearly realizable. Even with the most inclusive definitions, if we put some restrictions on the kind of state splitting we allow, we shall find some not linearly realizable finite sequential machines. So both the choice of allowable fields and the choice of definition of realization have a large effect on whether a given sequential machine is linearly realizable.

The present paper is self-contained in the sense that all definitions (except those of very basic algebra) will be explicitly given and all results used from other works will be stated in detail, though not proved. However, those without some basic knowledge of both abstract algebra and sequential machine theory will probably find this paper hard to follow. Probably the best single work for background reading is [7].

The remainder of this introduction will give formal definitions of the basic concepts used in the paper as well as our notational convention.

If Σ is a set, Σ^* denotes the set of all strings of finite length formed from elements of Σ, including the empty string, which we denote by Λ. $\Sigma^+ = \Sigma^* - \{\Lambda\}$.

If Σ and Δ are sets, $\Sigma \times \Delta$ denotes the set of ordered pairs with first element from Σ and second from Δ. $\phi : \Sigma \to \Delta$ indicates that ϕ is a function (mapping) from Σ into Δ.

Definition 1. A sequential machine is a 5-tuple $M = \langle Q, \Sigma, \Delta, \delta, \lambda \rangle$, where

(i) Q is a nonempty set of states;
(ii) Σ is a nonempty set of input symbols;
(iii) Δ is a nonempty set of output symbols;
(iv) $\delta : Q \times \Sigma \to Q$ is called the direct transition function;
(v) $\lambda : Q \times \Sigma \to \Delta$ is called the output function.

We shall say that a sequential machine $M = \langle Q, \Sigma, \Delta, \delta, \lambda \rangle$ is finite when Q, Σ, and Δ are finite.

It is necessary to extend both the transition function and the output function. This is done in the conventional manner as follows.

$\delta: Q \times \Sigma^* \to Q$. For each $q \in Q$, $x \in \Sigma^*$ and $a \in \Sigma$,

$$\delta(q, \Lambda) = q,$$

$$\delta(q, xa) = \delta(\delta(q, x), a).$$

$\lambda: Q \times \Sigma^+ \to \Delta$. For each $q \in Q$, $x \in \Sigma^*$ and $a \in \Sigma$,

$$\lambda(q, xa) = \lambda(\delta(q, x), a).$$

Furthermore, with each state $q \in Q$ we associate a function $\lambda_q: \Sigma^+ \to \Delta$, defined by

$$\lambda_q(x) = \lambda(q, x),$$

for all $x \in \Sigma^+$.

Definition 2. Let $M = \langle Q, \Sigma, \Delta, \delta, \lambda \rangle$ be a sequential machine. A machine $M' = \langle Q', \Sigma', \Delta', \delta', \lambda' \rangle$ is said to be a submachine of M if and only if

$Q' \subset Q$,

$\Sigma' \subset \Sigma$,

$\Delta' \subset \Delta$,

δ' is δ restricted to $Q' \times \Sigma'$,

λ' is λ restricted to $Q' \times \Sigma'$.

Definition 3. Let $M = \langle Q, \Sigma, \Delta, \delta, \lambda \rangle$ and $M' = \langle Q', \Sigma, \Delta, \delta', \lambda' \rangle$ be two sequential machines with the same input and output alphabet.

We say that a state q of M is equivalent to a state q' of M' if and only if

$$\lambda_q = \lambda'_{q'}$$

The machines M and M' are said to be <u>equivalent</u> if and only if

$$\{\lambda_q | q \in Q\} = \{\lambda'_{q'} | q' \in Q'\}$$

A sequential machine is said to be <u>minimal</u> if and only if it is not equivalent to any proper submachine of itself.

We shall use the following result in some of our proofs.

<u>Proposition 1</u>. If state q of sequential $M = \langle Q, \Sigma, \Delta, \delta, \lambda \rangle$ is equivalent to state q' of sequential machine $M' = \langle Q', \Sigma, \Delta, \delta', \lambda' \rangle$, then, for all $a \in \Sigma$, state $\delta(q, a)$ of M is equivalent to state $\delta'(q', a)$ of M'.

We shall assume that the reader knows the definition of a <u>field</u> [1; p.35] and <u>subfield</u> [1; p.36]. The <u>characteristic</u> of a field [1; p.388] is the least positive integer m such that the unity element of the field added to itself m times gives the zero element of the field. If there is no such positive integer m, we say that the field has characteristic ∞ (infinity). The following is easy to prove. (See e.g. [1; p.388, Theorem 11].)

<u>Proposition 2</u>. If a field has characteristic m, then <u>any</u> non-zero element added to itself m times gives the zero element of the field.

We now introduce the special class of machines with which we shall deal.

If F is a field and m is a non-negative integer, let F_m be the vector space of column vectors of dimension m over F. Note that $F_0 = \{0\}$. (The necessary algebra is discussed in [1; Chapters VII and VIII].)

Definition 4. A linear sequential machine M (LSM for short) is a sequential machine $M = \langle Q, \Sigma, \Delta, \delta, \lambda \rangle$ with the following special properties. There exists a field F and non-negative integers n, k, and l such that $Q = F_n$, $\Sigma = F_k$, and $\Delta = F_l$. Furthermore, there exists an $n \times n$ matrix $\underline{A}$, an $n \times k$ matrix $\underline{B}$, an $l \times n$ matrix $\underline{C}$ and an $l \times k$ matrix $\underline{D}$ such that for each $(q, a) \in Q \times \Sigma$,

$$\delta(q, a) = \underline{A}q + \underline{B}a,$$

$$\lambda(q, a) = \underline{C}q + \underline{D}a.$$

Such a linear sequential machine M will sometimes be denoted by $\langle F, n, k, l, \underline{A}, \underline{B}, \underline{C}, \underline{D} \rangle$ or $\langle F, \underline{A}, \underline{B}, \underline{C}, \underline{D} \rangle$, and we shall say that M is over the field F.

In some of the theorems, we shall talk about obtaining effectively the realization of a machine M over a field F. Since in all cases the realization will only involve elements of a computable subfield of F, the notion of effectiveness for such fields, developed by Rabin [11], will apply. A more general approach, which applies to all fields, but whose results are in accord with Rabin's in the special case of computable fields, can be found in [10]. We shall make no further direct reference to either of these works. Our terminology when talking about effective processes involving arbitrary fields will be that of Herman and Isard [10].

We shall give various definitions of realization. Any one of them will be referred to as "i-realization" where $i \in \{1,2,3,4,5\}$. For each of these concepts we shall adopt the following convention.

A sequential machine M is said to be i-realizable over the field F if and only if there exists an LSM M' over F such that M' is an i-realization of M.

1. The most general definition of realization.

The following definition of realization is the one used by Hartmanis & Stearns [8]. It is also the one adopted, for example, by Gallaire [3]. It has been shown in [9] that this definition is more general than other commonly used definitions of realization, i.e. if M' is a realization of M using another definition, then M' is also a realization of M using the one given below. The converse is not true in general. We shall see further examples of this in the present paper.

We shall call this realization 1-realization, in order to distinguish it from other definitions of realization which we shall discuss later on.

Definition 5. Let $M = \langle Q,\Sigma,\Delta,\delta,\lambda\rangle$ and $M' = \langle Q',\Sigma',\Delta',\delta',\lambda'\rangle$ be two sequential machines. M' is said to be a 1-realization of M if and only if there exist three mappings α_1, β_1, and ϕ_1 which satisfy the following conditions.

(i)$_1$ $\alpha_1 : \Sigma \to \Sigma'$.

(ii)$_1$ $\beta_1 : \Delta' \to \Delta$.

(iii)$_1$ ϕ_1 maps Q into nonempty subsets of Q'.

(iv)$_1$ For each $(q, a) \in Q \times \Sigma$ and $q' \in \phi_1 q$,

$$\delta'(q', \alpha_1 a) \in \phi_1 \delta(q, a).$$

(v)$_1$ For each $(q, a) \in Q \times \Sigma$ and $q' \in \phi_1 q$,

$$\beta_1 \lambda'(q', \alpha_1 a) = \lambda(q, a).$$

Theorem 1. For any finite sequential machine $M = \langle Q,\Sigma,\Delta,\delta,\lambda\rangle$ and any field F of characteristic ∞, there exists a LSM $M' = \langle F,1,1,1,\underline{A},\underline{B},\underline{C},\underline{D}\rangle$ such that M' is a

1-realization of M. Furthermore, given M, M' can be effectively obtained.

The proof of this and all other theorems in this paper will be omitted, since they will appear in a more complete publication in the Journal of Computer and Systems Sciences.

First we examine whether the condition that the field F is of characteristic ∞ is necessary. The answer to this question is that it depends on the field.

In any field F of finite characteristic p, p will be prime [1; p. 388, Theorem 12], and the additive subgroup generated by the unity element is a subfield isomorphic to the field J_p of integers modulo p [1; p. 389]. For notational convenience, we shall assume that J_p is actually a subfield of F and we shall denote its elements by 0, 1, 2, ..., p-1. An element z of F is said to be <u>algebraic</u> over J_p if there exists a positive integer n, and $c_0, c_1, \ldots, c_n$ in J_p such that

$$c_n z^n + c_{n-1} z^{n-1} + \ldots + c_1 z + c_0 = 0.$$

Otherwise z is said to be <u>transcendental</u> over J_p.

<u>Theorem 2</u>. For any finite sequential $M = \langle Q,\Sigma,\Delta,\delta,\lambda \rangle$, for any prime number p and for any field F of characteristic p which contains an element z which is transcendental over J_p, there exists a LSM $M' = \langle F,1,1,1,\underline{A},\underline{B},\underline{C},\underline{D} \rangle$ such that M' is a 1-realization of M. Furthermore, given M, M' can be effectively obtained provided we are given z.

Theorem 3. There exists a finite minimal sequential machine such that, for any field F of finite characteristic p in which every element is algebraic over J_p, and for any LSM M' over F, M' is not a 1-realization of M.

To summarize: If a field F has characteristic ∞ or if it is of finite characteristic p and there is an element of F which is transcendental over J_p, then every finite sequential machine is linearly 1-realizable over F. For all other fields G, there exists a finite sequential machine which is not linearly 1-realizable over G.

2. Realizations using homomorphic images.

There is another definition of realization which is frequently used in the literature (see e.g. Davis [2]). We shall call it, following Herman [9], 3-realization.

Definition 6. Let $M = \langle Q, \Sigma, \Delta, \delta, \lambda \rangle$ and $M' = \langle Q', \Sigma', \Delta', \delta', \lambda' \rangle$ be two sequential machines. M is said to be a homomorphic image of M' if and only if there exist three mappings α_3, β_3 and ϕ_3 which satisfy the following conditions.

$(i)_3$ α_3 maps Σ' onto Σ.

$(ii)_3$ β_3 maps Δ' onto Δ.

$(iii)_3$ ϕ_3 maps Q' onto Q.

$(iv)_3$ For each $(q', a') \in Q' \times \Sigma'$,

$$\phi_3\delta'(q', a') = \delta(\phi_3 q', \alpha_3 a').$$

$(v)_3$ For each $(q', a') \in Q' \times \Sigma'$,

$$\beta_3\lambda'(q', a') = \lambda(\phi_3 q', \alpha_3 a').$$

If, in addition, α_3, β_3, and ϕ_3 are one-to-one, M is said to be an <u>isomorphic image</u> of M'.

<u>Definition 7</u>. Let $M = \langle Q, \Sigma, \Delta, \delta, \lambda \rangle$ and $M' = \langle Q', \Sigma', \Delta', \delta', \lambda' \rangle$ be two sequential machines. M' is said to be a <u>3-realization</u> of M if and only if M is a homomorphic image of a submachine of M'.

It has been shown in [9] that 1-realization and 3-realization are not interchangeable concepts. An example is given (Theorem 4 (iv)) of a finite sequential machine M and a finite minimal LSM M' such that M' is a 1-realization of M, but there exist <u>no</u> finite LSM M" such that M" is a 3-realization of M. However, the similarity between the two definitions is great, as can be seen from the following theorem.

<u>Theorem 4</u>. Let M and M' be two sequential machines.

(i) If M' is a 3-realization of M, then M' is a 1-realization of M.

(ii) If M' is a 1-realization of M such that α_1 is one-to-one, β_1 is onto and ϕ_1 maps Q into disjoint subsets of Q', then M' is a 3-realization of M.

A consequence of this theorem is that as far as the results of the last section are concerned there is no difference between 1-realization and 3-realization. We summarize this in the following theorem.

<u>Theorem 5</u>. If a field F has characteristic ∞ or if it is of finite characteristic p and there is an element z of F which is transcendental over J_p, then every finite

sequential machine is linearly 3-realizable over F. For all other fields G, there exists a finite minimal sequential machine which is not linearly 3-realizable over G.

Theorem 5 provides us with an answer to two questions left open by Herman [9; p. 817 and p. 824]. These questions concerned themselves with the existence of 1-realizable, respectively 2-realizable, finite sequential machines which are not linearly 3-realizable. Since every finite sequential machine is linearly 3-realizable, the answer to both the questions in [9] is in the negative.

1-realization and 3-realization are probably the most generally accepted definitions of realization. In the remainder of the paper we shall investigate the effect on our basic theorems of some commonly used restrictions on realizations.

3. Realizations with restricted decoding.

Gallaire, Gray, Harrison & Herman [4] found that by restricting their attention to those realizations where the decoding function β_1 maps the relevant subset of Δ' one-to-one onto Δ, some rather interesting results can be shown which do not hold for 1-realizations in general. Their definition has also been adopted in the book on LSM's by Harrison [7].

<u>Definition 8</u>. Let $M = \langle Q,\Sigma,\Delta,\delta,\lambda\rangle$ and $M' = \langle Q',\Sigma',\Delta',\delta',\lambda'\rangle$ be two sequential machines. M' is said to be a <u>2-realization</u> of M if and only if there exist three mappings α_2, β_2, ϕ_2 which satisfy the following conditions.

$(i)_2$ $\alpha_2 : \Sigma \to \Sigma'$.

$(ii)_2$ $\beta_2 : \Delta \to \Delta'$ and β_2 is one-to-one.

$(iii)_2$ ϕ_2 maps Q into nonempty subsets of Q'.

$(iv)_2$ For each $(q, a) \in Q \times \Sigma$ and $q' \in \phi_2 q$, $\delta'(q', \alpha_2 a) \in \phi_2 \delta(q, a)$.

$(v)_2$ For each $(q, a) \in Q \times \Sigma$ and $q' \in \phi_2 q$, $\lambda'(q', \alpha_2 a) = \beta_2 \lambda(q, a)$.

The relation between 1-realization and 2-realization is discussed in Section 2, the relation between 2-realization and 3-realization is discussed in Section 4 of [9], while Chapter 4 of [7] is devoted to a discussion of 2-realizations. From the point of view of the present paper, the relevant result is that there exist finite sequential machines which are not linearly 2-realizable over any field.

Theorem 6. There exists a finite minimal sequential machine M and a finite minimal LSM M' such that M' is both a 1-realization and a 3-realization of M, and yet there exists no LSM M'' (over any field) such that M'' is a 2-realization of M.

4. Realizations with finite state splitting.

One particular objection which may be brought up to our proofs of Theorems 1, 2 and 5 is that we allow $\phi_1 q$ to be infinite, i.e. an infinite number of states in the realization correspond to the same state in the machine being realized. In this section we shall show that this condition is necessary, if we only allow $\phi_1 q$ to be finite, there will be finite sequential machines which are not linearly 1-realizable.

Definition 9. A sequential machine M' is said to be a 1-realization with finite state splitting of a sequential machine $M = \langle Q, \Sigma, \Delta, \delta, \lambda \rangle$ if and only if M' is a 1-realization of M and ϕ_1 can be chosen in such a way that $\phi_1 q$ is finite for all $q \in Q$. If, in addition, $\phi_1 q$ has exactly one element for all $q \in Q$, M' is said to be a 1-realization without state splitting of the sequential machine M.

In [9; Theorem 3] it was shown that there exists a finite minimal sequential machine M which is linearly 1-realizable with finite state splitting by a finite minimal LSM, but which is not linearly 1-realizable without state splitting. We shall now show that there are finite minimal sequential machines M which are not linearly 1-realizable with finite state splitting.

Theorem 7. There exists a finite minimal sequential machine M such that for any LSM M', over any field, M' is not a 1-realization with finite state splitting of M.

Thus there exist finite sequential machines which are not 1-realizable with finite state splitting. The notion of finite state splitting carries over to 3-realizations as well, and we shall now show that there exist finite sequential machines which are not 3-realizable with finite state splitting.

Definition 10. A sequential machine M' is said to be a 3-realization with finite state splitting of a sequential machine $M = \langle Q, \Sigma, \Delta, \delta, \lambda \rangle$ if and only if there exists a submachine $M'' = \langle Q'', \Sigma'', \Delta'', \delta'', \lambda'' \rangle$ of M' such that M is a homomorphic image of M'' in which for every $q \in Q$ the set of all $q'' \in Q''$ such that $\phi_3 q'' = q$

is finite. If ϕ_3 is actually one-to-one, then M' is said to be a <u>3-realization without state splitting</u> of M.

In [9; Theorem 5] it was shown that there exists a finite minimal sequential machine M which is linearly 3-realizable with finite state splitting by a finite minimal LSM, but which is not linearly 3-realizable without state splitting. We shall now show that there are finite sequential machines M which are not linearly 3-realizable with finite state splitting.

<u>Theorem 8</u>. There exists a finite minimal sequential machine M such that for any LSM M', over any field, M' is not a 3-realization with finite state splitting of M.

5. Realizations using isomorphic images.

Apart from Harrison's work [7], there are two other books (Reusch [12] and Gill [6]) entirely devoted to LSM's. Both of these books deal to some extent with the problem of linear realizability, both giving fairly restrictive definitions of realization. For the sake of completeness we examine how our results carry over to these definitions. In the present section, we discuss Reusch's work.

<u>Definition 11</u>. Let $M = \langle Q,\Sigma,\Delta,\delta,\lambda\rangle$ and $M' = \langle Q',\Sigma',\Delta',\delta',\lambda'\rangle$ be two sequential machines. M' is said to be a <u>4-realization</u> of M if and only if M is equivalent to an isomorphic image of a submachine of M'.

Although 4-realization at first sight appears to be a special case of 3-realization, that first impression is false. This is due to the fact that in a 4-realization M has to be only equivalent to an isomorphic image of a submachine of M'. Thus if M has lots of equivalent states, so that it has in fact more states than M', M can still be an equivalent to an isomorphic image of a submachine of M', but it cannot possibly be a homomorphic image of a submachine of M'. In a later work, Reusch [13] has redefined realization to be a special case of both 4-realization and 3-realization by saying that M' is a realization of M if and only if M is an isomorphic image of a submachine of M'.

For our present purpose, i.e. to decide whether all finite sequential machines are linearly realizable under given definitions of realizability, we need not get to the above mentioned further restriction. It is already the case for 4-realization that there exist finite sequential machines which are not linearly 4-realizable over any field. This will be a consequence of the following theorem.

Theorem 9. If a sequential machine M' is a 4-realization of a sequential machine M, then M' is a 2-realization of M.

Theorem 10. There exists a finite minimal sequential machine M and a finite minimal LSM M' such that M' is both a 1-realization and a 3-realization of M, and yet there exists no LSM M" (over any field) such that M" is a 4-realization of M.

We wish to note that the M' and M in the above theorem can be chosen so that M' is both a 1-realization and a 3-realization of M without state splitting.

Our definition of 4-realization is actually a slightly generalized version of Reusch's definition of realization. Reusch [12] only discusses isomorphic images in case of machines which have the same input and output alphabets. Hence his realizations are special cases of our 4-realizations and, in consequence, Theorem 10 is valid for his definition as well.

6. Realizations using equivalences.

Finally we turn to the definition in Gill [6]. This definition is very restrictive.

Definition 12. Let M and M' be two sequential machines. M' is said to be a 5-realization of M if and only if M' is equivalent to M.

Due to the restrictive nature of the definition, the following theorems require no proof.

Theorem 11. If the sequential machine M' is a 5-realization of M, then M' is a 4-realization of M.

Theorem 12. There exists a finite minimal sequential machine M such that there is no LSM M' (over any field) such that M' is a 5-realization of M.

7. Conclusions.

We have proved that under the most inclusive (as well as most popular) definitions of realization every finite sequential machine is linearly realizable over all fields of infinite characteristic and even over some fields of finite characteristic. In the proof we have allowed a state to split into infinitely many states. We have shown that this is necessary, that allowing only finite state splitting we get some finite sequential machines which are not linearly realizable. We have also proved that under more restrictive definitions of realization there exist some not linearly realizable sequential machines.

This paper mainly dealt with the problem whether or not every finite sequential machine is linearly realizable under a particular definition of linear realizability. There remains the problem of giving algorithms of the kind described in the introduction for those definitions for which not every finite sequential machine is linearly realizable. This is always the case if the field is finite, and most proposed algorithms were given to decide linear realizability over a finite field. The results of the present paper reinforce the claim of Herman [9] that there is a strong case for a survey of proposed algorithms with a careful examination of the definitions of realization for which they work. Due to the large amount of literature concerning such algorithms, this task will not be trivial.

Acknowledgement

The author is grateful to Professor Michael Harrison for the suggestion to investigate the existence of nonlinear machines with respect to the most general definition of realization.

References

1. G. Birkhoff and S. Maclane, "A Survey of Modern Algebra". Revised Edition. MacMillan Company, New York, 1953.

2. W. A. Davis, Linearity of sequential machines A critical review. IEEE Conference Record of 1968 Ninth Annual Symposium on Switching and Automata Theory, 427-430 (1968).

3. H. Gallaire, Decomposition of linear sequential machines II. Math. Systems Theory. 4, 168-190 (1970).

4. H. Gallaire, J. N. Gray, M. A. Harrison and G. T. Herman, Infinite linear sequential machines. J. Computer System Sciences. 2, 381-419 (1968).

5. H. Gallaire and M. A. Harrison, Decomposition of linear sequential machines. Math. Systems Theory. 3, 246-287 (1969).

6. A. Gill, "Linear Sequential Circuits". McGraw-Hill Book Company, New York, 1966.

7. M. A. Harrison, "Lectures on Linear Sequential Machines". Academic Press, New York, 1969.

8. J. Hartmanis and R. E. Stearns, "Algebraic Structure Theory of Sequential Machines". Prentice-Hall, Inc., Englewood, New Jersey, 1966.

9. G. T. Herman, When is a sequential machine the realization of another? Proceedings of the ACM International Computing Symposium, Bonn, 1970, pp. 792-827. (An updated version is to appear in Math. System Theory 5, (1971).)

10. G. T. Herman and S. Isard, Computability over arbitrary fields. J. London Math. Soc. (2). 2, 73-79 (1970).

11. M. O. Rabin, Computable algebra, general theory and theory of computable fields. Trans. Am. Math. Soc. 87, 341-360 (1960).

12. B. Reusch, "Lineare Automaten". Bibliographisches Institut, Mannheim, 1969.

13. B. Reusch, Zur Realisierung endlicher Automaten uber Algebren. Habilitationsschrift, University of Bonn, 1970.

ON THE LIMITS OF LINEARITY*

John F. Meyer**
Bernard P. Zeigler***

The University of Michigan
Ann Arbor, Michigan 48104

Introduction

It is generally acknowledged that linear systems and, in particular, linear sequential systems (see, for example, [3], [4], [6], and [7]) are limited in their behavioral capabilities, but the exact extent of such limitations has remained unclear. In this paper, we show that a very simple and fundamental sequential system, the common Set-Reset Flip-Flop, cannot be "realized" by any linear system. That this remains true for finite linear machines, even allowing such weakenings of the notion of "realization" as state splitting and computation rate slow down, suggests that we are exposing some rather basic limitations of linear systems. We also expand the notion of "linear system" to include the case where the input, state and output spaces are modules. We show that these ring based machines are more powerful than the common field based machines but they still suffer the basic limitations of linearity.

Simulation and Realization

Because the notions of "simulation" and "realization" have been given various formalizations in the context of

---

*This work was supported by National Aeronautics and Space Administration (Grant No. NGR-23-005-463), National Institutes of Health (Grant No. GM-12236) and the National Science Foundation (Grant No. GJ-519).

**Department of Electrical and Computer Engineering and Department of Computer and Communication Sciences.
***Department of Computer and Communication Sciences.

machine theory (cf. [1], [6], [8], and [9], for example), it is important that these concepts (and their various restrictions) be carefully established before addressing the question of whether a sequential machine is "simulatable" or "realizable" by some linear sequential machine. If $M = (I,Q,Z,\delta,\lambda)$ is a (Mealy) *sequential machine* and $\overline{\delta}$ and $\overline{\lambda}$ denote the natural extensions of δ and λ to $Q \times I^*$ and $Q \times I^+$, the *state behavior of M in q* ($q \in Q$) is the function $\alpha_q: I^* \to Q$ where $\alpha_q(x) = \overline{\delta}(q,x)$, for all $x \in I^*$ and the (input-output) *behavior of M in q* is the function $\beta_q: I^+ \to Z$ where $\beta_q(x) = \overline{\lambda}(q,x)$, for all $x \in I^+$. Accordingly, for all $q \in Q$, behavior is related to state behavior by $\beta_q(xa) = \lambda(\alpha_q(x),a)$, for all $x \in I^*$, $a \in I$. The most general notion of simulation considered here requires only that behavior (and not necessarily state behavior) be imitated by the simulating machine and permits arbitrary slow-down in the process of simulation. More precisely, if $M = (I,Q,Z,\delta,\lambda)$ and $M' = (I',Q',Z',\delta',\lambda')$ then

Definition 1: M' *simulates** M if there is a triple of functions $(\sigma_1,\sigma_2,\sigma_3)$ where $\sigma_1: I^+ \to (I')^+$ is a semigroup homomorphism, $\sigma_2: Q \to Q'$, $\sigma_3: Z'' \to Z$ where $Z'' \subseteq Z'$, such that, for all $q \in Q$ and all $x \in I^+$, $\beta_q(x) = \sigma_3(\beta'_{\sigma_2(q)}(\sigma_1(x)))$.†

We then reserve the term "realizes" for the special case where M' simulates M in "real time", that is:

Definition 2: M' *realizes* M if M simulates M' under some triple of functions $(\sigma_1,\sigma_2,\sigma_3)$ such that $\sigma_1(I) \subseteq I'$.

The restriction $\sigma_1(I) \subseteq I'$ is equivalent to requiring that $\ell g(x) = \ell g(\sigma_1(x))$, for all $x \in I^+$ ($\ell g(x)$ is the *length* of x), whence the interpretation as simulation in real time. As noted by [10] and others, this strictly behavioral definition is equivalent to the more structurally oriented definition of Hartmanis and Stearns [8] in terms of an "assignment" of M into M'. The above definition, however, is more general than the concept (bearing the same name) employed by Harrison [6] in the study of linear realizability. The latter requires a one-to-one output assignment and is equivalent to the following restricted type of realization:

*Termed "weakly simulates" by [1].

†Note that this condition implies $\{\beta'_{\sigma_2(q)}(\sigma_1(x)) | q \in Q, x \in I^+\} \subseteq Z''$.

Definition 3: M' *1-realizes* M if M' realizes M under some triple of functions $(\sigma_1,\sigma_2,\sigma_3)$ such that σ_3 is one-to-one. In the section that follows, we will establish that 1-realizations are indeed restrictive with regard to linear realizability (Theorem 4).

We also wish to consider "homomorphic" simulations wherein state behavior is simulated as well as input-output behavior, that is,

Definition 4: M' *homomorphically simulates* M if there is a triple of functions (η_1,η_2,η_3) where $\eta_1:I \to (I')^+$, $\eta_2:Q'' \to Q$ (onto) where $Q'' \subseteq Q'$, $\eta_3:Z'' \to Z$ where $Z'' \subseteq Z'$, such that, for all $q \in Q''$ and $a \in I$, i) $\alpha_{\eta_2(q)}(a) = \eta_2(\alpha'_q(\eta_1(a)))$, and ii) $\beta_{\eta_2(q)}(a) = \eta_3(\beta'_q(\eta_1(a)))$.†

If, in addition to the above conditions η_2 is one-to-one, then M' *isomorphically simulates* M.

Again, we reserve the term "realizes" for real time simulation, that is

Definition 5: M' *homomorphically (isomorphically) realizes* M if M' homomorphically (isomorphically) simulates M under some triple of functions (η_1,η_2,η_3) such that $\eta_1(I) \subset I'$.

It follows from the above definitions that if M' homomorphically simulates (realizes) M then M' simulates (realizes) M. Moreover, the homomorphic requirement is indeed a proper restriction, as evidenced by the following facts. Given any machine M and its reduced version M_R, M and M_R mutually realize one another. On the other hand, although M homomorphically realizes M_R, M_R need not homomorphically realize M (unless M is also a reduced machine). The connection between simulations (realizations) and their homomorphic restrictions can be precisely stated as follows (cf. [11]):

Theorem 1: If M and M' are sequential machines and M_R is a reduced machine equivalent to M then M' simulates (realizes) M if and only if M' homomorphically simulates (realizes) M_R.

†Note that i) implies $\{\alpha'_q(\eta_1(a)) \mid q \in Q'', a \in I\} \subseteq Q''$ and ii) implies $\{\beta'_q(\eta_1(a)) \mid q \in Q'', a \in I\} \subseteq Z''$.

Linear Sequential Machines

Let R be a ring (with a unit) and, if m is a nonnegative integer, let R^m denote the free R-module on m generators* ($R^0 = \{0\}$, where 0 is the additive unit of R). Then

Definition 6: A sequential machine $M = (I,Q,Z,\delta,\lambda)$ is a *linear sequential machine* (ℓsm) *over R* if there exist nonnegative integers k,n and ℓ such that $I = R^k$, $Q = R^n$, $Z = R^\ell$ and there exist module homomorphisms (linear transformations) $A:R^n \to R^n$, $B:R^k \to R^n$, $C:R^n \to R^\ell$ and $D:R^k \to R^\ell$ such that, for all $q \in R^n$ and $a \in R^k$, $\delta(q,a) = Aq + Ba$, and $\lambda(q,a) = Cq + Da$.

Accordingly, a ℓsm M over R can alternatively be specified as $M = (R,k,n,\ell,A,B,C,D)$ or simply $M = (R,A,B,C,D)$. The above definition is a generalization of the usual notion of an ℓsm over a field F (cf. [3], [4] or [6], for example) and is motivated by our desire to establish the "outer limits" of linearity. Certain well known properties of ℓsm's over a field hold for this more general class as well. In particular, the extended transition function $\bar{\delta}$ and the extended output function $\bar{\lambda}$ can be formulated as follows. If $M = (R,k,n,\ell,A,B,C,D)$ is a ℓsm, $q \in R^n$, and $a_1a_2\ldots a_t \in (R^k)^+$ then
$\bar{\delta}(q,a_1a_2\ldots a_t) = A^tq + \sum_{i=1}^{t} A^{t-i}Ba_i$ and $\bar{\lambda}(q,a_1a_2\ldots a_t) = C\bar{\delta}(q,a_1a_2\ldots a_{t-1}) + Da_t$.

To explore the limitations of linear structure and behavior, we will say that a given sequential machine M is *linearly simulatable (realizable, 1-realizable, homomorphically simulatable, homomorphically realizable) over R* if there is a linear machine M' over R such that M' simulates (realizes, 1-realizes, homomorphically simulates, homomorphically realizes) M. Basically our results state that the familiar Set-Reset Flip-Flop (SRF, Figure 1a) is not linearly simulatable. Actually, the results are established for the simpler Set Flip-Flop (SF, Figure 1b) which, since SF is a submachine of SRF, implies SRF is not linearly simulatable. It is also interesting to note that a delay-type network realization of SF involves multiplication in GF(2) (the two-element Galois field). Hence our results confirm the common belief that multiplication is essentially a nonlinear operation.

*Such a module is unique up to module isomorphism (cf. [5], p. 211, for example).

Linear 1-realizations

Considering first the most demanding type of realization (Definition 3) where the output decoding is required to be one-to-one, we show that the Set Flip-Flop cannot be realized by any ℓsm, whether finite or infinite over a ring or field. We need

Lemma 1: Let M be an ℓsm such that for some $q \in Q$, $a,b \in I$, $\beta_q(b^n a) = \beta_q(b^n)$ for all $n \geq 1$. (a acts as an identity for all strings of b's.) Then $\beta_q(b^{n+1}) = \beta_q(b) + nD(b-a)$ for $n \geq 0$.

Proof: $\beta_q(b^n) = \lambda(\alpha_q(b^{n-1}), b) = C\alpha_q(b^{n-1}) + Db$ for $n \geq 1$. Thus, $\beta_q(b^{n+1}) - \beta_q(b^n) = C\alpha_q(b^n) - C\alpha_q(b^{n-1})$. Now $\beta_q(b^n a) = \lambda(\alpha_q(b^n), a) = C\alpha_q(b^n) + Da$ so that $\beta_q(b^n a) = \beta_q(b^n)$ implies $C\alpha_q(b^n) + Da = C\alpha_q(b^{n-1}) + Db$. Hence $\beta_q(b^{n+1}) - \beta_q(b^n) = D(b-a)$ for $n \geq 1$. The unique solution of which is $\beta_q(b^{n+1}) = \beta_q(b) + n\,D(b-a)$ for $n \geq 0$ as claimed.

Remark: The only properties of ℓsm's relied upon above are the forms of the output and transition functions and the group nature of $(R^n,+,0)$.

Theorem 2: The Set Flip-Flop is not linearly 1-realizable.

Proof: Suppose that the SF of Figure 1b is 1-realizable by a ℓsm M' under $(\sigma_1, \sigma_2, \sigma_3)$. Let the σ_1 input encoding be given by $\sigma_1(0) = a$ and $\sigma_1(1) = b$, and let $q = \sigma_2(q_0)$. Since $\beta_{q_0}(1^n 0) = \beta_{q_0}(1^n)$ and σ_3 is 1-1, we have $\beta'_q(b^n a) = \beta'_q(b^n)$ for $n \geq 1$. Also since $\beta_{q_0}(1^2) = \beta_{q_0}(1)$ we have $\beta'_q(b^2) = \beta'_q(b)$. From Lemma 1 we must have $D(b-a) = 0$, i.e., $Db = Da$. Thus $\beta'_q(b) = Cq + Db = Cq + Da = \beta'_q(a)$, which contradicts the fact that $\beta_{q_0}(0) = 0$ and $\beta_{q_0}(1) = 1$.

To further explore the limits of linear 1-realizability, consider the m-state counter M_m of Figure 2 where M_m has the property that for every state q, $\beta_q(1^n 0) = \beta_q(1^n)$ for $n \geq 1$ and m is the least integer such that

$\beta_q(1^{m+1}) = \beta_q(1)$. Also note that the count mod m of the number of 1's in the input string appears as the output. We show that this class of counters is 1-realizable for all m by ℓsm's restricted to fields. It is interesting to note that the 1-realizability may not go through for the conventional {0,1} output counter (cf. Theorem 4).

Theorem 3: If m is the characteristic of a ring R then M_m is linearly 1-realizable over R. Conversely, M_m is linearly realizable over a ring only if m divides the ring characteristic.

Proof: Recall that the characteristic of a ring R with unit e is the additive order of e. Then we can 1-realize M_m by the ℓsm $M = (R,1,1,1,I,I,I,I)$ (whose structures are of the form $\delta(q,a) = q+a$, $\lambda(q,a) = q+a$) under $(\sigma_1,\sigma_2,\sigma_3)$ where $\sigma_1(0) = 0$, $\sigma_1(1) = e$, $\sigma_2(i) = ie$ and $\sigma_3(ie) = i$ $(0 \le i \le m-1)$.

Now suppose M_m is 1-realizable over R by a ℓsm M' under $(\sigma_1,\sigma_2,\sigma_3)$. Let $\sigma_1(0) = a$, $\sigma_1(1) = b$; then since σ_3 is 1-1 for $q = \sigma_2(q_0)$ we have $\beta'_q(b^n a) = \beta'_q(b^n)$ for $n \ge 1$ and m is the least integer such that $\beta'_q(b^{m+1}) = \beta'_q(b)$. By Lemma 1, m is the least integer such that $mD(b-a) = 0$. If $D(b-a) = 0$ then also from the lemma, $\beta_q(b^2) = \beta_q(b)$ so that $m = 1$ and m divides the ring characteristic. For $D(b-a) \neq 0$, m is the order of $D(b-a)$ in $(R^n,+,0)$ and hence the ℓcm of the additive orders of the elements appearing as components in a vector representation of $D(b-a)$. Since each of these divides the ring characteristic we have that m divides the ring characteristic as well.

Since fields have only prime characteristic we have

Corollary: The m-counter M_m is 1-realizable over a field if and only if m is a prime.

Corollary: For any integer m, M_m is 1-realizable by a ℓsm over a ring.

Proof: For every m, there is a residue class ring with characteristic m.

Corollary: For any ring (field) there is a counter not linearly 1-realizable over that ring (field).

At this point, a natural question to ask is whether the limitations implied by the above results are due basically to linearity or to restrictions imposed by 1-realizability. In other words, if slow-down and/or many-one output decoding are allowed (Definitions 1,2,4 and 5), it may be possible to linearly simulate the Set

Flip-Flop and to simulate all m-counters by field based ℓsm's. That this is indeed a possibility is evidenced by
Theorem 4: There exist machines that are linearly homomorphically realizable (over a finite field) but not linearly 1-realizable (over any ring).
Proof: Consider the machine M of Figure 4 and suppose M is 1-realizable by a ℓsm M', under $(\sigma_1,\sigma_2,\sigma_3)$. Let $a = \sigma_1(0)$, $b = \sigma_1(1)$, $q = \sigma_2(q_0)$, and $r = \sigma_2(q_1)$. Since $\beta_{q_1}(0) = \beta_{q_1}(1)$ and σ_3 is 1-1, we have $\beta'_r(a) = \beta'_r(b)$, that is, $Cr + Da = Cr + Db$. Thus $Da = Db$ which implies $\beta'_q(a) = Cq + Da = Cq + Db = \beta'_q(b)$ and consequently $\beta_{q_0}(0) = \beta_{q_0}(1)$. As this contradicts the behavior of M in q_0, M is not linearly 1-realizable over any ring.

To establish that M is linearly homomorphically realizable, consider the ℓsm M' = (GF(2),1,1,2,A,B,C,D) with the linear transformations A,B,C, and D as specified in Figure 5. Then it is easily verified that M' has the state graph of Figure 6 and, under the functions (η_1,η_2,η_3) specified in Figure 7, M' homomorphically realizes M.

Linear Simulations

Having shown that the SF is not linearly 1-realizable and that allowing many-one output mappings increases the set of realizations, it might be thought that the SF is linearly homomorphically realizable. This is not the case. Hartmanis and Davis [7] showed that if M is not a permutation machine and has no identical next state rows then M is not a homomorphic image of linear machine. In particular, the SF is not a homomorphic image of a finite linear machine since it satisfies the hypothesis of the theorem. In this section we strengthen the above result by establishing that the SF cannot be simulated (i.e., slow-down and submachines allowed) by any finite linear machine. More precisely,
Theorem 5: The Set Flip-Flop is not linearly simulatable over any finite ring.
Proof: Suppose to the contrary. Then, there exists a finite ring R and a ℓsm $M' = (R,k,n,\ell,A,B,C,D)$ such that M' simulates the SF of Figure 1b. If we let $\langle A\rangle$ denote the cyclic subsemigroup generated by the linear transformation A (in the semigroup of all linear transformations on R^n along with the operation of functional composition), then $\langle A\rangle$ has finite order (since R finite implies R^n finite)

and can be expressed in terms of its *index* r and *period* s [2] as $\langle A\rangle = \{A, A^2, \ldots, A^r, A^{r+1}, \ldots A^{r+s-1}\}$ where $A^{r+s} = A^r$. Consider now input sequences x and y (for the flip-flop M) defined as follows in terms of r,s, and the characteristic m of the ring R:

$$x = 1^{ms}0^{r+1} \text{ and } y = 0^{r+1}. \tag{1}$$

To examine the corresponding behavior of the simulating linear machine M', let $(\sigma_1, \sigma_2, \sigma_3)$ be a triple of functions under which M' simulates M, let $g = \ell g\sigma_1(0)$, $h = \ell g\ \sigma_1(1)$ and let v and w denote the encodings of the subsequences 1^{ms} and 0^r, i.e.,

$$v = \sigma_1(1^{ms}) = a_1a_2\ldots a_{msh} \text{ and } w = \sigma_1(0^r) = b_1b_2\ldots b_{rg} \tag{2}$$

where $a_i, b_i \in I' = R^k$ and we note that

$$a_i = a_{i+h} \quad (1 \le i \le (ms-1)h) \tag{3}$$

since σ_1 is a semigroup homomorphism. Then the state reached from $\sigma_2(q_0)$ under sequence vw is given by

$$\overline{\delta}'(\sigma_2(q_0), vw) = \overline{\delta}'(\overline{\delta}'(\sigma_2(q_0), v), w) =$$

$$A^{rg}[A^{msh}\sigma_1(q_0) + \sum_{i=1}^{msh} A^{msh-i}Ba_i] + \sum_{i=1}^{rg} A^{rg-i}Bb_i.$$

Since $\langle A\rangle$ has index r and period s, $A^{rg}A^{msh} = A^{rg+(mh)s} = A^{rg}$ and hence

$$\overline{\delta}'(\sigma_2(q_0), vw) = A^{rg}\sigma_1(q_o) + \sum_{i=1}^{rg} A^{rg-i}Bb_i + \alpha \tag{4}$$

where $\alpha = \sum_{i=1}^{msh} A^{rg+msh-i}Ba_i$. Decomposing this sum, we have

$$\alpha = \sum_{j=0}^{m-1} \left(\sum_{i=jsh+1}^{(j+1)sh} A^{rg+msh-i}Ba_i \right). \tag{5}$$

But if $1 \le i \le sh$ and $0 \le j \le m-1$, by (3),

$$a_i + jsh = a_i. \tag{6}$$

Moreover, since <A> has index r and period s

$$A^{rg+msh-(i+jsh)} = A^{rg+(m-j)sh-i} = A^{rg+sh-i}. \qquad (7)$$

Thus, by (6) and (7), the inner sum of (5) is independent of j, that is

$$\alpha = m[\sum_{i=1}^{sh} A^{rg+sh-i} B\, a_i]$$

and, since m is the characteristic of R, we have $\alpha = 0$.* Thus, from (4),

$$\overline{\delta}'(\sigma_2(q_0),vw) = A^{rg}\sigma_1(q_0) + \sum_{i=1}^{rg} A^{rg-i} B\, b_i$$

$$= \overline{\delta}'(\sigma_2(q_0),w).$$

Accordingly, from (1) and (2),

$$\beta'_{\sigma_2(q_0)}(\sigma_1(x)) = \lambda'(\overline{\delta}'(\sigma_2(q_0),vw),\sigma_1(0))$$

$$= \lambda'(\overline{\delta}'(\sigma_2(q_0),w),\sigma_1(0))$$

$$= \beta'_{\sigma_2(q_0)}(\sigma_1(y)).$$

Thus $\beta_{q_0}(x) = \sigma_3(\beta'_{\sigma_2(q_0)}(\sigma_1(x))) = \sigma_3(\beta'_{\sigma_2(q_0)}(\sigma_1(y))) = \beta_{q_0}(y)$ a contradition since in the SF, $\beta_{q_0}(x) = 1$ and

*In general, if M is an R-module generated by $\{\beta_1,\beta_2,...\}$ and $\alpha,\beta \in M$ such that $\alpha = m\beta$ where m is the characteristic R then $\alpha = m(\Sigma b_i\beta_i) = \Sigma(mb_i)\beta_i = \Sigma 0\beta_i = 0$.

$\beta_{q_0}(y) = 0$. Thus the SF is not linearly simulatable over any finite ring.

As a corollary of Theorem 5, and in view of Theorem 1, an equivalent result is the SF cannot be homomorphically simulated by a finite linear machine. It is interesting to note, however that the latter can be established directly by algebraic methods, as shown in the next section.

Linear Homomorphic Simulation

The general form of the semigroup S_M of a ℓsm M has been shown [9] to consist of a subset of $Q \times C_{r,s}$ where Q is the state space and $C_{r,s}$ is the cyclic semigroup of index r and period s (here $A^{r+s} = A^r$); this subset is closed under the associative multiplication:

$$(q_x,\ell_x)(q_y,\ell_y) = q_y + A^{\ell_y}q_x,\ell_x + \ell_y).$$

Thus S_M is anti-isomorphic to a subsemigroup of the semidirect product of the state space Q considered as an abelian group $(Q,+,0)$ and $C_{r,s}$. (S is *not* isomorphic to the semidirect product as stated in [9]). To see how this works consider the map from Σ^+ to $Q \times C_{r,s}$ where

$a_1a_2\ldots a_t \mapsto (\sum_{i=0}^{t} A^{t-i}Ba_i,t)$; i.e.,$x\mapsto(q_x,\ell_x)$; then note that the action of a string xy is mimicked by the semigroup multiplication, i.e., $\delta(q,xy) = \delta(\delta(q,x),y) = A^{\ell_x+\ell_y}q + A^{\ell_y}q_x+q_y$.

Lemma 2: A machine M is linearly homomorphically simulatable if and only if its semigroup S_M divides the semigroup $S_{\ell sm}$ of some ℓsm.

Proof: It is know that* if M is homomorphically simulatable by M' then S_M divides (is a homomorphic image of a subsemigroup of) $S_{M'}$. Conversely, if S_M divides $S_{M'}$ then M is homomorphically simulatable by a parallel composition of a number of copies of M'. Since the parallel composition of a number ℓsm's over a ring R is again a ℓsm over R, the lemma is proved.

Theorem 6: The Set Flip-Flop is not linearly homomorphically simulatable over any finite ring.

---

*"It is known" references may be found in [9] and in [12].

Proof: The semigroup of SF is the unit semigroup $U_1 = \{1,r\}$ where $xy = r$ unless $x = y = 1$. Suppose that the SF can be homomorphically simulated by a ℓsm. By Lemma 2 its semigroup U_1 must divide $S_{\ell sm}$. Thus the anti-isomorphic image of U_1 - which is U_1 since U_1 is abelian - must divide the semidirect product of $C_{r,s}$ and Q. But since U_1 is known to be irreducible it must divide either $C_{r,s}$ or Q. We now show this is impossible.

Claim: U_1 does not divide $C_{r,s}$. For let $C_{r,s} = \langle a \rangle$ and let $h(a^m) = 1$ and $h(a^n) = r$ where h is the associated homomorphism. Then $h(a^{mn}) = h((a^m)^n) = (h(a^m))^n = 1^n = 1$ and also $h(a^{mn}) = h((a^n)^m) = (h(a^n))^m = r^m = r$, a contradiction.

Claim: U_1 does not divide any finite group G. For let $h(x) = 1$ and $h(y) = r$ where x and y are in G and h is the associated homomorphism. Since G is finite there exist integers m and n such that $x^m = y^n = 1_G$ where 1_G is the identity of G. Then by the same argument as before $1 = h(x^m) = h(y^n) = r$, a contradiction. This completes the proof.

We now raise the question of whether there are in fact machines which are linearly homomorphically simulatable but not linearly homomorphically realizable. We have not been able to settle this question, however the following observation restricts the class of possibilities.

Observation: There is a machine which is linearly homomorphically *simulatable* but not linearly homomorphically *realizable* if, and only if, there is a machine $M_{S_{\ell sm}}$ which is not linearly homomorphically realizable. (Here $S_{\ell sm}$ is the semigroup of some linear machine and $M_{S_{\ell sm}}$ is the canonical machine having that semigroup.)

Proof: => Let M' be homomorphically simulated by a ℓsm M. It is known that M' can be homomorphically realized by M_{S_M}. If M_{S_M} is linearly homomorphically realizable then by transitivity of homorphic realization so is M'. Thus if M' is not linearly homomorphically realizable, M_{S_M} is not realizable in this way.

<= Conversely, suppose that M is a ℓsm and M_{S_M} is not linearly homomorphically realizable. Then M_{S_M} is the

desired example since M_{S_M} is homomorphically simulatable by M(S_M is the semigroup M_{S_M} and therefore by Lemma 2 it is homomorphically simulatable by M).

A realization of M_{S_M} as a parallel composition of machines $M_{C_{r,s}}$ and M_Q is shown in Figure 3. It is then apparent that all counters M_m are linearly simulatable even over fields since they can be embedded in $M_{C_{r,s}}$ machines. We have shown that only the prime counters are 1-realizable over fields but it remains open whether there are nonprime counters which are homomorphically realizable over fields.

The part of Figure 3 relating to M_Q can be put in the form of a transition function $\delta(q,a) = A^{f(a)}q + Ba$ where f is an integer valued function. When f is a constant function this reduces to a linear structure. When f is not constant, the machine is easily shown to be non-linear, but it is unknown whether it can always be homomorphically realized by a linear machine.

References

[1] Arbib, M.A., Theories of Abstract Automata, Prentice-Hall, Englewood Cliffs, New Jersey (1969).

[2] Clifford, A.H. and G.B. Preston, The Algebraic Theory of Semigroups, Vol. I., American Mathematical Society, Providence, Rhode Island (1961).

[3] Cohn, M. and S. Even, "Identification and Minimization of Linear Machines," IEEE Trans. Electronic Computers, EC 14, No. 3, pp. 367-376 (1965).

[4] Gill, A., Linear Sequential Circuits: Analysis, Synthesis, and Applications, McGraw-Hill, New York, (1967).

[5] Godement, R., Algebra, Hermann, Paris (1968).

[6] Harrison, M.A., Lectures on Linear Sequential Machines, Academic Press, New York, (1969).

[7] Hartmanis, J. and W.A. Davis, "Homomorphic Images of Linear Sequential Machines," J. of Computer and System Sciences, Vol. 1, pp. 155-165 (1967).

[8] Hartmanis, J. and R.E. Stearns, Algebraic Structure Theory of Sequential Machines, Prentice-Hall, Englewood Cliffs, New Jersey (1966).

[9] Kalman, R.E.;P.L. Falb; M.A. Arbib, Topics in Mathematical Systems Theory, McGraw-Hill, New York (1969).

[10] Leake, R.J., "Realization of Sequential Machines" (Correspondence), IEEE Trans. Computers, C17, No. 12, p. 1177 (1968).
[11] Zeigler, B.P. "Modeling and Simulation: Structure Preserving Relations for Discrete and Continuous Systems" To appear in "Computers and Automata" Brooklyn Polytechnic Press (1971).
[12] ___, "On the Feedback Complexity of Automata" University of Michigan Doctoral Dissertation, Technical Report No. 08226-6-T, (1969).

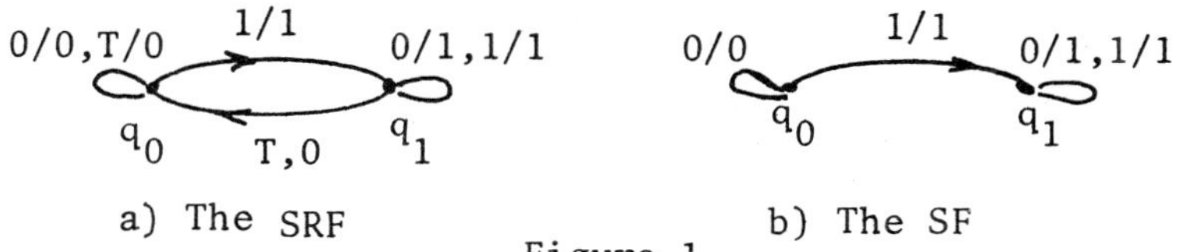

Figure 1

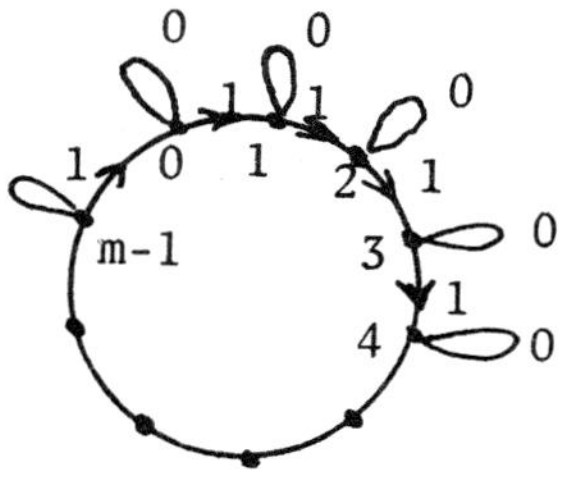

Figure 2: The M_m m-state counter

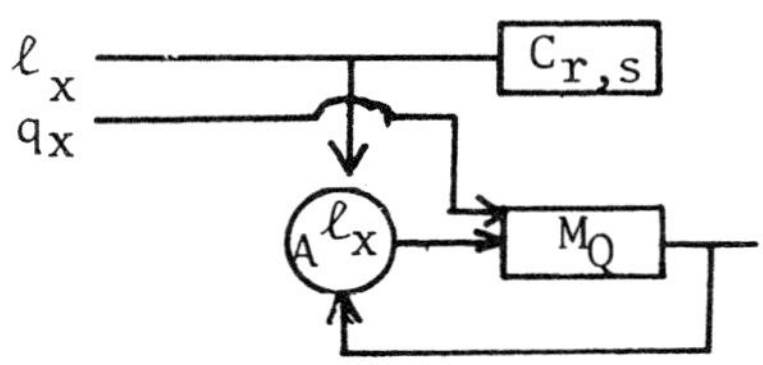

Figure 3

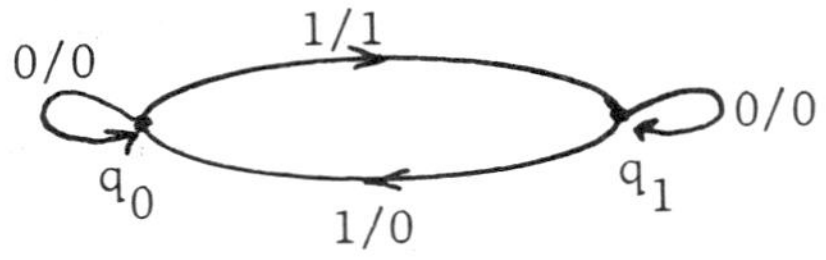

Figure 4

q	Aq
0	0
1	1

a	Ba
0	0
1	1

q	Cq
0	00
1	10

a	Da
0	00
1	01

Figure 5

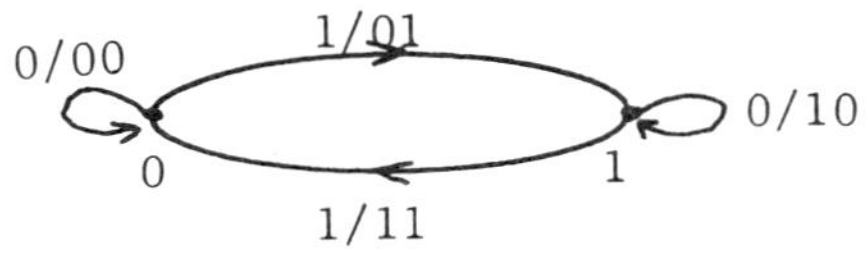

Figure 6

a	$\eta_1(a)$
0	0
1	1

q	$\eta_2(q)$
0	q_0
1	q_1

z	$\eta_3(z)$
00	0
01	1
10	0
11	0

Figure 7

THEOREMS ON ADDITIVE AUTOMATA

Bernd Reusch

Gesellschaft für Mathematik und Datenverarbeitung
Bonn, Germany.

1. Introduction.

The theory of linear automata is well developed and many papers appeared (and appear) on this topic. From early papers ([2]) on there is the hope to carry over ideas from linear automata to more general types of automata and there are some publications [1,4] in which generalizations are made. We want to add some more theorems which are known in the linear case and generalize them to what we call „additive automata".

DEFINITION 1,1: (X,S,Y,δ,λ) is an automaton

$:\Longleftrightarrow$ 1. X,S,Y are sets, resp. input-, state- and output-set, non-empty but not necessary finite.

2. $\delta : X \times S \longrightarrow S$, $\lambda : X \times S \longrightarrow Y$

The mappings δ and λ are extended to range over $X^* \times S$ in the usual way.

DEFINITION 1.2: (X,S,Y,δ,λ) is a linear automaton

$:\Longleftrightarrow$ 1. X,S,Y are finite dimensional vector-spaces over a field K .

2. δ and λ are linear mappings, i.e.

(*) $\delta(x,s) = As + Bx$, $\lambda(x,s) = Cs + Dx$,
where A,B,C,D are linear mappings:
$A : S \longrightarrow S$, $B : X \longrightarrow S$, $C : S \longrightarrow Y$, $D : X \longrightarrow Y$.

Arbib in [4] showed certain properties of linear automata to be equivalent to this definition and called this type „additive automata".

We would like to call an automaton additive, if (*) is meaningful. This is the case, if there are defined binary operations „+" on S and Y and there are mappings $A : S \longrightarrow S$, $B : X \longrightarrow S$, $C : S \longrightarrow Y$, $D : X \longrightarrow Y$. We want to use a little more although it must be statet that some theorems do not use <u>all</u> asumptions of the next definition.

<u>DEFINITION 1.3</u>: (X,S,Y,δ,λ) is an <u>additive automaton</u>

$:\Longleftrightarrow$ 1. X is a non-empty set, S and Y are semi-groups with neutral element 0.

2. There are mappings $A : S \longrightarrow S$, $B : X \longrightarrow S$, $C : S \longrightarrow Y$, $D : X \longrightarrow Y$, such that $\delta(x,s) = As + Bx$, $\lambda(x,s) = Cs + Dx$

3. A and C are homomorphisms and there is an element $0 \in X$ holding $B0 = 0$, $D0 = 0$.

4. There are operator-sets O_X, O_S, O_Y which work on resp. X,S and Y and there are mappings: $E : O_X \longrightarrow O_S$, $F : O_X \longrightarrow O_Y$, $G : O_S \longrightarrow O_Y$ such that $Aas = aAs$, $Bbx = EbBx$, $Cas = GaCs$, $Dbx = FbDx$ for all $s \in S$, $x \in X$, $a \in O_S$, $b \in O_X$.

We include the case where $O_S = O_X = O_Y =$ identity. Many well known results on linear automata can be generalized to additive automata. The following theorem is a simple exemple [3,5] .

<u>THEOREM 1.1</u>: Let (X,S,Y,δ,λ) be an additive automaton.

Then 1. $\delta(x_o \cdots x_{t-1},s) = A^t s + \sum_{i=o}^{t-1} A^{t-i-1} Bx_i$

2. $\lambda(x_o \cdots x_{t-1},s) = CA^{t-1} s + \sum_{i=o}^{t-2} CA^{t-i-2} Bx_i + Dx_{t-1}$

PROOF: 1. The formula is correct if $t = 1$. Now

$$\delta(x_o \cdots x_t , s) = \delta(x_t , \delta(x_o \cdots x_{t-1} , s)) =$$

$$= \delta(x_t , A^t s + \sum_{i=o}^{t-1} A^{t-i-1} Bx_i) =$$

$$= A(A^t s + \sum_{i=o}^{t-1} A^{t-i-1} Bx_i) + Bx_t =$$

$$= A^{t+1} s + \sum_{i=o}^{(t+1)-1} A^{(t+1)-i+1} Bx_i ,$$

$$2.\ \lambda(x_o\cdots x_{t-1}, s) = \lambda(x_{t-1}, \delta(x_o\cdots x_{t-2}, s)) =$$
$$= C(A^{t-1}s + \textstyle\sum_{i=o}^{t-2} A^{t-i-2} Bx_i) + Dx_{t-1} =$$
$$= CA^{t-1}s + \textstyle\sum_{i=o}^{t-2} CA^{t-i-2} Bx_i + Dx_{t-1} .$$

2. Reduction of Additive Automata.

It is well known that to every given automaton there belongs a unique (up to isomorphisms) minimal one, which is a homomorpic image of it. It is also known that the minimal automaton belonging to a linear automaton over a field K is again a linear automaton over the same field. The natural question to be answered in this section is, whether the minimal automaton belonging to an additive automaton is again additive with the same operator-sets.

DEFINITION 2.1: Let $M = (X,S,Y,\delta,\lambda)$ and $M' = (X,S',Y,\delta',\lambda')$ be automata. The mapping P of S onto S' ist an automaton-homomorphism if the following diagram is commutative:

$$\begin{array}{ccccc} Y & \xleftarrow{\ \lambda\ } & S \times X & \xrightarrow{\ \delta\ } & S \\ \downarrow{\scriptstyle id.} & & \downarrow{\scriptstyle P}\quad \downarrow{\scriptstyle id.} & & \downarrow{\scriptstyle P} \\ Y & \xleftarrow{\ \lambda'\ } & S' \times X & \xrightarrow{\ \delta'\ } & S' \end{array}$$

It can be shown that the diagram still commutes if we replace X by X^* .

DEFINITION 2.2: $M = (X,S,Y,\delta,\lambda)$ is minimal if every automaton-homomorphism P of M ist an isomorphism (i.e. a 1-1-mapping). We can now prove the following theorem

THEOREM 2.1: Let $M = (X,S,Y,\delta,\lambda)$ be an additive automaton and $M' = (X,S',Y,\delta',\lambda')$ a minimal homomorphic image of M under P . Then we can define a semigroup on S' and mappings A',B',C',D', such that M' is an additive automaton with the same operator-sets and P is a semigroup-homomorphism of S onto S' .

PROOF: 1. First of all we want to show that S' is a homomorphic image of S . We define:

$$\bigwedge_{s_i' \varepsilon S', i=1,2,3} (s_1'+s_2' = s_3' \iff (\bigvee_{s_i \varepsilon S, i=1,2,3} Ps_i=s_i', s_1+s_2=s_3))$$

We have to show that this definition does not depend on the choice of s_1, s_2 and s_3. This is done if we prove:

$$\bigwedge_{s_1, s_2 \varepsilon S} (Ps_1 = Ps_2 \Longrightarrow (\bigwedge_{s \varepsilon S} P(s_1 + s) = P(s_2 + s)))$$

Now, if $Ps_1 = Ps_2$ then $\lambda(s_1,x) = \lambda(s_2,x)$ for all $x \varepsilon X^\infty$, especially for all sequences of 0's. By the general answer-formula we get $CA^{t-1}s_1 = CA^{t-1}s_2$ for all natural numbers t.

Hence

$$CA^{t-1}s_1 + CA^{t-1}s + \sum_{i=o}^{t-2} CA^{t-i-2} Bx_i + Dx_{t-1}$$
$$= CA^{t-1}s_2 + CA^{t-1}s + \sum_{i=o}^{t-2} CA^{t-i-2} Bx_i + Dx_{t-1}$$

for all s and $x_o \cdots x_{t-1}$.

But this says $\lambda(s_1+s,x) = \lambda(s_2+s,x)$ for all $s \varepsilon S$ and all $x \varepsilon X^\infty$.

Since M' was minimal, we get $P(s_1 + s) = P(s_2 + s)$.

So S' is a semigroup and P is a homomorphism by definition.

In addition we show:

$$\bigwedge_{s_1, s_2 \varepsilon S} \bigwedge_{C \varepsilon O_S} (Ps_1 = Ps_2 \Longrightarrow Pcs_1 = Pcs_2)$$

If $Ps_1 = Ps_2$ then $\lambda(s_1, 0^t) = \lambda(s_2, 0^t)$ for all natural numbers t. This gives $CA^{t-1}s_1 = CA^{t-1}s_2$.

Hence
$$CA^{t-1}cs_1 + \sum_{i=o}^{t-2} CA^{t-i-2} Bx_i + Dx_{t-1}$$
$$= CA^{t-1}cs_2 + \sum_{i=o}^{t-2} CA^{t-i-2} Bx_i + Dx_{t-1}$$

for all $x_o \cdots\cdots x_{t-1}$. This again means:

$\bigwedge_{x \varepsilon X^+} \lambda(cs_1,x) = \lambda(cs_2,x)$. Since M' was minimal, we get $Pcs_1 = Pcs_2$.

2. Definition of mappings A', B', C', D' .

a) $B' := PB$, $D' := D$.
B' is a mapping of X into S', since first B maps X into S and then P maps S into S' . Since D maps X into Y , D' does the same.

b) We want to define a mapping A' of S' into S' such that $PA = A'P$. This equation can be taken as definition of A' , if the following holds:

$$\bigwedge_{s_1, s_2 \varepsilon S} (Ps_1 = Ps_2 \Longrightarrow PAs_1 = PAs_2)$$

Now, if $Ps_1 = Ps_2$ for some $s_1, s_2 \varepsilon S$, the following holds:

$$\begin{aligned} PAs_1 &= PAs_1 + PBo = P(As_1 + Bo) = \\ &= P\,\delta(s_1, o) = \delta'(Ps_1, o) = \delta'(Ps_2, o) = \\ &= P\,\delta(s_2, o) = PAs_2 + PBo = PAs_2 \end{aligned}$$

In addition we have to show that A' is a homomorphism of S' Let be $A's_1' = s_1''$ and $A's_2' = s_2''$. Because of the definition of A' there are elements s_1 and s_2 of S such that $Ps_1 = s_1'$, $Ps_2 = s_2'$, $PAs_1 = s_1''$ and $PAs_2 = s_2''$. Now let us look for $s = s_1 + s_2$. We get $Ps = s_1' + s_2'$ and $PAs = s_1'' + s_2''$ and conclude
$A'(s_1' + s_2') = s_1'' + s_2'' = A's_1' + A's_2'$. The last step is to prove that O_S operates on S' and that A' is compatible with the operations of O_S . We define

$$\bigwedge_{c \varepsilon O_S, s_1', s_2' \varepsilon S'} (cs_1' = s_2' :\Longleftrightarrow \bigvee_{s_1, s_2 \varepsilon S} (Ps_1 = s_1', Ps_2 = s_2', cs_1 = s_2))$$

This definition is valid because of the already shown property of P: $(Ps_1 = Ps_2 \Longrightarrow Pcs_1 = Pcs_2)$.

Now: $A'cs' = A'Pcs$ for some $s \varepsilon S$. Hence

$$A'cs' = PAcs = cPAs = cA'Ps = cA's ,$$

and we have proved A' to be compatible with the elements of O_S .

c) We want to define a mapping C' of S' into Y such that $C = C'P$. This equation again can be taken as <u>definition</u> of C' if the following holds:

$$\bigwedge_{s_1,s_2 \varepsilon S} (Ps_1 = Ps_2 \Longrightarrow Cs_1 = Cs_2)$$. If $Ps_1 = Ps_2$ we get

$$Cs_1 = Cs_1 + Do = \lambda(s_1,o) = \lambda'(Ps_1,o) = \lambda'(Ps_2,o) =$$
$$= \lambda(s_2,o) = Cs_2 + Do = Cs_2 .$$

Let us prove that C' is a homomorphism. Let be $C's_1' = y_2$ and $C's_2' = y_2$. Then there are $s_1, s_2 \varepsilon S$ holding $Ps_1 = s_1'$, $Ps_2 = s_2'$, $Cs_1 = y_1$ and $Cs_2 = y_2$. We look again for $s = s_1 + s_2$. We have $Ps = s_1' + s_2'$ and $Cs = y_1 + y_2$, hence $C'(s_1' + s_2' = y_1 + y_2 = C's_1' + C's_2'$. For all $c \varepsilon O_S$ we get $C'cs' = C'cPs = C'Pcs = Ccs =$ $= cC's = cC'Ps = cC's'$.

α) Next and last step is to prove
$\delta'(s',x) = A's' + B'x$, $\lambda'(s',x) = C's' + D'x$. We have
$$\delta'(s',x) = \delta'(Ps,x) = P\delta(s,x) = PAs + PBx = A'Ps + B'x =$$
$$= A's' + Bx .$$
$$\lambda'(s',x) = \lambda'(Ps,x) = \lambda(s,x) = Cs + Dx = C'Ps + D'x =$$
$$= C's' + D'x .$$

We have shown, that for every given additive automaton there is an equivalent minimal one such that its state-semigroup is a homomorphic image of the state-semigroup of the given automaton. The proof was by construction. The question arises, whether there are other equivalent minimal automata with an a priori additive structure and how the relation is to the constructed one.

<u>DEFINITION 2.3</u>: The additive automata $M = X,S,Y,\delta,\lambda)$ and $M' = (X,S',Y,\delta',\lambda')$ are <u>similar</u> if there is an isomorphism P of S and S' such that

$$A' = PAP^{-1}, B' = PB, C' = CP^{-1}, D' = D .$$

THEOREM 2.2: Let $M = (X,S,Y,\delta,\lambda)$ and $M' = (X,S',Y,\delta',\lambda')$ be minimal additive automata. They are automaton-isomorphic iff they are similar.

PROOF: 1) If M and M' are similar, then there is a semigroup-isomorphism P of S onto S' with the properties cited above. Now

$$P\delta(s,x) = PAs + PBx = A'Ps + B'x = \delta'(Ps,x)$$
$$\lambda(s,x) = Cs + Dx = C'Ps + D'x = \lambda'(Ps,x)$$

2) If P is an automaton-isomorphism, we have to show first that P is a semigroup-isomorphism of S onto S'.

Let be $Ps_1 = s'_1$, $Ps_2 = s'_2$ and $P(s_1 + s_2) = s'$. Since M and M' both are minimal, this is equivalent to

$CA^{t-1}s_1 = C'A'^{t-1}s'_1$, $CA^{t-1}s_2 = C'A'^{t-1}s'_2$ and

$CA^{t-1}(s_1 + s_2) = C'A'^{t-1}s'$ for all natural numbers t.

Hence $C'A'^{t-1}(s'_1 + s'_2) = C'A'^{t-1}s'$ for all t, which gives by the minimality of M' the equality of s' and $(s'_1 + s'_2)$. Thus we have $P(s_1 + s_2) = s' = s'_1 + s'_2 = Ps_1 + Ps_2$. We can now proceed:

$$\bigwedge_{s\in S, x\in X} (PAs + PBx = A'Ps + B'x \,,\; Cs + Dx = C'Ps + D'x\,.)$$

By setting $s = o$ we get

$$\bigwedge_{x\in X} (PBx = B'x \,,\; Dx = D'x)$$ which gives $B' = PB$, $D' = D$.

By setting $x = o$ we get

$$\bigwedge_{s\in S} (PAs = A'Ps \,,\; Cs = C'Ps)$$ which gives

$$A' = PAP^{-1} \,,\; C' = C'P^{-1}\,.$$

Hence M and M' are similar.

3. Realization over Semigroup with operators.

This section extends the author's work [6] on linear realization over rings and fields. The proofs are similar to those in [6] and will be omitted. Let $M = (X,S,Y,\delta,\lambda)$ be an automaton and H a commutative semigroup with a set of operators K working on it. We say A is (H,K)-realized, if the following diagram is commutative:

$$\begin{array}{ccccc} Y & \xleftarrow{\;\lambda\;} & X \times S & \xrightarrow{\;\delta\;} & S \\ \downarrow i_Y & & \downarrow i_X \qquad \downarrow i_s & & \downarrow i_S \\ H & \xleftarrow{\;\bar{\lambda}\;} & H^m \qquad H^n & \xrightarrow{\;\bar{\delta}\;} & H^n \end{array}$$

where i_Y, i_X, i_S are injections and $\bar{\lambda}$ and $\bar{\delta}$ are „linear" in the following sense: let i-proj o $\bar{\delta}$ be the mapping which is done by applying $\bar{\delta}$ and then the i-th projection of H^n. Then $\bar{\delta}$ and $\bar{\lambda}$ are linear if for $i = 1,\ldots,n, p = 1,\ldots 1$,

$$\text{i-proj} \circ \bar{\delta} = \sum_{j=1}^{n} a_{ij}\, s_j + \sum_{k=1}^{m} b_{ik}\, x_k$$

$$\text{p-proj} \circ \bar{\lambda} = \sum_{j=1}^{n} c_{pj}\, s_j + \sum_{k=1}^{m} d_{pk}\, x_k ,$$

where $a_{ij}, b_{ik}, c_{pj}, d_{pk} \in K$.

For the following we asume H to have a neutral element 0 and K to contain a o- and a 1-operator, where the 1-operator is the identity and the o-operator maps every element of H to its neutral element 0. Our problem is to find necessary and sufficient conditions for the (H,K)-realizability of an automaton M. We use H_M for the set of all mappings of a set M into H. It can be shown, that H_M is again a semigroup and H is imbeddable in H_M such that one can build the factor-semigroups $F_M = H_{M/H}$. The elements of H_M can be written as indexed partitions, which especially useful in the finite case.

DEFINITION 3.1: $P = (P_i)_{i \varepsilon H}$ is a H-indexed partition over M

$: \Longleftrightarrow$ 1. $\bigwedge_{i \varepsilon H} P_i \subseteq H$

2. $\bigwedge_{i \neq j} P_i \cap P_j = \emptyset$

3. $\bigcup_{i \varepsilon H} P_i = M$

For all $m \varepsilon M$ we write $P(m) = i$ iff $m \varepsilon P_i$.

LEMMA 3.1: $P = (P_i)_{i \varepsilon H}$, $Q = (Q_i)_{i \varepsilon H}$, $k \varepsilon K$.

1. $P + Q = (R_i)_{i \varepsilon H} \Longleftrightarrow \bigwedge_{i \varepsilon H} R_i = \bigcup_{k+1=i} (P_i \cap Q_1)$

2. $k \cdot P = (R_i)_{i \varepsilon H} \Longleftrightarrow \bigwedge_{i \varepsilon H} R_i = P_{ki}$

DEFINITION 3.2: $M = (X,S,Y,\delta,\lambda)$. $P = (P_i)_{i \varepsilon H} \varepsilon H_S$,
$T = (T_i)_{i \varepsilon H} \varepsilon H_Y$

1. $\bigwedge_{x \varepsilon X^*, i \varepsilon H} (\pi_x P_i := \{s \varepsilon S \mid \delta(x,s) \varepsilon P_i\}$ and
$\pi_x P = (\pi_x P_i)_{i \varepsilon H})$

2. $\bigwedge_{x \varepsilon X, i \varepsilon H} (\pi_x T_i := \{s \varepsilon S \mid \lambda(x,s) \varepsilon T_i\}$ and
$\pi_x T = (\pi_x T_i)_{i \varepsilon H})$

Actually the π_x are mapping of H_S resp. H_Y into H_S , which can be shown to be homomorphisms. Since for all $i \varepsilon I$ we hawe $\pi_x i = i$, we get induced homomorphisms $\bar{\pi}_x$ of the factor-semigroups. We need some more definitions.

DEFINITION 3.3: 1. $\bigwedge_{P \varepsilon H_M} m \equiv n(\alpha P) : \Longleftrightarrow P(m) = P(n)$

2. $\bigwedge_{V \subseteq H_M} \beta V := \prod_{P \varepsilon V} \alpha P$

DEFINITION 3.4: $H_Y^\infty := \{T \varepsilon H_Y \mid \bigwedge_{n} \bigwedge_{x,x' \varepsilon X^n} \bigvee_{h \varepsilon H} \pi_x T = \pi_{x'} T \oplus h\}$

(this means $\pi_x T$ and $\pi_{x'} T$ are in the same class of F_Y)

It can be shown, that H_Y^∞ is sub-semigroup of H_Y which is closed under the operations of K and contains H .
Our central theorem now is the following. (By „closed semigroup" we mean closed under K)

THEOREM 3.1: $M = (X,S,Y,\delta,\lambda)$ ist (H,K)-realizable

$\Longleftrightarrow$ There is a finitely generated closed semigroup $W \subseteq H_Y^\infty$ holding $\beta W = 0$, for which $[\pi_x W]_\pi$ for some $x \in X$ is a sub-semigroup of a finitely generated closed sub-semigroup of H_S . Here $[\pi_x W]_{\pi_x}$ is the smallest semigroup containing $\pi_x W$ and being closed under π_x.

Another consequence of the proof of this theorem is:

THEOREM 3.2: The finite automaton M is (H,K)-realizable

$\Longleftrightarrow$ M is $(H,\{0,1\})$-realizable.
This is a theorem not well known for linear realizations which gives realizations using the addition of the ring only.

COROLLARY 3.1: Let M be a finite automaton and H a finite semigroup. M is (H,K)-realizable $\Longleftrightarrow$ $\beta H_Y^\infty = 0$.

The remaining problem is how to construct H_Y^∞ .

DEFINITION 3.5:

1. $H_Y^n := \{T \in H_Y \mid \bigwedge_{r\leq n} \bigwedge_{x,x'\in X^r} \bigvee_{h\in H} \pi_x T = \pi_{x'} T \oplus h\}$

2. $H_S^n := \{P \in H_S \mid \bigwedge_{r\leq n} \bigwedge_{x,x'\in X^r} \bigvee_{n} \pi_x P = \pi_{x'} P \oplus h\}$

LEMMA 3.2: 1. $\bigwedge_{n\leq m} H_Y^m \subseteq H_Y^n$, $H_S^m \subseteq H_S^n$

2. $\bigwedge_{x\in X} \pi_x H_Y^{n+1} \subseteq H_S^n$

3. $H_Y^\infty = \bigcap_{n=1}^{\infty} H_Y^n$

4. $T \in H_Y^{n+1} \Longleftrightarrow \bigvee_{x\in X} (T \quad R_Y^1$ and $\pi_x T \in H_S^n,)$

LEMMA 3.3: 1. $H_S^{n-1} = H_S^n \Longrightarrow \bigwedge_{j=1,2,\dots} H_S^{n-1} = H_S^{n+j}$

2. $H_S^{n-1} = H_S^n \Longrightarrow H_Y^n = H_Y^\infty$

It is easy to show that in the finite case $H_S^{n-1} = H_S^n$ for some n. So we have an algorithm to construct H_Y^∞ at least for the finite case.

References.

[1] Doty, K.L., Frank, H.:
Discrete-Time Systems with the Decomposition Property.
IEEE C-19 , pp. 412-420, (1970) .

[2] Elspas, B.:
The Thory of Autonomous Linear Sequential Networks
IRE CT-6 , pp. 45-60, (1959) .

[3] Gill, A.:
Linear Sequential Machines
Mc Graw-Hill, New York (1966) .

[4] Kalman, R.E., Falb, P.L., Arbib, M.A.:
Topics in Mathematical System Theory
Mc Graw-Hill, New York (1969) .

[5] Reusch, B.:
Lineare Automaten
Bibliographisches Institut, Mannheim, (1969) .

[6] Reusch, B.:
On Liniar Realization of Automata over Arbitrary Rings.
to appear in J. of Computer and System Sciences.

CONNECTIVITY AND SEPARATION IN AUTOMATA

Zamir Bavel

University of Kansas*
Lawrence, Kansas

1. Introduction

Strong connectedness is a feature which has occupied almost exclusively the attention of many automata theorists. One likely motivation is the high desirability of strong connectedness in applications to sequential circuitry; another is the handsome harvest of behavior characteristics which such a strong condition implies.

In the past few years, interest has grown in a more general setting, one with weaker conditions, and many results known for strongly connected automata have been profitably generalized to arbitrary automata, finite and infinite (for example, [4], [5], and [6]). One result of this evolution is the recent interest in examining connectivity and reversibility conditions, as was done for example in [7], [8], [9], [10], [11], and in particular [4].

In some instances strong connectivity is too strong a condition to yield desired results. One such instance occurs in the investigation of homomorphisms of automata (see [1]), where connectivity and separation are the key issues, as we show below. This fact is not surprising, since an automaton is the disjoint union of its separated subautomata, and thus many if not most problems on automata are profitably reducible to the same or similar but easier problems on the separated parts.

In this article we present several characteristics of connectedness and of separation, examine their relationships to other connectivity properties and to the basic

*Department of Computer Science
This work was supported in part by the National Science Foundation under Grant GJ-639.

structure of automata, illustrate a method for finding the minimal separated subautomata of a finite automaton, and show its use in determining the homomorphisms, endomorphisms, isomorphisms, and automorphisms of finite automata.

2. Preliminaries

An <u>automaton</u> is a triple $A = (S,\Sigma,\delta)$, where S is a set (of <u>states</u>), Σ is a non-empty set (the <u>input alphabet</u>), and $\delta: S \times \Sigma^* \to S$ is the <u>transition function</u> satisfying: $\forall s \in S$ and $\forall x,y \in \Sigma^*$, $\delta(s,xy) = \delta[\delta(s,x),y]$, where Σ^* is the free monoid over Σ (the set of all strings of finite length of members of Σ, including the empty string ε, with $\delta(s,\varepsilon) = s$, $\forall s \in S$). The symbols A, S, Σ, and δ will be used generically, when no ambiguity arises; S_B denotes the set of states of the automaton B.

An automaton $B = (T,\Sigma,\delta')$ is a <u>subautomaton</u> of A ($B \leqslant A$) if and only if $T \subseteq S$ and δ' is the restriction of δ to $T \times \Sigma^*$. We shall use δ for δ', as no ambiguity arises. The set of <u>successors</u> of $R \subseteq S$ is $\delta(R) = \{\delta(r,x): r \in R$ and $x \in \Sigma^*\}$. When $R = \{r\}$, we permit $\delta(r)$ for $\delta(\{r\})$. The <u>automaton generated</u> by $R \subseteq S$ is $\langle R\rangle = (\delta(R),\Sigma,\delta)$; R is a <u>generating set</u> of (or for) $\langle R\rangle$. When $R = \{r\}$, we permit $\langle r\rangle$ for $\langle\{r\}\rangle$. An automaton A is <u>singly generated</u> if and only if $\exists s \in S$ such that $A = \langle s\rangle$, and in that event s is a generator of $\langle s\rangle$. The <u>empty automaton</u> is $\langle\phi\rangle = (\phi,\Sigma,\delta)$. B is a <u>proper subautomaton</u> of A if and only if $B \leqslant A$ and $\langle\phi\rangle \neq B \neq A$.

An automaton is <u>finite</u> if and only if its set of states is finite. (Unless otherwise stated, A is an automaton which is not necessarily finite.)

A <u>primary</u> of a nonempty finite automaton is a maximal singly generated subautomaton. An automaton A is <u>strongly connected</u> if and only if, $\forall s,t \in S$, $s \in \delta(t)$.

Where $A_i = (S_i,\Sigma,\delta_i) \leqslant A$, for some nonempty indexing set I, $\bigcup_{i\in I} A_i = (\bigcup_{i\in I} S_i,\Sigma,\delta')$ and $\bigcap_{i\in I} A_i = (\bigcap_{i\in I} S_i,\Sigma,\delta'')$, where δ' and δ'' are the respective restrictions of δ to $(\bigcup_{i\in I} S_i) \times \Sigma^*$ and $(\bigcap_{i\in I} S_i) \times \Sigma^*$.

The following results are straightforward consequences of the preceding definitions (see [2]) and thus are presented without proofs. They are used implicitly in the following sections.

Let A be an automaton. Then, $\forall R,T \subseteq S$; (i) $S_{\langle R\rangle} = \delta(R)$; (ii) $R \subseteq \delta(R)$; (iii) $R \subseteq T \Rightarrow \delta(R) \subseteq \delta(T)$; (iv) $\delta(R) = R \Leftrightarrow (R,\Sigma,\delta) \preccurlyeq A$; (v) $\delta(R \cup T) = \delta(R) \cup \delta(T)$; (vi) $\delta(R \cap T) \subseteq \delta(R) \cap \delta(T)$; (vii) $\delta(R) - \delta(T) \subseteq \delta(R - T)$.

The union and the intersection of subautomata of A are themselves subautomata of A.

3. Separated Subautomata and Connected Automata

Intuitively, a nonempty subautomaton B of A is separated when it cannot be reached from outside. The closure of the set of states of B under transitions prevents reaching from B a state which is not in B. On the other hand, a triple (T,Σ,δ) which is not a subautomaton cannot be separated since then T is not closed under transitions and a state outside T can be reached from T. These considerations motivate the following definition.

Definition 1. A nonempty subautomaton $B = (T,\Sigma,\delta)$ of A is said to be separated if and only if $\delta(S - T) \cap T = \phi$. A nonempty automaton A is said to be connected if and only if it has no separated proper subautomata.

The following lemma is used in the proof of one of the characterizations of Theorem 1.

Lemma 1. Let B be a separated subautomaton of a finite automaton A. Then, every primary of B is a primary of A.

Proof: Let $\langle s\rangle$ be a primary of B, and suppose it is not a primary of A. Then, $\exists t \in S - \delta(s)$ such that $\langle s\rangle \preccurlyeq \langle t\rangle$, since $\langle s\rangle$ cannot be maximal. Since $\langle s\rangle$ is a primary of B, $t \in S - S_B$. But $s \in \delta(t) \Rightarrow s \in \delta(S - S_B)$ and thus $\delta(S - S_B) \cap S_B \neq \phi$, contrary to the hypothesis. ▮

The first two characterizations of separation in Theorem 1 are both trivial to prove and easy to see intuitively. Since $\delta(R) = R$ is a necessary and sufficient condition for $R \subseteq S$ to be the set of states of a subautomaton, condition (ii) means that the set of states outside B is the set of states of a subautomaton (and hence closed under transitions). Condition (iii) states that the successors of no state of B meet those of any state outside B.

Condition (iv) characterizes the separation of B by the union of all subautomata of A which do not meet B. Condition (v) is a characterization of separation by primaries.

Theorem 1. Let A be an automaton, let $\langle\phi\rangle \neq B = (T,\Sigma,\delta) \ll A$, and let $C = \bigcup\{D \ll A: D \cap B = \langle\phi\rangle\}$. Then the following are equivalent.

(i) B is separated.

(ii) $\delta(S - T) = S - T$.

(iii) $\forall t \in T, \forall s \in S - T, \delta(t) \cap \delta(s) = \phi$.

(iv) $B = \langle S - S_C\rangle$.

If A is finite and B is a proper subautomaton of A, "B is separated" is equivalent to

(v) $S - S_B$ is the union of sets of all states of some primaries of A.

Proof: (i) $\Leftrightarrow$ (ii) is immediate from set algebra. (i) $\Leftrightarrow$ (iii): Condition (iii) is equivalent to $\delta(T) \cap \delta(S - T) = \phi$, which is equivalent to (i) by Definition 1 and the fact that $\delta(T) = T$, since $B \ll A$. (i) $\Rightarrow$ (iv): Let B be separated and let $s \in S - S_C$. Then, by hypothesis, $\langle s\rangle \cap B \neq \langle\phi\rangle$. But then, by (ii), $s \notin S - T$ since $\delta(S - T) \cap S_B = \phi$ and thus $s \in T$. Hence $S - S_C \subseteq T$, which implies $\delta(S - S_C) \subseteq \delta(T) = T$. On the other hand, $C \cap B = \langle\phi\rangle$ by hypothesis and thus $T \subseteq S - S_C \subseteq \delta(S - S_C)$. The double inclusion yields $T = \delta(S - S_C)$ and thus $B = \langle S - S_C\rangle$. (iv) $\Rightarrow$ (i): $B = \langle S - S_C\rangle \Rightarrow T = \delta(S - S_C) \Rightarrow S - T = S - \delta(S - S_C)$. But $S - \delta(S - S_C) \subseteq \delta(S - (S - S_C)) = \delta(S_C) = S_C$, since $C \ll A$. We thus have $S - T \subseteq S_C$. On the other hand, since $C \cap B = \langle\phi\rangle$, $S_C \subseteq S - T$ and hence $S - T = S_C$. But $C \ll A \Rightarrow S_C = \delta(S_C) \Rightarrow S - T = \delta(S - T) \Rightarrow B$ is separated, by (ii). (i) $\Rightarrow$ (v): Let B be a separated proper subautomaton of A. Then, by (ii), $S - S_B = \delta(S - S_B)$, which is the set of states of $\langle S - S_B\rangle$. Since B is proper, $\langle S - S_B\rangle \neq \langle\phi\rangle$ and hence it is the union of its primaries (Theorem 1, the Primary Decomposition Theorem, in [1]). Since $\delta(S - (S - T)) = \delta(T) = T = S - (S - T)$, by (ii), $\langle S - S_B\rangle$ is also separated and thus, by Lemma 1, its primaries are primaries of A. (v) ⇒ (i): Let B be a proper subautomaton of A such that $S - S_B$ is the union of sets of all states of some primaries of A. But then, $S - S_B$ is the set of states of a subautomaton of A and therefore $\delta(S - S_B) = S - S_B$. Hence, B is separated, by (ii). ▮

It is interesting to note that condition (v) with S_B replacing $S - S_B$ does not imply that B is separated. Also, if T is an arbitrary nonempty subset of S, condition (ii) does not imply that $\langle T\rangle$ is separated.

A fairly obvious consequence of part (ii) of Theorem 1 is that, if $B \lll A$ is separated, so is the "rest of A". I.e.,

<u>Corollary</u>. Let B be a proper subautomaton of A. Then, B is separated if and only if $C = (S - S_B, \Sigma, \delta)$ is a separated subautomaton of A.

<u>Proof</u>: Let B be separated. Then $\delta(S - S_B) = S - S_B$, by Theorem 1(ii). Thus, $S - S_B$ is the set of states of a subautomaton of A, i.e., $C \lll A$. Now, $S_B = S - (S - S_B)$ and $S_B = \delta(S_B)$ since $B \lll A$. Hence, $\delta(S - (S - S_B)) = \delta(S_B) = S_B = S - (S - S_B)$ and thus C is separated, by Theorem 1(ii). The converse follows by symmetry. ▮

Three characterizations of connectedness follow immediately from Theorem 1 by denying the existence of a separated proper subautomaton; we thus forego stating them formally. The following theorem interprets connectedness in terms of generating sets.

<u>Theorem 2</u>. A nonempty automaton A is not connected if and only if there exist two nonempty subsets, R and T, of S such that $\langle R\rangle \cap \langle T\rangle = \langle\phi\rangle$ and $\langle R\rangle \cup \langle T\rangle = A$; if and only if any generating set G of A may be partitioned into two nonempty subsets, R and T, such that $\langle R\rangle \cap \langle T\rangle = \langle\phi\rangle$.

<u>Proof</u>: To prove the first part we note that A is not connected ⇔ A has a separated proper subautomaton ⇔ $\exists T \subsetneq S$

such that $\phi \neq T \neq S$, $\delta(T) = T$, and $\delta(S - T) = S - T$. Since $(S - T) \cup T = S$ and $(S - T) \cap T = \phi$, T and $S - T = R$ satisfy the stated conditions. If R and T are nonempty subsets of S satisfying $\langle R\rangle \cap \langle T\rangle = \langle\phi\rangle$ and $\langle R\rangle \cup \langle T\rangle = A$, then $\delta(R) \cap \delta(T) = \phi$ and $\delta(R) \cup \delta(T) = S$. Hence, $\delta(R) = S - \delta(T)$ and $\delta(S - \delta(T)) = \delta(\delta(R)) = \delta(R) = S - \delta(T)$. Hence $\langle T\rangle$ is separated and A is not connected.

To prove the second part, let G be any generating set of A and let (Q,Σ,δ) be a proper separated subautomaton of A. Now, $G \cap Q = \phi \Rightarrow G \subseteq S - Q \Rightarrow \delta(G) \subseteq \delta(S - Q)$. But $\delta(G) = S$, since G is a generating set of A, and $\delta(S - Q) = S - Q$, since (Q,Σ,δ) is separated. Hence $S \subseteq S - Q$, which is impossible, as $Q \neq \phi$. Thus $R = G \cap Q \neq \phi$ and, by symmetry, $T = G \cap (S - Q) \neq \phi$. Now, $\delta(R) \cap \delta(T) \subseteq \delta(Q) \cap \delta(S - Q) = Q \cap (S - Q) = \phi$ and hence $\langle R\rangle \cap \langle T\rangle = \langle\phi\rangle$. Conversely, S is a generating set of A and therefore S can be partitioned into two nonempty subsets, R and T, such that $\langle R\rangle \cap \langle T\rangle = \langle\phi\rangle$. Since $S = R \cup T \subseteq \delta(R) \cup \delta(T)$, we also have $\langle R\rangle \cup \langle T\rangle = A$ and A is not connected, by the first part of the theorem. ▮

Theorem 2 can be reinterpreted in terms of primaries as follows:

<u>Corollary</u>. Let π be the set of primaries of a finite nonempty automaton A. Then A is not connected if and only if π may be partitioned into two nonempty subsets π_1 and π_2 such that $(\bigcup\{P: P \in \pi_1\}) \cap (\bigcup\{P: P \in \pi_2\}) = \langle\phi\rangle$.

The proof of the corollary is immediate from the theorem and is thus omitted.

The separated parts of an automaton may be regarded as unrelated automata with the same input alphabet. Many problems are profitably reducible to these natural building blocks, which are the subject of the following.

<u>Definition 2</u>. A nonempty subautomaton B of an automaton A is a <u>block</u> of A if and only if B is connected and separated.

<u>Lemma 2</u>. Let $\langle\phi\rangle \neq B \leqslant A$. Then, the following are equivalent:

(i) B is a block of A.

(ii) B is a minimal separated subautomaton of A.

(iii) B is a maximal connected subautomaton of A.

Proof: (i) $\Rightarrow$ (ii): If B is a block, it is separated. Moreover, since B is connected, no proper subautomaton of B is separated and hence B is minimal separated. (ii) $\Rightarrow$ (iii): Let B be a minimal separated subautomaton of A. Then B has no separated proper subautomata and is therefore connected. Any subautomaton C of A, such that B is a proper subautomaton of C, is not connected, by definition, and hence B is maximal connected. (iii) $\Rightarrow$ (i): Let B be a maximal connected subautomaton of A. By maximality, $\forall s \in S - S_B$, $\langle s \rangle \cap B = \langle \phi \rangle \Rightarrow \delta(s) \cap S_B = \phi \Rightarrow \delta(S - S_B) \cap S_B = \phi$ and B is separated. ∎

It follows immediately from the lemma that

Corollary. A nonempty automaton is connected if and only if it has exactly one block.

It may be intuitively clear that every nonempty automaton has blocks and is made entirely of blocks and, indeed, a simple induction argument suffices to prove this in the finite case. For arbitrary automata, more is needed, including the following two lemmas.

Lemma 3. The union of two nondisjoint connected subautomata is connected.

Proof: Let B and C be connected subautomata of A, let $B \cap C \neq \langle \phi \rangle$, and let D be a separated (nonempty) subautomaton of $B \cup C$. Then $D \cap (B \cup C) \neq \langle \phi \rangle$. Without loss of generality, let $D \cap B \neq \langle \phi \rangle$. Since D is separated in $B \cup C$, $S_D \cap \delta(S_{B \cup C} - S_D) = \phi$ and $\delta(S_{B \cup C} - S_D) = S_{B \cup C} - S_D$. Hence, $(S_D \cap S_B) \cap \delta(S_B - (S_D \cap S_B)) = \phi$ and $B \cap D$ is a separated subautomaton of B. But then $B \cap D = B$, since B is connected, and thus $B \leqslant D$. Now, $B \leqslant D$ and $B \cap C \neq \langle \phi \rangle$ imply $D \cap C \neq \langle \phi \rangle$ and hence, by symmetry, $C \leqslant D$. Consequently, no proper subautomaton of $B \cup C$ is separated and therefore $B \cup C$ is connected. ∎

Lemma 4. Let B be a separated subautomaton of A and let $C \leqslant A$ such that $B \cap C \neq \langle \phi \rangle$. Then $B \cap C$ is a separated subautomaton of C.

Proof: Since B is separated, $\delta(S - S_B) \cap S_B = \phi$ and $\delta(S - S_B) = S - S_B$. Hence, $\delta(S_C - S_{B \cap C}) \cap (S_{B \cap C}) = \phi$ and therefore $B \cap C$ is a separated subautomaton of C, since $B \cap C \neq \langle\phi\rangle$. ▮

As a consequence of Lemma 4 we have the following property of blocks (which is also shared by strongly connected subautomata), whose proof follows from Lemmas 2 and 4.

Corollary. Two blocks of a nonempty automaton are either identical or disjoint.

Theorem 3. Every state of a nonempty automaton A is in a block of A.

Proof: Let $s \in S$ and let $\mathcal{D}$ be the set of all connected subautomata of A in which s is a state. Then $\mathcal{D}$ is partially ordered by $\leqslant$. Since $\langle s\rangle \in \mathcal{D}$, $\mathcal{D} \neq \phi$. Let $\mathcal{C}$ be any chain in $(\mathcal{D},\leqslant)$ and let $D' = \bigcup\{D: D \in \mathcal{C}\}$. Suppose there exists a separated proper subautomaton B of D', and let $b \in S_B$ and $a \in S_{D'} - S_B$. Then, there exists $E \in \mathcal{C}$ such that $a,b \in S_E$, since $\mathcal{C}$ is totally ordered by $\leqslant$; moreover, $B \cap E \neq \langle\phi\rangle$, since b is a state of the intersection. Hence, by Lemma 4, $B \cap E$ is a separated subautomaton of E and, since $a \in S_E - S_B$, $B \cap E$ is proper in E, contradicting Lemma 3. Thus D' is connected. Since s is a state of D', $D' \in \mathcal{D}$. Clearly, D' is an upper bound for $\mathcal{C}$ and hence, by Zorn's lemma, $\mathcal{D}$ has a maximal element; i.e., there exists a block of A in which s is a state. Since s is arbitrary, the theorem follows. ▮

It now follows immediately from the theorem that

Corollary. Every nonempty automaton is the union of its blocks.

Lemmas 3 and 4 deal with the union of connected subautomata and the intersection of separated ones. The following lemma and remark relate to the union of separated subautomata and the intersection of connected ones.

Lemma 5. The union of separated subautomata of A is a separated subautomaton of A.

Proof: Let $\{B_i : i \in I\}$, for some nonempty indexing set I, be a family of (nonempty) separated subautomata of A, and let $B' = \bigcup\{B_i : i \in I\}$. If $B' = A$, it is separated, so let B' be a proper subautomaton of A, and let $s \in S_{B'}$ and $t \in S - S_{B'}$. Then, $t \notin S_{B_i}$, $\forall i \in I$, and $s \in S_{B_i}$, for some $i \in I$, and hence $\delta(s) \cap \delta(t) = \phi$, by Theorem 1(iii), since B_i is separated by hypothesis. Since s and t were arbitrarily chosen in their respective domains, B' is separated, again by Theorem 1(iii). ▮

Remark. The intersection of connected subautomata of A need not be connected, as may be easily verified with a simple counterexample.

Lemma 5 aids in proving yet another characterization of separation.

Theorem 4. A nonempty subautomaton C of A is separated if and only if C is the union of blocks of A.

Proof: Let $\langle\phi\rangle \neq C \lessdot A$. If C is the union of blocks of A, it is then the union of separated subautomata and is therefore separated, by Lemma 5. Conversely, let C be separated and let B be a block of C (justified by Theorem 3). Then we have $S_B \cap \delta(S_C - S_B) = \phi$ and, since $B \lessdot C$, $S_B \cap \delta(S - S_C) = \phi$. Hence, $\phi = (S_B \cap \delta(S - S_C)) \cup (S_B \cap \delta(S_C - S_B)) = S_B \cap (\delta(S - S_C) \cup \delta(S_C - S_B)) = S_B \cap \delta((S - S_C) \cup (S_C - S_B)) = S_B \cap \delta(S - S_B)$. Hence, B is separated in A and is therefore a block of A by minimality. By the corollary to Theorem 3, B is the union of its blocks, all of which are blocks of A. ▮

The following theorem is the basis of the procedure, which is described below, for obtaining the blocks of a finite automaton.

Theorem 5. A nonempty finite automaton A is connected

if and only if, for every ordered pair (s,t) of states of A, there exists a finite sequence of primaries $\langle s_1\rangle, \langle s_2\rangle, \ldots, \langle s_k\rangle$ of A with $s \in \delta(s_1)$ and $t \in \delta(s_k)$ such that $\langle s_i\rangle \cap \langle s_{i+1}\rangle \neq \langle\phi\rangle$, $\forall i \in \{1,\ldots,k-1\}$.

Proof: Let A be connected. Then, by the corollary to Theorem 2, any union of primaries of A which does not exhaust A has a nonempty intersection with a primary not in that union; since A is finite, the conclusion follows. Conversely, if A is not connected then, by the same corollary, there exist two unions B and C of primaries of A which exhaust A and which have no state in common. Let s and t be states of B and C, respectively, and let $\langle s_1\rangle$, $\langle s_2\rangle, \ldots, \langle s_k\rangle$ be any sequence of primaries such that $s \in \delta(s_1)$ and $\langle s_i\rangle \cap \langle s_{i+1}\rangle \neq \langle\phi\rangle$, $\forall i \in \{1,\ldots,k-1\}$. Then $\langle s_1\rangle \ll B$ and, by induction, $\langle s_i\rangle \ll B$ for each $i \in \{2,\ldots,k\}$, since $\delta(s_i) \cap \delta(s_{i-1}) \neq \phi$. Hence, for no such sequence of primaries do we have $t \in \delta(s_k)$ and the result follows. ∎

The procedure[1] for finding all blocks of a nonempty finite automaton, implied by Theorem 3, is the following: start with the first state s of the transition-table; find all predecessors of s and the successors of the result (to obtain all primaries having s as a state); continue to find the predecessors of the last result and their successors repeatedly until such double step yields no new state; at that point, the block containing s has been found and, if unused states still exist, start with the first such state and repeat the process until the entire automaton is exhausted.

4. Separation and Connectivity Related to Strong Connectedness and Retrievability

Among other connectivity properties, [4] presents a generalization of strong connectedness, whose definitions we reproduce here.

Definition 3. A nonempty automaton A is retrievable

[1] The detailed form of this procedure is a part of [3].

if and only if, $\forall s \in S$, $\forall x \in \Sigma^*$, $\exists y \in \Sigma^*$ such that $\delta(s,xy) = s$.

In essence, then, any starting point can be retrieved after leaving it. As is shown in [4], retrievability is weaker than strong connectedness only in that some states may not be reachable from others. Thus follows Lemma 6, which is also reproduced from [4] (Remark 1).

Lemma 6. A nonempty automaton is retrievable if and only if it is the (disjoint) union of strongly connected subautomata.

We use this lemma to prove the following characterizations of strong connectedness in terms of connectivity and separation.

Theorem 6. Let A be a nonempty automaton. Then the following are equivalent.

(i) A is strongly connected.

(ii) A is connected and retrievable.

(iii) Every (nonempty) separated subautomaton of A is strongly connected.

Proof: (i) ⇒ (ii): If A is strongly connected, it has no proper subautomaton and is therefore connected. A is then retrievable by Lemma 6. (ii) ⇒ (iii): If A is connected, the only separated subautomaton of A is A itself. If A is also retrievable, it is the disjoint union of strongly connected subautomata, by Lemma 6, and hence A, the only separated subautomaton, is itself strongly connected. (iii) ⇒ (i): If every separated subautomaton of A is strongly connected, since the entire automaton A is always separated, A is strongly connected. ∎

We conclude the section with characterizations of retrievability in terms of connectivity and separation.

Theorem 7. Let A be a nonempty automaton. Then the following are equivalent.

(i) A is retrievable.

(ii) Every block of A is strongly connected.

(iii) Every nonempty subautomaton of A is separated.

(iv) Every (nonempty) separated subautomaton of A is retrievable.

Proof: (i) ⇒ (ii): Let $\{C_i: i \in I\}$, for some nonempty indexing set I, be the set of all strongly connected subautomata of A. Then, by Lemma 6, $A = \bigcup\{C_i: i \in I\}$. Let B be a block of A. Then $B \cap A \neq \langle\phi\rangle \Rightarrow \exists j \in I$ such that $B \cap C_j \neq \langle\phi\rangle$. But, since $B \cap C_j \ll C_j$ and C_j has no proper subautomaton, $B \cap C_j = C_j$ and hence $C_j \ll B$. But C_j is separated, by Lemma 6, and B is minimal separated and hence $C_j = B$. (ii) ⇒ (iii): If every block of A is strongly connected then no block of A has a proper subautomaton. Hence, every nonempty subautomaton is the union of blocks of A and thus, by Theorem 4, it is separated. (iii) ⇒ (iv): Let every nonempty subautomaton of A be separated and let $s \in S$. Then, $\forall t \in \delta(s)$, $\langle t\rangle$ is not a proper subautomaton of $\langle s\rangle$; i.e., $\langle t\rangle = \langle s\rangle$. Hence, $s \in \delta(t)$ and therefore $\langle s\rangle$ is strongly connected. Let B be a (nonempty) separated subautomaton of A. Then $B = \bigcup\{\langle s\rangle: s \in S_B\}$ is the union of strongly connected subautomata and is, therefore, retrievable. (iv) ⇒ (i): Since A is (nonempty and) separated, it is retrievable, by (ii). ∎

5. Blocks and Homomorphisms

In [1] (Theorem 18), the set of homomorphisms on a finite automaton A to a finite automaton B has been shown to be precisely the set of nonempty extensions (see Definition 4, below) of homomorphisms on the primaries of A to B. Similar results were shown for endomorphisms, isomorphisms, and automorphisms. In order for a homomorphism f on a primary P of A to be extendable by a homomorphism g on a primary Q of A, where $P \cap Q \neq \langle\phi\rangle$, f and g must have identical images on the states of $P \cap Q$; otherwise, the extension $f \vee g$ is "empty."

Definition 4. Let $A = (S,\Sigma,\delta)$ and $B = (T,\Sigma,\gamma)$ be automata. A function on A to B is a mapping of S to T (and the identity mapping on Σ^*). A function $f: A \to B$ is a homomorphism if and only if it preserves transitions by Σ^*, i.e., $\forall s \in S$, $\forall x \in \Sigma^*$, $f(\delta(s,x)) = \gamma(f(s),x)$. We denote the set of all homomorphisms on A to B by $H(A \to B)$. An endomorphism of A is a homomorphism on A to A. We denote the set of all endomorphisms of A by $E(A)$. An isomorphism on A onto B is a monic and epic homomorphism on A onto B.

We denote the set of all isomorphisms on A onto B by $Is(A \to B)$. An automorphism of A is an isomorphism on A onto A. We denote the group of automorphisms of A by $G(A)$.

Let $A_i = (S_i, \Sigma, \delta) \ll A$ and let f_i be a function f_i: $A_i \to B$, for each i in some nonempty indexing set I. Let ε denote the empty state, a fictitious entity belonging to every set of states. The empty function on A to B is denoted by $\psi_{A,B}$ and is defined by $\psi_{A,B} = \{(s,\varepsilon) : s \in S\}$. The extension of f_i by f_j is denoted by $f_i \vee f_j$ and is defined as follows: if $A_i \neq \langle\phi\rangle$ and $f_i = \psi_{A_i,B}$, or if $A_j \neq \langle\phi\rangle$ and $f_j = \psi_{A_j,B}$, or if neither f_i nor f_j is the empty function but $f_i(r) \neq f_j(r)$ for some $r \in S_i \cap S_j$, then $f_i \vee f_j = \psi_{A_i \cup A_j, B}$; if neither f_i nor f_j is the empty function and if $f_i(r) = f_j(r)$, $\forall r \in S_i \cap S_j$, then

$$(f_i \vee f_j)(s) = \begin{cases} f_i(s), & \text{if } s \in S_i \\ f_j(s), & \text{if } s \in S_j. \end{cases}$$

A function f_i: $A_i \to B$ is extendable to A_j by a function f_j: $A_j \to B$ if and only if $f_i \vee f_j$ is nonempty; f_i is extendable to A_j if and only if $\exists g$: $A_j \to B$ such that $f_i \vee g$ is nonempty.

The extension $f_i \vee f_j$ is homomorphic if and only if f_i and f_j are (nonempty) homomorphisms; f_i is homomorphically extendable to A_j if and only if there exists a nonempty homomorphic extension of f_i to A_j.

Where H and K are classes of functions on A_i and A_j, respectively, to B, the class extension of H by K is denoted by $H \vee K$ and is defined by: if $H = \phi$ or if $K = \phi$, then $H \vee K = \{\psi_{A_i \cup A_j, B}\}$; if $H \neq \phi \neq K$, then $H \vee K = \{f \vee g : f \in H, g \in K\}$. Where R is a set of extensions, R^+ denotes the subset of all nonempty members of R.

Clearly, a nonempty homomorphic extension is a homomorphism. Moreover, the extension operation is commutative and associative, allowing the obvious generalization.

The main device in determining and characterizing transition-preserving functions on arbitrary finite automata is the reduction from functions on the entire automaton to corresponding functions on the primaries of the automaton. This reduction in the case of homomorphisms and endomorphisms was accomplished in Theorem 18 of [1], whose pertinent part is reproduced here for the readers' convenience.

Theorem 8. Let A and B be nonempty finite automata and let $A_1,\ldots,A_n$ be the primaries of A. Then,

(i) $H(A \to B) = \{\bigvee_{i=1}^{n} f_i : f_i \in H(A_i \to B)\}^+$;

(ii) $E(A) = \{\bigvee_{i=1}^{n} f_i : f_i \in H(A_i \to A)\}^+$.

The determination of all homomorphisms and endomorphisms on the entire finite automaton A was then accomplished in [1] in a simple process which, nevertheless, can become quite laborious at times. For the case where both domain automaton A and range automaton B are connected, we do not offer any improvement on Theorem 8. However, if either A or B is not connected, the process of finding all homomorphisms on A to B (respectively, all endomorphisms of A) is substantially reduced (and often drastically so) with the aid of the following two results (due to space restrictions, proofs of the remaining results are omitted; they will appear in an expanded version of this article):

Lemma 7. All extensions of homomorphisms on blocks are nonempty.

Lemma 8. Single-valued functions preserve connectedness.

Lemma 7 promotes a sizable reduction of effort in the event the domain automaton A is not connected: the homomorphisms on each block of A are computed as indicated in [1] (with the aid of Theorem 8, above), with special attention paid to eliminating all empty extensions. Then, the extension of any homomorphism on any block of A by any homomorphism on any other block of A is nonempty and therefore the set of all homomorphisms on A to B is precisely the set of all class extensions by blocks. Thus, no further computation of extensions is necessary; instead, it suffices to just indicate the class extensions of blocks by blocks.

Lemma 8 is responsible for a further reduction--in case the range automaton B is not connected. This reduction is accomplished by isolating the investigation of homomorphisms on a block of A to one block of B at a time. Thus, when the image by a subclass of homomorphisms of a primary of block A_i is in block B_j of B, all subclasses of homomorphisms of other primaries of A_i whose images are not in B_j may be ignored in the matching process, i.e., that of seeking nonempty extensions. This reduction from the entire range to the blocks of the range alone represents a sizable reduction in effort when the range automaton is not connected.

As an example, the 22,575 homomorphisms on A to B of Table 1 may be designated (following Lemma 7) as all the class extensions on the three blocks of A, whose respective numbers of homomorphisms are 25, 301, and 3. The effort is thus reduced from computing (25)(301)(3) = 22,575 individual homomorphisms to the computation of 25 + 301 + 3 = 329 homomorphisms on the corresponding blocks. Furthermore, as a result of Lemma 8, making use of the separation of the three blocks of B permits the low number of 35 matches of homomorphisms on single primaries of the second block of A to obtain the 301 functions on the entire second block. In fact, the total number of such matches for all three blocks of A is 37.

The implications of Lemmas 7 and 8, discussed in the preceding paragraphs, are summarized in the following theorem.

Theorem 9. Let A and B be nonempty finite automata and let $A_1,\ldots,A_n$ and $B_1,\ldots,B_m$ be the distinct blocks of A and B, respectively. Then,

(i) $$H(A \to B) = \bigvee_{i=1}^{n} H(A_i \to B) = \bigvee_{i=1}^{n} \Big(\bigcup_{j=1}^{m} H(A_i \to B_j)\Big);$$

(ii) $$\#(H(A \to B)) = \prod_{i=1}^{n} \#(H(A_i \to B)) = \prod_{i=1}^{n} \Big(\sum_{j=1}^{m} \#(H(A_i \to B_j))\Big).$$

(iii) $E(A) = \bigvee_{i=1}^{n} H(A_i \to A) = \bigvee_{i=1}^{n} (\bigcup_{j=1}^{n} H(A_i \to A_j))$;

(iv) $\#(E(A)) = \prod_{i=1}^{n} \#(H(A_i \to A)) = \prod_{i=1}^{n} (\sum_{j=1}^{n} \#(H(A_i \to A_j)))$.

6. Blocks and Isomorphisms

Here, as in the case of homomorphisms, the problem of finding all isomorphisms $Is(A \to B)$ on a finite automaton A onto a finite automaton B is reduced to the corresponding problem on primaries of the domain and the range automata. The essential identity (up to relabeling of states) between the two isomorphic automata and the preservation of primaries by isomorphisms ([1], Lemma 2) permit us to concentrate on mapping the primaries of the domain in a one-to-one fashion onto a permutation of the primaries of the range, as is indicated in the following.

Lemma 9. Let A and B be finite nonempty automata, let $A_1,\ldots,A_n$ and $B_1,\ldots,B_n$ be the (distinct) primaries of A and B, respectively, and let $f \in Is(A \to B)$. Then, for some permutation σ of $\{1,\ldots,n\}$, $f(A_i) = B_{\sigma(i)}$, $\forall i \in \{1,\ldots,n\}$.

The lemma constitutes both justification and motivation for establishing the following notational conventions, which aid in simplifying the statements of following results.

Notation. By Π_n we denote the set of permutations of $\{1,\ldots,n\}$, for each positive integer n.

Let A and B be nonempty finite automata, let $A_1,\ldots,A_n$ and $B_1,\ldots,B_n$ be the (distinct) primaries of A and B, respectively, and let $\sigma \in \Pi_n$. Then $Is(A \overset{\sigma}{\to} B)$ shall denote the subset of $Is(A \to B)$, each of whose members maps A_i to $B_{\sigma(i)}$, $\forall i \in \{1,\ldots,n\}$; i.e.,

$$Is(A \overset{\sigma}{\to} B) = \{f \in Is(A \to B)\colon f(A_i) = B_{\sigma(i)},\ 1 \leqq i \leqq n\}.$$

With Lemma 9, it is easy to show that the entire set $Is(A \to B)$ is precisely the union of all sets of the form $Is(A \overset{\sigma}{\to} B)$, where σ varies over all Π_n. That is,

Lemma 10. $\mathrm{Is}(A \to B) = \bigcup_{\sigma \in \Pi_n} \mathrm{Is}(A \overset{\sigma}{\to} B)$.

The lemma accomplishes part of the desired reduction, in that each class $\mathrm{Is}(A \overset{\sigma}{\to} B)$ of isomorphisms effecting a particular permutation σ remains uncharacterized. The remaining characterization is the subject of the following.

Lemma 11. Let $\sigma \in \Pi_n$. Then, where A has n primaries,

(i) $\mathrm{Is}(A \overset{\sigma}{\to} B) = \{\bigvee_{i=1}^{n} f_i\colon f_i \in \mathrm{Is}(A_i \to B_{\sigma(i)})$ and $\bigvee_{i=1}^{n} f_i^{-1} \neq \psi_{B,A}\}^+$;

(ii) If $\#(S_A) = \#(S_B)$, then $\mathrm{Is}(A \overset{\sigma}{\to} B) = \{\bigvee_{i=1}^{n} f_i\colon f_i \in \mathrm{Is}(A_i \to B_{\sigma(i)})\}^+$.

A combination of the preceding results yields the desired reduction in the following theorem.

Theorem 10. (i) $\mathrm{Is}(A \to B) = \bigcup_{\sigma \in \Pi_n} \{\bigvee_{i=1}^{n} f_i\colon f_i \in \mathrm{Is}(A_i \to B_{\sigma(i)})$ and $\bigvee_{i=1}^{n} f_i^{-1} \neq \psi_{B,A}\}^+$;

(ii) If $\#(S_A) = \#(S_B)$, then

$$\mathrm{Is}(A \to B) = \bigcup_{\sigma \in \Pi_n} \{\bigvee_{i=1}^{n} f_i\colon f_i \in \mathrm{Is}(A_i \to B_{\sigma(i)})\}^+;$$

(iii) $G(A) = \bigcup_{\sigma \in \Pi_n} \{\bigvee_{i=1}^{n} f_i\colon f_i \in \mathrm{Is}(A_i \to A_{\sigma(i)})\}^+$.

The indicated procedure for obtaining $\mathrm{Is}(A \to B)$ is then the following: first find $\mathrm{Is}(A \overset{\sigma}{\to} B)$, for each permutation σ of the primaries, and then obtain the union of all such sets. The absence of the second condition of the right-hand set of parts (i) from the right-hand set of parts (ii) of Lemma 11 and Theorem 10 is to be regarded with relief, since testing for this condition represents considerable effort (and a sizable disruption of the procedure whose details appear in [3]). At first glance, it may seem improper to consider, in the context of isomorphisms, domain and range automata whose respective numbers of states differ, and to express relief that a troublesome condition disappears when these numbers are the same. Yet, the domain and range automata may have equal size while key subautomata may not. In particular, when blocks of the two automata are mapped, even when all the individual primaries are mutually isomorphic, their union in the domain may not be isomorphic to the corresponding union in the range. It is thus fortunate that equality of size of the respective subautomata is sufficient to remove the need to check each extension for monicity.

The procedure indicated above for obtaining $Is(A \to B)$ is aided by many properties which are preserved under isomorphisms. Such devices are often crucial, since the total number n! of permutations of n primaries becomes prohibitively large very rapidly as n grows and, without drastically reducing the number of permutations we must consider, the task of obtaining all isomorphisms may become unprofitable and, at times, unattainable. In the event the two (isomorphic) automata are not connected, the number of permutations of the primaries which we must consider may be considerably reduced by the fact that <u>isomorphisms preserve separation</u>. I.e.,

<u>Lemma 12</u>. Let A and B be automata, let C be a separated subautomaton of A, and let $f \in Is(A \to B)$. Then f(C) is a separated subautomaton of B.

Together with the fact that single-valued functions preserve connectedness (Lemma 8), Lemma 12 implies that <u>isomorphisms preserve blocks</u>; i.e.,

<u>Lemma 13</u>. Let A and B be automata, let C be a block of A, and let $f \in Is(A \to B)$. Then, f(C) is a block of B.

As a consequence, it is not difficult to show that <u>isomorphisms permute blocks</u>, a fact on which the following theorem relies.

<u>Theorem 11</u>. Let A and B be nonempty isomorphic finite automata, let $A_1, \ldots, A_n$ be the (distinct) blocks of A, and let $B_1, \ldots, B_n$ be the (distinct) blocks of B. Then,

(i) $Is(S \to B) = \bigcup_{\sigma \in \Pi_n} (\bigvee_{i=1}^{n} Is(A_i \to B_{\sigma(i)}))^+$;

(ii) $G(A) = \bigcup_{\sigma \in \Pi_n} (\bigvee_{i=1}^{n} Is(A_i \to A_{\sigma(i)}))^+$.

Theorem 10 represents a reduction from entire finite automata to primaries. Theorem 11 is an intermediate reduction, from automata to blocks. The similarity between the two results may obscure the practical importance of this intermediate step. While Theorem 10 may give the impression that many, if not all, permutations of the primaries must be considered, Theorem 11 helps eliminate all such permutations which do not also permute the blocks. The technique implied by Theorem 11, then, is to obtain all the orderings of the blocks of B so that they are isomorphic in pairs to the blocks of A, and then, within each pairing of blocks, to obtain all permutations of the primaries of the range block which yield isomorphisms between the two blocks.

The reduction in effort which results is significant and is sufficient to justify the proposed procedure. An added justification is afforded by Theorem 12, which points out that extensions of isomorphisms on blocks to blocks are never empty and they always yield isomorphisms on the entire automaton, provided distinct blocks of the domain are mapped to distinct blocks of the range. In other words, the need for agreement on the common states does not exist in the case of blocks.

Theorem 12. Let the hypotheses of Theorem 11 hold, and, in addition, let $\sigma \in \Pi_n$ and let $n > 1$. Then the following are equivalent:

(i) $(\bigvee_{i=1}^{n} Is(A_i \to B_{\sigma(i)}))^+ \neq \phi$;

(ii) $\forall i \in \{1,\ldots,n\}$, $Is(A_i \to B_{\sigma(i)}) \neq \phi$;

(iii) $(\bigvee_{i=1}^{n} Is(A_i \to B_{\sigma(i)}))^+ = \bigvee_{i=1}^{n} Is(A_i \to B_{\sigma(i)})$.

References

1. Bavel, Z. "Structure and Transition-Preserving Functions of Finite Automata." J.ACM 15,1 (Jan. 1968), 135-158.

2. Bavel, Z. Introduction to the Theory of Automata and Sequential Machines. To appear.
3. Bavel, Z. "Algorithms in the Structure and Transition-Preserving Functions of Finite Automata." To appear.
4. Bavel, Z. and Muller, D. E. "Connectivity and Reversibility in Automata." J.ACM 17,2 (April 1970), 231-240.
5. Bavel, Z. and Thomas, J. W. "On the Decomposability of Monadic Algebras and Automata." 1967 IEEE Conf. Rec. on Switching and Automata Theory (Oct. 1967), 322-335.
6. Bayer, R. "Automorphism Groups and Quotients of Strongly Connected Automata and Monadic Algebras." 1966 IEEE Conf. Rec. on Switching and Automata Theory (Oct. 1966), 282-297.
7. Gluschkow, W. M. Theorie der Abstrakten Automaten (translation from the Russian). VEB Deutscher Verlag der Wissenschaften, Berlin (1963), 58-60.
8. Harrison, M. A. Introduction to the Theory of Finite-State Machines. McGraw-Hill Book Company (1965), 276-284.
9. Huzino, S. "On Some Sequential Machines and Experiments." Mem. Fac. Sci. Kyushu Univ., ser. A, 12 (1958), 136-158.
10. Huzino, S. "Theory of Finite Automata." Mem. Fac. Sci. Kyushu Univ., ser. A, 15 (1961), 97-159.
11. Trauth, C. A. "Group-Type Automata." J.ACM 13,1 (Jan. 1966), 170-175.

Table 1

Transition Tables of A and B

		a	b	c	d	e	f	g	h	i	j	k	l	m	n	o	p	q	r	s	t	u	v	w	x	y	z
A	0	b	a	c	d	f	e	e	i	h	k	j	l	m	o	n	n	d	s	r	u	t	v	x	w	y	z
	1	a	b	a	b	c	g	f	a	b	l	l	l	l	k	p	o	b	d	t	s	v	w	w	x	w	z

		a	b	c	d	e	f	g	h	i	j	k	l	m	n	o	p	q	r	s	t	u	v	w	x	y	z
B	0	a	b	c	e	e	f	h	g	i	j	p	m	m	o	n	k	q	r	s	u	t	v	x	w	z	y
	1	b	b	b	b	e	e	f	h	e	h	m	n	n	n	o	p	r	r	r	r	u	r	w	r	y	r

ALGEBRAIC THEORY OF m-ARY SYSTEMS

Y. Give'on

Department of Mathematics
University of the Negev, Beer-Sheva, Israel

1. Introduction

Systems are said to be "m-ary" whenever each input element is causing a transformation of the form $Q^m \to Q$ where Q is the state-space of the given system (m is a fixed positive integer and Q^m is the set of all m-tuples of elements of Q; the elements of Q^m will be denoted by symbols of the form $\vec{q}$, like vectors). The natural input structure of an m-ary system is that of a tree of a constant branching degree equal to m (those trees are going to be called "m-ary trees") labeled by the input letters. Thus m-ary systems are a special case of tree-automata (cf. [1],[2] and [3]).

In this paper the basic ideas of the algebraic study of finite-state m-ary acceptors, of finite-state m-ary automata, of m-ary linear systems and of m-ary phrase-structure grammars are presented in a very brief fashion assuming that the ordinary case (i.e., that of m = 1) is well known to the reader.

The purpose of the results presented in this paper is to demonstrate that ordinary automata theory possesses algebraic tools applicable to various domains of interest in the theories of machines and of mathematical systems. These tools should be studied as objects in an algebraic system theory which has yet to be developed.

The research leading to these results was carried out with M.A. Arbib, Department of Computer and Information Science, University of Massachusetts in Amhurst, and with Y. Zalcstein, Department of Computer Sciences, Carnegie-Mellon University.

2. m-ary Acceptors and Regular Events

(2.1) Let X and Q be sets. An m-ary transition map with state-set Q over the alphabet X is a map $\delta : Q^m \times X \to Q$. We say that δ is finite-state when both X and Q are finite, as we shall assume it throughout this paper unless stated to the contrary. The elements of Q are called states and the elements of X letters.

We define m-ary trees over X as formal expressions made of the letters in X and the integers $1,\ldots,m$ by the following recursion:
(2.2) Every single letter and every integer $1<j<m$ is an m-ary tree over X; if $\xi_1,\ldots,\xi_m$ are m m-ary trees over X such that the m-tuples $(\xi_1,\ldots,\xi_m)$ and $(1,2,\ldots,m)$ are not identical and if x is a letter then the expression $[\xi_1,\ldots,\xi_m]x$ is an m-ary tree over X. We denote by X* the set of all m-ary trees over X. An occurrence of a letter or an integer a in an m-ary tree ξ is terminal iff it is occurring in ξ immediately to the right of [or of a comma. The occurrence of any integer occurring in an m-ary tree ξ is always terminal.

(2.3) Given a transition map δ, it is expanded to become a map

$$\delta^* : Q^m \times X^* \to Q : (\vec{q},\xi) \mapsto \vec{q}\cdot\xi$$

by the "m-ary induction":

$$(q_1,\ldots,q_m)\cdot j = q_j \ , \ \vec{q}\cdot x = \delta(\vec{q},x)$$

$$\vec{q}\cdot[\xi_1,\ldots,{}_m]x = \delta((\vec{q}\cdot\xi_1,\ldots,\vec{q}\cdot\xi_m),x)$$

for all $1<j<m$, $\vec{q},(q_1,\ldots,q_m)\in Q^m$, $x\in X$ and $\xi_1,\ldots,\xi_m \in X^*$. δ^* is called the tree-expansion of δ.

(2.4) In X* we can define now an "m-ary concatenation" of an m-tuple of m-ary trees with an m-ary tree by the induction:

$$(\xi_1,\ldots,\xi_m)j = \xi_j \ , \ (1,2,\ldots,m)x = x$$

$$(\xi_1,\ldots,\xi_m)x = [\xi_1,\ldots,\xi_m]x$$

$$\vec{\xi}([\xi_1,\ldots,\xi_m]x) = (\vec{\xi}\xi_1,\ldots,\vec{\xi}\xi_m)x$$

whenever $[\xi_1,\ldots,\xi_m]x$ is defined, for all etc. Obviously, the m-ary concatenation is the tree expansion of the transition map

$$(X^*)^m \times X \to X^*: ((\xi_1,\ldots,\xi_m),x) \mapsto \begin{cases} x \text{ if } \xi_i = i \text{ for all } 1<i<m, \\ [\xi_1,\ldots,\xi_m]x \text{ otherwise.} \end{cases}$$

and it satisfies the following equations:

(m-ary identity:) $(1,2,\ldots,m)\xi = \xi$ for all $\xi \varepsilon X^*$

(m-ary projection:) $(\xi_1,\ldots,\xi_m)j = \xi_j$ for all $1<j<m, \xi_i \varepsilon X^*$

(m-ary associativity:) $\vec{\xi}((\eta_1,\ldots,\eta_m)\zeta) = (\vec{\xi}\eta_1,\ldots,\vec{\xi}\eta_m)\zeta$

for all m-tuples $\vec{\xi}$ of m-ary trees, $\xi_1,\ldots,\xi_m$, $\zeta \varepsilon X^*$.

(2.5) The following observation can illucidate the m-ary concatenation: The m-ary tree $(\xi_1,\ldots,\xi_m)\eta$ is derived from η by replacing each terminal occurrence of each letter x in η by the m-ary tree $(\xi_1,\ldots,\xi_m)x$ and each (necessarily terminal) occurrence of an integer j in η by ξ_j. The m-tuple $(1,2,\ldots,m)$ serves as an identity.

(2.6) Now, if δ^* is the tree expansion of a transition map δ then we have the following associativity:

$$\vec{q}\cdot((\xi_1,\ldots,\xi_m)\eta) = (\vec{q}\cdot\xi_1,\ldots,\vec{q}\cdot\xi_m)\cdot\eta$$

for all $\vec{q}\varepsilon Q^m$, $\xi_1,\ldots,\xi_m$, $\eta\varepsilon X^*$.

We define now "m-ary acceptors":

(2.7) An m-ary acceptor (over the alphabet X) is a triple $\mathfrak{A} = \langle\delta,\vec{q}_0,F\rangle$ where δ is an m-ary transition map, $\vec{q}_0$ an m-tuple of states and F a set of states of δ. The event defined by $\mathfrak{A}$ is denoted by $E(\mathfrak{A})$ and defined by

$$E(\mathfrak{A}) = \{\xi\varepsilon X^*: \vec{q}_0\cdot\xi\varepsilon F\}.$$

A subset E of X^* is an m-ary regular event over X iff $E = T(\mathfrak{A})$ for some m-ary acceptor over X with a finite-state transition map.

(2.8) The study of m-ary finite-state acceptors (i.e., with finite-state transition maps) can be developed in full analogy with Rabin-Scott theory of finite-state automata almost to the letter (cf. [4]). The class of all m-ary regular events over X is a Boolean algebra of sets, and it contains all the finite subsets of X*, and it is closed under the following two operations on subsets of X*:

(i) m-ary <u>product</u> of subsets of X*: for all $E_1,\ldots,E_m,E\epsilon X^*$:

$$(E_1,\ldots,E_m)E = \{(\xi_1,\ldots,\xi_m)\xi \ \ \xi_1\epsilon E_1,\ldots,\xi_m\epsilon E_m,\xi\epsilon E\}$$

(ii) m-ary <u>closure</u> of subsets of X*: for all $E\epsilon X^*$: E^* is the smallest subset of X* which contains E and which is closed under the m-ary concatenation. In fact, the class of all m-ary regular events over X is the smallest class of subsets of X* which contains the finite subsets and is closed under union of sets, m-ary products and the m-ary closure of subsets of X*. Thus, the m-ary analog of Kleene's Theorem is true.

(2.9) The main tool used in deriving these results is that of "invariant equivalences." An equivalence R in X* is said to be <u>right invariant</u> iff

$$\xi_1 R\xi_1',\ldots,\xi_m R\xi_m' \text{ implies } (\xi_1,\ldots,\xi_m)\eta R(\xi_1',\ldots,\xi_m')\eta$$

for all $\xi_1,\ldots,\xi_m,\xi_1',\ldots,\xi_m',\eta\epsilon X^*$. R is said to be <u>invariant</u> iff

$$\xi_1 R\xi_1',\ldots,\xi_m R\xi_m' \text{ and } \eta R\eta' \text{ implies } (\xi_1,\ldots,\xi_m)\eta R(\xi_1',\ldots,\xi_m')\eta'$$

for all $\xi_i,\xi_i',\eta,\eta'\epsilon X^*$. The precise method of applying these relations in order to derive the m-ary analogs of Narode's and Myhill's theorems will become clear from the minimization procedures to be detailed in the next section.

(2.10) As an example of a set which is not m-ary regular consider the following. Let X={a,b}, and for each n>0 let $[a^nba^n]$ denote the m-ary tree in which each maximal path is labeled by the string a^nba^n. The set $\{[a^nba^n]:n>0\}$ is not m-ary regular.

In order to prove a stronger statement, we introduce the following notation. For each <u>string</u> (i.e., 1-ary tree) over X let [s] denote the m-ary tree in which every maximal path is labeled by s. For each set S of strings over X, let $[S] = \{[s]:s\varepsilon S\}$. On the other hand, for each m-ary tree ξ let $|\xi|$ denote the set of all the strings labeling the maximal paths of ξ in which there is no occurrence of any integer. For each subset E of X* let $|E| = \{|\xi|:\xi\varepsilon E\}$

(2.11) Theorem. Let X be any finite alphabet then for each m-ary regular event E over X, $|E|$ is 1-ary regular over X, and for each 1-ary regular set E over X, [E] is m-ary regular over X.

Proof. Let E be an m-ary regular event over X, then $|E|$ is 1-ary regular because of the following properties of the mapping $E \mapsto |E|$ with respect to the Kleenean operations:

(i) if E is finite then $|E|$ is finite;

(ii) $|E_1 \cup E_2| = |E_2| \cup |E_2|$;

(iii) $|(E_1,\ldots,E_m)E| = (|E_1| \cup \ldots \cup |E_m|)E$;

(iv) $|E^*| = |E|^*$.

If E is a 1-ary regular event defined by the 1-ary acceptor $<\delta,q_0,F>$ with state-set Q, then add a new state q' to Q, let $Q' = Q \cup \{q'\}$ and define $\delta':(Q')^m \times X \to Q'$ by $\delta'((q,\ldots,q),x) = \delta(q,x)$ for all $q\varepsilon Q$ - otherwise let the value of δ' be q'. The m-ary regular event defined by $<\delta',(q_0,\ldots,q_0),F>$ is [E].

(2.12) Given an arbitrary subset E of X* and $1 \leq i \leq m$ we define $E|_i$ to be the set of the strings labeling the maximal paths derived from the trees in E by taking from each tree in E only that path which follows the i-th branch at each branching point. Obviously, we have:

(i) if E is finite then $E|_i$ is finite;

(ii) $(E_1 \cup E_2)|_i = E_2|_i \cup E_2|_i$;

(iii) $((E_1,\ldots,E_m)E)|_i = ((E_i)|_i)E|_i$;

(iv) $E^*|_i = (E|_i)^*$;

and therefore for any m-ary regular event E and any $1<i<m$, $E|_i$ is 1-ary regular.

(2.13) The "subset-expansion" is also used in order to convert "non-deterministic" m-ary transition maps into "deterministic" maps. 2^Q denotes the set of all subsets of Q. For each map $\delta: Q^m \times X \to 2^Q$ we define the map $2^\delta: (2^Q)^m \times X \to 2^Q$ by setting for all $Q_1, \ldots, Q_m \subseteq Q$ and any $x \in X$ $2^\delta((Q_1, \ldots, Q_m), x)$ to be the union of all the sets $\delta((q_1, \ldots, q_m), x)$ for all $q_i \in Q_i$; $1 \leq i \leq m$. The two maps δ and 2^δ are equivalent in the following sense: Extend δ into a map $\delta^{\circledast}: Q^m \times X^* \to 2^Q$ by the recursion

$$\delta^{\circledast}(\vec{q}, (\xi_1, \ldots, \xi_m)x) = \{\delta((q_1, \ldots, q_m), x) : q_i \in \delta^{\circledast}(\vec{q}, \xi_i), 1 \leq i \leq m\}$$

and extend 2^δ into its tree-expansion $(2^\delta)^*: (Q^Q)^m \times X^* \to 2^Q$; then for each $\vec{q} \in Q^m$ and each $\xi \in X^*$: $(2^\delta)^*(\vec{q}, \xi) = \delta^*(\vec{q}, \xi)$, where on the right-hand side $\vec{q}$ is taken to be also as an element of $(2^Q)^m$ (i.e., an m-tuple of singletons).

3. m-ary Automata

(3.1) An <u>m-ary</u> (finite-state) <u>automaton</u> $\mathfrak{A}$ <u>over</u> X with <u>output set</u> Y is a system $\mathfrak{A} = \langle \delta, \vec{q}_0, \beta \rangle$ where δ is an m-ary transition map (whose state-set Q is finite), $\vec{q}_0$ is an m-tuple of states and β is an arbitrary map of the form $\beta: Q \to Y$, called the <u>output map</u> of $\mathfrak{A}$. The map $b_{\mathfrak{A}}: X^* \to Y$ defined by $b_{\mathfrak{A}}(\xi) = \beta(\vec{q}_0 \cdot \xi)$, where $\vec{q}_0 \cdot \xi$ is the value of the tree-expansion of δ for $(\vec{q}_0, \xi)$, is called the behavior of $\mathfrak{A}$. Given a map $f: X^* \to Y$, we say that it is <u>realizable</u> iff $f = b_{\mathfrak{A}}$ for some m-ary finite-state automaton $\mathfrak{A}$ over X with output set Y, and in this case we say that $\mathfrak{A}$ is a <u>realization</u> of f.

(3.2) Given an arbitrary map $f: X^* \to Y$ we define two equivalences E_f and D_f in X^* as follows. Firstly, for each pair (ξ, η) of m-ary trees the set of <u>(ξ, η)-pairs</u> of m-ary trees is defined by the following induction: (ξ, η) itself is a (ξ, η)-pair; if $(\vec{\xi}, \vec{\eta})$ is a pair of m-tuples of m-ary trees which are identical except for one component ξ_i and η_i where (ξ_i, η_i) is a (ξ, η)-pair, then for all $x \in X$: $(\vec{\xi}x, \vec{\eta}x)$ is a (ξ, η)-pair. Right-invariant equivalences in X^* can be characterized by the property that if ξ is equivalent to η then ξ^α is equivalent to η^α for all (ξ, η)-pairs $(\xi^\alpha, \eta^\alpha)$. The equivalence E_f is defined by: $\xi E_f \eta$ iff $f(\xi^\alpha) = f(\eta^\alpha)$ for all (ξ, η)-pairs $(\xi^\alpha, \eta^\alpha)$. D_f is defined by $\xi D_f \eta$ iff $f(\zeta\xi^\alpha) = f(\zeta\eta^\alpha)$ for all $\zeta \in X^*$ and all (ξ, η)-pairs $(\xi^\alpha, \eta^\alpha)$. E_f is the smallest right-invariant equivalence E in X^* for which $\xi E \eta$ implies $f(\xi) = f(\eta)$. D_f is an invariant equivalence in X^* which implies E_f, and it is the smallest invariant equivalence D in X^* for which $\xi D \eta$ implies $f(\xi) = f(\eta)$.

(3.3) A map $f:X^* \to Y$ is realizable iff X^*/E_f is finite. The minimal realization of f (which is unique up to a naturally defined isomorphism of automata) is constructed by taking $Q_f = X^*/E_f$, defining δ_f by

$$\delta_f(([\xi_1],\ldots,[\xi_m]),x) = [(\xi_1,\ldots,\xi_m)x],$$

taking $\vec{q}_0 = ([1],[2],\ldots,[m])$, and β_f is defined by $\beta_f([\xi]) = f(\xi)$ (where now the square brackets denote E_f-equivalence classes). Obviously $\langle\delta_f,\vec{q}_0,\beta_f\rangle$ is a realization of f.

(3.4) The invariant equivalences on X^* respect the m-ary concatenation in the sense well defined by defining the category of m-ary monoids in which X^* is in fact the free m-ary monoid on the set X, and in which invariant equivalences are the morphic equivalences.

(3.5) An m-ary monoid W is defined by its carrier $\underset{\sim}{W}$ as a set, an m-ary operation $((w_1,\ldots,w_m),w) \mapsto (w_1,\ldots,w_m)w$ defined in $\underset{\sim}{W}$ and a distinguished m-tuple $\varepsilon = (p_1,\ldots,p_m)$ of elements of $\underset{\sim}{W}$ when the following conditions are met:

(i) m-ary associativity: $\vec{w}((w_1,\ldots,w_m)w) = (\vec{w}w_1,\ldots,\vec{w}w_m)w$;

(ii) m-ary identity: $\varepsilon w = w$ and $(w_1,\ldots,w_m)p_j = w_j$

for all $\vec{w},(w_1,\ldots,w_m)\varepsilon\underset{\sim}{W}^m, w\varepsilon\underset{\sim}{W}$ and $1\leq j\leq m$.

Given two m-ary monoids U and W a map $h:\underset{\sim}{U} \to \underset{\sim}{W}$ determines a morphism $h:U \to W$ iff $h(p_j) = p_j$ for all $1\leq j\leq m$, and $h((u_1,\ldots,u_m)u) = (h(u_1),\ldots,h(u_m))h(u)$ for all $u,u_1,\ldots,u_m\varepsilon U$. Composition of morphisms is defined in the obvious way and the class of all m-ary monoids with their morphisms under composition is a concrete category in which for every set X, X^* with the m-ary concatenation and the m-tuple $(1,2,\ldots,m)$ is a free m-ary monoid on X. For every set Q, the set of all maps $Q^m \to Q$ yields an m-ary monoid under the obvious m-ary composition of such maps with the m-tuple $(p_1,\ldots,p_m)$ of the obvious projections $p_j:Q^m \to Q:(q_1,\ldots,q_m) \mapsto q_j$ as the distinguished m-tuple.

The distinguished m-tuple of an m-ary monoid will be called the identity m-tuple.

The algebraic study of m-ary automata employing m-ary monoids can be pursued now in two equivalent directions as it is the case with ordinary automata:
(3.6) We may consider maps of the form $f:X^* \to Y$ as the objects under study. Such a map f determines an m-ary monoid W_f by taking the maximal factorization of f into a surjective morphism $H_f:X^* \to W_f$ of m-ary monoids followed by a map $h_f:W_f \to Y$. The monoid W_f can be constructed directly from f as the quotient m-ary monoid of X^* under the invariant equivalence D_f defined in (3.2). One has of course that f is realizable iff $W_f = X^*/D_f$ is finite. The definition of the simulation-relation between two maps $f_1:X_1^* \to Y_1$ and $g_1:X_2^* \to Y_2$, by analogy with Krohn & Rhodes' theory (cf.[5]), is defined by: f_1 can be simulated by f_2(in symbols $f_1 | f_2$) iff there exist maps $h_1:X_1 \to X_2$ and $h_2:Y_2 \to Y_1$ such that $f_1 = h_2 f_2 h_1^*$ where $h_1^*:X_1^* \to X_2^*$ is the morphism determined by h_1. It follows that any map $f:X^* \to Y$ can be simulated by the morphism $H_f:X^* \to W_f$ and that for any surjective morphism $H:X^* \to W$ we have $f | H$ iff W_f is a morphic image of an m-ary submonoid of W. Hence every property of simulation of maps of the form $f:X^* \to Y$ is represented by a property of m-ary monoids and, in particular, the study of realizable maps can be reduced to the study of finite m-ary monoids which is still open.

(3.7) We may leave the finite-state m-ary automata as our main object of study and follow the methods of Arbib, Zeiger and Ginzburg (cf.[5] and [6]) in order to develop the Krohn & Rhodes' decomposition theory of finite-state m-ary automata. In this fashion one reduces the study of automata (with output maps) to transition maps ("automata without output"), and associates with each map of the form $\delta:Q^m \times X \to Q$ the submonoid W_δ of the m-ary monoid of all maps $Q^m \to Q$ generated by the maps $\delta^x:Q^m \to Q:\vec{q} \mapsto \vec{q}\cdot x$ for all $x \in X$. Here W is the quotient monoid of X^* under the invariant equivalence defined in X^* by the statement $\vec{q}\cdot\xi = \vec{q}\cdot\eta$ for all $\vec{q} \in Q^m$. The decomposition of transition maps becomes possible due to the following construction which generalizes the "subset-expansion" discussed in (2.13): For any given transition map δ and any collection π of subsets B_i of Q which has the property that of any m-tuple $(B_{i_1},\dots,B_{i_m})$ of subsets in π and every $x \varepsilon X$ there exists $B \varepsilon \pi$ such that for all m-tuples $(q_1,\ldots,q_m)$ with $q_j \varepsilon B_j$, we have $(q_1,\ldots,q_m)\cdot x \varepsilon B$, there exists a transition map $\delta_\pi : \pi^m \times X \to \pi$ satisfying : for all m-tuples $(B_1,\ldots,B_m)$ in π^m, all m-tuples $(q_1,\ldots,q_m)$ with $q_j \varepsilon B_j$ and all $x \varepsilon X$: $\delta((q_1,\ldots,q_m),x) \varepsilon \delta_\pi((B_1,\ldots,B_m),x)$. This fact, together with the fact that simulation of m-ary transition maps (unlike simulation of maps as discussed in (3.6)) can be defined completely in terms of morphisms of transition maps (cf.[7]),establishes the foundation for a completely algebraic decomposition of m-ary finite-state automata.

4. Remark on m-ary Linear Systems

(4.1) Let R be a fixed commutative ring with a unit element. An m-ary R-linear transition system, with a state-space X and an input-space U is an R-linear map

$$\delta : X^m \times U \to X : ((x_i),u) \mapsto (x_i)\cdot u$$

where X and U are R-modules. An m-ary R-linear transition system can be regarded as the "input to states" part of an m-ary discrete-time, time-invariant linear dynamical system and its study can be developed in full analogy with the ordinary case (cf.[8]).

(4.2) For each $u \varepsilon U$ let $\delta^u : X^m \to X : (x_i) \mapsto (x_i)\cdot u$, then δ^u is R-affine with trace δ^0. The set $A^{\delta^0}(X^m,X)$ of all R-affine maps $X^m \to X$ with trace δ^0 forms an R-module isomorphic to X and such that the map $\hat{\delta} : U \to A^{\delta^0}(X^m,X) : u \to \delta^u$ is R-linear.

(4.3) We consider the free m-ary monoid U* on the set (carrier) of U. The set U* does not form an R-module compatible with U, but a family of R-modules U^μ, one for each "m-ary natural number" (i.e., element of the free m-ary monoid on a single generator, where any m-tuple of such "numbers" has a unique successor), together with a family of R-linear maps determined by the m-ary concatenation in U*. Thus the elements of U* are m-ary trees of elements of U treated like vectors in a most natural manner. The construction of U* is called for by the tree-expansion δ^* of δ and the consideration of U* as a family of R-modules is based on the intention of relating to δ^* an appropriate family of R-linear maps as a "tree-expansion" of the R-linear map $\hat{\delta}$.

(4.4) This leads us to the definition of the concept of an m-ary R-monoid as a family $\{W_\mu\}$ of disjoint R-modules indexed by the set of m-ary natural numbers (e.g., by the set $\{1\}^*$ of the elements of the free m-ary monoid on $\{1\}$) where for each $1 \leq i \leq m$, W_i is a trivial R-module, together with a family of surjective R-linear maps

$$\pi_{\vec{\mu},\nu} : (W_{\mu_1}, \ldots, W_{\mu_m}) \times W_\nu \to W_{\vec{\mu}\nu} : (\vec{w}, w) \to \vec{w}w$$

for each m-tuple $\vec{\mu} = (\mu_1, \ldots, \mu_m)$ of m-ary natural numbers and each m-ary natural number ν all satisfying the conditions which make UW_μ into an m-ary monoid. The definition of a morphism of m-ary R-monoids is natural and we get a category of m-ary R-monoids to serve the algebraic tools for the study of m-ary R-linear transition systems in the same way m-ary monoids serve m-ary transition maps.

(4.5) The significance in making this "m-ary exercise" in generalization and in analogy is in pointing at the crucial properties common to a wide domain of types of systems and in suggesting a general algebraic framework in which the various methods and constructions employed in the specific case become the main object of study.

5. Remark on m-ary Context-Free Languages

(5.1) The definition of an m-ary context-free grammar and of the language it generates should be obvious once the shift from ordinary concatenation to m-ary concatenation is understood. An m-ary context-free grammar over the terminal alphabet V_T is a triple $\mathcal{G} = \langle V_N, \sigma, P \rangle$ where V_N is a finite set disjoint from V_T (called the auxiliary alphabet of $\mathcal{G}$), $\sigma \varepsilon V_N$ and P is a finite set of ordered pairs of the form $P_i = (x, \xi)$ where $x \varepsilon V_N$ and $\xi \varepsilon (V_N \cup U_T)^*$ where $(V_N \cup V_T)^*$ is the free m-ary monoid on the union set $V_N \cup V_T$. Derivations by means of $\mathcal{G}$ are defined precisely as they are defined in the 1-ary case except for the fact that now we are dealing with strings of symbols taken from $V_N \cup V_T$ and of right and left bracket and of commas in a form which allows us to interpret these strings as m-ary trees. That is, the pairs in P (call the production rules of $\mathcal{G}$) are interpreted as substitution rules each (x,ξ) allowing the substitution of ξ instead of x in any place in an m-ary tree already derived by means of P from σ (the initial symbol of $\mathcal{G}$). Let us denote by $\mathcal{G}^*$ the set of all m-ary trees derived in this fashion from σ by means of P. Let $L(\mathcal{G})$ be the subset of $\mathcal{G}^*$ containing only m-ary trees that also belong to V_T^* (i.e., $L(\mathcal{G}) = \mathcal{G}^* \cap V_T^*$). The set $L(\mathcal{G})$ is called the language defined or generated by $\mathcal{G}$. A subset L of V_T^* is said to be an m-ary context-free language (in short m-ary c.f.l.) iff there exists an m-ary context-free grammar $\mathcal{G}$ over V_T such that $L = L(\mathcal{G})$.

(5.2) Every m-ary regular even over V_T is an m-ary c.f.l.. The subset $[a^n ba^n]$ given as an example for a set which is not m-ary regular, is not c.f.l. either for obvious reasons. On the other hand, consider the following m-ary grammar over $\{a,b\}$:

$$= <\{\sigma\},\sigma,\{(\sigma,[[a,a]\sigma,[a,a]\sigma]a),(\sigma,b)\}>$$

then $L(\mathcal{G})$ is not m-ary regular (note that $|L(\mathcal{G})|$ is the set of all string $a^n ba^n$ for $n \geqslant 0$ nevertheless).

(5.3) For each m-ary c.f.l. L over V_T the sets $|L|$ and $L|_i$ (for all $1<i<m$) are 1-ary c.f.l..

(5.4) Most of the well-known study of context-free languages (cf.[9]) can be copied into the m-ary case without any particular difficulty.

6. References

1. Mezei, J. and J. B. Wright (1965), Generalized ALGOL-like Languages, IBM Research Paper RC1528.
2. Arbib, M. A. and Y. Give'on (1968), Algebra Automata I, Information and Control, 12, 331-345.
3. Give'on, Y. and M. A. Arbib (1968), Algebra Automata II, Information and Control, 12, 346-370.
4. Rabin, M. O. and D. Scott (1959), Finite Automata and Their Decision Problems, IBM Journal, 3, 114-125.
5. Arbib, M. A. (ed.)(1968), Algebraic Theory of Machines, Languages and Semigroups, Academic Press.

6. Ginzburg, A. (1968), Algebraic Theory of Automata, Academic Press.
7. Give'on, Y. (1970), Algebraic Formulations of Simulation of Automata, University of the Negev Technical Note.
8. Give'on, Y. and Y. Zalcstein (1970), Algebraic Structures in Linear Systems Theory, J. Comput. System Sci., 4, 539-556.
9. Bar-Hillel, Y., M. Perles and E. Shamir (1960), On Formal Properties of Simple Phrase Structure Grammars, in: Y. Bar-Hillel (1964), Language and Information, Addison Wesley Series in Logic, 116-150.

GROUPS AND AUTOMATA

J-F. Perrot

Institut de Programmation
Université de Paris

Abstract

Four permutation groups are associated with any finite monogenic automaton $\underline{A}$, namely the Suschkewitsch group $G(\underline{A})$, the well known automorphism group $Aut(\underline{A})$, the maximal kernel group $\Gamma(\underline{A})$, and the maximal group homomorphic image $\Delta(\underline{A})$. Several results are given relating these groups to the algebraic structure of $\underline{A}$ and, in the case when $\underline{A}$ is the reduced acceptor $\underline{Ac}(A^*)$ associated with a prefix code A, to some properties of A. Proofs are not included and will be published elsewhere.

1. Automata and Prefix Codes

We call here automata what Ginzburg[8] calls semi-automata and Give'on[9] semi-modules or transition systems : a set X (the input alphabet), a set S (the set of states) together with an application of $S \times X$ into S (denoted by right multiplication: $s \in S$, $x \in X \longrightarrow sx \in S$) define an automaton $\underline{A} = \langle X, S \rangle$. As is well known, such an automaton can be viewed as an algebraic structure (monadic algebra), the states being the elements and the input letters the (unary) operators. Thus the traditional vocabulary of general algebra is relevant here, and accordingly we use the words subautomaton, congruence, quotient automaton, homomorphic image with their usual meaning.

Unless specifically stated otherwise, $\underline{A} = \langle X, S \rangle$ will denote a finite monogenic automaton, $\bar{S}$ the set of generators of $\underline{A}$ (i.e. the set of those states of $\underline{A}$, each of which generates $\underline{A}$), $C(\underline{A})$ the lattice of congruences of $\underline{A}$, and $Aut(\underline{A})$

the automorphism group of $\underline{A}$. An automaton $\underline{A}$ is <u>strongly connected</u> if $S = \bar{S}$, and is called here <u>0-connected</u> if it contains a state 0 such that $S = \bar{S} \cup \{0\}$ (0 is then a "sink").

Both strongly connected and 0-connected automata occur as reduced acceptors $\underline{Ac}(A^*)$ of submonoids generated by prefix codes. Recall that the following conditions on a subset P of the free monoid X^* generated by X are equivalent ([13], [16], [17]):

(i) P is a simple star event, i.e. the reduced (Rabin-Scott) acceptor $\underline{Ac}(P)$ has only one terminal state, which is the initial state ;

(ii) P is a right unitary submonoid of X^*, i.e. $u \in P$ implies $uv \in P \iff v \in P$;

(iii) P is the submonoid A^* of X^* generated by a prefix code $A \subset X^*$, i.e. by a subset A of XX^* such that $AXX^* \cap A = \emptyset$.

Let A be a prefix code : it follows from (i) that either $\underline{Ac}(A^*)$ is strongly connected, in which case A is said to be full, or $\underline{Ac}(A^*)$ is 0-connected. The main tool in investigating the relationship between A and $\underline{Ac}(A^*)$ is the following remark ([10], [11]):

<u>Theorem 1</u> : Let A be a prefix code, $\underline{A} = \underline{Ac}(A^*)$. Then to any non trivial congruence of $\underline{A}$ corresponds a prefix code B such that $A^* \subset B^*$. The converse is true if A is full and finite.

We shall give some results for finite prefix codes, which are consequences of

<u>Theorem 2</u> (M.P. Schützenberger [17]): If A is a finite prefix code such that $\underline{Ac}(A^*)$ is a group automaton, then A is a uniform code, i.e. $A = X^n$ for some integer n.

II. The transition monoid $T(\underline{A})$ and the Suschkewitsch group $G(\underline{A})$

An automaton $\underline{A}$ can also be considered as an application of X into the monoid S^S of all applications of S into itself, which is canonically extended to a monoid homomorphism of the free monoid X^* into S^S. The image of X^*, which is the submonoid of S^S generated by the transitions the input letters operate on S, is the <u>transition monoid</u> of $\underline{A}$, denoted by $T(\underline{A})$.

This paper is part of a general study of the relationships between monogenic automata and their transition monoids. Note that if $\underline{A}$ is the reduced acceptor $\underline{Ac}(L)$ of a regular event L, then $T(\underline{A})$ is isomorphic to the syntactic monoid of L, to the study of which our results are applicable.

Since $T(\underline{A})$ is represented by transformations of S, let us consider for $m \in T(\underline{A})$ the rank of m, i.e. $r(m) = |\{s \in S;\ s = tm \text{ for some } t \in S\}|$. For instance, the minimal two-sided ideal of $T(\underline{A})$ (see [5]) is exactly the set of elements of $T(\underline{A})$ having minimal rank, which makes it easy to compute (see [15]).

We now define a regular $\underline{D}$-class of $T(\underline{A})$ in which the properties of $\underline{A}$ are reflected, which we call the $\underline{D}$-class on which $\underline{A}$ depends and which we denote by $D(\underline{A})$:

Let a be a generator of $\underline{A}$, $P(a) = \{m \in T(\underline{A});\ am = a\}$ the submonoid of $T(\underline{A})$ that fixes a, and $Q(a)$ the minimal two-sided ideal of $P(a)$. Then $Q(a)$ is contained in a regular $\underline{D}$-class of $T(\underline{A})$ which is the same for all generators a of $\underline{A}$, and which is by definition the $\underline{D}$-class on which $\underline{A}$ depends.

Theorem 3: $m \in T(\underline{A})$ belongs to $D(\underline{A})$ iff m has minimal rank among those elements of $T(\underline{A})$ that map at least one generator onto another generator, i.e. such that $\bar{S}m \cap \bar{S} \neq \emptyset$.

The Suschkewitsch group $G(\underline{A})$ of $\underline{A}$ is defined as follows:

Let e be an idempotent element of $D(\underline{A})$. The maximal subgroup of $T(\underline{A})$ containing e acts transitively on the set $\bar{S}e \cap \bar{S}$. The various idempotents of $D(\underline{A})$ give in this way transitive permutation groups which are all equivalent by definition to the Suschkewitsch group $G(\underline{A})$.

Thus $G(\underline{A})$ is a homomorphic image of the structure group of $D(\underline{A})$.

If $\underline{A}$ is strongly connected, $D(\underline{A})$ is the minimal ideal of $T(\underline{A})$, the importance of which was first noted by Deussen[6]. If $\underline{A}$ is 0-connected, then $T(\underline{A})$ contains a zero element and $D(\underline{A})$ is the (completely 0-simple) 0-minimal ideal. In both cases $G(\underline{A})$ is isomorphic to the structure group of $D(\underline{A})$.

We shall see that $G(\underline{A})$ plays a major rôle in the present theory. In particular the three other groups associated with $\underline{A}$ that we consider here all divide $G(\underline{A})$. Moreover, much information on $G(\underline{A})$ can be obtained by an easy approximation of $T(\underline{A})$ [15]. For additional results and applications to reduced acceptors for full prefix codes see [10] and [14].

III. The automorphism group Aut($\underline{A}$) and the automorphism congruences

Whereas transition monoids seem to be a little-explored subject, automorphism groups have been widely studied (see Arbib[1]), especially in the strongly connected case (Deussen[6][7], Brauer[4], Barnes[2]) and also in the general monogenic case (Bavel[3]).

If s is a generator of $\underline{A}$, then any automorphism σ of $\underline{A}$ is entirely determined by $\sigma(s)$, which is too a generator of $\underline{A}$. Hence Aut($\underline{A}$) is faithfully represented by its restriction to $\bar{S}$, which is a semiregular group, i.e. if for some $s \in \bar{S}$ one has $\sigma(s) = s$ then σ is the identity automorphism. This amounts to saying that the order of Aut($\underline{A}$) is equal to the number of states in any of its transitivity classes in $\bar{S}$.

It follows that Aut($\underline{A}$) is transitive iff $\underline{A}$ is a group automaton such that T($\underline{A}$) is a regular group and that, unless it is of order two, it cannot be doubly transitive [4].

It has been noted [1] that Aut($\underline{A}$) must divide some subgroup of T($\underline{A}$). Indeed, we shall see that Aut($\underline{A}$) divides the Suschkewitsch group G($\underline{A}$), hence the structure group of D($\underline{A}$) . In the strongly connected case this follows from a result of [6].

Now let us denote by $\alpha(H)$ the transitivity equivalence of a subgroup H of Aut($\underline{A}$), α(Aut($\underline{A}$)) being abbreviated as $\alpha(\underline{A})$. Any equivalence $\alpha(H)$ is indeed a congruence of $\underline{A}$, let us say an "automorphism congruence", and the set of all automorphism congruences of $\underline{A}$ constitute a sublattice of the lattice C($\underline{A}$) of all congruences of $\underline{A}$, which is isomorphic to the lattice of all subgroups of Aut($\underline{A}$). The maximal element of this sublattice is of course $\alpha(\underline{A})$ and indeed if $\underline{A}$ is strongly connected or 0-connected then $\theta \in C(\underline{A})$ is an automorphism congruence iff $\theta \leq \alpha(\underline{A})$, i.e. the automorphism congruences of $\underline{A}$ constitute an ideal of the lattice C($\underline{A}$). This is in general not true, but we shall in the next section construct an ideal of C($\underline{A}$) containing all the automorphism congruences and still retaining some of their properties.

As regards the quotient automaton $\underline{A}/\alpha(\underline{A})$, Weeg[18] remarked that Aut($\underline{A}/\alpha(\underline{A})$) could be arbitrary. It can be shown that the automaton itself $\underline{A}/\alpha(\underline{A})$ can be arbitrary (see [12] for the strongly connected case).

IV. The group congruences and the maximal kernel group (A)

Clearly, any automorphism congruence is such that, for any $s \in S$, any $m \in T(\underline{A})$ verifying $sm \equiv s$ permutes the states that are congruent to s. We are thus led to the concept of group congruence, which was introduced and worked out in some detail for the strongly connected case in [12].

A congruence θ of $\underline{A}$ is a group congruence iff the submonoid of $T(\underline{A})$ leaving the class of a state s globally fixed induces on this class a permutation group. For $s \in \bar{S}$, all these groups are equivalent to the kernel group of θ.

Any automorphism congruence $\alpha(H)$ is a group congruence, its kernel group being isomorphic to H, subgroup of $Aut(\underline{A})$.

The set of all group congruences constitutes an ideal of the lattice $C(\underline{A})$, so that there exists a unique maximal group congruence which we denote by $\gamma(\underline{A})$. The kernel group of $\gamma(\underline{A})$ is by definition the maximal kernel group $\Gamma(\underline{A})$.

It is easy to see that if ζ and θ are group congruences and if $\zeta \leq \theta$, then the kernel group of ζ divides the kernel group of θ, hence that the kernel group of any group congruence of $\underline{A}$ divides $\Gamma(\underline{A})$. In particular, since $Aut(\underline{A})$ is isomorphic to the kernel group of $\alpha(\underline{A})$, we have

Theorem 4: $Aut(\underline{A})$ divides the maximal kernel group $\Gamma(\underline{A})$.

Furthermore it can be shown that

Theorem 5: $\Gamma(\underline{A})$ divides the Suschkewitsch group $G(\underline{A})$.

We then obtain the

Corollary : $Aut(\underline{A})$ divides $G(\underline{A})$.

(For these results in the strongly connected case, see [12].)

Now suppose $\underline{A}$ is the reduced acceptor $Ac(A^*)$ for a finite prefix code A. From Theorems 1 and 2 one can deduce that $\Gamma(\underline{A})$ is necessarily cyclic, say of order n, that $Aut(\underline{A})$ is indeed isomorphic to $\Gamma(\underline{A})$, and that $A = B^n$ for some (necessarily finite) prefix code B such that $Aut(Ac(B^*))$ is trivial. The converse is true, so that

Theorem 6 : For a finite prefix code A, $Aut(Ac(A^*))$ and $\Gamma(Ac(A^*))$ are isomorphic and necessarily cyclic. Both are of order n iff $A = B^n$ for some prefix code such that $\Gamma(Ac(B^*))$ is trivial.

Of course, Theorem 6 is no longer valid if we allow A to be infinite.

V. The maximal group homomorphic image $(\underline{A})$

A congruence θ of $\underline{A}$ is such that the quotient automaton $\underline{A}/\theta$ is a group automaton iff every $m \in T(\underline{A})$ permutes the classes mod. θ, i.e. iff for $s, t \in S$, $sm \equiv tm$ mod. θ implies $s \equiv t$ mod. θ. Hence if $\theta_1, \theta_2, \ldots, \theta_k$ are such congruences then $\theta_1 \wedge \theta_2 \wedge \cdots \wedge \theta_k$ is again such a congruence, so that there exists a unique minimal congruence of $\underline{A}$ the quotient of which is a group automaton, denoted by $\gamma(\underline{A})$. The <u>maximal group homomorphic image</u> is by definition $T(\underline{A}/\gamma(\underline{A}))$. Clearly, for any homomorphic image $\underline{B}$ of $\underline{A}$ which is a group automaton, $T(\underline{B})$ is a homomorphic image of $\Delta(\underline{A})$.

$\Delta(A)$ being a group and a homomorphic image of $T(\underline{A})$ is necessarily a homomorphic image of any maximal subgroup of the minimal ideal of $T(\underline{A})$.

<u>Theorem 7</u> : If $\underline{A}$ is strongly connected then $\Delta(\underline{A})$ is a homomorphic image of $G(\underline{A})$, and $\Delta(\underline{A})$ is isomorphic to $G(\underline{A})$ iff the minimal two-sided ideal $D(\underline{A})$ contains only one minimal right ideal.

Now let A be a full prefix code. From Theorem 1 follows that there exists a prefix code B such that $A^* \subset B^*$ and that $T(\underline{Ac}(B^*))$ is isomorphic to $\Delta(Ac(A^*))$. If A is finite, then B is necessarily finite too and we get from Theorem 2 that $\Delta(\underline{Ac}(A^*))$ must be cyclic and B uniform, which means that the greatest common divisor of the lengths of the words in A is equal to the order of $\Delta(\underline{Ac}(A^*))$.

REFERENCES

1. ARBIB, M.A.: Automaton Automorphisms, Inf. and Control <u>11</u> (1967) 147-154.
2. BARNES, B.: On the Group of Automorphisms of Strongly Connected Automata, Math. Systems Theory <u>4</u> (1970) 289-294.
3. BAVEL, Z.: Structure and Transition-Preserving Functions of Finite Automata, J.A.C.M. <u>15</u> (1968) 135-158.
4. BRAUER, W.: Gruppentheoretische Untersuchungen bei endlichen Automaten, Z.A.M.M. <u>48</u> (1968) T.113-T.115.
5. CLIFFORD, A.H., and G.B. PRESTON: The Algebraic Theory of Semigroups, American Math. Soc., t.1, 1961.
6. DEUSSEN, P.: On the Algebraic Theory of Finite Automata, ICC Bull. <u>4</u> (1966), 231-264.

7. DEUSSEN, P.: Some Results on the Set of Congruence Relations on a Finite, Strongly Connected Automaton, Computing 2 (1967) 353-367.
8. GINZBURG, A.: Algebraic Theory of Automata, Academic Press 1968.
9. GIVE'ON, Y.: Categories of Semimodules: The Categorical Structural Properties of Transition Systems, Math. Systems Theory 1 (1967) 67-78.
10. PERRIN, D.: Le langage engendré par un code préfixe et son monoïde syntactique, Thèse de 3e Cycle, Paris 1970.
11. PERRIN, D., et J-F. PERROT : Sur les codes préfixes complets finis, C.R. Acad. Sci. Paris 269 (1969) 1116-1118.
12. PERRIN, D.,et J-F. PERROT : Congruences et Automorphismes des automates finis, submitted to Acta Informatica (Springer).
13. PERROT, J-F.: Endliche Automaten und Prefixcodes, in J. Dörr u. G. Hotz (Herausgeber), Automatentheorie und formale Sprachen (Tagungsbericht, Oberwolfach 1969) 39-53.
14. PERROT, J-F.: On the Relationship between Finite Automata, Finite Monoids, and Prefixcodes, Proc. 2nd ACM Symposium on the Theory of Computing (1970), 217-220.
15. PERROT, J-F.: Sur le calcul effectif du monoide de transitions d'un automate fini, International Computing Symposium, Bonn 1970.
16. SCHÜTZENBERGER, M.P.: On an Application of Semigroup Methods to some Problems in Coding, IRE Trans. on Information Theory, IT-2 (1956) 47-60.
17. SCHÜTZENBERGER, M.P.: Une théorie algébrique du codage, Séminaire Dubreil-Pisot, Paris, Année 1955-56, n° 15.
18. WEEG, G.P.: The Automorphism Group of a Factor Automaton, mimeographed (1967).

AUTOMATON STRUCTURE PRESERVING MORPHISMS WITH APPLICATIONS TO DECOMPOSITION AND SIMULATION

Bernard P. Zeigler*

Department of Computer and Communication Sciences
Logic of Computers Group
The University of Michigan
611 Church Street
Ann Arbor, Michigan 48104

Introduction

We may view the problem of sequential machine decomposition in the following form:

Given an automaton M, a set of automata $\mathcal{M}$ and a simulation (or realization) criterion χ, find an automaton $M' \varepsilon \mathcal{M}$ which simulates M according to criterion χ.

In particular much attention has been given to the cases where $\mathcal{M}$ denotes a set of series-parallel compositions [e.g., Krohn and Rhodes (1965), Hartmanis and Stearns (1966)], or those for which $\mathcal{M}$ denotes a set of feedback shift register machines [e.g., Martin 1968].

Until recently however, the methods were developed to be generally applicable to any machine. Little attention was paid to intrinsic structural properties of the to-be-realized machine M, and their relations to properties of the machines M' in $\mathcal{M}$. A more structural approach is evident in recent work by Yamada and Amoroso (1969,1970) and Gallaire and Harrison (1969).

In this paper a basis is developed for the study of structured automata and the structure preserving morphisms by which they can be related.

Applied to the decomposition problem, the introduction of the structure preserving morphism permits the study of simulation criteria in which the simulatee M and the simulator M' are more intimately related than has been usual.

*This work was supported by the National Institutes of Health (Grant No. GM-12236) and the National Science Foundation (Grant No. GJ-519).

An automaton $M = \langle X,Q,Y,\delta,\lambda \rangle$ is *structured* by coordinatizing each of the sets X,Q,Y (input, state, and output), i.e., expressing each via a cross-product of a family of sets; and (consistent with this structure) expressing each of the functions δ,λ (transition and output functions) via a cross-product of a family of coordinate functions.

The relation which expresses the preservation of structure from a structured automaton M to a structured automaton M' is called a *structure preserving morphism*. Such a morphism preserves not only the transition and output functions of the abstract automaton but also the manner in which these functions arise out of the local coordinate functions in its structured representation.

A special class of such morphisms have been studied by Yamada and Amoroso (1970). Their attention was directed toward *isomorphic* preservation of the transition function of a tessellation automaton under various structural transformations with a view toward neighborhood reduction. The more general formulation in this paper facilitates discussion of truly *homomorphic* preservation of the transition function and the study of reduction of complexity for measures relevant to the simulation of structured automata (again including neighborhood reduction as a special case). The formulation of simulation given here facilitates discussion of both parallel and sequential simulation of structured automata.

Structured Functions

These concepts are most easily developed in terms of arbitrary functions $f:A \to B$.

The domain A is *structured* by injecting it into a cross-product of an indexed family $\{A_\alpha | \alpha \varepsilon D_A\}$, i.e., $A \subseteq \times_{\alpha\varepsilon D_A} A_\alpha$; D_A is the set of *coordinates** for A. (Similarly, the range $B \subseteq \times_{\beta\varepsilon D_B} B_\beta$.)

Associated with a structured set A is a family of *coordinate* projections $\{P_\alpha | \alpha\varepsilon D_A\}$ where $P_{\alpha_i}: A \to A_{\alpha_i}$ is defined by $P_{\alpha_i}(a_{\alpha_1}, a_{\alpha_2}, \ldots, a_{\alpha_i}, \ldots) = a_{\alpha_i}$.

*D_A is assumed to be a totally ordered set. Any subset of D_A is assumed to be presented in the order inherited from D_A.

Given an indexed family of functions $\{f_i : A \to B_i \mid i \varepsilon E\}$ the *cross-product* function $\underset{i\varepsilon E}{\times} f_i : A \to \underset{i\varepsilon E}{\times} B_i$ is defined by $\underset{i\varepsilon E}{\times} f_i(a) = (f_1(a), f_2(a), \ldots, f_{|E|}(a))$. [$|E|$ is the cardinality of E.]

Using the cross-product we can extend the projections of a structured set A to project on all nonempty subsets: we have the set $\{P_C \mid P_C = \underset{\alpha\varepsilon C}{\times} P_\alpha,\ \phi \neq C \subseteq D_A\}$. (Thus for example, $P_{\{1,3\}}(a_1,a_2,a_3) = (a_1,a_3)$.) For the empty set $\phi \subseteq D$ we set P_ϕ to be any constant function with domain A.

$f: A \to B$ is *structured* by first giving structures to A and B and then presenting an indexed family of functions $\{f_\beta \mid f_\beta : \underset{\alpha\varepsilon I_\beta}{\times} A_\alpha) \to B_\beta, I_\beta \subseteq D_A, \beta\varepsilon D_B\}$ such that $f = \underset{\beta\varepsilon D_B}{\times} f_\beta \circ P_{I_\beta}$.* The latter equation is in fact a set of $|D_\beta|$ equations of the form

$$P_\beta(f(a)) = f_\beta(P_{\alpha_1}(a), \ldots, P_{\alpha_{|I_\beta|}}(a))$$

or more compactly

$$P_\beta \circ f = f_\beta \circ P_{I_\beta}.$$

Example 1:

Let $A = \{a_0,a_1,a_2,a_3,a_4\}$, $B = \{b_0,b_1,b_2\}$ and $f: A \to B$ be given by

A	f
a_0	b_0
a_1	b_0
a_2	b_0
a_3	b_1
a_4	b_2

Let A be structured by $\{A_\alpha \mid \alpha\varepsilon D_A\}$ where $D_A = \{\alpha_0,\alpha_1,\alpha_2,\alpha_3\}$ and $A_\alpha = \{0,1\}$ for each $\alpha\varepsilon D_A$. This assignment is given by the identifications:

$$a_0 \leftrightarrow (0,0,0,0)$$
$$a_1 \leftrightarrow (0,0,1,1)$$
$$a_2 \leftrightarrow (0,1,0,1)$$
$$a_3 \leftrightarrow (0,0,1,0)$$

*The parentheses indicate that f_β need be defined only on $P_{I_\beta}(A)$. I will omit them hereafter. Also $h\circ g$ is the usual *composition* of h and g, namely $h\circ g(x)=h(g(x))$.

$$a_4 \leftrightarrow (1,1,1,1)$$

Similarly, let B be structured by $\{B_\beta | \beta \varepsilon D_B\}$ where $D_\beta = \{\beta_0, \beta_1, \beta_2\}$, each $B_\beta = \{0,1\}$ and the assignment is given by:

$$b_0 \leftrightarrow (0,1,0)$$
$$b_1 \leftrightarrow (0,1,1)$$
$$b_2 \leftrightarrow (1,0,0)$$

A structure assignment for f is given by $\{f_\beta | \beta \varepsilon D_B\}$ where

$$I_{\beta_0} = \{\alpha_0\} \text{ and } f_{\beta_0}(x) = x$$
$$I_{\beta_1} = \{\alpha_1, \alpha_2\} \text{ and } f_{\beta_1}(x,y) = \overline{x \wedge y}$$
$$I_{\beta_2} = \{\alpha_2, \alpha_3\} \text{ and } f_{\beta_2}(x,y) = x \wedge \bar{y}.^*$$

The validity of this assignment lies in the satisfaction of

$$f = \underset{\beta \varepsilon D_B}{\text{x}} f_\beta \circ P_{I_\beta}$$

i.e.,

$$f(a_{\alpha_0}, a_{\alpha_1}, a_{\alpha_2}, a_{\alpha_3}) = (f_{\beta_0}(a_{\alpha_0}), f_{\beta_1}(a_{\alpha_1}, a_{\alpha_2}), f_{\beta_2}(a_{\alpha_2}, a_{\alpha_3}))$$
$$= (a_{\alpha_0}, \overline{a_{\alpha_1} \wedge a_{\alpha_2}}, a_{\alpha_2} \wedge \overline{a_{\alpha_3}})$$

for all $(a_{\alpha_0}, a_{\alpha_1}, a_{\alpha_2}, a_{\alpha_3}) \varepsilon A$.

Given any function g with domain $X \subseteq \text{x}_{\alpha \varepsilon D} X_\alpha$, we say that g *depends* on a set $C \subseteq D$ if for all $x, x' \varepsilon X$

$$P_C(x) = P_C(x') \Rightarrow g(x) = g(x').$$

C is said to be a *location* for g, written loc g, if g depends on C and for any $C' \subseteq C$, if g depends on C' then C' = C (C is a minimal dependence set). More than one location for a function may exist (see Zeigler, 1968). A function g with domain $X \subseteq \text{x}_{\alpha \varepsilon D} X_\alpha$ is in *reduced* form if D is a location for g. Every function may be put in reduced form (nonuniquely).

The structured function f:A → B is in *reduced* form if

---

*(∧ = and, ∨ = or, - = not).

every f_β is in reduced form.

Example 1 (Cont'd):

Another structure assignment for $f:A \to B$, also reduced, is given by f_{β_0}, f_{β_2} as before but change f_{β_1} to $f_{\beta_1}(x) = \bar{x}$ where $I_{\beta_1} = \{\alpha_0\}$. This is possible because $P_{\alpha_0}(a) = P_{\alpha_1}(a) \wedge P_{\alpha_2}(a)$ for all $a \in A$. Here we have an (extreme) example of intervariable constraints which arise when not all elements of a cross-product are associated with elements of the structured set.

The dependencies underlying the structure of f can be displayed as a directed graph called the *dependency digraph representing* f. It has as points $D_A \cup D_B$ and there is a line from $\alpha \in D_A$ to $\beta \in D_B$ just in case $\alpha \in I_\beta$, i.e., coordinate α is in the *input* set of function f_β.

Example 1 (Cont'd):

The structure digraph for f (unmodified) is

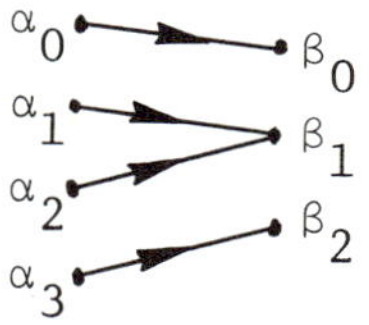

Structuring of functions can be done recursively. For example, for $f:A_1 \times A_2 \to B$, one assigns structures *separately* to A_1, A_2 and B. Thus, if $\{A^i_\alpha \mid \alpha \in D_{A_i}\}$ coordinatizes A_i, $i=1,2$ then $\bigcup_{i=1,2} \{A^i_\alpha\}$ coordinatizes $A_1 \times A_2$ via $A_1 \times A_2 \subseteq \times_{\alpha \in D_{A_1}} A^1_\alpha \times_{\alpha \in D_{A_2}} A^2_\alpha$.

In this way, one can assign a structure to an automaton $<X,Q,Y,\delta,\lambda>$.

Function and Structure Preserving Morphisms

We are concerned with preservation relations holding between functions $f:A \to B$ and $f':A' \to B'$ in their abstract and structured forms.

A *function preserving morphism* (briefly, *function morphism*) from f to f' is a pair (h_A, h_B) where $h_A:A \to A'$

(onto), $h_B: B \to B'$ (onto) and $f' \circ h_A = h_B \circ f$.

Applied to automata, the function morphism becomes the usual homomorphism.

A *structure preserving morphism* (briefly, *structure morphism*) from f to f' (structured functions) is a 4-tuple $(d_A, d_B, \{h_{\alpha'} | \alpha' \varepsilon D_{A'}\}, \{h_{\beta'} | \beta' \varepsilon D_{B'}\})$ where

1) $d_A: D_A \to D_{A'}$ (onto), $d_B: D_B \to D_{B'}$ (onto);

2) For each $\alpha' \varepsilon D_{A'}$, $h_{\alpha'}: \times_{\alpha \varepsilon (\alpha')} A_\alpha \to A'_{\alpha'}$ (onto) and for each $\beta' \varepsilon D_{B'}$, $h_{\beta'}: \times_{\beta \varepsilon (\beta')} B_\beta \to B'_{\beta'}$ (onto).
Here $(\alpha') = \{\alpha | d_A(\alpha) = \alpha'\}$ and $(\beta') = \{\beta | d_B(\beta) = \beta'\}$.

3) For each $\beta' \varepsilon D_{B'}$, $f'_{\beta'} \circ h_{I'_{\beta'}} = h_{\beta'} \circ f_{(\beta')}$.
Here $h_{I'_{\beta'}} = \times_{\alpha' \varepsilon I'_{\beta'}} h_{\alpha'} \circ P_{(\alpha')}$ and
$f_{(\beta')} = \times_{\beta \varepsilon (\beta')} f_\beta \circ P_{I_\beta}$.

4) For each $\beta' \varepsilon D_{B'}$, there exists a location for $f'_{\beta'} \circ h_{I'_{\beta'}}$ $(= h_{\beta'} \circ f_{(\beta')})$ call it loc $f'_{\beta'} \circ h_{I'_{\beta'}}$, such that loc $f'_{\beta'} \circ h_{I'_{\beta'}} \subseteq (I'_{\beta'}) \cap I_{(\beta')}$.
Here $(I'_{\beta'}) = \bigcup_{\alpha' \varepsilon I'_{\beta'}} (\alpha')$ and $I_{(\beta')} = \bigcup_{\beta \varepsilon (\beta')} I_\beta$.

Example 2:

Let $A' = \{a'_0, a'_1, a'_2, a'_3\}$ be structured by $\{A'_{\alpha'} | \alpha' \varepsilon D_{A'}\}$ where $D_{A'} = \{\alpha'_0, \alpha'_1, \alpha'_2\}$. The assignment is

$$a'_0 \leftrightarrow (0,0,1)$$
$$a'_1 \leftrightarrow (0,1,0)$$
$$a'_2 \leftrightarrow (0,0,0)$$
$$a'_3 \leftrightarrow (1,1,1).$$

Let $B' = \{b'_0, b'_1\}$ be structured by $\{B'_{\beta'} | \beta' \varepsilon D_{B'}\}$ where $D_{B'} = \{\beta'_0, \beta'_1\}$. The assignment is

$$b'_0 \leftrightarrow (0,0)$$
$$b'_1 \leftrightarrow (1,1).$$

Let $f':A' \rightarrow B'$ be structured by $\{f_{\beta'} | \beta' \varepsilon D_{B'}\}$ where

$$I'_{\beta'_0} = \{\alpha'_0\} \quad \text{and} \quad f'_{\beta'_0}(x) = x$$

$$I'_{\beta'_1} = \{\alpha'_1, \alpha'_2\} \text{ and } f'_{\beta'_1}(x,y) = x \equiv y.*$$

There is a structure morphism $(d_A, d_B, \{h_{\alpha'}\}, \{h_{\beta'}\})$ from f of Example 1 (unmodified) to f' as follows:

1. $d_A:D_A \rightarrow D_{A'}$, $d_B:D_B \rightarrow D_{B'}$ are given by

D_A	d_A
α_0	α'_0
α_1	α'_1
α_2	α'_2
α_3	α'_2

D_B	d_B
β_0	β'_0
β_1	β'_1
β_2	β'_1

This pair of mappings is best visualized as relating the structure digraphs:

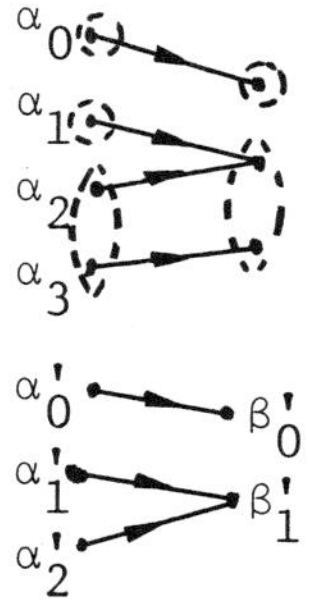

2. $\{h_{\alpha'_0}, h_{\alpha'_1}, h_{\alpha'_2}\}$ and $\{h_{\beta'_0}, h_{\beta'_1}\}$ are given by

$(\alpha'_0) = \{\alpha_0\}$ and $h_{\alpha'_0}(x) = x$

$(\alpha'_1) = \{\alpha_1\}$ and $h_{\alpha'_1}(x) = x$

$(\alpha'_2) = \{\alpha_2, \alpha_3\}$ and $h_{\alpha'_2}(x,y) = x \equiv y$;

$(\beta'_0) = \{\beta_0\}$ and $h_{\beta'_0}(x) = x$

*$x \equiv y = 1 \iff x = y$.

$(\beta'_1) = \{\beta_1, \beta_2\}$ and $h_{\beta'_1}(x,y) = x \equiv y$

3. For structure morphism we must have

$$\begin{cases} f'_{\beta'_0} \circ h_{I'_{\beta'_0}} = h_{\beta'_0} \circ f_{(\beta'_0)} \\ f'_{\beta'_1} \circ h_{I'_{\beta'_1}} = h_{\beta'_1} \circ f_{(\beta'_1)} \end{cases}$$

where

$$\begin{cases} h_{I'_{\beta'_0}} = h_{\alpha'_0} \\ h_{I'_{\beta'_1}} = h_{\alpha'_1} \circ P_{\alpha_1} \times h_{\alpha'_2} \circ P_{\{\alpha_2, \alpha_3\}} \end{cases}$$

$$\begin{cases} f_{(\beta'_0)} = f_{\beta_0} \\ f_{(\beta'_1)} = f_{\beta_1} \circ P_{\{\alpha_1, \alpha_2\}} \times f_{\beta_2} \circ P_{\{\alpha_3\}} \end{cases}$$

In other words

$$\begin{cases} f'_{\beta_0}(h_{\alpha'_0}(a_{\alpha_0})) = h_{\beta'_0}(f_{\beta_0}(a_{\alpha_0})) \\ f'_{\beta'_1}(h_{\alpha'_1}(a_{\alpha_1}), h_{\alpha'_2}(a_{\alpha_2}, a_{\alpha_3})) = h_{\beta'_1}(f_{\beta_1}(a_{\alpha_1}, a_{\alpha_2}), \\ \qquad f_{\beta_2}(a_{\alpha_2}, a_{\alpha_3})). \end{cases}$$

We leave the final substitutions and verification as an exercize for the reader.

4. It is readily checked that there are locations

$$\begin{cases} \text{loc } f'_{\beta_0} \circ h_{\alpha'_0} = \{\alpha_0\} \\ \text{loc } f'_{\beta_1} \circ h_{I'_{\beta'_1}} = \{\alpha_1, \alpha_2, \alpha_3\} \end{cases}$$

and since

$$\begin{cases} (I_{\beta'_0}) \cap I_{(\beta'_0)} = \{\alpha_0\} \cap \{\alpha_0\} = \{\alpha_0\} \\ (I_{\beta'_1}) \cap I_{(\beta'_1)} = \{\alpha_1, \alpha_2, \alpha_3\} \cap \{\alpha_1, \alpha_2, \alpha_3\} = \{\alpha_1, \alpha_2, \alpha_3\} \end{cases}$$

condition 4 is satisfied.

Remark

Condition 4 *cannot* be satisfied with the *modified* structure of Example 1. Since Condition 3 is still satisfied we have a proof that Condition 4 is not a consequence of Condition 3. The special condition where 4 follows 3 can be precisely identified but is omitted because of space limitations.

We proceed to demonstrate a strong distinction between structure and function preserving morphisms.

Theorem 1: Let (h_A,h_B) be a function morphism from $f:A \to B$ to $f':A' \to B'$. Then there are partitions τ,ρ on A,B respectively such that for all $a_1,a_2 \in A$

$$a_1 \tau a_2 \Rightarrow f(a_1)\rho f(a_2) \qquad \ldots *)$$

Conversely, if $f:A \to B$ and there exist partitions τ,ρ on A,B respectively such that *) holds, then there exists a corresponding function $f':A' \to B'$ and a morphism (h_A,h_B) from f to f'.

Theorem 2: Let $(d_A,d_B,\{h_{\alpha'}\},\{h_{\beta'}\})$ be a structure morphism from $f:A \to B$ to $f':A' \to B'$. Then the following are true:

a) there are partitions τ,ρ on A,B respectively such that *) holds;

b) there are partitions μ,ν on D_A,D_B respectively;

c) to each block $[\alpha]$ of μ there corresponds a partition $\tau_{[\alpha]}$ on A such that $\tau_{[\alpha]} \geq \pi_{[\alpha]}$; similarly, to each $[\beta]$ of ν, there is a partition $\rho_{[\beta]}$ on B such that $\rho_{[\beta]} \geq \pi_{[\beta]}$,

d) $\bigcap_{[\alpha]\in\mu} \tau_{[\alpha]} = \tau$; $\bigcap_{[\beta]\in\nu} \rho_{[\beta]} = \rho$.

Conversely, given a structured function $f:A \to B$ and that a)...d) hold, there exists a (not unique) structured function $f':A' \to B'$ and a structure preserving morphism from f to f'.

Proof: (Only the forward direction is given here)

a) follows from Theorem 2 with $\tau = \pi_{h_A}$, $\rho = \pi_{h_B}$. For b) take $\mu = D_A|d_A$, $\nu = D_B|d_B$; thus $[\alpha] = (\alpha')$ where $d_A(\alpha) = \alpha'$; and $[\beta] = (\beta')$ where $d_B(\beta) = \beta'$.

We show that c) can be satisfied by setting $\tau_{[\alpha]} = \pi_{h_{\alpha'}}$ and $\rho_{[\beta]} = \pi_{h_{\beta'}}$. To have this, we have $a_1 \pi_{[\alpha]} a_2 \Leftrightarrow P_{[\alpha]}(a_1) = P_{[\alpha]}(a_2) \Rightarrow h_{\alpha'} \circ P_{[\alpha]}(a_1) = h_{\alpha'} \circ P_{[\alpha]}(a_2) \Rightarrow a_1 \pi_{h_{\alpha'}} a_2$, i.e., $\pi_{h_{\alpha'}} \geq \pi_{[\alpha]}$ as required. Similarly $\pi_{h_{\beta'}} \geq \pi_{[\beta]}$.

Also d) holds since $a_1 \pi_{h_A} a_2 \Leftrightarrow h_A(a_1) = h_A(a_2)$

$\Leftrightarrow (\forall\alpha' \varepsilon D'_{A'})(h_{\alpha'} \circ P_{(\alpha')}(a_1) = h_{\alpha'} \circ P_{(\alpha')}(a_2))$

$\Leftrightarrow (\forall\alpha' \varepsilon D'_{A'})(a_1 \pi_{h_{\alpha'}} a_2)$, i.e., $\pi_{h_A} = \bigcap_{\alpha' \varepsilon D'_{A'}} \pi_{h_{\alpha'}}$ or

equivalently $\tau = \bigcap_{[\alpha]\varepsilon\mu} \tau_{[\alpha]}$ as required. Similarly

$\pi_{h_B} = \bigcap_{\beta' \varepsilon D_{B'}} \pi_{h_{\beta'}}$ so that $\rho = \bigcap_{[\beta]\varepsilon\nu} \rho_{[\beta]}$.

Structured function concepts are open to a number of specializations. We consider the case of *autonomous* machines $M = \langle Q, \delta \rangle$ where $\delta: Q \rightarrow Q$. M is *structured* when Q is a structured set and $\delta: Q \rightarrow Q$ is structured consistently with respect to the structure of Q. Thus if Q is structured by $\{Q_\alpha | \alpha\varepsilon D\}$ then δ is structured by $\{\delta_\alpha | \alpha\varepsilon D\}$ where $\delta_\alpha: \underset{\beta\varepsilon I_\alpha}{X} Q_\beta \rightarrow Q_\alpha$, $I_\alpha \subseteq D$ and $\delta = \underset{\alpha\varepsilon D}{X} \delta_\alpha \circ P_{I_\alpha}$.

Let M and M' be structured machines $(d, \{h_{\alpha'}\})$ is a *structure morphism* from M to M' if

1) $d: D \rightarrow D'$ (onto) and for each $\alpha' \varepsilon D'$
2) $h_{\alpha'}: \underset{\alpha\varepsilon(\alpha')}{X} Q_\alpha \rightarrow Q_{\alpha'}$ (onto)
3) $h_{\alpha'} \circ \delta_{(\alpha')} = \delta'_{\alpha'} \circ h_{(I_{\alpha'})}$
4) there is a location loc $h_{\alpha'} \circ \delta_{(\alpha')}$ such that loc $h_{\alpha'} \circ \delta_{(\alpha')} \subseteq (I_{\alpha'}) \cap I_{(\alpha')}$.

Specializing Theorem 2 we have

Theorem 3: Let $(d, \{h_{\alpha'}\})$ be a structure morphism from M to M' (structured machines). Then the following are true:

a) there is a partition τ on Q with S.P. (substitution property),
b) there is a partition μ on D,
c) to each block $[\alpha]$ of μ there corresponds a partition $\tau_{[\alpha]}$ such that $\tau_{[\alpha]} \geq \pi_{[\alpha]}$,
d) $\bigcap_{[\alpha]\varepsilon\mu} \tau_{[\alpha]} = \tau$.

The converse holds in like manner to Theorem 2.

It is not difficult to exhibit pairs of structured machines M,M' such that M' is a homomorphic image of M but such that M' is not a structure morphic image of M. With Theorem 3 in hand however, we can exhibit pairs which make a much stronger distinction between structure and function morphisms. Let us say that a set Q is *nontrivially* structured by $\{Q_\alpha | \alpha \varepsilon D\}$ if $|D| \geq 2$. A machine M is *nontrivially structured* if Q is nontrivially structured.

Theorem 4: There are pairs M,M' such that a) M is structured (nontrivially) b) there is a homomorphism from M to M' considered as abstract machines but c) no nontrivial structure assignment exists for M' which will enable a structure morphism to run from M to M'.

Proof: The structure (logical net, if you wish) shown in Figure 1a) gives rise to the cycle of order 6 in the state transition graph shown in Figure 1b). The partition $\tau = \{0,3;1,4;2,5\}$ has S.P. and represents a homomorphism of the 6-cycle on a 3-cycle. The 6-cycle and 3-cycle represent a pair M,M' which satisfy Conditions a) and b) of the Theorem. We now show that c) is also true in this case.

Suppose that there is a nontrivial structure for the 3-cycle and a structure morphism corresponding to it. Since $|D'| \geq 2$, the partition μ of Theorem 3 must separate at least one pair of the coordinates $D = \{\alpha,\beta,\gamma\}$ (Recall $\mu = D/d$). But this means that some coordinate is the only element in its block; for example if $\mu = \{\gamma;\alpha,\beta\}$ then $[\gamma] = \{\gamma\}$. Since $\tau = \bigcap_{[\alpha]\varepsilon\mu} \tau_{[\alpha]}$ we have that $\tau \leq \tau_{[\alpha]}$ for each block $[\alpha]$ in μ. Now consider the single element block, $[\gamma]$ say. By d) of Theorem 3, $\tau_{[\gamma]} \leq \pi_{[\gamma]}$ but since $|\pi_{[\gamma]}| = 2$ we have $\tau_{[\alpha]} = I$ or $\tau_{[\gamma]} = \pi_{[\gamma]}$.

<u>Case 1</u>: $\tau_{[\gamma]} = \pi_{[\gamma]}$

We have $\tau \leq \pi_{[\gamma]}$. But this is a contradiction case since 0,3 are in the same τ block but are in different $\pi_{[\gamma]}$ blocks. The same contradiction occurs for the cases where $[\alpha]$ or $[\beta]$ are single element blocks.

Thus we must have

<u>Case 2</u>: $\tau_{[\gamma]} = I$

Since $\tau = \bigcap_{[\alpha]\varepsilon\mu} \tau_{[\alpha]}$ we have $\tau = \tau_{[\alpha]} \cap \tau_{[\beta]}$ since $\pi_{[\alpha]} \leq \tau_{[\alpha]}$ and $\pi_{[\beta]} \leq \tau_{[\beta]}$ we have $\tau = \tau_{[\alpha]} \cap \tau_{[\beta]} \geq \pi_{[\alpha]} \cap \pi_{[\beta]} = \pi_{\{\alpha,\beta\}}$.

But this is a contradiction since 0,5 are in the same $\pi_{\{\alpha,\beta\}}$ block but in different τ blocks. The same contradiction occurs for the cases where $[\alpha]$ or $[\beta]$ are singleton blocks.

Thus there is no nontrivial structure assignment for the 3-cycle which will enable a structure morphism to run from the 6-cycle to the 3-cycle.

Application to Decomposition and Simulation

Space permits only a brief sketch of the applications of the structure morphism concept.

The decomposition statement already introduced informally may be rephrased:

Given an automaton M and a set of automata $\mathcal{M}$, find an automaton $A' \varepsilon \mathcal{M}$ such that $A' \overset{m}{\rightarrow} A$, i.e., a morphism of kind m runs from A' to A where m can denote either a structure or function preserving morphism (according to the criterion of simulation, χ).

By examining the functions defining an automaton this formulation can be shown to reduce to:

Given a function f and a set of functions F, find a function $f^c \varepsilon F$ such that $f^c \overset{m}{\rightarrow} f$ where m denotes a structure or function preserving morphism.

Beyond the question of the existence of a simulator $f^c \varepsilon F$ for f we are interested in the relative complexity of f and f^c and the selection of simulators of minimal complexity when more than one exists.

A simulation is *parallel* if the coordinate functions in the family $\{f^c_\beta\}$ structuring f^c are computed simultaneously and synchronously.

A simulation is *sequential* if $\{f^c_\beta\}$ is a (totally) ordered set and the computation of the f^c_β proceeds according to this order.

Appropriate complexity measures are introduced as follows:

μ_G will denote a functional, parameterized by G, a set of functions, such that $\mu_G(f)$ is a measure of the complexity of a function f.

G is to satisfy the conditions:

1) For each $n \varepsilon N$ (the nonnegative integers) there is a (unique) $g_n \varepsilon G$ such that $g_n : N^{n+2} \rightarrow N$.
2) The $\{g_n\}$ are nondecreasing in the sense that if $n \geq m$, and $x_i \geq y_i$ for $i=1,2,\ldots m$ then $g_n(x_1, x_2, \ldots x_m, \ldots x_n) \geq g_m(y_1, y_2, \ldots y_m)$. To see how this works, let f be a

function of n variables; e.g., $f: \underset{\alpha \varepsilon I}{X} A_\alpha \rightarrow B$, where $|I| = n$. Then $\mu_G(f) = g_n(n, |B|, |A_{\alpha_1}|, \ldots, |A_{\alpha_n}|)$.

The complexity measures under consideration can be sensitive to the number of function variables n, the cardinalities of their ranges $|A_{\alpha_i}|$ and the cardinality of the image range $|B|$. Because they are functionals assumed to be everywhere defined these measures do not satisfy the Blum size or step-counting axioms (Blum, 1967); see also Strong (1970).

These complexity measures subsume as special cases a number of measures studied in the literature including Winograd (1967), Spira (1969), Minsky and Papert (1969) and Strong (1970), Yamada and Amoroso (1970).

This notion is extended to structured functions using the measures M_Σ, M_{max} where $M_\Sigma(f) = \sum_{\beta \varepsilon D_B} \mu(f_\beta)$ and $M_{max}(f) = \max_{\beta \varepsilon D_B} \{\mu(f_\beta)\}$.

The interprelation in terms of time and space is indicated in Table 1.

Let $M \varepsilon \{M_{max}, M_\Sigma\}$, and let $f \overset{m}{\to} f'$ indicate that a morphism of type m (function preserving, structure preserving, etc.) runs from f to f'.

M will be *nonincreasing* with type m morphisms if

$$f \overset{m}{\to} f' \Rightarrow M(f') \leq M(f),$$

M will be *nondecreasing* with type m morphisms if

$$f \overset{m}{\to} f' \Rightarrow M(f) \leq M(f'),$$

M will be *ambivalent* with type m morphisms if it is neither nonincreasing nor nondecreasing (with type m morphisms).

The results shown in Table 2 have been established.

Conclusions

The introduction of the structure morphism concept makes possible improved prediction of the relative complexities of an automaton and its simulators, Also since the number of possible simulators is controlled by the simulation criterion, more efficient search methods (decomposition schemes) may be developed using structure morphisms.

References

Blum, M. (1967) "A Machine-Independent Theory of the Complexity of Recursive Functions," J. Assoc. Comp. Mach., Vol. 14.

Gallaire, H. and Harrison, M.A. (1970) "Decomposition of Linear Sequential Machines," Math. System Theory, Vol. 3, No. 3.

Hartmanis, J. and Stearns, R.E. (1966) Algebraic Structure Theory of Sequential Machines, Prentice-Hall, New Jersey.

Martin, R.L. (1968) *Studies in Feedback Shift Register Synthesis of Sequential Machines*, MIT, Cambridge.

Minsky, M. and Papert, S. (1969) *Perceptrons*, MIT, Cambridge

Spira, P.M. (1969) "The Time Required for Group Multiplication," *J. Assoc. Comp. Mach.*, Vol. 16.

Strong, H.R. (1970) "Depth-Bounded Computation," *J. of Computer and System Sciences*, Vol. 4.

Winograd, S. (1967) "On the Time Required to Perform Multiplication," *J. Assoc. Comp. Mach.*, Vol. 14.

Yamada, H. and Amoroso, S. (1970) "Structural and Behavioral Equivalences of Tessellation Automata," To appear.

Zeigler, B.P. (1968) "On the Feedback Complexity of Automata," University of Michigan Doctoral Dissertation.

___, (1971) "On the Formulation of Problems in Modelling and Simulation in the Framework of Mathematical System Theory," *Proceedings of Sixth Annual International Assoc. of Cybernetics*, Namur, Belgium.

TABLE 1

Interpretation of Complexity Measures M_{max} and M_{Σ}.

Mode of Simulation \ Measure	Time	Space: Function Storage	Space: State Storage
Sequential	M_{Σ}	M_{max};M_{Σ}	M_{Σ}
Parallel	M_{max}	M_{Σ}	M_{Σ}

TABLE 2

Behavior of complexity measures under morphisms.

Type of Morphism \ Measure of Complexity		M_{Σ}	M_{max}
Structure Preserving	D-morphism*	Nonincreasing	Nonincreasing
	General,** Admissible***	Nonincreasing	Ambivalent
Function Preserving		Ambivalent	Ambivalent

*d_A,d_B are one-one as well as onto.

**Measures dependent only on the number of variables [$g_n(x_1,\ldots x_{n+2}) = g(x_1)$] and assumed to be growth

bounded by $g(n+m) \leq g(n)+g(m)$.
***Morphisms limited to $f \overset{m}{\to} f'$ where $f \in C_p$, $f' \in C_q$ and $q \leq p$ where $C_r = \{f:A \to B | A \subseteq \{0,1,\ldots,r-1\}^n, B \subseteq \{0,1,\ldots,r-1\}^m$ for some $m,n\}$.
Measures growth bounded by $g_n(x_1+y_1,x_2,\ldots,x_{n+2}) \leq g_n(x_1,x_2,\ldots,x_{n+2}) + g_n(y_1,x_2,\ldots,x_{n+2})$.

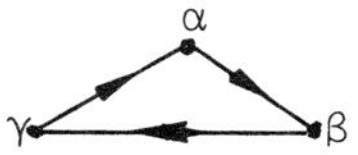

γ	δ_α
0	1
1	0

α	δ_β
0	0
1	1

β	δ_γ
0	0
1	1

(a)

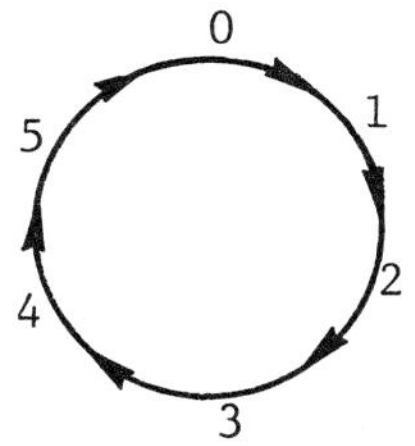

	α	β	γ
0	0	0	0
1	1	0	0
2	1	1	0
3	1	1	1
4	0	1	1
5	0	0	1

(b)

Figure 1: A structured machine which has a nontrivial homomorphic image but no nontrivial structure morphic image.

SECTION IV

FAULT-DETECTION EXPERIMENTS

AN ALGORITHM FOR GENERATING A FAULT DETECTION TEST FOR A CLASS OF SEQUENTIAL CIRCUITS

Melvin A. Breuer*

Electrical Engineering Department
University of Southern California
Los Angeles, California 90007

Abstract

In this paper we consider the problem of generating a fault detection sequence for sequential circuits. We employ a three valued logic system which allows us to handle race and hazard conditions. The main result of this paper is an algorithm for constructing a minimal length input sequence $\underline{X}$ such that $g^0(Y^0, \underline{X}) \neq g^1(Y^1, \underline{X})$, where $g^0(g^1)$ is the output of the circuit containing no fault (fault i), starting in state $Y^0(Y^1)$, when input sequence $\underline{X}$ is applied. Both synchronous and asynchronous circuits are considered. Asynchronous circuits are mapped into "equivalent" combinational switching functions by introducing new input and output variables associated with the present and next state of the element. The solution to the sequential circuit test generation problem is shown to require the ability to generate a test to detect a multiple fault in a combinational circuit.

Introduction

In this paper we will consider the problem of generating a fault detection sequence for sequential circuits.

---

*This work was supported by the Joint Services Electronics Program (U. S. Army, U. S. Navy, and U. S. Air Force) under Grant AFOSR-69-1622-B, by the National Science Foundation under Grant No. 4386, and by the Office of Naval Research under Grant No. N00014-67-A-0269-0019.

We assume knowledge of the circuit structure only, and not the state flow table. We will restrict our attention to permanent, nonredundant, single failures, usually of the stuck-at (s-a) variety, though only the assumption of a permanent failure is essential to the results obtained.

Notation and Definitions

Let SC be a sequential circuit having m primary input (pi) lines labeled $x_1, x_2, \ldots, x_m$, and n primary output (po) lines, labeled $z_1, z_2, \ldots, z_n$. Those lines which represent the state of SC are labeled $y_1, y_2, \ldots, y_p$, and will include the state of all memory devices such as latches and clocked flip flops.

A signal line r can take on one of three values, namely 0, 1 or u, where u indicates an unknown value. The value u is required due to a number of reasons, such as:

a) some inputs to the circuit may not be controllable nor observable, and hence their value is unknown (u);
b) the initial state of some devices may be unknown;
c) u's may be generated during test generation due to races and hazards.

One can associate with SC a set of permanent logical faults. We enumerate the faults, and let $F = \{1, 2, \ldots, I\}$ be the set of all (irredundant) faults of interests. For example, fault i may correspond to "gate j s-a-1". Each fault $i \in F$ defines a circuit SC^i in a natural way. Let SC^0 be the fault free circuit.

We label the value of line r in SC^i by r^i. Let $X = (x_1, x_2, \ldots, x_m)$, $Z^i = (z_1^i, z_2^i, \ldots, z_n^i)$ and $Y^i = (y_1^i, y_2^i, \ldots, y_p^i)$ where X is a (0, 1, u) m-tuple, Z^i is a (0, 1, u) n-tuple, and Y^i is a (0, 1, u) p-tuple. If Y^i is the present state of SC^i and X is the input, let Z^i be the output and $W^i = (w_1^i, w_2^i, \ldots, w_p^i)$ be the next state of SC^i, where W^i is a (0, 1, u) p-tuple. Let $f^i(Y^i, X) = W^i$ and $g^i(Y^i, X) = Z^i$.

Given two line values a_j, $b_j \in \{0, 1, u\}$, we say that a_j and b_j are <u>incompatible</u>, denoted by $a_j \nmid b_j$, if and only if $a_j = 1$ and $b_j = 0$ or vice versa. Let $a = (a_1, a_2, \ldots, a_t)$ and $b = (b_1, b_2, \ldots, b_t)$ be two (0, 1, u) t-tuples. We say that a is equivalent to b, denoted by $a \equiv b$, if and only if for all j we have that $a_j, b_j \in \{0, 1, u\}$ and $a_j = b_j$. Otherwise $a \not\equiv b$. If $a \not\equiv b$ and there exists a j such that $a_j \nmid b_j$, then a and b are said to be incompatible, denoted by $a \nsim b$, otherwise they are compatible, denoted by $a \sim b$. For example, $(01) \equiv (01)$, $(u0) \equiv (u0)$, $u0) \sim (00)$, and $(u0) \nsim (u1)$. If either $a \equiv b$ or $a \sim b$, then we write $a \cong b$.

We assume that SC^0 can be partially reset to a known initial state Y_1^0 by applying some process R. By partially reset we mean that Y_1^0 is a (0, 1, u) p-tuple. Total reset requires Y_1^0 to be a (0, 1) p-tuple. The process R may be, for example, an input pulse or sequence. Let Y_1^i be the state of SC^i after R is applied. It is possible that $Y_1^i \not\equiv Y_1^0$.

Let $\underline{X} = \underline{X}_K = X_1 X_2 \ldots X_K$ be an input sequence. Then the output sequence and next state sequence of SC^i when $\underline{X}$ is applied, starting in state Y_1^i, are denoted by $\underline{Z}^i = Z_1^i Z_2^i \ldots Z_K^i$ and $\underline{W}^i = W_1^i W_2^i \ldots W_K^i$. The present state sequence is denoted by $\underline{Y}^i = Y_1^i Y_2^i \ldots Y_K^i Y_{K+1}^i$, where $Y_{k+1}^i = W_k^i$ for $k = 1, 2, \ldots, K$. We have that $\underline{Z}^i \nsim \underline{Z}^j$ if and only if there exists a k, $1 \leq k \leq K$, such that $Z_k^i \nsim Z_k^j$.

Input sequence X is said to be a fault detection test for SC^0 with respect to F and $\{Y_1^0, Y_1^1, \ldots, Y_1^I\}$, where $F \subseteq F_1$, if for each $i \in F$ we have that $\underline{Z}^0 \nsim \underline{Z}^i$. $\underline{X}$ is said to be a complete test if $F = F_1$.

The problem which we will be concerned with in this paper is the following: Determine a general procedure which will dictate how to construct a fault detection test $\underline{X}$ for SC^0 with respect to F_1 and $\{Y_1^0, Y_1^1, \ldots, Y_1^I\}$.

We assume the reader is familiar with the D-algorithm including the concepts of primitive cubes (pc), primitive d-cubes (pdc), and primitive d-cubes of a failure (pdcf), and the operations of d-drive, implication and consistency [1], [2].

In generating a test for fault i one must work with two circuits, namely SC^0 and SC^i. When considering these two circuits, line values will be represented as r^0/r^i. The possible line value pairs of interest are shown below.

Line Value Pairs r^0/r^i	Line Value Pairs r^0/r^i	Shorthand Notation
0/u	0/0	0
1/u	0/1	$\overline{d}$
u/1	1/1	1
u/0	1/0	d
	x/x	x
	u/u	u

The interpretation of $d(\bar{d})$ is the same as given by Roth [1], [2].

Let $a^0 = (a_1^0, a_2^0, \ldots, a_t^0)$ and $a^1 = (a_1^1, a_2^1, \ldots, a_t^1)$, where $a_k^1, a_k^0 \in \{0, 1, u\}$ are line values. Then we define the <u>composite cube</u> $a^1(d) = a^0/a^1$ by the equation

$$a^1(d) = (a_1^0/a_1^1, a_2^0/a_2^1, \ldots, a_t^0/a_t^1).$$

Note that the cube $a^1(d)$ contains at least one $d(\bar{d})$ component if and only if $a^0 \nmid a^1$. The cube $Y^1(d)$ formed from Y^0 and Y^1 is called the <u>composite state cube</u>.

Two cubes $a^1(d) = (a_1, a_2, \ldots, a_t)$ and $b^1(d) = (b_1, b_2, \ldots, b_t)$ are said to <u>intersect</u> according to the following rules, where $k = 1, 2, \ldots, t$:

a) if for some k neither a_k nor b_k is x, and $a_k \neq b_k$, then the intersect does not exist, otherwise;
b) the intersect is $a^1(d) \cap b^1(d) = (c_1, c_2, \ldots, c_t)$, where if $a_k = b_k$ or if $b_k = x$, then set $c_k = a_k$; otherwise set $c_k = b_k$.

For example

$$\begin{array}{rl} & (0\ d\ 0/u\ x) \\ \cap & \underline{(x\ d\ 0/u\ \bar{d})} \\ & (0\ d\ 0/u\ \bar{d}) \end{array}$$

Given a combinational circuit C having inputs X, Y and outputs Z and W, one can define two subcircuits C_Z and C_W associated with C. C_Z is called the output subcircuit of C, and consists of all elements and interconnections of C which exist along any path from a line in X or Y to Z. The next state subcircuit C_W of C is defined analogously.

Consider the sequential circuit SC shown in Figure 1, where C_1 and C_2 are combinational logic networks implementing multiple output switching functions f and g, and F/F is a set of clocked delay flip-flops.

<u>Theorem 1</u>: A necessary and sufficient condition for detecting a fault i in C_1 is that $g^0(Y^0, X) \nmid g^0(Y^1, X)$ for some X. This condition implies that SC^i be driven into a state Y^1 such that $Y^0 \nmid Y^i$.

<u>Proof</u>: This result is obvious for (0, 1) logic values. For (0, 1, u) logic values the necessity of the condition

$Y^o \nparallel Y^1$ follows from the fact that changing an input to a gate from 0 or 1 to u cannot change the output from 0 to 1 or 1 to 0.

Theorem 2: A necessary and sufficient condition for detecting a fault i in C_2 is that the circuit be driven to a state Y such that $g^o(Y, X) \nparallel g^1(Y, X)$ for some X.

The state-input pair (Y, X) can be found in a number of ways, such as by employing the D-algorithm to the circuit C_2. If we allow feedback to occur from the output of C_2 to the input of C_1, then Theorem 2 should be modified to state that the circuits SC^o and SC^i are driven to states Y^o and Y^1 such that $g^o(Y^o, X) \nparallel g^1(Y^1, X)$.

It is seen that testing sequential circuits differs from testing combinational circuits in three main aspects. For combinational circuits one seeks an input X such that $g^o(X) \nparallel g^1(X)$, while for sequential circuits the following three problems exist:

P1 - Find X such that $g^o(Y^o, X) \nparallel g^1(Y^1, X)$

P2 - Find Y^o, Y^1 and X such that $g^o(Y^o, X) \nparallel g^1(Y^1, X)$

P3 - Find an input sequence $\underline{X}$ which will drive the circuit from a state $Y^i_k(d)$ to a state $Y^i_q(d)$.

In the next section we will describe a procedure, called the S-algorithm, for constructing a test for a given failure.

Sequential Test Generation

In this section we will consider testing circuits SC of the form shown in Figure 2, which we call a Class 1 circuit. We assume the clocked delay flip flops are fault free. The circuit C consists of an acyclic combinational network formed by interconnecting basic elements called atoms, where an atom is any multi-input multi-output combinational circuit. An atom is processed according to its functional characteristics, not by its circuit implementation. For example, the circuit shown in Figure 3a is defined by the atom shown in Figure 3b. The functional effect of a fault on an atom is obtained by analyzing the circuit realization of an atom. For example, if fault i corresponds to "D s-a-0", then the resulting atom is defined in Figure 3c.

Consider the latch circuit shown in Figure 5, which is a sequential device. In Figure 5b we indicate its state diagram, and in Figure 5c we show its representation as an atom. It is seen that we have transformed a two input two output sequential device into a four input four output combinational device.

In general, if S is an asynchronous circuit defined by the next state function f(s, x) and output function g(s, x), then we can model this circuit by the atom having input (s, x) and output (f(s, x), g(s, x)). The result of this transformation T is the switching function T(S). Of course, timing is not preserved in this transformation. To reduce problems caused by this transformation, it is best that each output line of S undergo at most one change in value when S goes from stable state s to stable state f(s, x).

For the latch, f(s, x) = g(s, x), but in general this need not be the case.

Clocked flip flops are transformed as shown in Figure 4.

Using the T transformation, the circuit shown in Figure 7a is transformed into the Class 1 circuit shown in Figure 7b. It is clear that not all cyclic circuits can be accurately modeled by a Class 1 circuit. This procedure is best suited for circuits where the asynchronous feedback is restricted to small circuits such as latches, and where global feedback occurs through clocked paths. This class of circuit is used almost exclusively in the design of modern digital computers.

Below we indicate a few cubes associated with the atom representation L+ of the NOR latch.

pdc's

RS	Q	Q^+
0d	01	dd
$\overline{d}$1	d$\overline{d}$	d0
0$\overline{d}$	0$\overline{d}$	u/1 u/0 (race)

pdcf's

RS	Q	Q^+	Fault
00	xx	d$\overline{d}$	F s-a-1
10	xx	$\overline{d}$d	T s-a-1
01	xx	d0	T s-a-0
10	xx	0$\overline{d}$	F s-a-0

In addition to pdc's and pdcf's, we require a new type of cube, called primitive fault d cubes (pfdc's), which indicate how signals of the form a^0/a^1 propagate through atoms of the form A^0/A^1, where A^0 is the fault free atom and A^1 is the faulty atom. For example, for the latch, one pfdc for the failure "F s-a-0" is $d_R x_S xx_Q \bar{d}0_{Q+}$. Here we see that for the fault free case d = 1 hence $Q^+ = 00$, while if the fault is present d = 0 and $Q^+ = 10$. It is not difficult to derive the corresponding pc's, pdc's, pdcf's and pfdc's where some input components have the value u. This extension will not be given in this paper.

In the D-algorithm the process of test generation begins by selecting a pdcf as the initial test cube tc^0. The algorithms thus drive the d's forward using pdc's, where $tc^{i+1} = tc^i \cap pdc \cap \partial I^i(tc^i, pdc)$. When a d is driven to a po, then all 0 and 1 line values are justified by the consistency operation, where $tc^{i+1} = tc^i \cap pc \cap \partial I^i(tc^i, pc)$.

We will now consider problem P1, i. e., find X such that $g^0(Y^0, X) \nleftrightarrow g^1(Y^1, X)$, where g^1 is the output function defined by the output subcircuit C_Z^1 of C^1. This problem can be solved by employing the D-algorithm after making all appropriate modifications for u's, modeling acyclic subcircuits using the T transformation, and use of pfdc's as previously discussed. We refer to the revised version of the D-algorithm containing these modifications as the DM-algorithm.

One additional modification is required to solve problem P1, namely the selection of the proper initial test cube tc^0. This modification is given by Theorem 3, the proof of which requires the following definitions.

A <u>d-chain</u> is a path in a circuit where every signal line along this path has value d or $\bar{d}$. A d-chain is <u>maximal</u> if it is not contained in any other d-chain. The first $d(\bar{d})$ in a maximal d-chain is called the source.

<u>Theorem 3</u>: Starting with the initial test cube tc^0 and employing the DM-algorithm, a test X will be derived if it exists. The initial test cubes are determined as follows.

Case 1 – If $Y^1(d)$ contains no d or $\bar{d}$ components, then activate the fault, i. e., set $tc^0 = pdcf \cap Y^1(d) \cap \partial I^0(pdcf, Y^1(d))$.

Case 2 – If $Y^1(d)$ contains one or more d or $\bar{d}$'s, then

1. Activate the fault, i. e., set $tc^0 = pdcf \cap Y^1(d) \cap \partial I^0(pdcf, Y^1(d))$.
2. Ignore the fault, i. e., set $tc^0 = Y^1(d) \cap \partial I^0(Y^1(d))$.

Proof: Case 1 corresponds to the case of combinational logic where certain inputs have constrained values. For case 2 it is clear that this selection of initial cubes tc^0 are necessary. To prove sufficiency, assume X is a test and $z_k^i(d) = d$. Given the value of each line defined by $Y^i(d)$ and X, we can determine all maximal d-chains terminating at line z_k. For each such chain, the source is either a d or $\bar{d}$ on line j created by a pdcf for fault i, or by a state input line y_q. There are no other sources of d's, i.e., a $d(\bar{d})$ can be created only by a pdcf; the pdc's and pfdc merely propagate d's through atoms. If there is no maximal d-chain from line j to line z_k, then there must be a maximal d-chain from a state input variable to z_k, hence setting $tc^0 = Y^i(d) \cap \partial I^0(Y^i(d))$ will generate a test.

Note that in determining tc^{i+1}, if we are driving a d through a faulty gate, then a pfdc is used in place of a pdc, or if we are attempting to justify a 0 or 1 value on the output of a faulty gate, a pfdc is used instead of a pc.

Let the set of all pdcf's corresponding to a fault i be denoted by S_i, and the addition of the cube xx...x to this set define the extended set of pdcf S_i^+. For example, for the AND gate defined by the equation $A = B \cdot C$, and the fault i defined by "A s-a-1", we have $S_i^+ = S_i \cup \{x_A x_B x_C\}$, where $S_i = \{0_A x_B \bar{d}_C, x_A 0_B \bar{d}_C\}$.

Ignoring the fault (Theorem 3, Case 2, part 2) is equivalent to employing the pdcf U_n which contains x's on every line. If we append this cube to the set of all pdcf of a failure, then we obtain the following result.

Corollary 1: The DM-algorithm will construct a test X, if one exists, if we set $tc^0 = c \cap Y^i(d) \cap \partial I^0(c, Y^i(d))$ for each $c \in S_i^+$.

In some cases there exists no X such that $g^0(Y_k^0, X) \nmid g^i(Y_k^i, X)$. In this case it is necessary to generate a sequence of inputs $X_k, X_{k+1}, \ldots$ inorder to detect the fault i.

To solve this problem, we note that a time domain analysis of a sequential circuit can be mapped into a spacial domain analysis. To accomplish this mapping, we first transform the circuit SC into an iterative array as shown in Figure 6. To accomplish this transformation, we first make L copies of C, labeled C(k), C(k+1), ..., C(k+L-1) and interconnect the state outputs of C(q) to the state inputs of C(q+1). For test generation, we then replace C(q) by $C_W(q)$ for $k \leq q \leq L-2$, and C(k+L-1) by $C_Z(k+L-1)$. The resulting network C^L is a combinational circuit, and $X_k, X_{k+1}, \ldots, X_{k+L-1}$ are primary inputs. Note that a single fault in C corresponds to a multiple fault in the iterative circuit C^L, or more precisely is a fault of multiplicity L. We define the extended set of pdcf's associated with C^L by the equation $S_i^+(L) = \{\bigcap_{q=k}^{k+L-1} c(q) \mid c(q) \in S_i^+(q)\}$, where $S_i^+(q)$ is the extended set of pdcf associated with C(q). Note that except for the multiplicity of the fault, the final circuit is again of the form considered in Theorem 3, hence this result is still valid. From Theorem 3 and Corollary 1 we can state the following algorithm for construction a minimal length test sequence $X_k, X_{k+1}, \ldots, X_{k+L-1}$ for fault i starting in state $Y_k^i(d)$.

S-algorithm: Generation of a minimal length test sequence for fault i in a Class 1 sequential circuit starting in initial state $Y_k^i(d)$.

Step 1: Set L = 1 and determine C from SC using the T transformation.

Step 2: Construct the acyclic combinational iterative network C^L.

Step 3: Generate a test for fault i by employing the DM-algorithm, where $tc^o = c \cap Y_k^i(d) \cap \partial I^o(c, Y_k^i(d))$ and $c \in S_i^+(L)$. If no test is found for each $c \in S_i^+(L)$ go to step 4, otherwise exit with a test $X_k, X_{k+1}, \ldots, X_{k+L-1}$.

Step 4: If $L < B$, set $L+1 \rightarrow L$ and return to step 2, otherwise exit and no test exists.

The parameter B is an upper bound on the length of a test. Let p' be the total number of state input lines to C.

Theorem 4: $B = 9^{p'}$.

Proof: Each state input line can take on one of nine values, namely $0, 1, d, \bar{d}, u, u/0, u/1, 1/u$ or $0/u$. In a minimal length test sequence each cube of state input values to $C_W(q)$ or $C_z(k+L-1)$ is unique, therefore $B = 9^{p'}$. If u values are not used, then we can set $B = 4^{p'}$.

For many circuits of practical interest, this bound is quite large, and if a test is not found for a small value of L, it is usually not computationally feasible to consider larger values. It is interesting to note that this algorithm generates a minimal length test in a quite natural way, i.e., it appears to be more work to generate a non-minimal length test.

We should note that the transformation of an asynchronous sequential circuit into an iterative array for the purpose of testing has previously been suggested by Roth et.al. [3], [4] in their discussion of the C-algorithm. Some important differences between the C-algorithm and the S-algorithm presented here are the following:

1. The C-algorithm requires the equivalent of $Y_k^i(d) = uu \ldots u$; i.e., the test sequence $X_k, X_{k+1}, \ldots, X_{k+L-1}$ must detect the fault i independent of the initial states of C^0 and C^i. This implies a rather strong connectivity requirement on the structure of the circuit. It does not necessarily imply that the original circuit is strongly connected. The relation between the existence of tests for these two approaches of selecting the initial state $Y_k^i(d)$ is given in the following theorem. Let $Y(d)$ be any arbitrary composite state vector, and $Y(u) = uu \ldots u$.

Theorem 5: If $\underline{X}$ is a test for fault i starting in state $Y(u)$, then $\underline{X}$ is also a test for fault i starting in state $Y(d)$. The converse is not necessarily true.

Therefore, the S-algorithm may find a minimal length test for a fault where the C-algorithm fails to find any test.

2. The S-algorithm employs the extended set $S_i^{+(L)}$ on pdcf's.

3. The S-algorithm employs state line values of u, hence will not generate a test which is invalid due to race conditions.

We will now demonstrate the necessity of employing the extended set of pdcf $S_i^{+(L)}$. Consider the sequential circuit SC shown in Figure 8a, and its transformed equivalent iterative network shown in Figure 8b for L = 2.

Let the initial state of the flip flop be u. Then since one input to gate E is a u, we cannot drive a d to line E, hence this circuit cannot be tested for L = 1. For L = 2 we first employ the pdcf $0_{B1}d_{C1}$ for C1 s-a-0. To drive d_{C1} through gate E2 using a pdc requires 1_{D2}. By by consistency $1_{D2} \Rightarrow 1_{C2}$ which contradicts the condition C2 s-a-0.

However, if we employ the pdcf $0_{B2}d_{C2}$ for C2 s-a-0, then by the pdc $1_{A2}d_{C2}d_{D2}$ we obtain $d_{D2}d_{G2}$ which implies d_{E2}, hence $\underline{X}$ = (x, 0), (1, 0) is a test, where $X_k = (Ak, Bk)$. We see that the actual pdcf employed is $0_{B1}d_{C1} \cap 0_{B2}d_{C2}$. Employing the pdcf $x_{B1}x_{C1} \cap 0_{B2}d_{C2}$ or $0_{B1}d_{C1} \cap x_{B2}x_{C2}$ do not lead to a test. If the false (F) output of the delay flip flop were used as an input to E rather than the true (T) output, then we would have an inverter between C1 and G2, and employing the pdcf $x_{B1}x_{C1} \cap 0_{B2}d_{C2}$ would lead to a test.

Consider a combinational circuit containing a multiple fault defined by the set $\mathcal{S} = \{i_1, i_2, \ldots, i_E\}$, of single faults. Set $S^+(\mathcal{S}) = \{\bigcap_{e=1}^{E} c(e) \mid c(e) \in S^+_{i_e}\}$. From the previous discussion we obtain the following result.

Theorem 6: The D-algorithm will obtain a test for the multiple fault $\mathcal{S} = \{i_1, i_2, \ldots, i_E\}$, if one exists, if we set $tc^0 = c \cap \partial I^0(c)$ for each $c \in S^+(\mathcal{S})$.

References

[1] J. P. Roth, "Diagnosis of Automata Failures: A Calculus and a Method", IBM J. of Res. and Dev., vol. 10, pp. 278-291, July 1966.

[2] J. P. Roth, W. G. Bouricius, P. R. Schneider, "Programmed Algorithms to Compute Tests to Detect and Distinguish Between Failures in Logic Circuits", IEEE TEC, vol. EC-16, pp. 567-580, October 1967.

[3] G. R. Putzolu, J. P. Roth, "An Algorithm and a Program for Generation of Test Patterns for Sequential Circuits", Proc. of the Third Hawaii Int'l Conference on System Sciences, pp. 64-67, January 1970.

[4] K. A. Duke, G. R. Putzolu and J. P. Roth, "A Heuristic Algorithm for Sequential Circuit Diagnosis", IBM Research Report RC2639, October 1969.

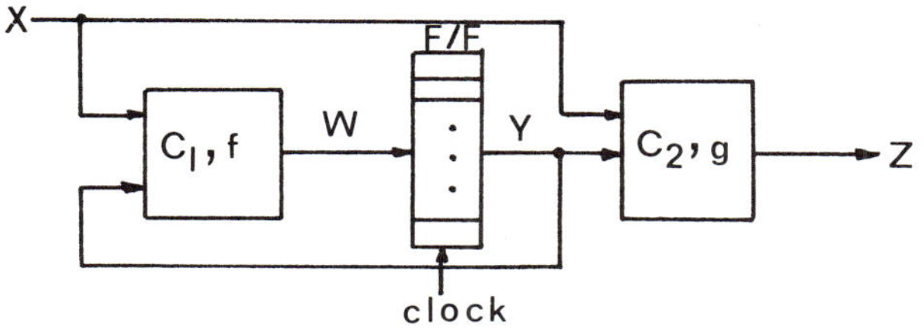

Fig. 1 Sequential circuit SC

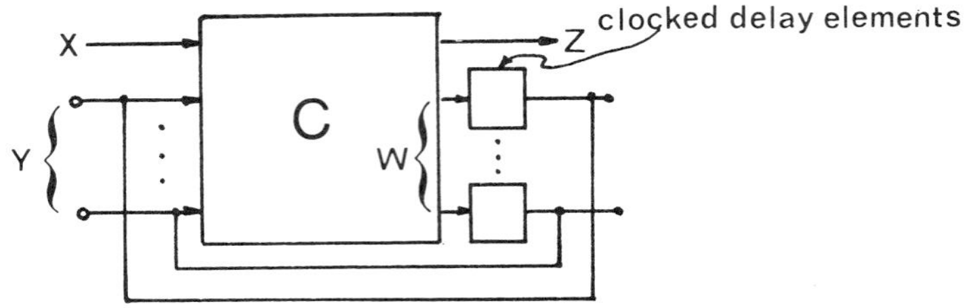

Fig. 2 General form of circuit SC being tested

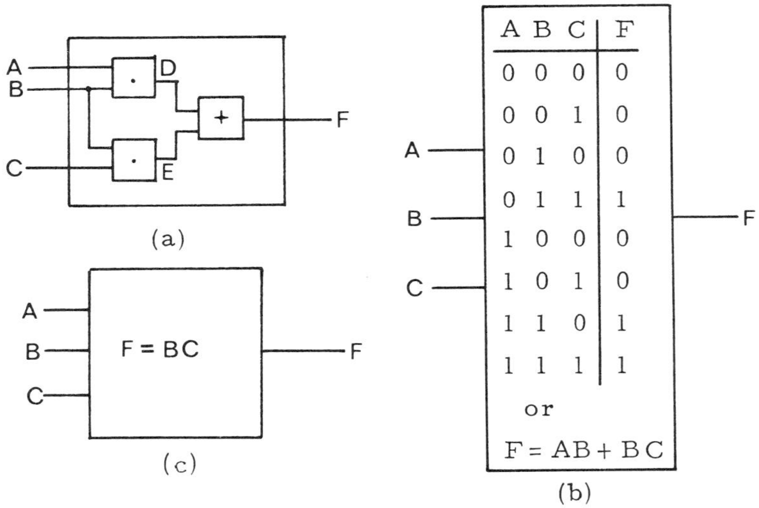

Fig. 3 (a) Circuit (b) Representation as atom (c) Representation as atom for fault "D s-a-0".

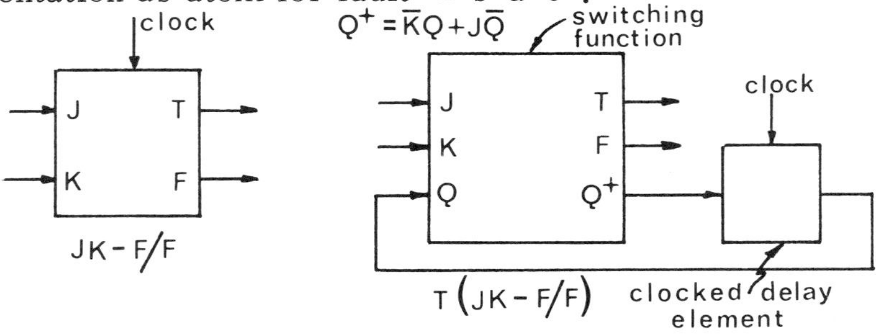

Fig. 4 Transformation of a clocked JK flip flop.

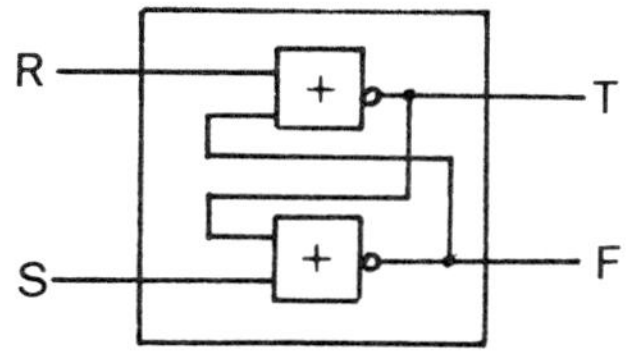

(a)

INPUT

Q = TF \ RS	00	01	10	11
present state 00	$y\bar{y}$	10	01	00
01	01	10	01	00
10	10	10	01	00
11	$y\bar{y}$	10	01	00

next state = output

$Q^+ = TF^+$

$y \in \{0,1\}$. State $(y, \bar{y})$ is represented by (u,u) in all computations

(b)

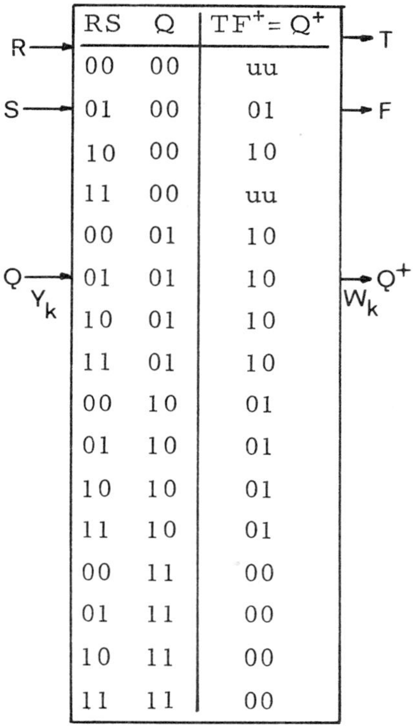

RS	Q	$TF^+ = Q^+$
00	00	uu
01	00	01
10	00	10
11	00	uu
00	01	10
01	01	10
10	01	10
11	01	10
00	10	01
01	10	01
10	10	01
11	10	01
00	11	00
01	11	00
10	11	00
11	11	00

function

(c)

Fig. 5 (a) NOR LATCH (b) State table (c) (Combinational) Atom L^+ corresponding to the NOR LATCH.

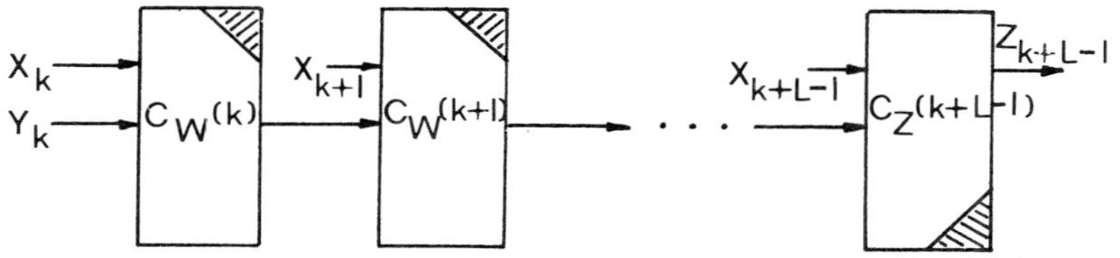

Fig. 6 Circuit C^L pruned for test purposes.

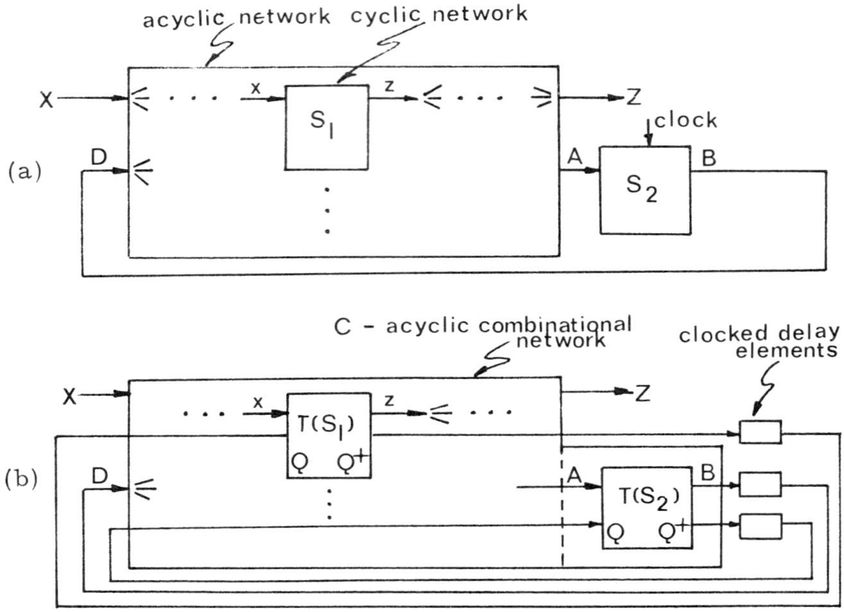

Fig. 7 Transformation of cyclic network into a Class1 circuit.

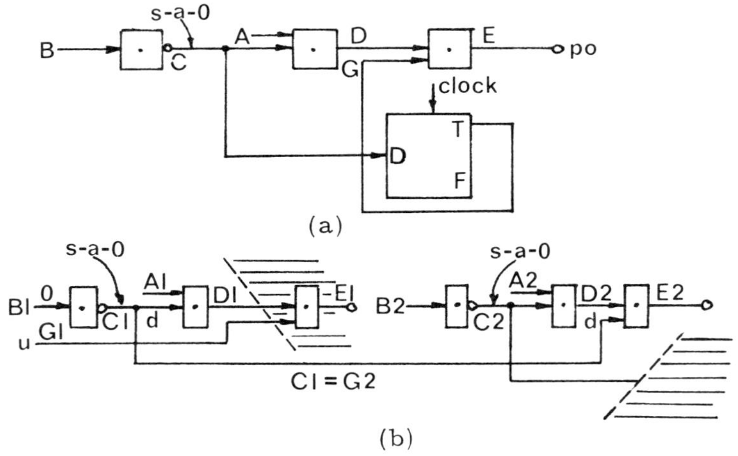

Fig. 8 (a) SC (b) C^2

FAULT LOCATION IN ITERATIVE LOGIC ARRAYS

A. D. Friedman and P. R. Menon

Bell Telephone Laboratories, Incorporated
Murray Hill, New Jersey

Abstract

In this paper we consider the problem of locating a faulty module in a one-dimensional array. Kautz has previously considered this problem and derived a set of sufficient conditions for fault location which were also claimed to be necessary. We show that these conditions are not necessary for fault location and that in some cases a faulty module can be located even if it contains no external output. Specifically, we define the concept of masking inputs of degree k, which is useful for locating the faulty module within k units. This concept is then generalized to obtain necessary and sufficient conditions to locate the faulty module within k units. Making use of these concepts, we introduce a simple design procedure whereby the addition of one external binary input to each module enables fault location to within two modules for an arbitrary array. These techniques may be applicable to some systems of interconnected modules other than one dimensional arrays.

Introduction

Previous papers [1], [2] have considered the problem of detecting faults in iterative arrays of combinational cells. Sufficient conditions for locating the fault in a one-dimensional array to within two cells were also presented in [1]. These conditions were obtained under the assumptions that all cell input combinations are necessary for detecting all faults in a cell and the fault may cause the output of the faulty cell to change in any arbitrary way. We shall refer to these as the general fault assumptions.

In this paper, we first consider the fault location problem in one-dimensional arrays under the assumption that the realization of each cell in the array is known. This implies that the set of tests for detecting every fault in the cell as well as the normal and faulty outputs for each test and fault are known. Necessary and sufficient conditions are derived for fault location in one-dimensional arrays under these assumptions and also under the general fault assumptions. The latter conditions improve upon those of Kautz [1]. A method of realizing individual cells for fault locatability in one-dimensional arrays of cells is also presented.

As in the earlier papers, we assume that the cells in the array are identical and that the size of the array is arbitrarily large, but finite. The results derived here will be applicable to all arrays composed of these cells, independent of the size of the array. The array can have at most one fault at any given time. The notation to be used is shown in Fig. 1. A typical cell receives the input x from its left hand neighbor and an external input z. It generates an external output $\hat{z}$ and transmits an output $\hat{x}$ to its right hand neighbor. The controllable inputs consist of the x input to the first (left most) cell and the z inputs to all cells in the array. All $\hat{z}$ outputs and the $\hat{x}$ output of the last cell are observable. We assume that the z input to cell i is independent of the z input to cell j for $i \neq j$. We shall use subscripts to refer to specific inputs or outputs where necessary. The behavior of a cell can be described by a flow table, which has a row for each x input (also referred to as state) and a column for each z input. The entries in the table consist of pairs of cell outputs $(\hat{x}, \hat{z})$ for each combination (x, z) of cell inputs. The entries in row x_i, column z_j will be represented functionally as $\hat{x}(x_i, z_j), \hat{z}(x_i, z_j)$. Note that the variables are not necessarily binary and may represent combinations of binary variables.

We shall first present a few definitions and results from an earlier paper [2], which will be useful in the following discussion.

Definition 1. Two states x_i and x_j of a cell are ultimately distinguishable if and only if there exists at least one combination of z inputs to the array such that some observable output is different when x_i and x_j are applied to the first cell of the array. A procedure for obtaining the set of all ultimately distinguishable pairs of states in a flow table is given in [2]. A test $t_i = (x_i, z_i)$ for detecting a fault f_i in an individual cell detects the same fault when the cell is part of a one-dimensional array if and only if the $\hat{z}$ outputs of the normal and faulty cells are ultimately distinguishable. t_i is said to be usable for detecting the fault f_i.

Definition 2. For any set A of x inputs (states) applicable to a cell, we denote the set of all obtainable $\hat{x}$ outputs by N(A).

$$N(A) = \{x_i | x_i = \hat{x}(x_j, z_k),\ x_j \in A \text{ and any applicable } z_k\}$$

Also, $N^0(A) = A$ and $N^{k+1}(A) = N(N^k(A))$. It was shown in [2] that if $N^{k+1}(X) = N^k(X)$, where X is the set of all x inputs, then $N^m(X) = N^k(X)$ for all $m > k$. Thus the set of x inputs $N^k(X)$ is applicable to all cells in the array, independent of size.

Sufficient Conditions for Fault Location

In [1] Kautz has shown how $\hat{z}$ outputs can be used to locate faults in an array. We shall now show that a faulty cell can sometimes be located even if the basic cell has no $\hat{z}$ output.

Definition 3. Let $t_i = (x_i, z_i)$ be a test for detecting a fault f_i in an individual cell. An input combination $m(t_i, f_i) = (x_m, z_m)$ is said to be a masking input for the test t_i and fault f_i if the $\hat{x}$ outputs of the normal and faulty cells with the masking input applied are the same as the output of the normal cell with the test applied. That is,

$$\hat{x}_{f_i}(x_m, z_m) = \hat{x}(x_m, z_m) = \hat{x}(x_i, z_i),$$

where $\hat{x}_{f_i}$ is the $\hat{x}$ output of a cell containing the fault f_i.

<u>Theorem 1</u>. The faulty cell in a one-dimensional array can be located if there exist a set of usable tests T and a corresponding set of masking inputs M such that for every allowable fault f_i, there is a test $t_i \in T$ which detects f_i and a masking input $m(t_i, f_i) \in M$, and $N^k(X) = N^{k+1}(X) \supseteq T_X \cup M_X$, for some k, where T_X and M_X are the sets of x inputs of T and M.

<u>Proof</u>. $N^k(X) = N^{k+1}(X) \supseteq T_X \cup M_X$ implies that a set of usable tests for detecting all faults and their masking inputs can be applied to any cell in the array. We show the sufficiency of the two conditions by demonstrating how the faulty cell can be located.

Let us assume that the application of a test t_i indicated that there is a faulty cell in the array and that one of the faults which could have produced the observed response is f_i in the first cell. We now change the cell inputs to the first cell only to a set of masking inputs $m(t_i, f_i)$ which, by definition, guarantees the $\hat{x}$ output of the first cell to be correct if the fault is f_i or if it is normal. If the observed output is now correct, this implies that the $\hat{x}$ output of the first cell changed, because the inputs to the second cell onwards are kept unchanged when the masking inputs were applied to the first cell. Hence the first cell must be faulty. If the observed output with the masking inputs applied to the first cell is incorrect, then the fault f_i is not present in the first cell.

If the observed incorrect output could have been produced by any one of more than one fault in the first cell, it will be necessary to apply the masking inputs for each of these faults. We can conclude that the first cell is faulty if the correct output is observed for at least one masking input. If all masking inputs produce incorrect outputs, the fault is not in the first cell, because the appropriate masking input insures a correct $\hat{x}$ output from the first cell and the single fault assumption guarantees correct operation of the rest of the array. Note that we may not be able to determine which fault is present in the first cell even if we can establish that it is faulty.

If the first cell is not faulty, the second cell can be checked in a similar manner by applying masking inputs to it and keeping the z inputs to the succeeding cells unchanged. Since the first cell has been proven to be fault-free, masking inputs can be applied to the second cell. The same procedure is repeated for all succeeding cells until the faulty cell is located. This procedure and hence Theorem 1 are valid whether or not the cells have $\hat{z}$ outputs.

Example 1. The flow table and a realization of the exclusive-OR function are shown in Fig. 2. If the set of faults is restricted to stuck at zero (s-a-0) and stuck at one (s-a-1) at the inputs to gates other than the OR gate, the set of tests and masks shown in Table I are obtained. The masks for each test and fault are determined by analyzing the circuit.

$$X = \{0,1\}$$

$$T = M = X = N^k(X) \qquad \text{for all } k.$$

The faulty cell in the array can therefore be located by observing the output of the last cell. If the output (or any input) of the OR-gate in any cell may also be stuck at zero or one, the faulty cell cannot be located using the method given in the proof of Theorem 1, because there are no masking inputs for these faults.

The procedure given in the proof of Theorem 1 is valid only if masking inputs exist for all faults that may occur in a cell. In the above example, fault location was possible because we excluded the possibility of one of the inputs to the OR gate being stuck at one. In general, any combinational circuit realized with ANDs, ORs, NANDs, NORs and NOTs will have such faults for which no masking inputs exist. For, if the output gate is an OR or NOR, s-a-1 faults on any input of this gate cannot be masked. Similarly, a s-a-0 fault on an input of an output AND or NAND gate cannot be masked. It is therefore useful to extend the concept of masking inputs to blocks of two or more cells in order to locate any fault to such a block.

Definition 4. The $\hat{x}$ output of an array of p cells with input x_i applied to the left most cell and z inputs $z_{j1}, z_{j2}, \ldots, z_{jp}$ will be denoted by $\hat{x}^p(x_i, \underline{z}_j)$.

$$\hat{x}^p(x_i, \underline{z}_j) = \hat{x}(\hat{x}(\ldots(\hat{x}(x_i, z_{j1}), z_{j2})\ldots), z_{jp}).$$

where $\underline{z}_j = z_{j1}, z_{j2}, \ldots, z_{jp}$.

Definition 5. Let $t_i = (x_i, z_{i1})$ be a test for detecting a fault f_i in a cell and let $z_{i2}, z_{i3}, \ldots, z_{ip}$ be the inputs to the following p - 1 cells so that the effect of the fault is propagated to the $\hat{x}$ output of the pth cell. An input combination $m(t_i, f_i) = (x_m, \underline{z}_m)$, where $\underline{z}_m = z_{m1}, z_{m2}, \ldots, z_{mp}$ is said to be a masking input of degree p for the test t_i and fault f_i if the $\hat{x}$ outputs of the normal and faulty p-cell block with $(x_m, \underline{z}_m)$ applied are the same as the output of the normal p-cell block with $(x_i, \underline{z}_i)$ applied. That is,

$$\hat{x}^p_{f_i}(x_m, \underline{z}_m) = \hat{x}^p(x_m, \underline{z}_m) = \hat{x}^p(x_i, \underline{z}_i),$$

where the subscript f_i denotes the presence of the fault f_i and $\underline{z}_i = z_{i1}, z_{i2}, \ldots, z_{ip}$. Note that the masking input of Definition 3 is a masking input of degree 1.

In order to derive a masking input $m(t_i, f_i)$ of degree p, we first determine the $\hat{x}$ outputs of an array of p cells with the test t_i applied to the first cell and the propagating z inputs to the succeeding cells. We then determine the $\hat{x}$ outputs that can be produced by an individual cell containing the fault f_i. For each such output, we determine the possible outputs of the succeeding cells, using the information contained in the flow table. If any possible output of the kth cell, $k \leq p$ is the same as the normal output of that cell, then a masking input of degree k is the combination of inputs that produced that output with the fault present in the first cell. If a masking input of degree k exists for $k < p$, then a masking input of degree p can be obtained by making the z input to the jth cell equal to the propagating z input to this cell, for all j, $k < j \leq p$.

The following corollary of Theorem 1 gives sufficient conditions for locating a fault to a p-cell block.

Corollary 1.1. A fault in a one-dimensional array can be located to a block of p cells if there exist a set of tests T and a corresponding set M of masking inputs of degree p, such that for every fault f_i, there is a test $t_i \in T$ which detects f_i and a masking input $m(t_i, f_i)$ of degree p and $N^k(X) = N^{k+1}(X) \supseteq T_X \cup M_X$, for some k, where T_X and M_X are the sets of x inputs of T and M.

Proof. Follows from Theorem 1 by treating p-cell blocks as single cells.

Existence of Masking Inputs

Although the existence of masking inputs of degree 1 depends not only on the flow table but also on its realization and the class of faults, some sufficient conditions for the existence of masking inputs of higher degree may be stated in terms of the properties of the flow table. If a test (x_i, z_i) for detecting a fault f_i has no masking input of degree 1, let $\hat{x}(x_i, z_i) = x_j$ and $\hat{x}_{f_i}(x_i, z_i) = x_k$. Let the z input to the next cell for propagating the effect of the fault through it be z_j. A masking input $m(t_i, f_i)$ of degree 2 exists if there exists an input z_k such that $\hat{x}(x_j, z_k) = \hat{x}(x_k, z_k) = \hat{x}(x_j, z_j)$. This condition can be extended in an obvious manner to masking inputs of higher degree.

The conditions for the existence of masking inputs can be applied also under the general fault assumptions. Without the knowledge of the realization of a cell or the class of faults, we cannot obtain masking inputs of degree 1. Masking inputs of degree 2 exist for every detectable fault if for every ordered pair of states (x_i, x_j), there exist z inputs z_k and z_m such that $\hat{x}(x_j, z_k) \neq \hat{x}(x_i, z_k) = \hat{x}(x_i, z_m) = \hat{x}(x_j, z_m)$. If the normal and faulty $\hat{x}$ outputs of a cell are x_i and x_j respectively, $\hat{x}(x_i, z_k) \neq \hat{x}(x_j, z_k)$ ensures propagation of the change through the next cell whereas $\hat{x}(x_i, z_m) = \hat{x}(x_j, z_m) = \hat{x}(x_i, z_k)$ enables masking in the next cell.

Theorem 2. Fault location is possible to a 2-cell block under the general fault assumptions, if all x-states appear as $\hat{x}$ entries in the table and for every ordered pair of states (x_i, x_j), there is some z input, z_k such that $\hat{z}(x_i, z_k) \neq \hat{z}(x_j, z_k)$ or there are inputs z_k and z_m such that $\hat{x}(x_j, z_k) \neq \hat{x}(x_i, z_k) = \hat{x}(x_i, z_m)$.

Proof. If there is some z input for which the $\hat{z}$ outputs are different, then any fault which produces an $x_i \rightarrow x_j$ change in the $\hat{x}$ output will cause the $\hat{z}$ outputs of the next cell to change. However, a fault in the latter cell may also produce the same $\hat{z}$ output change and therefore fault location is possible only to a 2-cell block. If the condition on $\hat{z}$ outputs is not satisfied, the second condition is sufficient for the existence of masking inputs. The procedure given in the proof of Theorem 1 can be used to locate the faulty 2-cell block. Note that the first condition of this theorem is the same as that in Theorem 4 of [1]. Thus, Theorem 2 implies that fault location is possible to a 2-cell block in some cases, even in the absence of $\hat{z}$ outputs.

Necessary and Sufficient Conditions

We shall derive necessary and sufficient conditions for locating the faulty cell in an array without $\hat{z}$ outputs and generalize them for locating the fault to a block of two or more cells, when the faulty cell itself cannot be located.

Theorem 3. A faulty cell which realizes $\hat{x}'(x, z)$ instead of $\hat{x}(x, z)$ can be located if and only if there exist two input combinations x_1, z_1 and x_1', z_1' applicable to any cell in the array, such that

(1) $\hat{x}(x_1, z_1) = \hat{x}(x_1', z_1') = x_m$

(2) $\hat{x}'(x_1, z_1) = x_k$

$\hat{x}'(x_1', z_1') = x_k'$

where x_k and x_k' are ultimately distinguishable.

Proof. It can be shown that if the conditions of the theorem are satisfied, x_1, z_1 and/or x_1', z_1' will be a usable test for detecting the fault under consideration. To prove the sufficiency of these conditions for locating the faulty cell, consider a block of two cells, where the first cell realizes $\hat{x}'$ instead of $\hat{x}$. This fault will be indistinguishable from some fault in the second cell which causes it to realize $\hat{x}''$ instead of $\hat{x}$, if and only if

$$\hat{x}''(\hat{x}(x_1, z_1), z_2) = \hat{x}(\hat{x}'(x_1, z_1), z_2) \qquad \text{for all } x_1, z_1, z_2.$$

Let $z_{p_1}, z_{p_2}, \ldots$ be a sequence of z inputs that will propagate an $x_k \to x_k'$ change to the right-hand boundary. If x_k and x_k' are ultimately distinguishable, such a sequence of inputs exists. If the first cell realizes $\hat{x}'$ instead of $\hat{x}$, application of $x_1, z_1, z_{p_1}, z_{p_2}, \ldots$ will produce an output (at the right-hand boundary) that is different from the output produced by $x_1', z_1', z_{p_1}, z_{p_2}, \ldots$ If the first cell is not faulty, it will produce the same $\hat{x}$ output for both x_1, z_1 and x_1', z_1', and it is impossible for any fault in the second cell (or any succeeding cell) to produce different outputs for the inputs $x_1, z_1, z_{p_1}, z_{p_2}, \ldots$ and $x_1', z_1', z_{p_1}, z_{p_2}, \ldots$

To prove the necessity of these conditions, we show that $\hat{x}''$ can be defined so as to make faults in the first and second cell indistinguishable if any condition is not satisfied. If condition (1) is not satisfied for some pair of input combinations, i.e., $\hat{x}(x_1, z_1) = x_m$ and $\hat{x}(x_1', z_1') = x_m' \neq x_m$, we define $\hat{x}''(x_m, z_j) = \hat{x}(x_k, z_j)$ and $\hat{x}''(x_m', z_j) = \hat{x}(x_k', z_j)$ for all z_j, whether or not condition (2) is satisfied. If condition (2) is not satisfied, but condition (1) is, we define $\hat{x}''(x_m, z_j) = \hat{x}(x_k, z_j)$ or $\hat{x}(x_k', z_j)$ for all z_j. With $\hat{x}''$ defined in this way, a fault in the first cell which causes it to realize $\hat{x}'$ instead of $\hat{x}$ cannot be distinguished from a fault in the second cell which causes it to realize $\hat{x}''$ instead of $\hat{x}$.

In Theorem 3, the special case where $x_m = x_k$ or x_k' corresponds to the masking input discussed earlier. For fault location under the general fault assumptions, the conditions of Theorem 3 should be satisfied for all faulty $\hat{x}$-functions. This is clearly impossible because there exist faulty $\hat{x}$-functions for which condition (2) cannot be satisfied; e.g., $\hat{x}'(x_i, y_j) = x_k$, for all x_i, y_j. The following corollary to Theorem 3 gives necessary and sufficient conditions for location of the fault to a two-cell block, which can then be extended for fault location to two-cell blocks under the general fault assumptions.

Corollary 3.1. A fault which causes a cell to realize a function $\hat{x}'(x, z)$ instead of $\hat{x}(x, z)$ can be located to a two-cell block if and only if there exist two input combinations x_1, z_1, z_2 and x_1', z_1', z_2' applicable to any cell in the array, such that

(1) $\hat{x}(\hat{x}(x_1, z_1), z_2) = \hat{x}(\hat{x}(x_1', z_1'), z_2') = x_m$

(2) $\hat{x}(\hat{x}'(x_1, z_1), z_2) = x_k$

$\hat{x}(\hat{x}'(x_1', z_1'), z_2') = x_k'$

where x_k and x_k' are ultimately distinguishable.

The proof of Corollary 3.1 is similar to that of Theorem 3. Necessary and sufficient conditions for fault location to k-cell blocks, $k > 2$, can be obtained by similar extensions of the theorem.

Example 2. Consider the normal and faulty flow tables of a cell shown below:

$\hat{x}$:

x \ z	0	1
1	3	1
2	2	1
3	2	4
4	2	2

$\hat{x}'$:

x \ z	0	1
1	2	1
2	2	1
3	2	4
4	2	2

The following tables give the output of a two-cell block when both cells are normal and when the first cell realizes $\hat{x}'$ instead of $\hat{x}$:

x \ z_1z_2	00	01	11	10
1	2	4*	1	3
2	2	1	1	3
3	2	1	2	2
4	2	1	1	2

$\hat{x}(\hat{x}(x, z_1), z_2)$

x \ z_1z_2	00	01	11	10
1	2	1*	1	3
2	2	1	1	3
3	2	1	2	2
4	2	1	1	2

$\hat{x}(\hat{x}'(x, z_1), z_2)$

The two tables agree everywhere except the starred entries. Hence the two conditions of Theorem 3 cannot be satisfied simultaneously by any pair of input combinations, excluding the circled entry. However, $\hat{x}(\hat{x}(1,0),1) = 4$ and there is no other entry 4 in the table. Hence $x=0$, $z_1=0$, $z_2=1$ cannot be a member of a pair of input combinations satisfying condition (1) of Theorem 3. Thus, there exists no pair of input combinations which satisfies the conditions of the theorem and the fault cannot be located to a two-cell block. The fault in the first cell cannot be distinguished from a fault in the third cell which causes it to realize $\hat{x}''$ constructed using the method given in the proof of Theorem 3 and shown below:

x \ z	0	1
1	3	1
2	2	1
3	2	4
4	3	1

$\hat{x}''$

Consider another faulty function $\hat{x}'$ such that $\hat{x}'(2,0) = 1$ and $\hat{x}' = \hat{x}$ elsewhere. The conditions of the theorem are satisfied for the pair of input combinations $x=2$, $z_1=z_2=0$ and $x=1$, $z_1=z_2=0$ and the fault is locatable to a two-cell block.

Satisfaction of the conditions of Theorem 3 for all faulty $\hat{x}$-functions is necessary and sufficient for locating a faulty two-cell block in the absence of $\hat{z}$ outputs, under the general fault assumptions. Theorem 3 also leads to the following simpler sufficient conditions for fault location to a two-cell block, under the general fault assumptions. All states appear as next-state entries in the flow table and for every pair of states (x_i, x_j) there exist inputs z_k and z_k' such that

$$\hat{x}(x_i, z_k) = \hat{x}(x_i, z_k'); \quad \hat{x}(x_j, z_k) \neq \hat{x}(x_j, z_k') \text{ or}$$

$$\hat{x}(x_i, z_k) \neq \hat{x}(x_i, z_k'); \quad \hat{x}(x_j, z_k) = \hat{x}(x_j, z_k').$$

Cell Realizations for Fault Locatability

We now show how any flow table can be realized to have masking inputs of degree 2, by adding one z input (i.e., doubling the number of columns in the table). Coding of the states of the flow table is employed. This implies an increase in the number of states, because noncode points are assigned specific outputs in order to obtain the desired masking property.

Let us code the states of the flow table (x inputs and $\hat{x}$ outputs) using a code in which any pair of code points differs in three or more variables. We shall refer to this as a distance-3 code. If the flow table is realized in the two-level sums-of-products form with no shared logic, any single fault will affect only one output. The distance-3 code enables us to correct any output error due to a single fault.

For any given flow table M, we construct a new flow table M′ with one adiitional z input z_t. M′ will have twice as many columns as M. For each state represented by a code point, the next state $(\hat{x})$ entries for both $z_t = 0$ and $z_t = 1$ are assigned to be the same as in M. For input combinations adjacent to code points (differing in only one variable), the next state entries are made the same as those of the state represented by the code point nearest to the input combination, for $z_t = 0$. For the same case with $z_t = 1$, the next state entries are assigned values adjacent to the correct coded output.

If M′ defined above is realized in the two-level sums-of-products form and the array is operated with $z_t = 0$ for all cells, any single fault will be masked. For fault detection, we set $z_t = 1$ for all cells, thereby allowing propagation through all cells. In order to locate the fault, we set $z_t = 0$ to the first two cells. If the output is correct, we can conclude that the fault is in the first cell or the second cell. If the output is incorrect, the fault is not in the first cell. We then set $z_t = 0$ to the first cell and locate the fault to cells 2 or 3, or establish that the fault is not in cell 2. This procedure can be repeated until the fault is located to some 2-cell block.

Conclusion

In this paper, we have derived necessary and sufficient conditions for the location of faults in one-dimensional arrays under the general fault assumptions as well as restricted fault assumptions. A method of augmenting any flow table and realizing the augmented table for fault location to 2-cell blocks is also presented.

The concepts presented in this paper may also be useful for developing methods for locating faults in circuits other than iterative arrays. These extensions would probably be relatively straightforward for circuits without reconvergent fanout, such as tree-type circuits. However, the presence of reconvergent fanout, in circuits such as two-dimensional iterative arrays, leads to additional problems which have not been considered here.

References

1. W. H. Kautz, "Testing for Faults in Combinational Cellular Logic Arrays," Conf. Record 8th Annual Symposium on Switching and Automata Theory, pp. 161-174, October 1967.

2. P. R. Menon and A. D. Friedman, "Fault Detection in Iterative Logic Arrays," IEEE Trans. on Computers C-20, pp. 524-535, May 1971.

Table I

Fault		Test		Mask	
Wire	Stuck at	x	z	x	z
a	0	0	1	1	0
b	0	0	1	1	0
c	0	1	0	0	1
d	0	1	0	0	1
e	0	1	1	0	0
f	0	1	1	0	0
a	1	0	0	1	1
b	1	1	1	0	0
c	1	1	1	0	0
d	1	0	0	1	1
e	1	0	1	1	0
f	1	1	0	0	1

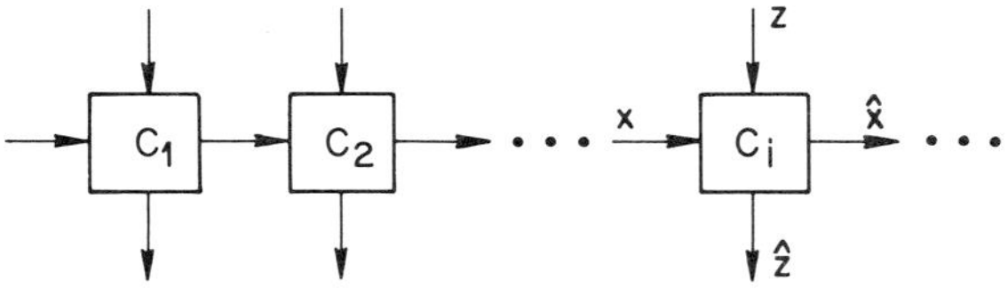

Fig. 1 A one-dimensional array.

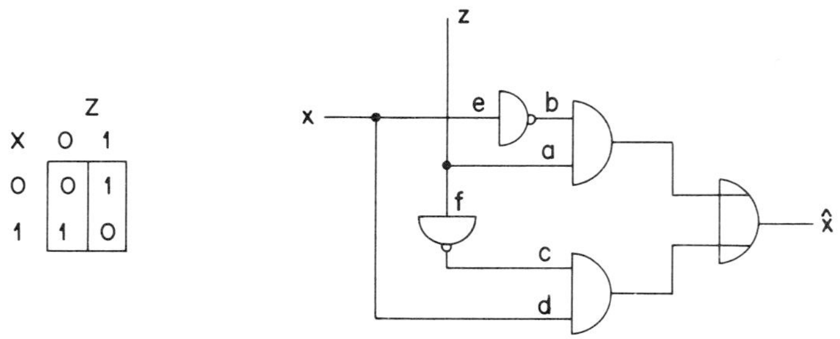

Fig. 2 Flow table and realization of Example 1.

AN APPROACH TO DESIGNING CHECKING EXPERIMENTS BASED ON A DYNAMIC MODEL

Charles L. Seitz

University of Utah
Computer Science

MACHINE IDENTIFICATION AND CHECKING EXPERIMENTS

In the usual form of *machine identification experiment* the experimenter is to determine the behavior of an unknown sequential machine by applying an input sequence and recording the output sequence. The problem of finding an input sequence which allows the experimenter to characterize completely the behavior of the unknown machine cannot be solved unless the machine is strongly connected and an upper bound on the number of its distinguishable states is known. Given this bound alone, it is always possible to devise an experiment which allows one to predict all future behavior of the machine. This can be shown as follows: Suppose that the unknown machine has "n" or fewer distinguishable states. Form the direct sum of *all* machines with n or fewer states. Although the direct sum machine is not strongly connected, it still possesses a (quasi-) homing experiment which leaves the direct sum machine in one of a set of equivalent states, thus allowing the future behavior to be predicted.

This well-known trick of finding a homing experiment on a direct sum machine is theoretically applicable to the problem of determining which (if any) of a finite number of state diagrams represents the behavior of an unknown machine. Through this connection, the practical application of machine identification experiments is as a *checking* or *fault detection experiment,* to determine whether the unknown (untested) machine behaves in accordance with its state diagram specification. In order to test a machine thoroughly, it is necessary to devise a machine identification experiment which assures that the machine under test has a given state diagram, to the exclusion of all other state diagrams which might result from a fault. Of course, we assume that the fault is persistant, rather than intermittent.

The experimenter must know enough about the internal structure of the untested machine to determine what he feels includes "all other state diagrams which might result from a fault." If, for example, no fault could give the machine more than n states, he can resort to using a machine identification experiment based on the direct sum of all machines with n or fewer states. Unfortunately, the very rapid growth of the number of machines with n makes this direct approach impractical, even with a computer, if n is larger than about four. A more plausible approach, still based on the direct sum, is to list in the direct sum only those state tables that would result from each circuit element fault. This approach has the advantage of determining in most cases the location of the fault.

Instead of trying to find a *minimal* checking sequence, one can use a heuristic approach which relies on the existence of a distinguishing experiment (or experiments) for the machine being tested [1,2,3]. The checking experiment consists of a homing experiment followed by a series of tests which check the response to each state and transition by means of the distinguishing experiment(s). Usually the test can be made shorter by cleverly superimposing different parts of the test. Lacking a distinguishing experiment this problem is difficult [4], and the checking experiment can be very much simplified by augmenting the output mapping so that the machine possesses a distinguishing experiment [5].

The heuristic approaches outlined above generate reasonably short checking sequences, which are constructed by testing each feature of the machine's state table with the distinguishing sequence(s). The approach suggested here is also heuristic, but does not rely on the existence of a distinguishing sequence, and does not even refer to the features of the machine's state table. The state table is used only to determine the response to input sequences. This may seem to resemble some form of parlor trick, which might be explained as follows: Checking sequences tend to be surprizingly short considering how difficult they are to compute by the direct sum technique. Certainly given a sequence, it is much easier to determine for what (if any) machine this is a checking sequence than vice-versa. Thus we use an approach of finding machines which explain a given behavior, rather than searching for a behavior which characterizes a given machine.

PASSIVE MACHINE IDENTIFICATION

The gedanken-experiments on machines [6] are usually classified as either *preset* or *adaptive*. In order to concentrate on the analysis of behavior without diverting attention (initially) to the synthesis of experiments, we consider first another type of experiment, called *passive*, in which the experimenter has no control over the inputs. We assume that the experimenter has no knowledge of the initial state of the machine (the state the machine was in when first encountered), but must know the input and output alphabets. We consider here, without particular loss of generality, only machines whose input and output alphabet is {0,1}.

Passive machine identification experiments are reminicent of the approach of the behavioral scientist who prefers to observe some creature in its natural inhabitation rather than to capture the creature and subject it to a controlled experiment. If one has no control over the stimuli, it is not necessary to devise revealing experiments, but one merely hopes that the natural environment of the creature will provide circumstances which reveal its behavior. As the experimenter accumulates behavior records, he might be expected to form a model for this behavior. In the case in which the creature is a finite state machine, this model naturally takes the form of a set of state diagrams, each of which might explain the behavior observed up to that point in time. In order to formalize this idea, some notation is required:

M is the machine the experimenter is observing. M is a transition output (Mealy) machine with #(M) states. The states of M are denoted as $S_0, S_1, S_2, \ldots$.

k denotes the present length of the experiment.

Σ_k $= \sigma_1\sigma_2\ldots\sigma_k$ is the input sequence after the kth input symbol has been applied.

Ω_k is similarly the output sequence.

m_k is the set of valid models for M based on the behavior Σ_k/Ω_k. The states of some particular m_k are denoted as $s_0, s_1, s_2, \ldots$, where s_0 is the state m_k was in when the experiment began. Each machine in the set must be a *valid* model for M in the sense that the application of Σ_k to any machine in m_k starting in s_0 yields Ω_k.

m_k' is a subset of m_k, consisting of those machines which are minimal in the set with respect to the number of states, $\#(m_k')$.

For any behavior Σ_k/Ω_k it is a simple matter to construct the set m_k'. It is revealing, however, to look at an example of the development of m_k' in the course of a passive experiment.

For example, let $\Sigma_1/\Omega_1 = 0/0$; then m_1' is as shown below. Now let $\Sigma_2/\Omega_2 = 01/00$; then m_2' is like m_1' except that it is furthur constrained. Properly, each of these incompletely specified tables is a representation for a set of completely specified machines. It is clear that if $\#(m_i') = \#(m_j')$ and $i \leq j$, then the set m_j' is included by m_i'. This fact is a direct consequence of the phenomenon that additional inputs can only furthur constrain the behavior. If you regard each machine in m_k' as a possible theory of M's behavior, a continuation of the experiment can only have the effect of disproving none, some, or all of the previously valid theories.

	x=0	x=1
s_0	-/0	-

m_1'

	x=0	x=1
s_0	s_0/0	-/0

m_2'

Continuing with the example, next let $\Sigma_3/\Omega_3 = 010/001$. This evidence is inconsistent with all machines in m_2', so evidently m_3' contains machines with more than one state. It is easily shown that $1 \leq \#(m_k') \leq \#(m_{k+1}') \leq k+1 \leq \#(M)$.

The following procedure may always be used to determine m_k', and is particularly useful when $\#(m_{k-1}') < \#(m_k')$. The behavior record (here 010/001) is written as an incompletely specified machine with k states, as shown below, which can by the Paull-Unger technique [7] be reduced to yield all minimal state representations. While the reduction of an incompletely specified machine does not neces-

	x=0	x=1
s_0	$s_1/0$	-
s_1	-	$s_2/0$
s_2	$-/1$	-

(om_3)

sarily yield a unique machine, it does yield a unique set of minimal state representations.

Kella [8] recently* published a fast algorithm for reduction of incompletely specified machines of the form shown above, which he called "original machines" (and which we now denote by om_k). Since the state graph for an original machine possesses no circuits, the conditional compatibilities represented on a compatibility graph are also circuit free. This fact permits the reduction to be accomplished somewhat more efficiently.

The reduction in our example yields for m_3' a set of 16 two-state machines. In the process of doing quite a few examples by hand, we stumbled on an interesting result which is the same as one proved by Kella in [8]; namely, that in examining the closed coverings of compatibles, only those that are partitions need be used to create the reduced machines. This special feature of the reduction of "original machines" can be verified in a manner rather less tedious than an argument based on the compatibility graph by using the following interpretation. The states of each (fully specified) machine in m_k' induce a partition on the states of the k-state original machine, this partition being the same as a closed covering from which this table is generated from the original machine. The result of having a partition rather than a cover is to assign to each state of the original machine, or to each step in Σ_k, a unique state of the reduced machine. When some state s_{i+1} of the original machine appears in more than one block of a *cover*, the successor (there is but one) of the block containing s_i of the original machine may be assigned to any of the states corresponding to the blocks in which s_{i+1} appears. Thus the cover may assign to each state of the original machine, or to each step in Σ_k, a non-unique state

*In fact, Kella's paper appeared between this paper's 2nd and final drafts, and inspired the latter.

of the reduced machine. This amounts to a set of possible state sequences, but each of these must have been included before in the partitions.

In our present example, the partitions are $\{\overline{s_0,s_1};\overline{s_2}\}$ and $\{\overline{s_0};\overline{s_1,s_2}\}$. The closed cover $\{\overline{s_0,s_1};\overline{s_1,s_2}\}$ may be ignored by the argument above as generating no new tables. The partitions may generate several state tables each, since certain transitions are not exercised by Σ_3. The 16 machines in m_3' can be represented by two two-state tables resulting from the respective partitions:

	x=0	x=1
s_0	$s_0/0$	$s_1/0$
s_1	-/1	-

	x=0	x=1
s_0	$s_1/0$	-
s_1	-/1	$s_1/0$

(m_3')

As the passive experiment proceeds furthur, it is possible to construct the m_k' in the same way m_3' was produced, but it is not necessary to do that much work. Upon the observation of additional input-output pairs, each machine in the current m_k' may be checked to determine whether it is consistent with the observed behavior $\Sigma_{k+1}/\Omega_{k+1}$, and may be discarded if inconsistent.

Eventually, one may find that there are no more valid machines left. For example, Σ_6/Ω_6 = 010001/001001 is not consistent with any of the machines in m_3', and the experimenter would have to conclude that $\#(m_6') > 2$. On the other hand, for Σ_8/Ω_8 = 01000110/00100011, only one machine remains from m_3', and if it is known that #(M) = 2, then $m_8' = M$, since m_8' is the only two-state machine which can account for the behavior Σ_8/Ω_8. It is only in these conditions that a passive experiment can terminate.

DESIGN OF CHECKING EXPERIMENTS

A dynamic model, such as m_k', in a passive experiment is of little use unless the experimenter is permitted to choose the next input symbol. However, the fiction of a passive experiment has allowed us to introduce all the analytical tools, and all that is necessary to extend this discussion to the design of checking experiments is a way of choosing the input sequence.

Surely every scientist is familiar with the ways in

which his models serve as preconceptions which influence his experiments. It is in this way that we use the model machines m_k', to guide the experiment by this incomplete knowledge of M, rather than by its desired behavior.

For a genuine machine identification experiment, in which M is completely unknown except for #(M), the experimenter can choose the next (k+1)th input on the basis of m_k', as long as this is a set with more than one element. A procedure which can always be applied here is to form the direct sum of all the machines in m_k', and to find a (quasi) homing experiment for the direct sum machine. This will always permit m_k' to be reduced to a single machine, or in pathological cases to set of equivalent states in different machines which still permits the future behavior to be "predicted." Since M is not necessarily contained in the set m_k', the application of the complete homing experiment may yield an "impossible" response -- which implies that the number of states in m_k' be increased. Thus it is appropriate to apply the homing sequence one symbol at a time, or to generate it adaptively, if the number of symbols used is to be decreased.

When m_k' consists of only one machine, or a set of machines with equivalent submachines, the experimenter has no clue about how to choose an input sequence which produces a contradiction to his model, which is the only way in which the number of states can be increased. Similarly, there seems to be no very systematic way to choose the first several input symbols.

For a checking experiment, the experimenter has a description of the desired behavior of M, which we denote as M', and his task is to confirm that M = M'. We assume here as is customary that the number of states in M does not exceed the number of states in M'. The experimenter can use an heuristic approach to devising a fault-detection or checking experiment which is guided by both m_k' and by M'. This particular heuristic does not require that M' possess a distinguishing experiment, and is computationally quite simple.

In order to demonstrate the convergence of this technique, we separate the experimenter's activities into two parts (which will later be combined). This also illustrates a dilemma to the experimenter: whether to try for a contradiction between the behavior record and his current set of models m_k' so that (1) all the machines in m_k' become disqualified, or (2) all but one machine in m_k' becomes disqualified. Assume that he attempts first goal, which is to increase the number of states, only after reducing the number of elements of m_k' to one, and assume that he attempts the second goal, which is reduce the set m_k' to a single element, only when it contains more than one machine. If the experimenter proceeds in this fashion, always able to accomplish his current goal until $m_k' = M'$, the procedure obviously converges.

Suppose that m_k' has more than one element. Then the technique outlined above for machine identification will always reduce this set to a single element. In the pathological case of equivalent states from different components any component will serve as the single element of the shrunken set, since it carries forth the same future behavior.

Assume that m_k' consists of only a single element. To produce a contradiction between m_k' and M', form the direct sum of these two machines and find a homing experiment, which has Σ_k as a preamble, to distinguish between m_k' and M'. If no such experiment can be found, then $m_k' = M'$, and the experiment is concluded.

Now let us point out that the proper way for the experimenter to resolve his dilemma between the two goals is probably not as outlined above. Furthur, it makes no difference for convergence which he is pursuing, so long as he is progressing on either one. The best way for the experimenter to resolve this dilemma is to form the direct sum of all the machines in m_k' *and* M'. In this way he is able to reduce the population of machines in m_k' through a homing experiment until the opportunity arises to follow the homing tree into an ambiguity contained entirely in M'. At this point the experimenter must recreate his model set and form a new direct sum, or else he is done.

We assume in this discussion that the actual checking experiment includes a short prefix to home M' to S_0. While the checking experiments designed by this technique may appear to be adaptive, they are in fact preset experiments because the behavior is demonstrated to be unique to M'.

CONCLUSIONS

We have used the model machine technique for designing checking experiments for numerous examples. The resulting experiments *tend* to be shorter or about the same in length as those devised by other techniques [3,4]. The character of the experiments does not depend very strongly on the "cleverness" of the experimenter, but are somewhat difficult to relate to the structure of the machine being tested.

REFERENCES

[1] Hennie, Frederick C., *Finite-State Models for Logical Machines,* John Wiley & Sons, 1968. (3.3)

[2] Kohavi, Zvi, *Switching and Finite Automata Theory,* McGraw-Hill, 1970. (13.4-13.7)

[3] Kohavi, Igal and Zvi Kohavi, "Variable-length Distinguishing Sequences and their Application to the Design of Fault-detection Experiments," *IEEE TC,* vol C-17, pp. 792-795. (August 1968)

[4] Hennie, Frederick C., "Fault Detecting Experiments for Sequential Circuits," *Proceedings of the Fifth Annual Symposium on Switching Circuit Theory and Logical Design,* pp. 95-110, Princeton, November 1964.

[5] Kohavi, Zvi and Pierre Lavallee, "Design of Sequential Machines with Fault-Detection Capabilities," *IEEE TEC,* vol. EC-16, pp. 473-484. (August 1967) (See also [2] sections 13.6,7.)

[6] Moore, E. F., "Gedanken-experiments on Sequential Machines," *Automata Studies,* pp. 129-153, Princeton University Press, 1956.

[7] Paull, M. C., and S. H. Unger, "Minimizing the number of states in incompletely specified sequential switching circuits," *IRE TEC,* vol. EC-8, pp. 356-367. (September 1959)

[8] Kella, J., "Sequential Machine Identification," *IEEE TC,* vol. C-20, pp. 332-338. (March 1971)

SECTION V

SWITCHING THEORY

TREE-THRESHOLD-SYNTHESIS OF TERNARY FUNCTIONS

H. Arango, J. Santos and M. Pascual

Departamento de Electrotecnia
Universidad Nacional del Sur
Bahía Blanca, Bs. As., Argentina

Abstract

The paper describes a method for the synthesis of ternary functions using diagonal negation and two threshold operations. Main advantages over previous methods are a reduction in the number of required inputs and a distribution of input functions over input nodes that automatically takes care of fan-in limitations. It is also shown that in the case of self-dual functions a more economical synthesis is possible by a change in the representation basis and finally the electronic circuits implementing the method are described.

Introduction

In 1963, Hanson defined and developed a Ternary Algebra [1] using diagonal negation and certain threshold operations in its generating set. The representation basis defined in the paper is called the r-set and a recursive tabular algorithm was given for the synthesis of any ternary function. However, the r-set is not totally disjoint and this fact complicates the synthesis by imposing the necessity of compensations when the effect of an r corresponding to a certain element of the domain is propagated to other elements of the domain. Moreover, the method has two important shortcomings: in the first place a rather high number of inputs (up to 5^{ν}, ν being the order of the operation) may be required in the circuit implementing the function. In the second place, the limited fan-in of threshold gates complicates the final design by imposing a careful distribution of input functions over input nodes.

For instance two functions that may take simultaneously the value 1 or the value $\bar{1}$ can not be inputs to the same gate in the first layer of logic; a similar requirement exists at every level of combinational logic and this fact certainly makes the final steps of the design procedure rather cumbersome.

The original approach is hereby improved by the development of a tree-synthesis method that reduces the number of inputs to a maximum of 2.3^{ν}, and automatically takes care of the distribution of input functions over input nodes. Finally it is shown that a simplifying relation can be systematically applied in the case of self-dual operations allowing a more economical synthesis by a change to a representation basis simply formed by the (negated or unnegated) variables.

The method leads naturally to modular tree-structures.

The Tree-Synthesis Method

The set $S = \{\bar{1},0,1\}$ will be used. $f(D)$ will denote the value of the function f in its domain element D. The constant operation c_s is defined as having the value $c_s(D) = s$ for every $s \in S$, $D \in S^{\nu}$. The variable operation x_{λ} is defined as having the value $x_{\lambda}(D) = d_{\lambda}$, $D = \langle d_1 d_2 \ldots . d_{\lambda} \ldots . d_{\nu} \rangle \in S^{\nu}$. $\bar{x}_{\lambda}$ will denote diagonal negation on x_{λ} according to Table I.

Two threshold operations $\triangle$ and ∇, called majority and unanimity will be used. They are defined as follows: $\triangle(D)$ equals $\bar{1}$, 0 or 1 according to the number of $\bar{1}$'s in D being greater, equal or smaller than the number of 1's. $\nabla(\bar{1}\bar{1}\ldots\bar{1}) = \bar{1}$; $\nabla(11\ldots1) = 1$; the value of ∇ for every other element of the domain is 0.

Complementary functions Θ_E, $E \in S^{\nu}$ are defined as the tape $f_1 f_2 \ldots . f_{\nu}$ of operations f_{α} such that f_{α} equals $\bar{x}_{\alpha}$, c_1 or x_{α} according to d_{α} being $\bar{1}$, 0 or 1 respectively. The vectors r_E, $E \in S^{\nu}$ of the representation basis are defined as:

$$(\forall D)_{S^{\nu}}, \qquad r_E = \nabla(\Theta_E \; c_1)$$

Each node of a (μ levels, γ degree) tree [3] can be associated with a vector of μ elements $\langle 00..01a_1 a_2 ..a_{\rho} \rangle$ in such a way that the number of zeros before the first 1 indicates its level (counted from left to right) and the subvector $\langle a_1 a_2 \ldots a_{\rho} \rangle \in \{0,1,\ldots,(\gamma-1)\}^{\rho}$ indicates its position in the level (counted from the top). The raising function $\uparrow$ is defined as $\uparrow(n_1 n_2 \ldots n_\mu) = n_1 n_2 \ldots.(n_\mu - 1)$, for $n_\mu > 0$, and $\uparrow(n_1 n_2 \ldots 0) = \Phi$, Φ being the empty set. The <u>shifting</u> function $\rightarrow$ is defined as $\rightarrow(n_1 n_2 \ldots n_\mu) = 0 n_1 n_2 \ldots n_{\mu-1}$, for $n_1 n_2 \ldots n_\mu \neq 00\ldots.1$, and $\rightarrow(00\ldots.1) = \Phi$.

In a tree circuit, the output of any non-leaf node with vector T may be obtained recursively from the outputs of the nodes with vectors in $\rightarrow^{-}(T)$. The output of the root is the output of the circuit.

In what follows, $\gamma=2$ will be assumed. A typical step of the tree synthesis method involves the selection of a set of inputs into which operations r_D or $\bar{r}_D$ must be injected. The resultant of the actions exerted by the new and the previous inputs must be (just) the necessary to bring the output to the desired value f(D). In order to secure convergence in the compensation procedure mentioned in the Introduction, the domain elements must be considered in a sequence $\subset$ verifying the following property: $D \subset D' \Leftrightarrow \Leftrightarrow \&(D') < \&(D)$ (where $\&(D)$ is the number of zeros in D). Now, if T is the input last used and T' the nex input, the <u>influenced</u> nodes are those in the intersection of the descendences $B_{TT'} = (\hat{\rightarrow}(T)) \wedge (\hat{\rightarrow}(T'))$, (where $\hat{\rightarrow}$ indicates the closure of $\rightarrow$); the <u>correcting</u> nodes belong to the set $C_{T'} = (\uparrow^{-} \rightarrow B_{TT'} \wedge \bar{B}_{TT'}$; the <u>perturbating</u> nodes belong to the set $P_{T'} = (\uparrow \rightarrow^{-} B_{TT'}) \wedge \bar{B}_{TT'}$, and the problem may be simply stated as <u>how to select correcting nodes in such a way that a proper compensation over the perturbating nodes takes place</u>. Fig.1 illustrates the sets $B_{TT'}$, $C_{T'}$ and $P_{T'}$, for T = (10100) and T'= (10101) in a $\mu=5$, $\gamma=2$ tree. The selection of correcting nodes depends on the level-ordered sequence σ of outputs from the perturbating nodes. $\sigma' \dashv \sigma$ indicates that σ' is a solid subtape of σ. σ is opaque if max $\{|\sum_{\sigma'} \sigma_\alpha| \sigma' \dashv \sigma\} > 1$ (where $\sum_{\sigma'} \sigma_\alpha$ indicates the sum of the components of σ' and the set covers the sums for every σ' being a solid subtape of σ); it must be noted that it is impossible to correct the output of an opaque subtape from nodes situated at its left.

Therefore, the first task is to find the maximal non-opaque suffix σ^* of σ. Compensating nodes at the left of σ^* are disregarded; the compensative action depends on:

a) The extremal left and right non-zero elements of σ^*.

b) The required aoutput value f(D).

The action to be performed is indicated in Table II. When $\sigma^* = \langle 00\ldots0 \rangle$ and r_D (or $\bar{r}_D$) must be entered, node T' is directly used as input. Node (10....0) is used as input for the first r_D such that $f(D) \neq 0$.

Once the correcting node W (at level α) has been chosen, the only remaining question is the selection of the input node in the set $\rightarrow^{-\alpha}(W)$. This is easily done starting from the selected correcting node and tracing back from it the highest level available input node.

Example: Let us synthetize the function defined in Table III. $\gamma=2$ is adopted and a $\mu=5$ tree assumed necessary. The successive steps are:

1) $f(00) = 0$ implies that r_{00} will not appear as input.

2) $f(0\bar{1}) = 1$; the construction is started with $r_{0\bar{1}}$ as input at leaf (10000).

3) $f(01) = \bar{1}$; $T = (10000)$; $T' = (10001)$; $B_{TT'} = \{(01000), (00100), (00010), (00001)\}$; $P_{T'} = (10000)$; $C_{T'} = \{(10001), (01001), (00101), (00011)\}$. $\sigma_{01} = \langle 0 \rangle = \sigma^*_{01}$, and therefore it suffices to enter $\bar{r}_{01}$ as a second input at leaf (10001).

4) $f(\bar{1}0) = \bar{1}$; $T = (10001)$; $T' = (10010)$; $B_{TT'} = \{(00100), (00010), (00001)\}$; $P_{T'} = (01000)$; $C_{T'} = \{(01001), (00101), (00011)\}$; $\sigma_{\bar{1}0} = \langle 0 \rangle = \sigma^*_{\bar{1}0}$, and therefore it suffices to enter $r_{\bar{1}0}$ as input at leaf (10010).

5) $f(10) = 0$; $T = (10010)$; $T' = (10011)$; $B_{TT'} = \{(01001), (00100), (00010), (00001)\}$; $P_{T'} = \{(10010), (01000)\}$; $C_{T'} = \{(10011), (00101), (00011)\}$; $\sigma_{10} = \langle 0 \rangle = \sigma^*_{10}$, and having in mind that $f(10) = 0$, it follows that r_{10} is not necessary as input.

6) $f(\bar{1}\bar{1}) = \bar{1}$; T, T', $B_{TT'}$, $C_{T'}$, and $P_{T'}$ as in step 5); $\sigma_{\bar{1}\bar{1}} = \langle \bar{1}1 \rangle = \sigma^*_{\bar{1}\bar{1}}$, and therefore according to row 4 in Table II, compensative action must be taken at the right of node (00100). This is possible from the correcting node (00101), and the input leaf (10100) is easily traced back. $r_{\bar{1}\bar{1}}$ enters then as input there.

7) $f(\bar{1}1) = 1$; $T = (10100)$; $T' = (10101)$; $B_{TT'} = \{(01010), (00101), (00010), (00001)\}$; $P_{T'} = \{(10100), (00100)\}$; $C_{T'} = \{(10101), (01011), (00011)\}$; $\sigma_{\bar{1}1} = \langle 00 \rangle = \sigma^*_{\bar{1}1}$; no compensative action is required and therefore it suffi-

ces to enter $r_{\bar{1}1}$ as input at leaf (10101).

8) $f(1\bar{1}) = 0$; $T = (10101)$; $T' = (10110)$; $B_{TT'} = \{(00101), (00010), (00001)\}$; $P_{T'} = \{(01010), (00100)\}$; $C_{T'} = \{(01011), (00011)\}$; $\sigma_{1\bar{1}} = \langle 00 \rangle = \sigma^*_{1\bar{1}}$, and having in mind that $f(1\bar{1}) = 0$, it follows that $r_{1\bar{1}}$ is not necessary as input.

9) $f(11) = 1$; T, T', $B_{TT'}$, $C_{T'}$ and $P_{T'}$ as in step 8). $\sigma_{11} = \langle 0\bar{1} \rangle = \sigma^*_{11}$. According to row 3 in Table II, a compensative action must be taken at right of (00011). From the correcting nodes, the leaves (10110) and (11000) are easily traced back.

Step 9 finishes the synthesis process. The modular tree-structure of Fig.2 may be reduced to the tree in Fig. 3. The same function, synthetized in [1] with the original method requires 10 inputs and 9 gates, while the new method allows its synthesis with 7 inputs and 6 gates.

Table I

x	$\bar{1}$	0	1
$\bar{x}$	1	0	$\bar{1}$

Table II

case	Extremal nonzero elements of		Desired output	Compensative action	Input function
	left	right	f(D)	$\sum^*$	
1	$\bar{1}$	$\bar{1}$	$\bar{1}$	o------o	-
2	$\bar{1}$	$\bar{1}$	0	o------o ↗	r_D
3	$\bar{1}$	$\bar{1}$	1	o------o ↗ ↗	r_D
4	$\bar{1}$	1	$\bar{1}$	o------o ↗	$\bar{r}_D$
5	$\bar{1}$	1	0	o------o	-
6	$\bar{1}$	1	1	↗ o------o	r_D
7	1	$\bar{1}$	$\bar{1}$	↗ o------o	$\bar{r}_D$
8	1	$\bar{1}$	0	o------o ↗	-
9	1	$\bar{1}$	1	o------o	r_D
10	1	1	$\bar{1}$	o------o ↗ ↗	$\bar{r}_D$
11	1	1	0	o------o ↗	$\bar{r}_D$
12	1	1	1	o------o	-

Table III

x_1	x_2	f
$\bar{1}$	$\bar{1}$	$\bar{1}$
$\bar{1}$	0	$\bar{1}$
$\bar{1}$	1	1
0	$\bar{1}$	1
0	0	0
0	1	$\bar{1}$
1	$\bar{1}$	0
1	0	0
1	1	1

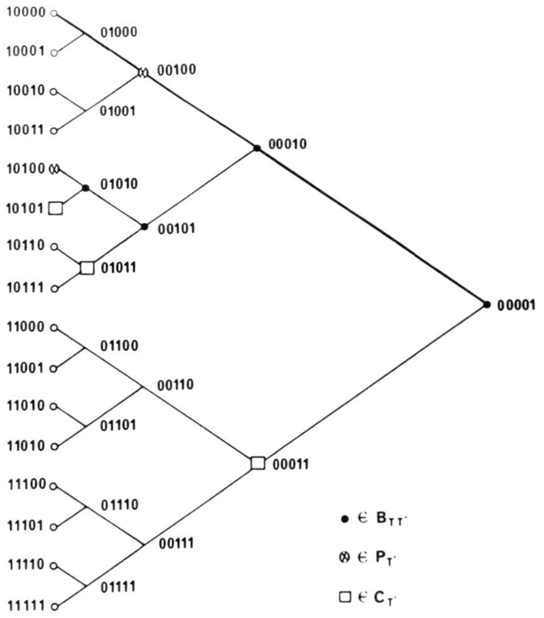

Fig. 1 A $\mu=5$, $\gamma=2$ tree and the sets $B_{TT'}$, $C_{T'}$, $P_{T'}$, for T= (10100) and T' = (10101).

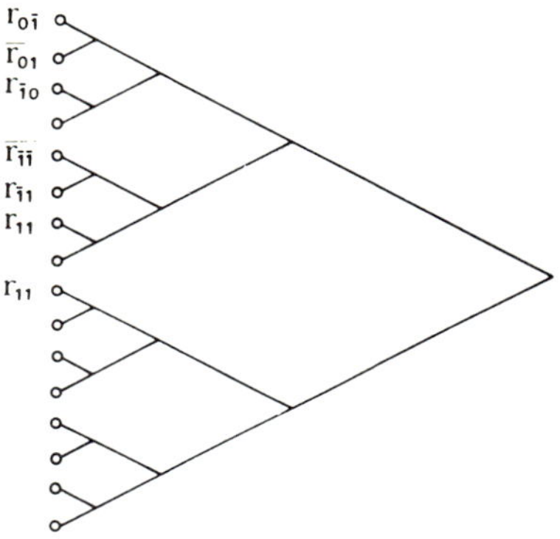

Fig. 2 Original Tree

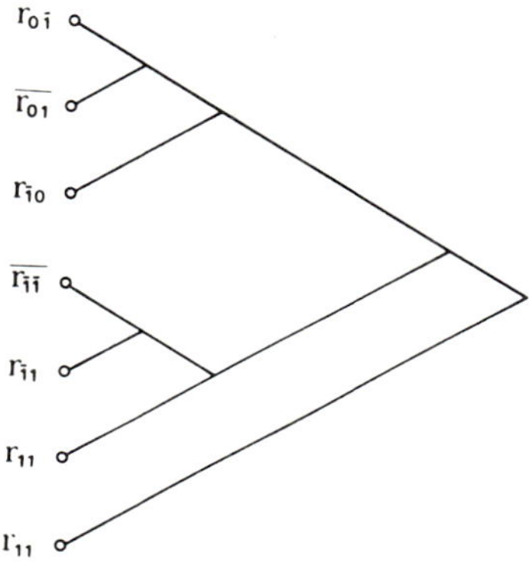

Fig. 3 Reduced Tree

Θ-Basis Synthesis

The r and Θ are related by

$$(\forall E)_S, \qquad \Delta(r_{\bar{E}}\, r_E) = \nabla \Theta_E \qquad 4.1$$

<u>Proof</u>: By definition

$$\Delta(\bar{r}_{\bar{E}}\, r_E) = \Delta(\nabla(\Theta_{\bar{E}}\, c_1), \nabla(\Theta_E\, c_1))$$

By Theorem 8 in [1]

$$\Delta(\nabla(\Theta_{\bar{E}}\, c_1), \nabla(\Theta_E\, c_1)) = \Delta(\nabla(\Theta_E\, c_{\bar{1}}), \nabla(\Theta_E\, c_1))$$

And finally, by Theorem 12 in [1]

$$\Delta(\nabla(\Theta_E\, c_{\bar{1}}), \nabla(\Theta_E\, c_1)) = \Delta\nabla\Theta_E = \nabla\Theta_E$$

If the function to be synthetized is self dual (i.e., $f\Theta_{\bar{E}} = \bar{f}\Theta_E$), forms of the type in the left-hand member of 4.1 will appear and therefore a more economical synthesis (on Θ-basis) is possible.

Example: The function defined in Table IV is self dual. Therefore it admits a Θ-basis as well as an r-basis as shown in Fig.4 .

Table IV

x_1	x_2	f
$\bar{1}$	$\bar{1}$	$\bar{1}$
$\bar{1}$	0	0
$\bar{1}$	1	0
0	$\bar{1}$	$\bar{1}$
0	0	0
0	1	1
1	$\bar{1}$	0
1	0	0
1	1	1

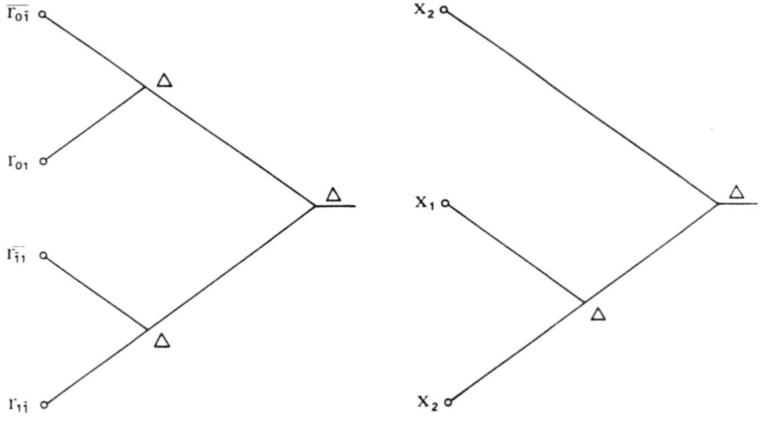

Fig. 4 r-basis and Θ-basis trees of function f.

Electronic Implementation

Fig.5 shows the circuits implementing the $\triangle$ and ∇ operations. It also shows the implementation of the diagonal negation with a circuit applying non-linear load techniques analogous to those described in [4] . The ternary multivibrator obtained by a proper connection of two diagonal negators is specially suited to the implementation of functions synthetized in r-basis and Θ-basis.

Note that the codification of electrical values <-6V, 0V, +6V> into algebraical values <1, 0, 1> is used. The output of a threshold circuit is regenerated through a negator circuit. A proper application of De Morgan law.

$$\triangle(x_1 x_2 \ldots x) = \overline{\triangle(\bar{x}_1 \bar{x}_2 \ldots \bar{x})}$$

allows regeneration at every level of the tree.

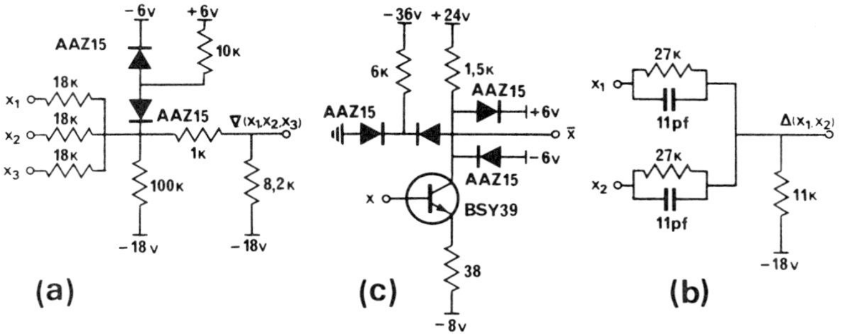

Fig. 5 Implementation of logical operations; (a) ∇ -operation (b) $\triangle$-operation (c) Diagonal negation

References

1. W. H. Hanson, IEEE Trans. Elec. Comp., EC-12, 191 (1963).
2. A. R. Meo, IEEE Trans. on Comp., C-17, 5, 432 (1968).
3. K. E. Iverson, John Wiley & Sons, N.Y., (1962).
4. H. Arango, M. Pascual, M. Valentinuzzi and J. Santos, IEEE, Trans. on Elec. Comp., EC-15, 4, 661, (1966).

A MINIMIZATION METHOD FOR 3-VALUED LOGIC FUNCTIONS

Claudio R. Moraga

Universidad Técnica Federico Santa María
Valparaíso, Chile

Abstract

A Minimization Method for 3-valued Logic Functions, (Ternary Functions), is proposed, by means of the intersection of two binary functions obtained from original Ternary Function. Redundant elements of the intersection are eliminated, in a similar procedure than in the Quine McCluskey binary method, to give the simplified function.

The Method uses a ternary extension of Karnaugh maps, which limits its applications up to 4 variables, but this means up to 81 different states, what should be enough for Ternary Digital systems applications.

The proposed Method has been evaluated by comparison with other existing minimization methods. Good results have been obtained.

Introduction

The constituents of the Ternary Algebra used in this paper are:

0,1,2 : Constants
(A,B,...): Set of symbols to represent Variables
V = (0,1,2): Set of states for the ternary variables
S = (0,1): Binary subset of V ; $s \in S$
T = (1,2): Binary subset of V ; $t \in T$
U = (0,2): Binary subset of V ; $u \in U$
M = (α,β,γ,...): Set of symbols to indicate Mappings
P : Set of Permutations of the states of a given variable.

Operations:

$$X + Y = \mathrm{Max}\ (X,Y) \qquad (1)$$
$$X \cdot Y = XY = \min\ (X,Y) \qquad (2)$$

(It follows that $(V,+,\cdot)$ is a Lattice, then idempotent, associative, conmutative and absorption laws hold. [1]).

TABLE 1

Permutations of X

Symbol	States	Name
$\underline{X}$	0 1 2	Identity
$\overline{X}$	2 1 0	Negation
X^c	1 2 0	Cyclic
X^a	2 0 1	Acyclic
X^o	0 2 1	Zero
X^2	1 0 2	Two

Proposed Method

This method uses two auxiliar binary functions obtained from the truth table of the ternary function to be simplified. The binary functions are intersected and the resulting expression is simplified eliminating redundant elements. The simplified function is represented by means of Instrumental Matrices or Permuted Variables, (p-variables), from the set P of mappings of V onto V. Mappings of V onto any of its binary subsets define Truncated Variables, (t-variables), that may be represented as a function of p-variables. (see Appendix 1).

Fundamentals, Definitions and Notation

Let L be a Ternary function such that $L = L(A,B,C,\ldots)$ Its truth table will be defined as a map α

$$\alpha: \quad L \longrightarrow V \ , \quad \alpha = \alpha\ (A,B,C,\ldots) \qquad (3)$$

Let

$$\beta : L \xrightarrow{\text{onto}} T \quad ,$$

such that $(L=2)\beta = 2$
and $(L=1)\beta = 1$ (4)
and $(L=0)\beta = t$
then $(L)\beta = L_2$ (5)

Let

$$\gamma : L \xrightarrow{\text{onto}} U \quad ,$$

such that $(L=0)\gamma = 0$
$(L=1,2)\gamma = 2$ (6)
then $(L)\gamma = L_0$ (7)

from (4) and (6), it is clear that

$$L_2 \cdot L_0 = L \tag{8}$$

Def. 1: A Karnaugh [2] Ternary map, (K-T map), is an array representation of the truth table of a given ternary function. Each cell of the map has for coordinates, one of the possible states of the variables of the function. Each cell has for entry, the state of the function under the conditions given by the coordinates.
Def. 2: Side Adjacency: 3^m cells from a K-T map are side adjacents, iff in each one of them, m coordinates take a different combination out of the possible 3^m combinations of states of m ternary variables.
Def. 3: Square Adjacency: An even number of cells from a K-T map for n variables are square adjacents iff they form an n-dimentional rectangular parallelepid.

Equations may be obtained for L_2 and L_0 by joining adjacent cells with a 2, t or ø entry, until all 2's of the maps are considered. However, since L_2 and L_0 are only auxiliar functions, no literal simplified expression for then is required, but some expression that allows a simple solution for equation (8). A minimum number of arrays of 2's is desired, yet each array does not require to be the largest possible. (Size of each array becomes some sort of ø condition for the minimization procedure.)
Def. 4: An Instrumental Matrix, (InMat), is an (n)x(3) Matrix, where each row represents respectively the set of images of V onto V, S, T or U for each variable; such

that the entries of an array of adjacent cells from a K-T map may be expressed as the (•) operation among the images of the states of the coordinates. (see figure 1)
Def. 5: (•) operation for InMat's is defined between corresponding elements from each InMat.

$$\text{let} \quad f_m = \left[f_{m_{ij}} \right] \quad , \quad f_n = \left[f_{n_{ij}} \right] \tag{9}$$

$$\text{then} \quad f_m \cdot f_n = \left[f_{m_{ij}} \right] \cdot \left[f_{n_{ij}} \right] = \left[(f_{m_{ij}})(f_{n_{ij}}) \right]$$

Def. 6: (+) operation for InMat is defined, (i.e. a resultant InMat may be obtained), iff n-1 rows are respectively identical. In this case the operation is defined between corresponding elements of the non-identical rows. Identical rows remain as such in the resulting Matrix.
Def. 7: Inclusion: InMat f_j includes InMat f_k, ($f_j > f_k$), iff every element in f_j is greater than or equal to the corresponding element in f_k.
Def. 8: An InMat is redundant if it defines cells which have already been defined by other InMat or group of InMats. (Inclusion is a particular case of redundancy).
Def. 9: Literals: A literal is a variable in some ternary formulation. (States are obtained as images of V into V).

A p-literal is a variable in ternary formulation, where states are obtained as images of V onto V.

A t-literal is a variable in binary formulation, where states are obtained as images of V onto some of its binary subsets.

Procedure

The following procedure is suggested to obtain a simplified ternary function:

a) Given the truth table of a Ternary Function, draw the corresponding K-T map.
b) With equations (4) and (6), obtain K-T maps for L_0 and L_2.
c) Select arrays of adjacent cells with a 2, t or ∅ entry to cover both maps.

d) Read from the maps the InMats for the corresponding arrays and obtain equations for L_0 and L_2, as was shown in Fig. 1.
e) Solve equation (8) according to Def. 5 and Def. 6.
f) Delete included Matrices. It should be noticed here that if all the elements of a row of an InMat belong to s = (0,1) , then all the non zero elements of the InMat may be considered as "1s", since from def. 4 this InMat represents a sub map whose entries are only 1s and 0s.
g) Check against the original K-T map to find other redundant InMats, to be deleted. (See Example 1).
h) Write literal expressions for the final InMats. (See Appendix 1).

<u>Example 1</u>: Simplify the Ternary function whose truth table may be represented by the K-T map shown in fig.2.

Maps for $L_2(A,B,C)$ and $L_0(A,B,C)$ may be found in figures 3 and 4.

Reading from the maps:

$$L_2 = \begin{matrix} 2 & 2 & 1 \\ 2 & 2 & 1 \\ 2 & 2 & 2 \end{matrix} + \begin{matrix} 2 & 2 & 2 \\ 1 & 1 & 2 \\ 2 & 2 & 1 \end{matrix} \qquad (10)$$

$$L_0 = \begin{matrix} 2 & 0 & 0 \\ 2 & 0 & 0 \\ 2 & 2 & 2 \end{matrix} + \begin{matrix} 2 & 2 & 0 \\ 0 & 2 & 2 \\ 2 & 0 & 0 \end{matrix} + \begin{matrix} 2 & 2 & 2 \\ 0 & 0 & 2 \\ 2 & 0 & 2 \end{matrix} + \begin{matrix} 0 & 0 & 2 \\ 0 & 2 & 2 \\ 0 & 2 & 2 \end{matrix} \qquad (11)$$

Equation (8) may be evaluated in array from as shown in fig. 5.

It may be seen that:

$$\begin{matrix} 2 & 2 & 0 \\ 0 & 2 & 1 \\ 2 & 0 & 0 \end{matrix} + \begin{matrix} 2 & 2 & 0 \\ 0 & 1 & 2 \\ 2 & 0 & 0 \end{matrix} = \begin{matrix} 2 & 2 & 0 \\ 0 & 2 & 2 \\ 2 & 0 & 0 \end{matrix} \qquad (12)$$

$$\begin{matrix} 2 & 0 & 0 \\ 2 & 0 & 0 \\ 2 & 2 & 2 \end{matrix} \rangle \begin{matrix} 2 & 0 & 0 \\ 1 & 0 & 0 \\ 2 & 2 & 1 \end{matrix} \qquad (13)$$

$$\begin{matrix} 2 & 2 & 2 \\ 0 & 0 & 2 \\ 2 & 0 & 1 \end{matrix} \quad \rangle \quad \left(\begin{matrix} 2 & 2 & 1 \\ 0 & 0 & 1 \\ 2 & 0 & 2 \end{matrix} = \begin{matrix} 1 & 1 & 1 \\ 0 & 0 & 1 \\ 1 & 0 & 1 \end{matrix} \right) \qquad (14)$$

$$\begin{matrix} 0&0&2\\ 0&1&2\\ 0&2&1 \end{matrix} \quad \rangle \quad \begin{pmatrix} 0&0&1 & & 0&0&1\\ 0&2&1 & = & 0&1&1\\ 0&2&2 & & 0&1&1 \end{pmatrix} \tag{15}$$

<u>Check for redundancy</u>: A procedure similar to the Quine McCluskey method, [22], [23], to obtain prime implicants may be used: To each non included InMat assign one letter; enter with that letter in a Map to cover all the cells represented by the InMat; use high case letter for a 2, and low case letter for a 1. After doing this with all the InMats, all the non-zero cells of the original K-T Map should be properly covered. Cells of the check Map containing a single letter or a single high case letter, imply they are covered by an esential InMat. All other cells covered by the esential InMats should be crossed out. For the remaining lettered cells, a test may be done to select the most convenient set of Matrices to complete the map. Most times this can be done by inspection, however, for a given complex case, an algorithm similar to the one used in the above mentioned references could be used.

This procedure allows both deletting redundant matrices and searching alternatives for possible optimization, as later will be seen.

From the array in fig. 5 and eqs. (12) to (15), non included InMats are:

$$\begin{matrix} 2&2&0\\ 0&2&2\\ 2&0&0 \end{matrix} \;,\; \begin{matrix} 2&0&0\\ 2&0&0\\ 2&2&2 \end{matrix} \;,\; \begin{matrix} 2&2&2\\ 0&0&2\\ 2&0&1 \end{matrix} \;\text{and}\; \begin{matrix} 0&0&2\\ 0&1&2\\ 0&2&1 \end{matrix}$$

Let them be named W,X,Y, and Z. The check for redundancy may be seen in fig. 6. Comparing with fig. 2 it is also clear that all the InMats are esential. then:

$$L = \begin{matrix} 2&2&0\\ 0&2&2\\ 2&0&0 \end{matrix} + \begin{matrix} 2&0&0\\ 2&0&0\\ 2&2&2 \end{matrix} + \begin{matrix} 2&2&2\\ 0&0&2\\ 2&0&1 \end{matrix} + \begin{matrix} 0&0&2\\ 0&1&2\\ 0&2&1 \end{matrix} \tag{16}$$

or

$$L = (\bar{A} + A^c)(B + B^o)\bar{C}C^a + \bar{A}A^a\bar{B}B^a + BB^2C^a + AA^2BC^o \tag{17}$$

<u>Evaluation:</u> This example has formerly been solved [3], using an adaptation of the Scheinman's Binary Method

[4], obtaining a simplified function with 23 literals, 1 constant and 17 operations. The present method gives a simplified function with 17 p-literals and 9 operations, or 10 literals and 7 operations.

Optimization

The assignment of states to the ∅ conditions, and the proper selection of arrays for the K-T maps will affect the degree of simplification of a given ternary function.

However, even if a good selection of ∅ conditions and arrays has been made, some times it is possible to improve the final solution after the method has been applied.

Two situations may arise that allow final improvement:

a) If an InMat of the final function is essential to represent one or more cells with a 1 entry, all 1's and 2's of such InMat may be revised to reformulate a consecuent Matrix with a simpler expression.

b) If a cell with a 2 entry in the original map is covered by more than one InMat of the final solution, in one of them is essential but in the others may be considered ∅ condition, and a simpler Matrix may result.

The map check for redundancy also allows a check for existence and selection of improvement possitilities.

Example 1 (Cont.): It may be seen in eqs. (16), that both the first and third InMats define a same couple of cells with a 2 entry, as shown in the K-T Map of fig.6.

This affects the B variable in the first InMat, and the A variable in the third InMat. Since the third InMat is already independent of A no further improvement is possible. For the first InMat, the following transformation is possible if minimization of p-literals is desired:

$$\begin{matrix} 2 & 2 & 2 \\ 0 & 2 & 2 \\ 2 & 0 & 0 \end{matrix} \text{ becomes } \begin{matrix} 2 & 2 & 0 \\ 0 & 2 & \emptyset \\ 2 & 0 & 0 \end{matrix} \text{ to give } \begin{matrix} 2 & 2 & 0 \\ 0 & 2 & 1 \\ 2 & 0 & 0 \end{matrix} \qquad (18)$$

Then L becomes:

$$L = (\overline{A} + A^c)B^o\overline{C}C^a + \overline{A}A^a\overline{B}B^a + BB^2C^a + AA^2BC^o \qquad (19)$$

So, L has been reduced to only 16 p-literals and 8 operations.

Conclusions

a) General Conclusions: A Minimization Method for Ternary functions has been devised. Results obtained are usually simpler than those obtained by other methods known to the author [3], [6], [17], [18]. Comparative results are found in [5] if threshold implementation is considered.

The Method is recommended up to 4 variables, since it uses K-T maps, and larger maps would become difficult to operate with.

b) Digital Systems: The fact that the proposed method seems to be convenient up to 4 variables, is not a severe limitation from the point of view of a Ternary Digital System, since up to 81 different states of a system could be represented with the 4 variables, what seems to be well over average.

The Method allows to decide by the end of the problem whether p-gates only, p/t-gates [7] to [16], or other means of implementation [5], [19], [20], [21] will be used. From the integrated circuit point of view, the cost of both type of gates should be about the same, however, from a normalization point of view, only 5 different p-gates, but 23 p/t-gates would be required. On the other hand, for a discrete solution for a particular circuit, it might be more economic to select gates that require minimum number of components.

It has been shown [19], that in some cases more economic implementation may be obtained with threshold gates to realize a full Instrumental Matrix.

Acknowledgement

The author would like to express his appreciation to Miss Carmen-Gloria Palacios for her typing of this Paper.

Appendix 1

TABLE 2

Relationship between t-variables and p-variables

States	Function of p-variables to satisfy the set of states
000	Null Constant
001	$X^a X^o = X^2 X^o = X^a X$
002	$X^2 X$
010	$X\bar{X} = XX^c = \bar{X}X^o$
011	XXo
012	X (Identity)
020	$X^c X^o$
021	X^o (Zero)
022	$X + X^o$
100	$\bar{X}X^2 = X^a X^c = X^c X^2$
101	$X^a X^2$
102	X^2 (Two)
110	$\bar{X}X^c$
111	Limitting Constant
112	$X + X^2$
120	X^c (Cyclic)
121	$X^{\bar{c}} + Xo$
122	$X + X^c = X^c + X^2 = X^o + X^2$
200	$\bar{X}X^a$
201	X^a (Acyclic)
202	$X^a + X^2$
210	$\bar{X}$ (Negation)

States	Function of p-variables to satisfy the set of states
211	$\overline{X} + X^a$
212	$X + \overline{X} = X + X^a = \overline{X} + X^2$
220	$\overline{X} + X^c$
221	$\overline{X} + X^o = X^a + X^c = X^a + X^o$
222	Universal Constant

References

1. Prather R.E., Introduction to Switching Theory: A Mathematical Approach Allyn and Bacon, Inc. (1967)
2. Karnaugh M., Transaction AIEE, Part I, 72, pp.593-599, (1953).
3. Yoeli M. and Rosenfeld G., IEEE Transactions on E. Computers, EC-14, pp.19-28, (1965)
4. Scheinman A.H., BSTJ, 41, pp.1337-1346, (1962).
5. Merril D.R. Jr., IEEE Trans. on E. Computers, EC-15, pp.578-585, (1966).
6. Moraga C.R., Technical Report EA6802 UCV, Valparaíso, Chile.
7. Friichtenicht R.D., An Experimental Study of the uses of Ternary Logic in Digital Computers, Master Thesis, USN Postgraduate School, 1964. (AD 621976).
8. Rozmarich T.A., Synthesis of three-level Logic Circuits with application to a Radix three Computer Arithmetic Unit, Master Thesis, University of Illinois, 1965. (AD 617298).
9. Baskin H.B., AIEE Conference Paper CP-62-500.
10. Hurst S.L., Electronic Engineering, 40 Nº 482, and 40 Nº 483, (1968).
11. Santos J., Arango H., and Lorenzo F., IEEE trans. on E. Computers, EC-15, pp 105-107, (1966).
12. Arango H., Pascual M., Valentinuzzi M.E., and Santos J., IEEE Trans. on E. Computers, EC-15, 6, pp. 661-662, (1966).
13. Bardell P.H., Maley G.A., and McAnney W.H., IBM Tech. Disclosure Bull. 4, pp.25-27, (1961).

14. Gruodis A.J., IBM Tech. Disclosure Bull. 4, pp.28-30, (1961).
15. Groudis A.J., IBM Tech. Disclosure Bull, 4, pp.31-33, (1961).
16. Trampel K.M., IBM Tech. Disclosure Bull. 4, pp.34-35, (1961).
17. Allen C.M. and Givone D.D., IEEE Trans. on Computers, C-17, pp.182-184, (1968).
18. Herrmann R.L., Selection and Implementation of a Ternary Switching Algebra, SJCC, (1968).
19. Moraga C., Ternary Threshold Implementations. To be published.
20. Moraga C., A Tristable Switching Circuit for Synchronized Sequential Machines. Symposium on the Theory and Applications of Multiple-Valved Logic Design. SUNY/Buffalo, N.Y., USA, (May 27-28,1971)
21. Moraga C., Informe de Investigación EOSD 7101, Universidad Técnica Federico Santa María, Valparaíso, Chile (1971).
22. Quine W.V., Am. Math. Monthly, 59, pp.512-531, (1952).
23. McCluskey E., BSTJ 35, pp.1417-1444, (1956).

X \ Y	0	1	2
0	2	2	1
1	2	2	1
2	1	1	2

$$f_1 = \begin{matrix}221\\221\end{matrix} \qquad f_2 = \begin{matrix}112\\112\end{matrix}$$

$$f(X,Y) = f_1 + f_2$$

Fig 1. A K-T Map and corresponding InMats.

A \ B	0	1	2	0	1	2	0	1	2
0	2	2	2	2	0	0	2	0	1
1	0	2	2	0	0	0	∅	∅	∅
2	0	0	2	0	1	2	0	1	1
C	0			1			2		

Fig 2. K-T Map for L(A,B,C) example 1

A \ B	0	1	2	0	1	2	0	1	2
0	2	2	2	2	t	t	2	t	1
1	t	2	2	t	t	t	t	t	t
2	t	t	2	t	1	2	t	1	1
C	0			1			2		

Fig 3. K-T Map for L_2(A,B,C) example 1

A	B								
	0	1	2	0	1	2	0	1	2
0	2	2	2	2	0	0	2	0	2
1	0	2	2	0	0	0	u	u	u
2	0	0	2	0	2	2	0	2	2
C	0			1			2		

Fig 4. K-T Map for $L_0(A,B,C)$ example 1

L_2 \ L_0	2 0 0 2 0 0 2 2 2	2 2 0 0 2 2 2 0 0	2 2 2 0 0 2 2 0 2	0 0 2 0 2 2 0 2 2
2 2 1 2 2 1 2 2 2	2 0 0 2 0 0 2 2 2	2 2 0 0 2 1 2 0 0	2 2 1 0 0 1 2 0 2	0 0 1 0 2 1 0 2 2
2 2 2 1 1 2 2 2 1	2 0 0 1 0 0 2 2 1	2 2 0 0 1 2 2 0 0	2 2 2 0 0 2 2 0 1	0 0 2 0 1 2 0 2 1

Fig 5. Array for the evaluation of L_0 L_2

A	B								
	0	1	2	0	1	2	0	1	2
0	X	W	WY	X			X		y
1		W	WY						y
2			Y		z	Z		z	yz
C	0			1			2		

Fig 6. Check Map for redundancy.

THE MINIMIZATION OF CONTROL VARIABLES IN ADAPTIVE SYSTEMS

Tomas Lang and Mario Schkolnick

Department of Electrical Engineering
University of Chile, Santiago, Chile

Abstract

An upper bound is given to the number of control variables necessary to realize every boolean function which is partially specified. This bound is attained by minimizing this number over a reduced class of solutions. A circuit realization using almost this number of controls is presented.

Introduction

A digital combinational switching network is said to be adaptive if it is capable of realizing several boolean functions. To acomplish this it requires a certain number of control variables besides the input variables. The control variables allow for the specification of the particular boolean function that is desired. If a learning mechanism is attached to this system we can utilize it to perform classification tasks. An adaptive network with n input variables is said to be universal if it is capable of realizing every boolean function of the n variables. In order to do this, 2^n control variables are required to select one of the 2^{2^n} possible functions. The number of control variables is thus quite large even for small values of n. It is then attractive to study what can be done with nonuniversal adaptive systems. In many practical situations where patterns are to be classified, the boolean function which is desired is highly non-specified. We are only interested in the value of the function for certain input combinations (or stimulus) and the output for the rest of the stimulae is undefined. The number of stimulae for which the function is specified is usually very small. This bring us to the question of studying the adaptive systems which are used in the classification processes. In this paper we study the problem of finding out the minimum number of control variables which are necessary to realize every boolean function whose value is specified for c stimulae and not specified for the remaining 2^n-c stimulae. An upper bound for this number is found by minimizing over a reduced class of solutions. We then describe an economical adaptive network which can be used for classification.

Section 1

In this section we present the problem we are studing and show an equivalent one. Using this equivalence we produce a solution to a restricted problem which gives us the desired upper bound. To begin with, we define the objects we are studying.

Definition 1. Let $f \subseteq \{0,1\}^{n+1}$ be an n+1 ary relation on the set {0,1} such that for every $(x_1, x_2, .., x_n)$ there is at most one y such that $(x_1, x_2, .., x_n, y) \varepsilon f$. The set $A = \{(x_1, x_2, .., x_n) | \exists y, (x_1, x_2, .., x_n, y) \varepsilon f\}$ will be called the domain of f. If $A = \{0,1\}^n$, f will be called a total boolean function of n variables. If $A \subset \{0,1\}^n$, f will be called a partial boolean function of n variables. If f is a partial function with domain A such that $|A|$=c then f will be called a c-specified function. If f is a partial boolean function and g is a total function then g is an extension of f if $\forall x \varepsilon \{0,1\}^n$, $x \varepsilon$ domain (f) $\Rightarrow f(x)=g(x)$.

Using the definitions given in 1 we now state the problem we are analyzing.

Problem 1. Let F_c be the set of all c-specified functions from $\{0,1\}^n$ to {0,1}. Find the number n of elements in a set G_c of total functions from $\{0,1\}^n$ to {0,1} such that i) ($f \varepsilon F_c$)($g \varepsilon G_c$)(g is an extension of f) ii) $n = |G_c|$ is minimal.

Example. Let n=2, c=2. We can represent all the 2-specified functions of 2 variables by a table as follows where an x is placed to indicate that f is undefined for that value of (x_1, x_2). Below this table we exhibit two sets of total functions which satisfy condition i) of problem 1

x_1	x_2	f_1	f_2	f_3	f_4	f_5	f_6	f_7	f_8	....	f_{22}	f_{23}	f_{24}
0	0	0	0	0	x	x	x	0	0		1	x	x
0	1	0	x	x	0	0	x	1	x		x	1	x
1	0	x	0	x	0	x	0	x	1		x	x	1
1	1	x	x	0	x	0	0	x	x		1	1	1

		G						G'				
x_1	x_2	g_1	g_2	g_3	g_4	g_5	g_6	g_1'	g_2'	g_3'	g_4'	g_5'
0	0	1	1	1	0	0	0	0	1	0	1	0
0	1	1	0	0	1	1	0	0	1	0	0	1
1	0	0	1	0	0	1	1	0	1	1	0	0
1	1	0	0	1	1	0	1	0	0	1	1	1

It can be shown that the set G' also satisfies the condition ii) of problem 1.

We now introduce a map ϕ from the set of partial functions to the set of subcubes of an m-cube so that an extension of a partial function maps into a point of its image.

Let $m=2^n$ and f a partial function of n variables. Define ϕ as follows: $\phi(f)=\{(z_o, z_1,\ldots,z_{m-1}) \mid z_i \varepsilon \{0,1\}$ for all $0 \leq i < m$ and $(\forall x=(x_1, x_2,\ldots,x_n) \varepsilon \{0,1\}^n)(x \varepsilon$ domain f$)$ $(z_{i_k}=f(x)$ for $i_k=(x_1, x_2,\ldots, x_n)_2)\}$

We have the inmediate result.

<u>Lemma 1:</u> Let f be a c-specified function of n variables, g a total function of n variables. Then, $\phi(g)\varepsilon\phi(f) \Longleftrightarrow$ g is an extension of f.

Using lemma 1 we may restate problem 1 in terms of points and subcubes of the 2^n-cube as follows:

<u>Problem 2.</u> Find the number of points n in a set G of points of the 2^n cube such that i) for every (2^n-c) subcube there is a point in G which belongs to this subcube, ii) $n=|G|$ is minimal.

We introduce one last set of definitions so as to simplify writing.

<u>Definition 2.</u> Any set G of points of the 2^n cube satisfying condition i) of problem 2 is called a <u>delegation.</u> A

delegation G which satisfies the property that $\forall x\varepsilon G$, $G-\{x\}$ is not a delegation is called a perfect delegation.

Clearly, any delegation which solves problem 2 is perfect. (The converse is not true: in the above example the delegations $\Delta=\{\phi(g)|g\varepsilon G\}$ and $\Delta'=\{\phi(g')|g'\varepsilon G'\}$ are both perfect). So to solve problem 2 we must only consider perfect delegations.

There is a special class of delegations which are images of sets of functions which can be implemented in a very simple way. We will now focus our attention on them and solve problem 2 for this class. This will produce an upper bound on the solution of problem 2 while giving at the same time a nice set of functions to use in solving problem 1.

Let $x\varepsilon\{0,1\}^m$ represent a point in the $m(=2^n)$ cube, $\delta=m-c+1$, $x_0=(0,0,0,\ldots,0)\varepsilon\{0,1\}^m$, and let $d(x,y)$ be the distance between two points x,y of the m-cube. Now consider the following set of points:

$$\Delta_q=\bigcup_{0\leqslant j\leqslant\left\lfloor\frac{m-q}{\delta}\right\rfloor}\{x|d(x,x_0)=q+j\delta\}$$

The set Δ_q consists of all the points in the spheres whose center is x_0 and whose radius are q, $q+\delta$, $q+2\delta,\ldots$, $q+\left\lfloor\frac{m-q}{\delta}\right\rfloor\delta$ (We use the convention that $\lfloor r\rfloor$ is the greatest integer less than or equal to r).

We have the following fact concerning the sets Δ_q.

Lemma 2. For every integer q, $0\leqslant q<\delta$, the set Δ_q is a perfect delegation. Proof: Consider a (m-c) subcube $S=\{(k_1, k_2,\ldots,k_c, x_{c+1},\ldots, x_m)|k_1, k_2,\ldots,k_c$ are constants in $\{0,1\},x_i\varepsilon\{0,1\}\}$ (There is no loss of generality assuming this because it can be easily seen that the property of being a perfect delegation is invariant under permutation of the variables x_i). Then, there are two points in S, namely $p_1=(x_1, x_2,\ldots, x_c, 0, 0,\ldots,0)$ and $p_2=(x_1, x_2,\ldots, x_c, 1, 1,\ldots, 1)$ such that $d(p_2, x_0)=d_0+(m-c)$, $d(p_1, x_0)=d_0$ and $d_0=$ number of x_i's $(1\leqslant i\leqslant c)$ such that $x_i=1$.

Choose $j_0=\left\lfloor\frac{d_0+(m-c)-q}{\delta}\right\rfloor$. Then we have: $d_0\leqslant q+j_0\delta\leqslant d_0+(m-c)$ and $0\leqslant j_0\leqslant\lfloor(m-q)/\delta\rfloor$. This implies that there is a point p in S such that $d(x_0,p)=q+j_0\delta$. So p is in Δ_q. Then Δ_q is a delegation. To see that Δ_q is perfect, remove a point $p=(p_1,p_2,\ldots,p_m)$ with $d(x_0,p)=d_p=q+j_0\delta$ for some $0\leqslant j_0\leqslant\lfloor(m-q)/\delta\rfloor$. We assume with no loss of generality that $p_i=1$ for all $1\leqslant i\leqslant d_p$. Let $0\leqslant j_0<\lfloor(m-q)/\delta\rfloor$ so that $j_0+1\leqslant(m-q)/\delta$. Then $\delta+d_p\leqslant m$ and replacing m for $\delta+c-1$ we have $d_p<c$. Consider the subcube $S=\{(k_1,k_2,\ldots,k_{d_p},k_{d_p+1},\ldots,k_c,x_{c+1},\ldots,x_m)\mid k_1=k_2=\ldots=k_{d_p}=1,$ $k_{d_p+1},\ldots,k_c=0,\ x_i\varepsilon\{0,1\}\}$. This subcube contains the point p. Moreover p is the only point in the sphere with center x_0 and radius d_p. The remaining points of S have distances d such that $d_p<d\leqslant d_p+(m-c)<d_p+m-c+1=d_p+\delta=q+(j_0+1)\delta$. This means that p is the only point of S contained in Δ_q. (A similar argument holds for the case $j_0=\lfloor(m-q)/\delta\rfloor$. In this case we consider the subcube $S=\{(x_1,x_2,\ldots,x_{d_p},k_{d_p+1},\ldots,k_m\mid k_i=0,\ x_j\varepsilon\{0,1\}\})$.

We consider now the problem of finding a Δ_q-type set with least number of elements. This will provide us with an upper bound for the solution of problems 1 and 2. The first thing to do is to count the elements in Δ_q.

<u>Lemma 3</u>: For a given n and c, let $k_q(c,n)$ be the number of elements in Δ_q. Then $k_q(c,n)=\sum_{0\leqslant j\leqslant\lfloor(m-q)/\delta\rfloor} C^m_{q+j\delta}$ where $m=2^n$ and C^r_s is the number of combinations or r elements taken s at a time.

The proof of lemma 3 is trivial.

Let $k(c,n)=\min_{0\leqslant q<\delta} k_q(c,n)$. We will prove the following result.

<u>Theorem</u>: $k(c,n)=k_p(c,n)$ where $p=\lfloor c/2-\delta\lfloor(c-2)/2\delta\rfloor\rfloor$, $\delta=m-c+1$, $m=2n$.

The proof of the theorem requires an intermediate result.

<u>Lemma 4</u>: Let $S_q=k_{q+1}(c,n)-k_q(c,n)$. Then $S_q\geqslant 0$ if

$q+r\delta+1/2<m/2\leq q+r\delta+1/2+\delta/2$ for some r and $S_q\leq 0$ if $q+r\delta+1/2+\delta/2\leq m/2<q+(r+1)\delta+1/2$ for some r.

To follow the proof of the lemma and the theorem the reader is referred to figure 1. We can write S_q as

$S_q=\sum_{k=0}^{m} \alpha(m,k)C_k^m$, $m=2^n$, where $\alpha(m,k)=1$ for all k such that $k\equiv q+1 \mod \delta$, $\alpha(m,k)= -1$ for all $k \equiv q \mod \delta$ and $\alpha(m,k)=0$ for all other values of k. Using the identity $C_k^j = C_k^{j-1} + C_{k-1}^{j-1}$ we can write a general expression for S_q as: $S_q = \sum_{k=0}^{j} \alpha(j,k)C_k^j$. For j=0 we have $S_q=\alpha(0,0)C_0^0=\alpha(0,0)$ so it remains to find the sign of $\alpha(0,0)$.

Let $L(r,j)=q+r\delta+1/2-(m-j)/2$. We will say that a point (j,k) is on a line of symmetry and that k is on a line of symmetry at the jth level if either $k=L(r,j)$ or $k=L(r,j)+\delta/2$. We say that a point (j,k) is within two lines of symmetry if either $L(r,j)<k<L(r,j)+\delta/2$ or $L(r,j)+\delta/2<k<L(r+1,j)$ for some r. Now we make the following claim: For all j, $0\leq j\leq m$, $\alpha(j,\ell-i/2)= -\alpha(j,\ell+i/2)$ for all $0\leq i<\delta$ such ℓ is on a line of symmetry at the jth level, $0\leq\ell-i/2$, $\ell+i/2\leq j$.

The claim is valid when j=m. To see why is it so, consider $\ell=L(r,m)$. For i=1 we have $\alpha(m,q+r\delta)= -1$ and $\alpha(m,q+r\delta+1)=1$. For all other values of i, $\alpha(m,\ell-i/2)= -\alpha(m,\ell+i/2)=0$. A similar argument holds if $\ell=L(r,m)+\delta/2$. Now assume the claim to be true for j. We will prove it is true for j-1. We use the fact that $\alpha(j-1,k)=\alpha(j,k)+\alpha(j,k+1)$. Consider $\alpha(j-1,\ell'-i/2)$ for ℓ' on a symmetry line at the $(j-1)^{st}$ level, $0\leq i<\delta$, $0\leq\ell'-i/2$, $\ell'+i/2\leq j-1$. Note that $\ell'=\ell-1/2$. Then, $\alpha(j-1,\ell'-i/2)=\alpha(j,\ell'-i/2)+\alpha(j,\ell'-i/2+1)= \alpha(j,\ell-(i+1)/2)+\alpha(j,\ell-(i-1)/2)=-\alpha(j,\ell+(i+1)/2)- \alpha(j,\ell+(i-1)/2)=-[\alpha(j,\ell'+i/2+1)+\alpha(j,\ell'+i/2)]=-\alpha(j-1,\ell'+i/2)$ which completes the proof of the claim.

An important corolary of our claim is the following Corolary: For all points (j,k) which lie within the same two consecutive symmetry lines we have that $\alpha(j,k)$ has the same sign (or is equal to zero).

The proof is an induction on j. Between two lines of symmetry there is just one point (m,k) such that $\alpha(m,k)\neq 0$ so the corolary holds for j=m. Now assume it holds for j. We have $\alpha(j-1,k)=\alpha(j,k)+\alpha(j,k+1)$. But either $\alpha(j,k)$ and $\alpha(j,k+1)$ have the same sign or one of them is 0. In any case $\alpha(j-1,k)$ preserves the sign.

We were after the sign of $\alpha(0,0)$. By the corolary, we have to see between which lines of symmetry lies the point (0,0) and then check if $\alpha(m,k)=1$ or $\alpha(m,k)=-1$ for the unique (m,k) within these lines. The lines are determined by the value of r for which $L(r,0)<0\leqslant L(r,0)+\delta/2$ or $L(r,0)+\delta/2\leqslant 0<L(r,0)$ (If $L(r,0)+\delta/2=0$ for some r then (0,0) is on a symmetry line and $\alpha(0,0)=0$). This determines the value of r for which $q+r\delta+1/2<m/2\leqslant q+r\delta+1/2+\delta/2$ or $q+r\delta+1/2+\delta/2\leqslant m/2<q+(r+1)\delta+1/2$. By the corolary we know that $\alpha(0,0)$ has the same sign as the unique $\alpha(m,k)$ within the same two consecutive lines. But $\alpha(m,k)\geqslant 0$, if $L(r,m)<k\leqslant L(r,m)+\delta/2$ and $\alpha(m,k)\leqslant 0$ if $L(r,m)+\delta/2\leqslant k<L(r+1,m)$. This completes the proof of lemma 4.

To conclude the proof of the theorem we note two facts. The first is that since q varies from 0 to $\delta-1$ there are at most two sign inversions of the function S_q. The second fact is that the function k_q has certain symmetries. We have $k_q=k_{q+m-2\ell+1}$ where $\ell=L(r,m)$ for some r such that both q and $q+m-2\ell+1$ are within 0 and $\delta-1$. Also, $k_q=k_{q+m-2\ell+\delta+1}$ where $\ell=L(r,m)+\delta/2$ for some r such that both q and $q+m-2\ell+\delta+1$ are within 0 and $\delta-1$. Using these facts it is straightforward to realize that the minimum of $k_q(c,n)$ occurs for a value of q for which $S_{q-1}\leqslant 0$ and $S_q\geqslant 0$. Using lemma 4 we have that q must satisfy $m/2\leqslant q+r\delta+1/2+\delta/2\leqslant m/2+1$ where r is the value for which $r\delta+1/2+\delta/2\leqslant m/2\leqslant (r+1)\delta+1/2+\delta/2$. Choose r to be the largest integer such that $r\delta+1/2+\delta/2\leqslant m/2$. Then $r=\lfloor(m-\delta-1)/2\rfloor = \lfloor(c-2)/2\delta\rfloor$. We get that q is the largest integer such that $q+r\delta+1/2+\delta/2\leqslant m/2+1$ or $q=\lfloor(m+1-\delta)/2-r\delta\rfloor=\lfloor c/2-\delta\lfloor(c-2)/2\delta\rfloor\rfloor$, $\delta=m-c+1$, $m=2^n$. This concludes the proof of the theorem.

Section 2

In this section we study the special case when c is small compared with m. This is the usual situation in a recognition problem. For this case we obtain a simple realization.

Based on the result of section 1, a circuit that realizes all c-specified functions would consist of one implementing all total functions of weight $q+j\delta$ for $0\leq j\leq \lfloor(m-\delta)/q\rfloor$, where q is obtained from the theorem. If $c<(2m+4)/3$ this set consists only two elements, so that it is necessary to implement all total functions of weight $\lfloor c/2\rfloor$ and of weight $\lfloor c/2\rfloor+\delta$. The minimum number of control variables for any such circuit would be $\log_2 k(c,n)$. We now show how to build a circuit which for small values of c uses essentially the same number of control variables as this one and is easy to implement.

Consider the circuit of figure 2. Each box realizes the identity function $(xz+\bar{x}\bar{z})$ for inputs x and z. If we think of the x's as being inputs and the z's as being controls variables we can see that this circuit realizes all the functions with weight $p=\lfloor c/2\rfloor$ or less (for $z_0=1$) and all functions with weight $2^n-\lfloor c/2\rfloor$ or more (for $z_0=0$). This set of functions includes the set of functions mentioned before, so that this circuit realizes all c-specified functions. This circuit uses $n.c/2+1$ control variables. Let us compare this number with the upper bound we obtained in the theorem. We have $\log k(c,n)\geq\log C^m_p$. Using Stirling's approximation formula and making $p<<m$ we get $\log C^m_p \simeq np-p\log p+(\log p/2\pi)/2$. The ratio between this number and the number of control variables we are using is $(np-p\log p+(\log p/2\pi)/2)/(1+np)$ which is of the order of 1 as n grows and p/n remains constant.

Using the implementation of fig. 2 it is also easy to specify a total function that is an extension of the c-specified function one wants to realize. If the number of 1's that the function takes for the c-specified arguments is less than or equal to c/2 then we put $z_0=1$ and we specify with the other z's the arguments of the function for which it takes the value 1. If the number of 1's is greater than c/2 then we put $z_0=0$ and we specify the arguments of the function for which it takes the value 0. The circuit presented is modular in the sense that the number of variables n and the specification c can be easily increased. Notice the a_i inputs which are used to connect other modules to increase the number of variables.

Conclusions

In this paper an upper bound on the number of control variables necessary to realize any c-specified function, was obtained. Although we know that this is not the minimum number of control variables required (an example was studied for n=3, c=2 obtaining $\log_2 7$ where the upper bound gives $\log_2 9$) we conjecture that this bound is close.

A circuit realization was described which is easy to implement and where the control variables are sistematically assigned. The circuit is modular and can be expanded for any n and c. The number of control variables obtained is much less than the number required for a universal adaptive system, but never the less becomes quite large for big n and c. It would be interesting to study an even more restricted class of function, may be the class of c-specified functions where the specified stimulae are separated by a minimum distance k (this would be called the class of (c,k) specified functions). In order to make this class useful for recognition problems, probably it would be convenient to assign values to the function corresponding to the non specified stimulae to be the same as the one the function has at the nearest specified stimulus.

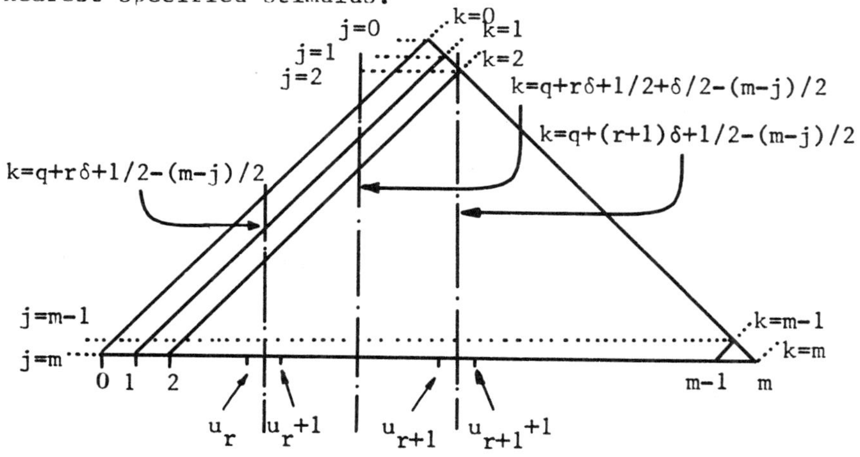

$u_r=q+r\delta$; $u_{r+1}=q+(r+1)\delta$

Figure 1

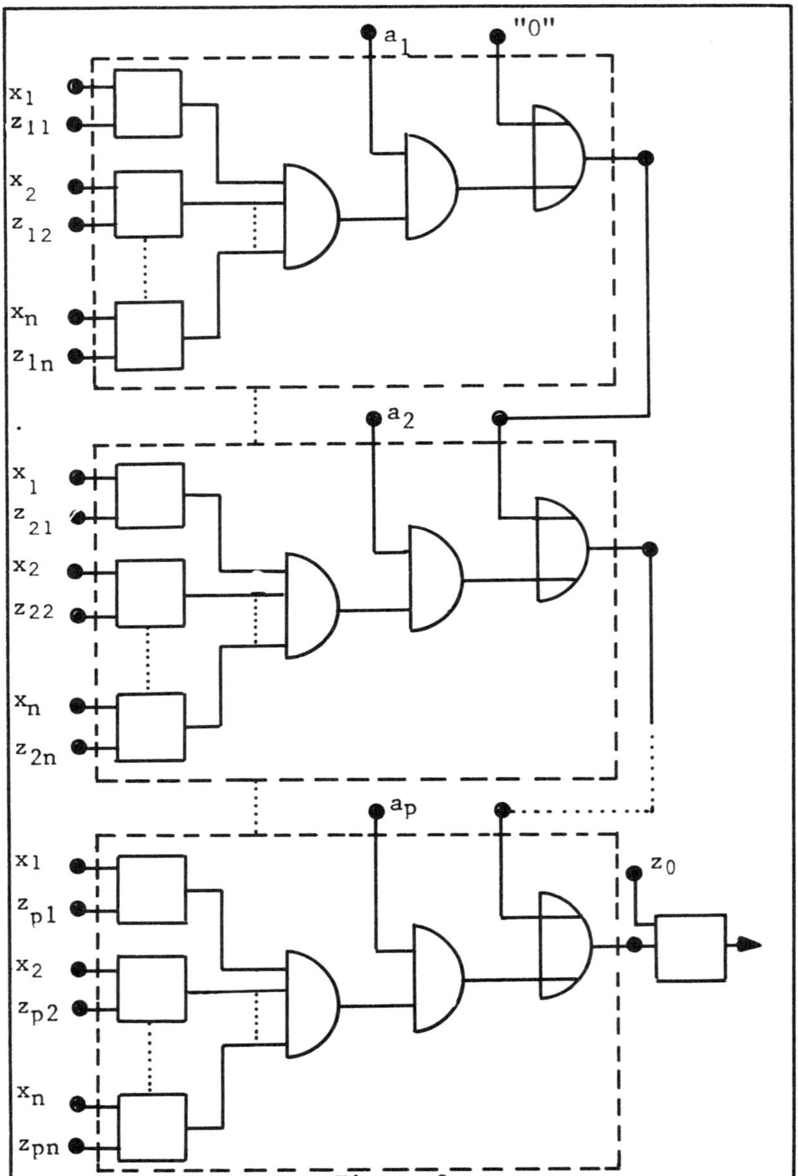
a1
"0"
x1
z11
x2
z12
xn
z1n
a2
x1
z21
x2
z22
xn
z2n
ap
x1
zp1
x2
zp2
xn
zpn
z0

Figure 2

ON COMPLETENESS OF A SET OF AMBIGUOUS LOGIC PRIMITIVES

Amar Mukhopadhyay
Department of Computer Science

Sudhakar M. Reddy
Department of Electrical Engineering

The University of Iowa

Abstract

A logic primitive is said to be ambiguous if for some input configurations, the output of the primitive is not definitely specified. This paper is concerned with the problem of building switching circuits for arbitrary switching functions by using a set of ambiguous logic primitives. A set of necessary conditions and a set of sufficient conditions for a set of ambiguous logic primitives to be complete, are given.

Introduction

A logic primitive is said to be <u>ambiguous</u> if for some input configurations, the output of the primitive is not definitely specified; the output values for these configurations could be either 1 or 0 due to some transient or permanent fault. A logic module realizing an ambiguous function $f(x_1,\ldots,x_n)$ ($x_i = 0$ or 1, $1 \le i \le n$) can be specified by giving the definite part $h(x_1,\ldots,x_n)$ of f and the uncertain part $g(x_1,\ldots,x_n)$ of f such that $h \cdot g = 0$ and at any instant the behavior of the module corresponds to $f' = h + a$ where a is contained in g, that is, $a \le g$.

This paper is concerned with the problem of building switching circuits for arbitrary switching functions by using a set of ambiguous logic primitives. We assume that the primitives are interconnected to form a well-formed net such that no two outputs of primitives are connected together, there is no feedback loop in the circuit, and the inputs of the primitives could be identified and/or connected to outputs of other primitives. The inputs to the circuit are x_i's and possibly constant functions 1 and 0 and there is only a single output of the circuit realizing the function $f(x_1,\ldots,x_n)$.

A set of ambiguous logic primitives is said to be strong complete if any arbitrary function $f(x_1,\ldots,x_n)$ can be realized without any uncertainty as the output of a circuit which contains a finite number of primitives from the given set and whose inputs are identified with the set of variables $x_1,\ldots,x_n$. If the requirement for the realizability of constant functions 1 and 0 is removed and if these constants can be applied to the inputs whenever necessary, then the set of ambiguous primitives is said to be weak complete.

Several authors have studied the problem of completeness of a set of logic primitives each of which produces a nonambiguous function. The original theorem was obtained by Post (1921). Yablonskii (1958), Butler (1960), Nozaki (1970), Mukhopadhyay (1971) and Reddy and Mukhopadhyay (1971) have obtained simplified proofs of Post's Theorem. Muchnik and Gindikin (1962) obtained an extension of Post's Theorem in which the system of primitives consists of a completely reliable set and an unreliable set each element of which has a finite probability of failure. Using a redundant construction with the elements of the reliable set very similar to that used by von Neumann (1956), they have proved the necessary and sufficient conditions for completeness such that the overall system will have a probability of failure less than arbitrarily small value with proper amount of redundancy.

The approach that we propose to take in this paper is to assume that each one of the primitives is unreliable but that the primitives exhibit reliable behavior for some input configurations. We propose to study the nature and properties of ambiguities such that an overall fault-free network can be designed.

Fault-tolerant Function

An ambiguous logic module is said to be fault-tolerant with respect to a property P if $f' = h + a$ preserves the property P under all variations of a, $a \le g$. For example, the following two-variable module, where ? denotes ambiguous

x \ y	0	1
0	0	1
1	1	?

output, is fault-tolerant with respect to non-self-duality. This is because when ? = 0, the function is Exclusive OR ($x \oplus y$) and when ? = 1, the function is Inclusive OR ($x + y$), both of which are non-self-dual.

Theorems

The following theorems give conditions under which a fault-tolerant function preserves certain properties which are useful in proving the theorems on completeness (Theorems 6, 7 and 8).

Let A,B,C denote binary n-tuples. If $A = (a_1, \ldots, a_n)$, by f(A) we mean the value of the function $f(x_1, \ldots, x_n)$ when $x_i = a_i$ for all $i, 1 \leq i \leq n$. If $B = (b_1, \ldots, b_n)$, then we say $A \leq B$ if and only if $a_i \leq b_i$ ($0 \leq 0$, $0 \leq 1$ and $1 \leq 1$).

Theorem 1. The function $f(x_1, \ldots, x_n)$ is fault-tolerant with respect to non-zero [or non-one] preservation if and only if $f(0,0,\ldots,0) = 1$ [or $f(1,1,\ldots,1) = 0$] and this output is definitely specified.

Theorem 2. A function is fault-tolerant with respect to non-monotonicity if and only if there exist n-tuples A and B such that $A \leq B$ and $f(A) = 1$ and $f(B) = 0$ are definitely specified.

Theorem 3. The function is fault-tolerant with respect to non-self-duality if and only if there exist n-tuples A and B such that B is obtained by complementing each bit of A and $f(A) = e$, $f(B) = e$ are definitely specified where e is 0 or 1.

Theorem 4. A necessary condition that a function $f(x_1, \ldots, x_n)$ is fault-tolerant non-linear is that there exist three n-tuples A,B,C such that $f(A) = f(B) = e$ where $e = 0$ or 1, $f(C) = \bar{e}$ (complement of e) and A has odd number of 1's in it whereas B has an even number of 1's in it.

The proofs of the above theorems are simple and are omitted in this paper. We now give a sufficient condition for fault-tolerant non-linearity in the next theorem and use that to arrive at sufficient conditions for completeness of ambiguous primitives. We define a sublattice with respect to an n-tuple A to be the collection of n-tuples X such that $X \leq A$.

Theorem 5. A sufficient condition that a function $f(x_1,\ldots,x_n)$ is fault-tolerant non-linear is that it is definitely specified for a sublattice containing at least four n-tuples such that the function is definitely specified to be 1 for an odd number of n-tuples in the sublattice.

Proof: To prove this theorem, we will use the complement-free ring-sum expansion of a function

$$f(x_1,\ldots,x_n) = \sum\nolimits^{\oplus} c_i\, x_{j_1} x_{j_2} \ldots x_{j_n} \tag{1}$$

where c_i is 0 or 1, $0 \leq i \leq 2^n-1$, $0 \leq k \leq n$, $j_i < j_{i+1}$ and $(x_{j_1}, x_{j_2}, \ldots x_{j_k})$ is a subset, proper or improper (when $k = 0$), of $(x_1,\ldots,x_n)$ and $\sum^{\oplus}$ denotes extended Exclusive OR operation. The non-linearity of the function $f(x_1,\ldots,x_n)$ can be guaranteed under all fault conditions if it can be insured that the above expansion of f contains a product term such that $k \geq 2$ under all variations of a. But c_i can be expressed as

$$c_i = \sum\nolimits^{\oplus} f(A) \tag{2}$$

where $A \leq B$ and B is an n-tuple such that $x_{j_1} = x_{j_2} = \ldots = x_{j_k} = 1$ and $x_{j_{k+1}} = \ldots = x_{j_n} = 0$. The set of n-tuples A obviously forms a lattice whose maximal n-tuple is B. Obviously, an odd number of terms in the right-hand side of Eqn. (2) must be definitely specified to be 1 and the rest 0 in order that $c_i = 1$. The lattice is assumed to have at least four n-tuples in order that the trivial case of a single variable function, which is always linear, is excluded.

Using Theorems 2 and 5 we can now state sufficient conditions for weak completeness as Theorem 6.

Theorem 6. A set of ambiguous logic modules is weak complete if it has at least one fault-tolerant non-monotonic primitive and at least one fault-tolerant non-linear primitive which satisfies Theorem 5.

The proof of this theorem is very similar to the corresponding proof for non-ambiguous logic primitives as described by Mukhopadhyay (1971) and will be omitted here.

We now prove a set of necessary conditions and a set of sufficient conditions for a set to be strong complete.

<u>Theorem</u> 7. A set of necessary conditions such that a set of ambiguous primitives is strong complete is that the set includes

1) at least one primitive fault-tolerant non-self-dual,
2) at least one primitive fault-tolerant non-zero-preserving,
3) at least one primitive fault-tolerant non-one-preserving,
4) at least one primitive fault-tolerant non-monotonic,
5) at least one primitive fault-tolerant non-linear,
6) at least one of the three types of functions, given below. The three types of functions are specified by their definite portions.

$$\text{I} \qquad \begin{array}{cccccc|c} x_{j_1}x_{j_2} & \cdots & \cdots & \cdots & & x_{j_n} & f \\ \hline 00\ldots0 & 11\ldots1 & 00\ldots0 & dd\ldots d & dd\ldots d & dd\ldots d & 0 \\ \underbrace{11\ldots1}_{k_1} & \underbrace{dd\ldots d}_{k_2} & \underbrace{dd\ldots d}_{k_3} & \underbrace{00\ldots0}_{k_4} & \underbrace{11\ldots1}_{k_5} & \underbrace{dd\ldots d}_{k_6} & 0 \end{array}$$

$$\text{II} \qquad \begin{array}{cccccc|c} x_{j_1}x_{j_2} & \cdots & \cdots & \cdots & & x_{j_n} & f \\ \hline 00\ldots0 & 11\ldots1 & 00\ldots0 & dd\ldots d & dd\ldots d & dd\ldots d & 1 \\ \underbrace{11\ldots1}_{k_1} & \underbrace{dd\ldots d}_{k_2} & \underbrace{dd\ldots d}_{k_3} & \underbrace{00\ldots0}_{k_4} & \underbrace{11\ldots1}_{k_5} & \underbrace{dd\ldots d}_{k_6} & 1 \end{array}$$

$$\text{III} \qquad \begin{array}{cccccc|c} x_{j_1}x_{j_2} & \cdots & \cdots & \cdots & & x_{j_n} & f \\ \hline 00\ldots0 & 11\ldots1 & 00\ldots0 & dd\ldots d & dd\ldots d & dd\ldots d & 1 \\ \underbrace{11\ldots1}_{k_1} & \underbrace{dd\ldots d}_{k_2} & \underbrace{dd\ldots d}_{k_3} & \underbrace{00\ldots0}_{k_4} & \underbrace{11\ldots1}_{k_5} & \underbrace{dd\ldots d}_{k_6} & 0 \end{array}$$

where d is 0 or 1, $0 \leq k_i \leq n$ $(1 \leq i \leq 6)$ such that the sum of k_i's is n and $x_{j_1}, x_{j_2}, \ldots, x_{j_n}$ is some arbitrary ordering of $x_1, x_2, \ldots, x_n$. The column f denotes the function values associated with the sets of inputs.

Proof: The necessity of conditions 1) through 5) is proved using arguments similar to those used in proving Post's Theorem. We note that if a function is fault-tolerant self-dual or fault-tolerant linear, it has to be specified without ambiguity. On the other hand, fault-tolerant monotonic, zero-preserving and one-preserving functions could be truly ambiguous. Conditions 1) through 5) follow if one notes that a linear function of linear functions is a linear function and this statement is true if one replaces "linear" by "monotonic," "self-dual," "zero-preserving," and "one-preserving." The necessity of condition 6) is obtained by contradiction as discussed below.

Consider a logic net built with primitives satisfying conditions 1) through 5), but not 6). Obtain an equivalent tree logic net by duplicating each primitive whose outputs are connected to more than one primitive such that the resulting network does not have a primitive whose output is connected to more than one point. We can now talk in terms of the distinct levels of the net: the primitives in the first level have inputs which are only primary inputs; primitives in the jth level have inputs from lower than the jth level and at least one input from (j-1)th level, etc. Contrary to the theorem, assume that the network can produce all functions of the inputs, including the constant functions 0 and 1. If it is producing a constant function 0, we must have $f(0,0,\dots,0) = f(1,1,\dots,1) = 0$. Apply inputs $x_1 = x_2 = \dots = x_n = 0$ to the net; outputs of the first level network could be 0, 1 or d. Then apply $x_1 = x_2 = \dots = x_n = 1$; again the possible outputs are 0,1 or d. Of these, the combination 0 output for both input states or 1 output for both input states or 1 for the first input and 0 for the second input state is not permissible for any primitive since this will violate the hypothesis that no primitive of type I through III is present in the set. Therefore the possible inputs to the second level primitives for primary inputs $x_1 = \dots = x_n = 0$ and $x_1 = \dots = x_n = 1$ are given by the sets described in I. Notice that the general description of the possible input states applied to primitives in any level will also be described by I and, therefore, it should be applicable to the primitives at the final level whose output cannot be 0 again for both input states. This contradicts the assumption that the network produces the constant function 0. The contradiction is resolved if and only if we assume the existence of a primitive which produces 0 output with respect to inputs described by I.

Theorem 8. A set of sufficient conditions such that a set of ambiguous primitives is strong complete is that the set includes the four primitives described by 1) through 4) and 6) in Theorem 7 plus

5) at least one primitive fault-tolerant non-linear which satisfies Theorem 5.

Proof: The sketch of the proof is as follows. We will first show that the constant functions 1 and 0 are producible and then appeal to the weak completeness Theorem 6.

Suppose a primitive P of type I is in the set of primitives. Connect the k_1 inputs of P to the variable input x. Connect x to a fault-tolerant non-zero-preserving primitive whose output is connected to the k_2 inputs of P. Connect x to k_3, k_5 and k_6 inputs of P. Connect x to a fault-tolerant non-one-preserving primitive whose output is then connected to k_4 inputs of P. Since the primitive is of type I, the output will always be 0 independent of the value of x, thereby producing the constant function 0. The output of P is then connected to a fault-tolerant non-zero-preserving primitive of the set which generates the constant function 1. Once we have the constant functions 0 and 1, we can use the fault-tolerant non-monotonic function to synthesize NOT operation. By using the fault-tolerant non-linear primitive we can now synthesize AND or OR function. By similar arguments, if we have a type II primitive we can first synthesize 1, then 0 and then NOT operation, and ultimately AND or OR operation. If we have a type III primitive, using connections identical to those described for type I, we synthesize the NOT of x ($\bar{x}$) at the output. Now, we take a fault-tolerant non-self-dual primitive, identify a subset of the inputs to $\bar{x}$, the remaining inputs to x, thereby producing a constant function e (0 or 1) at the output of the non-self-dual primitive. We can now use another copy of the NOT primitive to produce $\bar{e}$ (1 or 0). We then proceed to synthesize AND or OR operation as before. The details of the construction of NOT from fault-tolerant non-monotonic primitives, and AND or OR from fault-tolerant non-linear primitives are similar to those for non-ambiguous primitives as described by Mukhopadhyay (1971).

The problem of obtaining a set of necessary and sufficient conditions for completeness (weak or strong) for a set of ambiguous logic primitives is still open.

Acknowledgments

The work of the first author (AM) has been supported by National Science Foundation grant GJ-723. The work of the second author (SMR) has been supported by National Science Foundation grant GK-10025.

References

J. W. Butler (1960), "On Complete and Independent Sets of of Operations in Finite Algebra," Pacific J. Math., Oct., 1169-1179.

A. A. Muchnik and S. G. Gindikin (1962), "The Completeness of a System Made Up of Nonreliable Elements Realizing a Function of Algebraic Logic," Soviet Physics Dokl. 7, 447-479, Dec.

A. Mukhopadhyay (1971), "Complete Sets of Logic Primitives," Chapt. I of Recent Developments in Switching Theory (Ed. A. Mukhopadhyay), Academic Press.

A. Nozaki (1970), "Réalisation des fonctions definies dans un ensemble à l'aide des organes élémentaires d'entrée-sortie," Proc. Japan Acad. 46, 478-482, June.

E. L. Post (1941), "Two-valued Iterative Systems of Mathematical Logic," Princeton Univ. Press, Princeton, N. J.

S. M. Reddy and A. Mukhopadhyay (1971), "Simple Proofs of Two Theorems on Completeness of Logic Primitives." Unpublished manuscript.

J. von Neumann (1956), "Probabilistic Logics and Synthesis of Reliable Organisms from Unreliable Components," Automata Studies, 43-98, Princeton Univ. Press, Princeton, N. J.

S. V. Yablonskii (1958), Trudy Mat. Inst. Steklov AN SSSR 51, 5.

MINIMIZING THE NUMBER OF INTERNAL STATES IN INCOMPLETELY SPECIFIED PULSE INPUT ASYNCHRONOUS SEQUENTIAL MACHINES

G. Frosini G.B. Gerace
Istituto di Elaborazione dell'Informazione del C.N.R.
Pisa, Italy

1. Introduction

The synthesis of asynchronous sequential circuits has been extensively treated in the literature [1]. In this paper we shall consider the synthesis of that restricted class of asynchronous circuits characterized by the fact that in every input sequence each input state I_i $(i=1,2,...,n)$ is immediately followed by a special input state I_0 called null input state. Therefore, in the asynchronous circuits discussed here only input sequence of the form I_h, I_0, I_k, I_0 are allowed. When in such a circuit every two successive input state changes $I_0 - I_i$, $I_i - I_0$ produce one input pulse, the circuit is called *pulse input asynchronous sequential circuit* (PA circuit). A comprehensive treatment of the general properties ad applications of PA circuits can be found in [2].

As for any sequential circuits, the first step in the synthesis of a PA circuit is the description of the circuit behaviour. It is customary to describe the behaviour of an asynchronous circuit by a *primitive flow table* where each row contains one stable state only. Due to the mentioned restriction on the input sequences, any primitive flow table for a PA circuit (primitive PA table) having more than one state I_i contains some optional (don't care) next-state entries. One primitive PA table where optional entries result only from such a restriction is shown in Fig. 1, where the superscript of a next state indicates the associated output state.

Another step in the synthesis of a sequential circuit is state reduction. When the flow table is incompletely specified, the procedures for obtaining the minimum-state sequential circuit are very laborious [3] - [6]. For restricted classes of incompletely specified flow tables, where optional entries depend only on certain constraints in input sequences, McCluskey [7] and Unger [8] have demonstrated that more efficient pro cedures can be devised.

The aim of this paper is to describe new semplified procedures for minimizing incompletely specified primitive PA tables belonging to the following two classes:

a) *Complete primitive PA tables*, where optional entries result only from the restriction on the input sequences of the form "input state I_i is immediately followed by input state I_0";

b) *Incomplete primitive PA tables*, where optional entries result from the restriction in a) and from the further restriction on the input sequences of the form "any input state I_i following input state I_0 is different from input state I_i preceding input state I_0" (e.i. for any $I_h I_0 I_k I_0$, I_k is different from I_h).

The importance of types a) and b) of PA tables are not discussed here. The reader may refer to a previous paper [2] where we show that for any pulse input synchronous circuit fully specified we can realize a PA circuit, with identical input-output specifications, described by a complete primitive PA table; and that any asynchronous circuit described by a flow table F fully specified can always be realized by using a PA circuit described by an incomplete primitive PA table derived from F.

In the following, the theory of state minimization for incompletely specified flow tables studied by Paul and Hunger and then extended by other authors [4] - [6], is assumed to be known.

2. Structure of complete and incomplete primitive PA tables

The procedures to reduce incompletely specified flow tables are heavy and awkward to carry. This chiefly derives from the fact that the compatibility relation is not transitive. However, for complete and incomplete primitive PA tables the compatibility relation has some transitive properties which allow to strongly simplify the reduction process. Before discussing this, a precise definition of the internal structure of these PA tables is necessary. For both types of primitive PA tables we assume the following: 1) PA tables are normal (each unstable state leads directly to a stable state); 2) each unstable state has the same output as the corresponding stable state in the same column; 3) the output state is unspecified whenever the next-state is unspecified.

Let us call *start-state* and *end-state* of a PA table an internal state that results to be unstable and stable for input state I_0, respectively, and *start-row* and *end-row* the corresponding rows. Moreover we shall say that start-state *a* (start-row *a*) such that $\delta(I_0, a) = b$ is *associated* to end-state *b* (end-row *b*). Note that an end-state not associated to any start-state cannot exist, since any input sequence starts from input I_i. Then the restrictions on the input sequences defined in the Introduction induce unspecified entries as follows.

In complete primitive PA tables, any start-row contains unspecified entries in all columns I_i except that column containing the stable state. No unspecified entry exists in end-rows. As an example see table in Fig. 1.

In incomplete primitive PA tables, unspecified entries of the start-rows are defined as in complete primitive PA tables. In order to define the unspecified entries of the end-rows some assumption is necessary. We assume that "two start-states *a* and *b* stables for different input states are associated with different end-states", that is, no preliminary reduction has implicitely occurred in constructing the primitive PA table. Thus better results in the reduction process may be achieved. Because of this assumption and the general condition $I_k \neq I_h$ in any input sequence $I_h I_0 I_k I_0$, if *a* is the start-state stable for input I_h then the associated end-state $b = \delta(I_0, a)$ is unspecified for input I_h. As an example, Fig. 2 shows an incomplete primitive PA table where unspecified entries are defined as above.

3. State reduction of complete primitive PA tables

McCluskey has shown [7] that for normal primitive flow tables operating in fundamental mode, if optional entries result only from the restriction of the form "input I_h can never immediately followed by input I_k" (flow tables of type A), the compatibility relation has the following transitive property: if s_l, s_m and s_n are three internal states stable for the same input I, and $s_l \sim s_n$, $s_m \sim s_n$, then $s_l \sim s_m$. Because of this, it is possible to obtain a minimal cover for tables of type A using only the maximal compatibility classes.

Complete primitive PA tables are evidently flow tables of type A. However, because of their particular structure a further transitive property, defined by the following theorem, can be stated.

Theorem 1. In any complete primitive PA table let *a* be an end-state, and S_1 and S_2 two other states. If $S_1 \sim a$ and $S_2 \sim a$, then $S_1 \sim S_2$.

Proof. Denote by I the generic input state for which $\delta(I, S_1)$ and $\delta(I, S_2)$ are both specified. Note that next-states of *a* are specified for every inputs. If $S_1 \sim a$ and $S_2 \sim a$, then for every I

(1) $\delta(I, S_1) \sim \delta(I, a)$ $\qquad$ $\delta(I, S_2) \sim \delta(I, a)$

(2) $\lambda(I, S_1) = \lambda(I, a)$ $\qquad$ $\lambda(I, S_2) = \lambda(I, a)$

because of compatibility definition. Moreover, $\delta(I, S_1)$, $\delta(I, S_2)$ and $\delta(I, a)$ are evidently stables for input I. Therefore $\delta(I, S_1) \sim \delta(I, S_2)$ because of the transitive property shown by McCluskey. Consequently $S_1 \sim S_2$, since $\lambda(I, S_1) = \lambda(I, S_2)$ from relation 2).

From the transitive property illustrated by Theorem I it follows:

Theorem 2. In any complete primitive PA table any end-state is contained in only one maximal compatibility class.

Proof. Let *a* be an end-state and suppose that there are two maximal compatibility classes C_{M_1} and C_{M_2} containing *a*. If S_1 and S_2 are two other states contained in C_{M_1} and C_{M_2}, respectively, $S_1 \sim S_2$ for Theorem 1, since $S_1 \sim a$ and $S_2 \sim a$. Each state of C_{M_1} is therefore compatible with all the states of C_{M_2} and viceversa. C_{M_1} and C_{M_2} cannot be maximal classes.

Starting from a complete primitive PA table, the following procedure is to obtain a minimal cover:

1) Find all the maximal compatibility classes.
2) Select all the maximal classes containing end-states.
3) Among the set of remaining classes select the smallest subset that contain all start-states not contained in classes selected in 2). These classes and those contained in the selected subset form a minimal covering.

As an example, all the maximal classes of the primitive PA table shwn in Fig. 1 are listed in the left hand-side of Table 1. Classes selected in Step 2) are marked by an asterisk. Classes forming the minimal cover are listed in the right hand-side of the table.

The corresponding reduced PA table is shown in Fig. 3.

4. State reduction of incomplete primitive PA tables

In order to simplify the reduction process for an incomplete primitive PA-table (denoted by [A]) it is convenient to carry out the state reduction throught two steps [8]:

1) reduction of [A] into a PA table [A eq] in which all the equivalent states have been eliminated;
2) reduction of [A eq.] to obtain a minimum-row flow table [A'eq].

It has heen shown by Hunger that the preliminary state reduction of [A] into [A eq.] does not foreclose the possibility of further reductions [8].

In order to reduce equivalent states, the following can be easly stated for a flow table [A]:

– two start-states stable for the same input state are equivalent if

they are compatible;
- two end states with next-state unspecified for the same input state are equivalent if they are compatible;
- a start-state and an end-state cannot be equivalent.

For example, in table [A] shown in Fig. 2, the pairs of states 8, 14 and 11,15 are equivalent, and reduce to states 8 and 14, respectively, in table [A eq] in Fig. 4.

For any table [A eq] the general results on state minimization are specialized as follows.

Lemma 1. Two states, S_1 and S_2, are compatibles if and only if the following conditions hold:

(1) $\delta(I_i, S_1) = \delta(I_i, S_2)$, (2) $\lambda(I_i, S_1) = \lambda(I_i, S_2)$

for every input I_i for which $\delta(I_i, S_1)$ and $\delta(I_i, S_1)$ are both specified;

(3) $\delta(I_0, S_1) \sim \delta(I_0, S_2)$, (4) $\lambda(I_0, S_1) = \lambda(I_0, S_2)$.

Proof. If the conditions hold, compatibility relation $S_1 \sim S_2$ is evidently verified. Assume that condition 1) is not truth. In this case states $\delta(I_i, S_1)$ and $\delta(I_i, S_2)$ are start-states that are stable for the same input. Therefore, if they were compatible, they would be equivalent too, which is excluded for any [A eq]. If they are not compatible, S_1 and S_2 are not compatible.

Not that, if S_1 and S_2 are both end-states, only conditions 1), 2) and 4) must be verified, since condition 3) reduces to $S_1 \sim S_2$.

Lemma 2. Let C be a compatibility class with two states at least, and denote by S_i the generic state of C. The class-set P_C implied by C is formed by at most one class C_0 whose elements are the end-states $S(I_0, S_i)$.

Proof. All classes C_i implied by C for inputs I_i $(I_i \neq I_0)$ are not contained in P_C, since they are formed by only one state because of Lemma 1. If C_0 exists (that is, P_C is not void), it is formed as stated in the Lemma.

Note that, since in a table [A eq] two start-states associated with the same end-state cannot be compatible (if they where compatible they would be equivalent) a class C cannot contain two start-states associated with the same end-state. If a class C for each start-state contains the associated end-state, then the P_C in void ($P_C = \emptyset$) since $C \supset C_0$. If the P_C of a class C is not void, each subclass of C implies a class-set contained in P_C.

The following theorem states a transitive property among the states

of a table [A eq].
Theorem 3. Let a and b be two end-states such that $a \sim b$, and S_1 and S_2 two other states. If conditions

$$(1) \qquad S_1 \sim a \qquad \text{and} \qquad S_1 \sim b \; ;$$

$$(2) \qquad S_2 \sim a \qquad \text{and} \qquad S_2 \sim b \; ;$$

hold, then $S_1 \sim S_2$.
Proof. Since $a \sim b$, let us denote by c the state corresponding to the compatibility class {a, b}. Note that the corresponding row c obtained by merging rows a and b of table [A eq] is fully specified, since states a and b cannot be equivalent. Conditions 1) and 2) of the theorem can therefore be replaced by

$$(1') \qquad S_1 \sim c \qquad\qquad (2') \qquad S_2 \sim c$$

From 1'), 2') and Lemma 1 it follows:

$$(3) \qquad \delta(I_i, S_1) = \delta(I_i, c) = \delta(I_i, S_2)$$

$$(4) \qquad \lambda(I_i, S_1) = \lambda(I_i, c) = \lambda(I_i, S_2)$$

whenever $\delta(I_i, S_1)$ and $\delta(I_i, S_2)$ are both specified, and

$$(5) \qquad \delta(I_0, S_1) \sim \delta(I_0, c) \; ; \; \delta(I_0, S_2) \sim \delta(I_0, c)$$

$$(6) \qquad \lambda(I_0, S_1) = \lambda(I_0, c) = \lambda(I_0, S_2) \; .$$

From (5) it derives that $S_1^* = \delta(I_0, S_1)$ and $S_2^* = \delta(I_0, S_2)$ - if S_1 and S_2 are end-states $S_1^* = S_1$ and $S_2^* = S_2$ - are end-states compatible with state $c = \delta(I_0, c)$. That is S_1 and S_2 satisfy the hypothesis of the theorem. Consequently relations (3), (4) and (6) with S_1 and S_2 replaced by S_1^* and S_2^*, respectively, are satisfied. End-states S_1^* and S_2^* are compatible because of Lemma 1, and, consequently, $S_1 \sim S_2$.

In the following we shall consider all the possible prime compatibility classes for a PA table [A eq]. We first consider a special subset of them.
Theorem 4. All prime compatibility classes that contain two end-states at least, imply a class-set void and are maximal ones.
Proof. Let C be a prime compatibility class that contains two end-states a and b at least. If states of C are end-states only, class-set P_C is void (see Lemma 2). Otherwise, let s be the generic start-state contained in C. Since $s \sim a$ and $s \sim b$, then end-state $c = S(I_0, s)$ associated to

s is also compatible with *a* and *b*. Therefore, c is compatible with all the states of C because of Theorem 3. Assume that $c \notin C$, and denote by $\bar{C}$ the class that contains the states of C and the end-states associated to start-states (such as *s*) contained in C. Then $P_{\bar{C}} = \emptyset$ because of Lemma 2 ($\bar{C}$ contains end-states and pairs of associated states), and consequently C is excluded by $\bar{C}$. In order that C be a prime compatibility class, $C \equiv \bar{C}$. P_C is therefore void.

Assume now that C is not a maximal compatibility class. Then, there exists a class C_M that implies a void class-set and such that $C_M \supset C$. Therefore, if class C is not a maximal one it cannot be a prime class.

Theorem 5. Let C be a prime compatibility class that implies a not void classe-set P_C, and let C_0 be the unique class of P_C. Then, C_0 either is a maximal compatibility class that implies a void class-set or is excluded by one and only one maximal compatibility class C_M that implies a void class-set.

Proof. Since $P_C \neq \emptyset$, C must contain at least two states not associated and C_0 at least two end-states (see Lemmas 1, 2 and notes). Then, C_0 either is a maximal compatibility class which implies a void class-set or is not a prime class (Theorem 4). If C_0 is not a prime class, there is a class C_M excluding C_0. Then, C_M is a maximal compatibility class that implies a void class-set (see proof of Theorem 4). To demonstrate that there is one and only one class as C_M, assume that two maximal compatibility classes, C_{M_1} and C_{M_2}, excluding C_0, exist. Since C_{M_1} and C_{M_2} contain an identical pair of end-states, each state of C_{M_1} is compatible with all the states of C_{M_2} and viceversa (see Theorem 3). Therefore, classes C_{M_1} and C_{M_2} cannot be maximal ones.

Theorem 6. Let K be a minimal closed collection of prime compatibility classes and C a class not maximal of K which implies a class-set not void. Then, there is a maximal compatibility class C* that can replace C in K.

Proof. Since P_C is not void, let C_0 be the class implied by C, and C_M be the maximal compatibility class excluding C_0 (see Theorem 5).
It may happen that $C_M \doteq C_0$. Then K contains C and C_M. Let C* be a maximal compatibility class such that $C^* \supset C$. Since C is a prime class and $C^* \supset C$, P_{C^*} is not void. Let C_0^* be the class of P_{C^*}, and C_M^* the maximal compatibility class excluding C_0^*. Since $C_0^* \supset C_0$ for Lemma 2, C_M and C_M^* contain a same pair of end-states. Therefore each state of C_M is compatible with all the states of C_M^* and viceversa (theorem 3). Therefore $C_M = C_M^*$. Replacing C by C*, all states covered by C are also covered by C* and closure conditions imposed by C* are satisfied by

C_M. Therefore, K remains a minimal cover.

Up to now all the prime compatibility classes have been considered, except the classes that imply a void class-set and contain less than two end-states. Because of Lemma 2 these classes could be the ones formed by a pair of associated states (classes C_p) or by only one state (classes C_s). Since for each class C_s there is a class C_p excluding C_s (each start-state is always compatible with its associated end-state), only classes C_p must be taken into account as possible prime classes. As a first result of the previous discussion and theorems the following can be stated:
A minimal cover for a flow table [A eq] exists which can always be obtained by a selection from the maximal compatibility classes and from the prime classes formed by one pair of associated states.

The following theorems are to show that a subset of maximal compatibility classes can be neglected when searching for a minimal cover.
Theorem 7. Let C be a maximal compatibility class that contains only one end-state *a* and implies a not void class-set P_C. Let C_0 be the class of P_C. Then the maximal compatibility class C_M excluding C_0 contains *a* and all the start-states contined in C and not associated with *a*.
Proof. Since $P_C \neq \emptyset$, C contains at least one start-state *s* not associated with *a* for Lemma 2. Since $C_M \supset C_0$, C_M contains at least the end-states *a* and $b = \delta(I_0, s)$. Since $s \in C$, $s \sim a$. Moreover $s \sim b$, since *s* and *b* form a pair of associated states. Consequently *s* is compatible with all states of C_M and, therefore, is contained in C_M.
Theorem 8. Let C be a maximal compatibility class that contains only one end-state *a*. Then C contains a start-state associated with *a*.
Proof. If C implies a void class-set it must contain a start-state associated with *a*. If C implies a class-set not void, Theorem 7 holds. Assume that C not contains a start-state associated with *a*. Then C is excluded by C_M and, therefore, cannot be a maximal compatibility class.
Theorem 9. A minimal cover for a table [A eq] exists which can always be obtained by a selection from the following classes:

1) Maximal compatibility classes that imply a void class-set.
2) Maximal compatibility classes not containing end-state (they imply a not void class-set).
3) Prime compatibility classes formed by one pair of associated states.

Proof.. With respect to the statement enounced after Theorem 6, points 1), 2) and 3) do not consider the maximal compatibility classes that contain only one end-state and imply a not void class-set. Let C be one of them and denote by K a minimal closed collection of prime classes formed by C and by classes of the types specified in 1), 2) and 3). Let *a* be the end-state contained in C. We shall demonstrate that C can be replaced by a class of type 3) that contains *a*. Because of Theorem 8 class C contains a pair of associated states $C_p = \{s, a\}$, with $a = \delta(I_0, s)$. Since K contains C, K must contain the class C_M that excludes the class C_0 implied by C. Therefore, C_M contains i) all start-states contained in C and not associated with *a* and ii) state *a* (Theorem 7). Moreover C does not satisfy any closure condition for the other classes of K, since it contains only one end-state. Consequently C can be replaced by C_p.

Because of Theorem 9 the work for reducing the tables [A eq] is considerably shortened. Let us call *useful classes* the classes specified in points 1), 2) and 3) of this theorem. A procedure to find the set of useful classes follows:

a) Find all the maximal compatibility classes;
b) Replace each maximal class containing only one end-state by class C_p containing this state.

After finding the set of useful classes the selection for finding a minimal closed selection K is facilitated by noting that i) only classes containing start-states only (specified in point 2) of the theorem) have a class-set not void, ii) this class-set is composed by only one class and iii) this class must be contained into a class (specified in point 1) of the theorem) forming K.

As an example, the maximal compatibility classes of table [A eq] shown in Fig. 4 are listed in Table II. This table shows also the useful classes and the classes selected for a minimal cover. Using this selection the reduced table [A′eq] is shown in Fig. 5.

References

[1] D.A. Huffman, "The synthesis of sequential switching circuits", *J. Franklin Inst., 257*, pp. 161-190, 275-303 (1954).

[2] G. Frosini, G.B. Gerace, "Pulse input asynchronous sequential circuits", *IEEE Trans. on Computers,* Vol. c-20, April 1971, pp. 436-442.

[3] M.C. Paul, S.H. Unger, "minimizing the number of states in incompletely specified sequential switching functions", *IRE Trans. on Electronic Computers*, Vol. EC-8, pp. 356-367, September 1959.

[4] A. Grasselli, F. Luccio, "A method for minimizing the number of internal states in incompletely specified sequential networks", *IEEE Trans. on Electronic Computers*, Vol. EC-14, pp. 350-359, June 1965.

[5] R.E. Miller, *Switching Theory Sequential Circuits and Machines,* Vol. 2, New York: Wiley, 1965, Chapter 7.

[6] W.S. Meizel, "A note on internal state minimization in incompletely specified sequential networks", *IEEE Trans. on Electronic Computers,* Vol. EC-16, pp. 508-509, August 1967.

[7] E.J. McCLuskey, "Minimum state sequential circuits for a restricted class of incompletely specified flow tables", *Bell System Tech. J.;* Vol. 41, pp. 1759-1768, December 1962.

[8] S.H. Unger, "Flow table simplification. Some useful aids", *IEEE Trans. on Electronic Computers*, Vol.EC-14, pp. 472-475, June 1965.

Maximal compatibility classes	Selected classes
1, 10, 11 *	1, 10, 11
2, 5, 8	2, 5, 8
1, 5, 11	
3, 9 *	3, 9
4 *	4
6	6
7	7

Table I

Maximal compatibility classes	Useful Classes	Class-set	Selected Classes
1, 2, 3	1, 2	∅	1, 2
2, 3, 4	2, 3, 4	∅	
3, 4, 5	3, 4	∅	
3, 5, 9	3, 5, 9	4, 6, 10	3, 5, 9
4, 5, 6, 10	4, 5, 6, 10	∅	4, 5, 6, 10
5, 9, 10	9, 10	∅	
7, 11	7, 11	8, 12	7, 11
7, 8	7, 8	∅	
11, 12, 13	11, 12	∅	
8, 12, 13	8, 12, 13	∅	8, 12, 13

Table II

	I_0	I_1	I_2	I_3
1	2^{1}	–	$\textcircled{1}^{2}$	–
2	$\textcircled{2}^{1}$	3^{1}	4^{1}	5^{1}
3	6^{1}	$\textcircled{3}^{1}$	–	–
4	7^{1}	–	$\textcircled{4}^{1}$	–
5	8^{1}	–	–	$\textcircled{5}^{1}$
6	$\textcircled{6}^{1}$	11^{2}	4^{1}	10^{2}
7	$\textcircled{7}^{1}$	9^{1}	1^{2}	5^{1}
8	$\textcircled{8}^{1}$	9^{1}	4^{1}	5^{1}
9	6^{1}	$\textcircled{9}^{1}$	–	–
10	2^{1}	–	–	$\textcircled{10}^{2}$
11	8^{1}	$\textcircled{11}^{2}$	–	–

Fig. 1 - A complete primitive PA table.

	I_0	I_1	I_2	I_3
1	2^{0}	$\textcircled{1}^{1}$	–	–
2	$\textcircled{2}^{0}$	–	3^{1}	11^{2}
3	4^{0}	–	$\textcircled{3}^{1}$	–
4	$\textcircled{4}^{0}$	5^{2}	–	15^{2}
5	6^{0}	$\textcircled{5}^{2}$	–	–
6	$\textcircled{6}^{0}$	–	7^{3}	11^{2}
7	8^{0}	–	$\textcircled{7}^{3}$	–
8	$\textcircled{8}^{0}$	1^{1}	–	9^{1}
9	10^{0}	–	–	$\textcircled{9}^{1}$
10	$\textcircled{10}^{0}$	5^{2}	7^{3}	–
11	12^{0}	–	–	$\textcircled{11}^{2}$
12	$\textcircled{12}^{0}$	1^{1}	13^{2}	–
13	14^{0}	–	$\textcircled{13}^{2}$	–
14	$\textcircled{14}^{0}$	1^{1}	–	9^{1}
15	12^{0}	–	–	$\textcircled{15}^{2}$

Fig. 2 - An incomplete primitive PA table.

	I_0	I_1	I_2	I_3	
a	b^{1}	$\textcircled{a}^{2}$	$\textcircled{a}^{2}$	$\textcircled{a}^{2}$	(1, 10, 11)
b	$\textcircled{b}^{1}$	c^{1}	d^{1}	$\textcircled{b}^{1}$	(2, 5, 8)
c	e^{1}	$\textcircled{c}^{1}$	–	–	(3, 9)
d	f^{1}	–	$\textcircled{d}^{1}$	–	(4)
e	$\textcircled{e}^{1}$	a^{2}	d^{1}	a^{2}	(6)
f	$\textcircled{f}^{1}$	c^{1}	a^{2}	b^{1}	(7)

Fig. 3 - The minimum-row flow table which covers the PA table in Fig. 1.

	I_0	I_1	I_2	I_3	
1	2^{0}	**1** ^{1}	–	–	
2	**2** ^{0}	–	3^{1}	11^{2}	
3	4^{0}	–	**3** ^{1}	–	
4	**4** ^{0}	5^{2}	–	11^{2}	
5	6^{0}	**5** ^{2}	–	–	
6	**6** ^{0}	–	7^{3}	11^{2}	
7	8^{0}	–	**7** ^{3}	–	
8	**8** ^{0}	1^{1}	–	9^{1}	(8-14)
9	10^{0}	–	–	**9** ^{1}	
10	**10** ^{0}	5^{2}	7^{3}	–	
11	12^{0}	–	–	**11** ^{2}	(11-15)
12	**12** ^{0}	1^{1}	13^{2}	–	
13	8^{0}	–	**13** ^{2}	–	

Fig. 4 - The reduced PA table $[A_{eq}]$ equivalent to the PA table in Fig. 2.

	I_0	I_1	I_2	I_3	
a	**a** ^{0}	**a** ^{1}	c^{1}	e^{2}	(1,2)
b	**b** ^{0}	**b** ^{2}	e^{3}	e^{2}	(4,5,6,10)
c	b^{0}	**c** ^{2}	**c** ^{1}	**c** ^{1}	(3,5,9)
d	**d** ^{0}	a^{1}	**d** ^{2}	c^{1}	(8,12,13)
e	d^{0}	–	**e** ^{3}	**e** ^{2}	(7,11)

Fig. 5 - The minimum-row flow table $[A'_{eq}]$ which covers $[A_{eq}]$.

ON THE ANALYSIS OF AUTONOMOUS SEQUENTIAL NETWORKS OF ITERATIVE ADAPTIVE ELEMENTS

E.H. Mamdani,
Department of Electrical Engineering
Queen Mary College, Mile End Road,
London, E.1. England.

I. Aleksander,
Electronics Laboratory,
University of Kent at Canterbury,
Canterbury, Kent, England.

Abstract

Autonomous networks of universal logic elements which can perform any function of its inputs are studied. The effects of both the structure of the network as well as its function for a given structure are considered. The behaviour of the network is interpreted in terms of the "topology" of the state diagram realized.

From the structure of the network an equivalence relation yields the partitions of the set of states into blocks of *maximal independent sets*. It is shown that if the next state is defined for each of the states in a maximal independent set, the function of the network is completely defined. Certain considerations also reveal the necessary condition for the network to realize a permutation machine.

ASSIGNMENT AND NEXT STATE EQUATIONS OF ASYNCHRONOUS SEQUENTIAL MACHINES

G. SAUCIER

Institut de Mathematiques Appliquees
Universite de GRENOBLE (France)

A B S T R A C T

Interested for a long time in the problem of encoding asynchronous machines, the author wants to show what result we can expect from using the algebraic structures defined by HARTMANIS especially the theorem of variable dependance (2). The problem consists of searching a critical race free encoding which gives us simple internal variables equations. This can be well illustrated by the encoding method proposed by LIU (4) and the systematic form of the equations can be easily justified by HARTMANIS theorem. More generally, we can deduce an encoding rule, finding again more easily TRACEY'S results (6).

AUTHOR INDEX

In parentheses are the reference numbers on the indicated pages.